I0823024

SAUL STEINBERG'S LITERARY JOURNEYS

Saul Steinberg's Literary Journeys

Nabokov, Joyce, and Others

JESSICA R. FELDMAN

University of Virginia Press
CHARLOTTESVILLE AND LONDON

University of Virginia Press

Printed in the United States of America on acid-free paper

First published 2021

9 8 7 6 5 4 3 2 1

Library of Congress Cataloging-in-Publication Data

Names: Feldman, Jessica R. (Jessica Rosalind), author.
Title: Saul Steinberg's literary journeys : Nabokov, Joyce, and others / Jessica R. Feldman.
Description: Charlottesville : University of Virginia Press, 2021. | Includes bibliographical references and index.
Identifiers: LCCN 2020028771 (print) | LCCN 2020028772 (ebook) | ISBN 9780813945118 (hardcover ; acid-free paper) | ISBN 9780813945125 (epub)
Subjects: LCSH: Steinberg, Saul—Criticism and interpretation. | Nabokov, Vladimir Vladimirovich, 1899–1977—Influence. | Joyce, James, 1882–1941—Influence. | Art and literature—History—20th century.
Classification: LCC NC1429.S588 F45 2021 (print) | LCC NC1429.S588 (ebook) | DDC 700.9/04—dc23
LC record available at https://lccn.loc.gov/2020028771
LC ebook record available at https://lccn.loc.gov/2020028772

Cover art: Untitled, Saul Steinberg, c. 1949–54, ink on paper, 7½ × 10 ½ in. (Beinecke Rare Book and Manuscript Library, Yale University; © The Saul Steinberg Foundation/Artists Rights Society, New York); background daboost/iStock

For George

CONTENTS

Part IV. Assembling Steinberg and Joyce

ACKNOWLEDGMENTS

Sheila Schwartz, Research & Archives Director at the Saul Steinberg Foundation, provided excellent support for this project. I thank the staff at Alderman Library, University of Virginia, and the Beinecke Rare Book and Manuscript Library, Yale University, especially Eve Neiger and Anne Marie Menta. The Pace Gallery and Aram Jibilian, Director of Photography Archives at Pace, supplied important images. For help of exactly the kind I needed, I thank Paul Barolsky, Mary McKinley, Farzaneh Milani, Christina Ball, Michael Rutherglen, Susannah Rutherglen, Claire A. Nivola, Christine Taylor, David Berson, Tim Morton, Julia Stone, Lucy Stylianopoulos, Steve Arata, and John O'Brien. All errors are my own.

All Saul Steinberg images © The Saul Steinberg Foundation/Artists Rights Society (ARS), New York.

Figure 43 courtesy of Cornell University, PJ Mode Collection of Persuasive Cartography.

Charles Baudelaire, excerpts from "Correspondences" and "Crowds" from *Flowers of Evil and Paris Spleen,* translated by William H. Crosby. Translation © 1991 by William H. Crosby. Reprinted with the permission of The Permissions Company, LLC on behalf of BOA Editions, Ltd., boaeditions.org.

Elizabeth Bishop, excerpt from "The Map" from *The Complete Poems, 1927–1979.* Reprinted with permission from Farrar Straus Giroux. © 1983 by Alice Helen Methfessel. All rights reserved.

Vladimir Nabokov, "North America on Antiterra," from *Ada oder Das Verlangen.* Reprinted with the permission of Rowohlt Verlag GmbH, copyright © 1974. All rights reserved.

Arthur Rimbaud, excerpts from "Memory" from *Rimbaud: Complete Works, Selected Letters,* translated by Wallace Fowlie. © 1966, University of Chicago Press. All rights reserved.

ABBREVIATIONS

Saul Steinberg

LAB	*Lettere a Aldo Buzzi;* English translation, *Letters to Aldo Buzzi,* typescript at Saul Steinberg Foundation
NY	*New Yorker* magazine
RS	Saul Steinberg, with Aldo Buzzi, *Reflections and Shadows*
SS: I	Joel Smith, *Saul Steinberg: Illuminations*
SSF	The Saul Steinberg Foundation
YCAL	Saul Steinberg Papers, Yale Collection of American Literature, Beinecke Rare Book and Manuscript Library, mss. 1053; with box number (b.) and file number (f.)

Note: In referring to works by Saul Steinberg that are not reproduced in this book, those bequeathed by the artist to the Saul Steinberg Foundation are cited as SSF followed by five digits, e.g., "SSF 00222." Those bequeathed to the Beinecke Rare Book and Manuscript Library, Yale University, are cited as "YCAL inv. no." followed by four digits, e.g., "YCAL inv. no. 0222."

Vladimir Nabokov

Ada	*Ada, or Ardor: A Family Chronicle*
AnL	*The Annotated Lolita*
LL	*Lectures on Literature*
PF	*Pale Fire*
RLSK	*The Real Life of Sebastian Knight*
SM	*Speak, Memory: An Autobiography Revisited*
SO	*Strong Opinions*

James Joyce

P	*A Portrait of the Artist as a Young Man*
U	*Ulysses*

Part I

Introduction

1

Thought Images

Steinberg Praises Joyce and Nabokov

Saul Steinberg's mingling of the visual and the verbal, based on his fascination with—and reworking of—the fiction of Vladimir Nabokov and James Joyce, indicates that modernism developed in part through a bold exploration of inter-art energies. Steinberg deserves an honored place both in the vanguard of mid-twentieth-century artists and in our understanding of modernism. In order to give him his due, it's necessary to explore further the notion that *he regarded his drawing as a form of writing*—a statement that, as we'll see, both he and his astute admirers often make.[1] It is time to explore with specificity what Steinberg's understanding of himself as a writer meant to his actual making of art, image by image.

Luckily, Steinberg gave us an important clue. In 1977 Grace Glueck, for *ARTnews,* asked some one hundred artists, "heavily weighted on the American side," to answer this question: "What specific work(s) of art—or artist(s)—of the past 75 years have you admired or been influenced by—and why?" Saul Steinberg carefully wrote out his reply: "The artist is an educator of artists of the future—of artists who are able to understand and in the process of understanding perform unexpected—the best—evolutions. In this sense James Joyce and Vladimir Nabokov are our great teachers." He goes on to name and praise three visual artists: Pablo Picasso, Walker Evans, and Andy Warhol. This was an unusual response to the survey: Pablo Picasso, Henri Matisse, Jackson Pollock, and Constantin Brâncuși dominated, in that order, and only a few of the artists polled mentioned writers.[2]

By naming Joyce and Nabokov, Steinberg announces his literary culture. Visual artists are not necessarily fervent readers, much less readers of difficult texts. He also epitomizes with these two names a lifetime of intense reading—had the "past 75 years" limit not been placed on him, he would likely have listed Leo Tolstoy, Nikolai Gogol, Gustave Flaubert, and Charles Baudelaire among his personal greats.

Not only did Steinberg have a literary bent, but he also thought of himself as a writer. "Drawing is like writing," he explained. "Or, you do it instead of writing. Drawing is actually the necessity to explain something. In a writer's drawing, a line is a line. Like a written word is seen letter by letter and then it is translated. I draw to explain things to myself."[3] Let us then consider the works of his two "great teachers," Nabokov and Joyce, in relation to Steinberg's own oeuvre.

We don't yet have a comprehensive examination of Steinberg's place in the history of art, nor will this study provide one.[4] Books and writers who mattered most to him will predominate here. Steinberg, Nabokov, and Joyce, taken together, will reveal a modernist triad in which literary art and visual art cast light on each other and even challenge those categories themselves. From Simonides's "Painting is silent poetry, poetry is eloquent painting" to Horace's "As is painting so is poetry," through G. E. Lessing's *Laokoön* and Charles Baudelaire's *The Painter of Modern Life,* to many twentieth- and twenty-first-century critical and theoretical works, analyses of the relation of visual art to literary art abound.[5] Saul Steinberg joins this analytic tradition, himself writing and speaking about the relation of writing and drawing. But it is through his visual oeuvre—his drawings, paintings, prints, sculptures, and assemblages—that he most eloquently makes the case for the inseparability of his own visual and verbal artistry.

From the multitude of possible approaches to Steinberg's work I have chosen to begin with two simple questions. First, when we think about the works of Nabokov and Joyce, what do we begin to see and understand in Steinberg's works? And second, when we think about Steinberg's works, what do we begin to see and understand in the works of Nabokov and Joyce? What I promote, then, is an interpretive circle. If we are ever fully to tease out Steinberg's debts and gifts to literature—and this study is just a beginning—this circle is one that we must travel. Steinberg himself liked to collapse the distinction between visual and verbal (not to mention musical) art: "my idea of the artist, poet, painter, composer, etc., is the novelist."[6]

The question of the ground of comparison between visual and verbal art arises, and I believe that the answer lies less in abstract formulation than in pragmatically attending to actual practices of the artist's drawing and writing as well as to the audience's viewing and reading. As Wendy Steiner writes, "There can be no final consensus about whether and how the two arts resemble each other, but only a growth in our awareness of the process of comparing them, of metaphoric generation and regeneration."[7] We can begin with Steinberg's own statement of their necessary relation: "In art everything has a literary origin—except Abstract Expressionism, which pretended to grow out of the activity of the body, not out of thought. However, even action painting is the intelligence of the body. Anything that implies some sort of intelligence, of whatever kind, belongs at least partly to the realm of literature."[8]

This study of Steinberg's explorations in that realm does not provide a complete compendium of literary sources for Steinberg's works, although several, beyond Joyce and Nabokov, will be mentioned. Instead, it teases out the affinities among the works and lives of Nabokov, Joyce, and Steinberg. While the very word "affinities" may seem to lack authority, the search for them requires strong reading and viewing. By "strong," I mean interpretation made possible only through our imaginative and informed collaboration with the works of art before us. We bring them to life. Such interpretations must always be based on the "facts" before us: actual texts, whether visual or literary. Steinberg himself hoped for such readings of his work; he counted on our moving beyond perception of his works to *understanding.* "The bourgeoisie is happy with perceptions," he notes. "They see a Vasarely, their eyeballs twitch and they're happy. I am concerned with the memory, the intellect, and I do not wish to stop at perception. Perception is to art what one brick is to architecture."[9] As we'll see, Nabokov and Joyce too, in their letters, conversations, and essays, and especially in their works of art, themselves promote that kind of reader/viewer participation.

Such strong reading requires multiple faculties. John Ashbery, in his essay "Saul Steinberg: Callibiography," has argued that such a requirement is in any case always fulfilled, because "our eyes, minds and feelings do not exist in isolated compartments but are part of each other, constantly cross-cutting, consulting and reinforcing each other."[10] Here we might usefully swivel for the first time to Nabokov, who, in a passage from *The Real Life of Sebastian Knight,* describes simultaneously a writer, the masterpiece of this writer, and the interpretation of this work by its reader (and supposed narrator of the novel), declaring, "One thought-image, then another, then another, breaks upon the shore of consciousness" (*RLSK,* 175). It's no accident that such a statement reflexively tells us how to read the very novel we hold in our hands: by choosing to accept its combined sensory images and ideas, its "thought-images," as naturally as we accept the gifts of the tides, by readying ourselves to both perceive and conceive, view and read and think. Steinberg's works require nothing less.

Finding the "thought-images" or verbal/visual presence in Steinberg's work requires first of all a recognition that he loved books and read widely. In a 1986 letter to his close friend Aldo Buzzi, Steinberg writes, "These days I'm creating a library of books I've read. Books made out of wood, Russian books in Romanian, French books in Italian, etc., a kind of autobiography . . . I should end up making at least fifty or so books" (*LAB,* September 25, 1986). This project culminated in *Library* (fig. 1), an assemblage

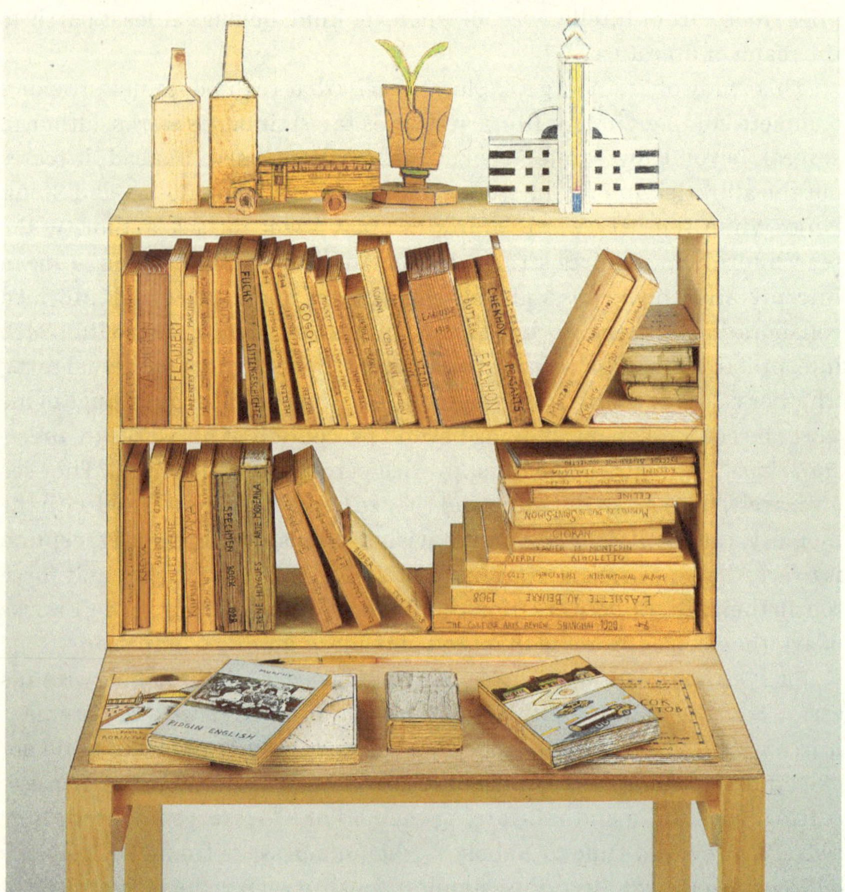

Fig. 1. *Library,* 1986–87. Pencil and mixed media on wood assemblage, 68½ × 31 × 23 in. (Collection of Carol and Douglas Cohen)

of fifty-six books, a "carpenter's sketch of a desk" (*SS: I,* 216), and a few flattish versions of domestic items—bottles, houseplant, miniature bus—along with an architectural model.

While the books Steinberg fashions for this piece seem a haphazard collection, a "canon of . . . Steinberg's idiosyncrasy," it is also true that the assemblage moves toward both autobiographical and "mysterious" ends (*SS: I,* 216). Like all gifted writers, Steinberg is also a reader, and *Library* is an account of the intertwining of his life with books. One untitled mock volume, simply labeled "Nabokov" on its spine and presenting a portrait of a woman on its cover, opens onto a subject of this study: the "unexpected evolutions"[11] that Steinberg made after "studying" Nabokov. The Gogol and Flaubert volumes also made themselves felt throughout his career.

As readers of *Library* as a whole, however, we can find further evidence of affinities among our triad. With his description of *Library* for Buzzi—again, "Russian books in Romanian, French books in Italian, etc."—Steinberg emphasizes the importance of translation to a man who is both an immigrant and a cultured, multilingual cosmopolitan, as were Nabokov and Joyce.

Thirteen of the books in *Library* appear in translation, such as Gogol's *Nose,* Kipling's *Il Libro della Jungla,* Erskine Caldwell's *Le Petit Arpent Du Bon Dieu* (*God's Little Acre*), and "Dostoievschi's" *Crima si Pedeapsa.* Several more might well be translations: any of the books that have an author's name without a title, such as "Suetonius" or "Céline." Steinberg delighted in reading works translated into several languages, not just English: "I read Anatole France in Italian, Hemingway in French (funnily enough), *I Promessi Sposi* in English, and in 1927 I saw in Bucharest *Les Précieuses Ridicules* performed in Yiddish," he reported.[12]

Multiple languages and translation mattered enormously to those other émigrés Joyce and Nabokov. Nabokov not only oversaw the translations of some of his own works but also translated the work of other writers, his beloved Pushkin first and foremost. His fictional characters sometimes engage in translation. Translating, and also finding better and worse translations by others (he collected "howlers"), led Nabokov to theorize translation as well, in both his essays and fiction. Joyce translated from Latin, French, Italian, and (less successfully) German. He taught himself some Norwegian in order to read Ibsen, spoke good enough Danish, lived for many years in polyglot Trieste and Switzerland, and wrote the "*poly*- and *meta*-language" of *Finnegans Wake.*[13] In both *A Portrait of the Artist as a Young Man* and *Ulysses,* Stephen Dedalus enjoys the act of translation. Leopold Bloom muses on the subject.

Furthermore, multiple kinds of translation order the worlds of Joyce, Nabokov, and Steinberg: not just translations between languages. Translation is a subtype of metamorphosis, and, as I'll show, Steinberg, Nabokov, and Joyce widen the notion of translation to include movements between the imaginary and the real, between verbal and visual art, and even between what appears on a canvas or a page and viewers' and readers' responses to those markings. Steinberg tells Jean vanden Heuvel, "The purpose of the drawing is to make people feel that there is something else beyond the perception. That is essentially what I am playing with—the voyage between perception and understanding."[14] For these modernists, translation, always involving movement, can shrink to the size of a word and expand to the size of a book, an artistic medium, or even human understanding in the face of the work of art.

If *Library* is, as Steinberg announces, "a kind of autobiography," then we learn that he loved fiction (the largest category of books, at twenty-one volumes). Much could be made of the crafted models of bottles, a bus, a planter, and an Art Deco building that sit atop the book shelves, those shelves themselves sitting on a table. Suffice it for the moment to say that these items announce that books for him are continuous with the everyday world of things, not privileged objects to be worshipped. Were we sorting *Library*'s books into stacks of four or five, travel books, works of satire, and volumes of art practice and criticism would appear. Telephone directories from Oxford, Mississippi, and Johnson City, Tennessee, wittily depict Steinberg the American wanderer; a Samarkand telephone directory reminds us of Steinberg the world traveler. Like Nabokov and Joyce, he never stopped traveling, even after escaping from the Italian Fascists. Exile and travel will be central themes of this study.

It will close with an analysis and appreciation of a few of Steinberg's other assemblages, many of which are constructed drawing tables on which he places facsimiles of the tools of his art, including pens and pencils, as well as samples of his previous works. Taken together, *Library* and these tables depict a self-described reading and writing artist. They are self-portraits, but self-portraits as parodic as those books that don't open, that miniature wooden school bus going nowhere or that static wooden plant. Parody, as we'll see, enables Steinberg, Nabokov, and Joyce simultaneously to suggest and to hide the intimate self, thus exercising the modernist turn to impersonality.

I begin my study with Nabokov for two reasons. First, he and Steinberg knew each other, and we have evidence of "real world" interactions between the two men. Leading with such facts lends a solidity to my arguments from the outset. But, second, I want also to disrupt any inferred notions of aesthetic timetables: chronologically, of course, Joyce precedes Nabokov, but I want to emphasize that Joyce and Nabokov were contemporaries in Steinberg's imaginative world.

"I consider myself a good artist and a writer manqué," Steinberg writes. "Manqué in the sense not of a failure but of a person who, while having gifts for writing, understands that he cannot attain the highest level and therefore decides to 'move one step down.' However, these writer's gifts are a great help to me in drawing."[15] In a mirror image, Nabokov viewed himself as a weak painter: "I think I was born a painter—really!—and up to my fourteenth year, perhaps, I used to spend most of the day drawing and painting and I was supposed to become a painter in due time. But I don't think I had any real talent there" (*SO,* 17). Nabokov studied with various drawing masters, and one of them, Mstislav Dobuzhinsky, himself a prominent artist, encouraged the young Nabokov to write: "You have a talent for painting, but you must write."[16] He became instead a writer with an acute sense of visual beauty. In his works he refers by name to over a hundred visual artists, ranging from Apelles to Zurbarán, some of them more than once.[17] The presence of Nabokov's visual imagination in his works only begins with such explicit references to artists. He liked comic strips and devised chess puzzles.[18] He drew butterflies as a part of his lepidopteral research, peopled his fictions with artists and aesthetes, and brilliantly figured forth the appearance of real and imaginary worlds, detail by brilliant detail. As he told his students, "In reading, one should notice and fondle details" (*SO,* 335). Perhaps most importantly for this study of his affinities with Steinberg, we shall see that he claimed to write novels requiring a spatial viewing-reading much like that accorded to visual art.

By 1948, when works by Steinberg and Nabokov appeared together in three issues of the *New Yorker,* the two certainly were acquainted with each other. Saul Steinberg's name appears twice in Nabokov's work: in his introduction to *Bend Sinister,* where he suggests that the "urchins in the yard (Chapter Seven) have been drawn by Saul Steinberg,"[19] and in *Strong Opinions,* in which he comments on a Festschrift in his honor that included one of Steinberg's mock documents: "There is magic in every penstroke and curlicue of the delightful diploma that Saul Steinberg has drawn for my wife and me" (*SO,* 297).

We have a letter from Nabokov to Steinberg, written in October 1965, thanking him for Steinberg's gift of his recently published book, *The New World.*[20] Nabokov calls it a "magic ledger" and pays him the compliment of writing about details of the drawings. The postscript reads, "Please do come and see us when you are again in Europe," and in 1966 Steinberg does just that. Nabokov reports, "a wonderful time with wonderful Saul Steinberg."[21] Steinberg saw it this way: "[Nabokov] looked at me with tenderness and disbelief. I suspect he thought I was a drawing. Having lunch and dinner with a drawing was heaven for Nabokov, a playful man. He inscribed for me a book, made me a butterfly drawing, and dated it March, 1966, Mont Roux. (Mont Roux, formerly Rosenberg, laundered finally to Montreux)."[22]

Steinberg received an undated postcard of two arms dipping bread into cheese fondue, inscribed, "Thanks for the beautiful purple-and-green landscape. Joyeux Noel et bon appétit V. and V. Nabokov."[23] Nabokov had drawn a small butterfly on the postcard's dividing line.

Steinberg would later say, "A few days after the death of Nabokov, Amagansett was invaded by butterflies. Probably this always happens, and the reason I noticed the butterflies this time was, precisely, the presence, or the absence, of Nabokov."[24]

When Steinberg and the Nabokovs got together, visual wit mattered:

"To the 1964 Bollingen Press reception for *Eugene Onegin* Véra—who had done so much to research the circumstances of Pushkin's duel—carried a beaded evening bag with a mother-of-pearl handle. Steinberg, whose grasp of images the couple thought unrivaled, attended the festivities, probably at Nabokov's request. At the end of the party, the three found themselves alone on the Upper East Side street, with Steinberg's date. 'Véra, show him what you have in your handbag,' Vladimir directed, with what Steinberg recognized as immense pride. Véra extracted the Browning."[25]

Nabokov seemed to enjoy in Steinberg's book *The New World* his ability to place not only human characters on a stage (the gentleman doffing his Stein/Hom-berg) but also personified abstractions: Mr. Pi, 3.14159265, appears as an elegantly slim and erect 3, his post-decimal ornamentation gracefully arrayed in his wake. That Steinberg's numbers and letters themselves strolled, balanced, explored the hills in the company of an infinity sign, or physically supported lackluster men in their careful excursions, would have amused a writer who himself played with numbers and their relation to human identity in his fiction, and whose frequent puns and alliterations always call attention to the individual words and letters that make them happen.

Nabokov would have also seen in Steinberg's book a drawing of one of his own favorite writers, Gogol, and a punning drawing at that: the words Gogol, Vincent Van Gogh, and Gauguin circulate about a plinth, with only the two G's of Gogol and Gogh touching down upon it. Steinberg glosses this drawing: "Names are important; artist's name[s] determine half of what they do. Gogol, Van Gogh, Gauguin—the 3 Gogs. Celan, Céline, Cioran. The three caryatids, supporting the world of wartime disaster and misery. The other apparition that comes in the night is the strange tango of Lorca and Rilke. They are uneasily related, of course, to Kafka, who we see in the background, observing them. The phonetically reasonable is often the most reasonable of all."[26]

He would also have seen Steinberg's drawing (fig. 2) of a man holding a balloon-like collection of largely literary characters' names spelled out in large, looping letters across the air: Leopold Bloom, Ahab, Pavel Ivanovich Chichikov, Emma Bovary, Gulliver, Papageno, Julien Sorel, Candide, and "Rodion R[omanovich] Raskolnikov" (from Dostoevsky's *Crime and Punishment*) with its deliciously resonant trio of Rs. Three of these characters appear in some of Nabokov's favorite books—*Ulysses, Dead Souls* (Chichikov), and *Madame Bovary.* Furthermore, Nabokov plays on the triple Rs of Raskolnikov's full name in his own *Invitation to a Beheading,* in which the characters Rodion, Roman, and Rodrig prominently appear. Given Nabokov's interest in American popular culture, he would have ap-

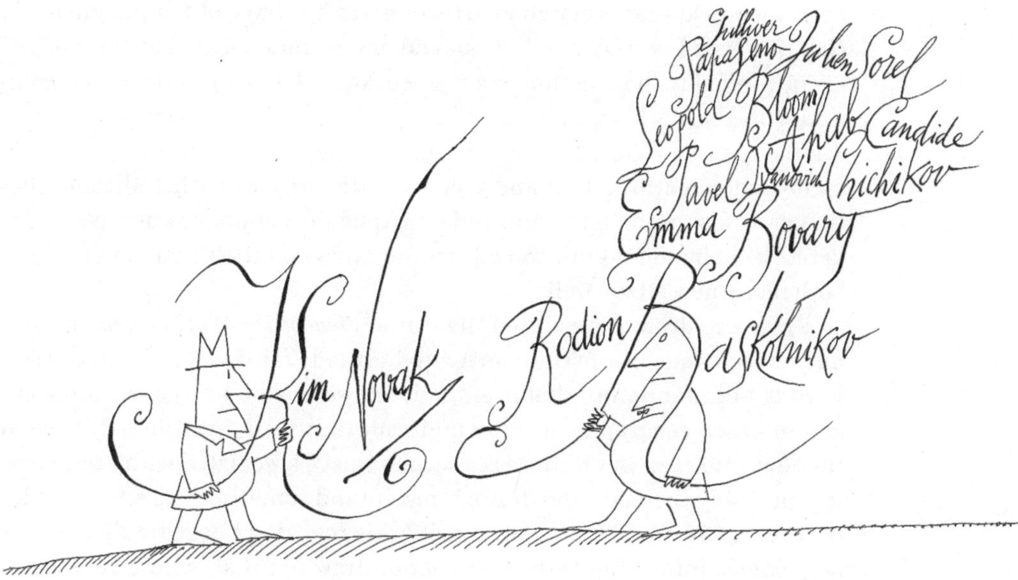

Fig. 2. Untitled, 1964. Ink on paper. Originally published in the *New Yorker*, November 7, 1964.

preciated the man holding aloft the words "Kim Novak," as if the actress's physical being had metamorphosed into the sprightly k's and short syllables of her name. Nor would the faux-elegant prominence of Steinberg's carefully drawn letters have been wasted upon Nabokov. In his Russian autobiography, Nabokov explains that, for him, the "physical shape of a letter representing the same sound in different languages" actually sounds different: the sound spelled out in Roman letters is duller than its Slavic version.[27] He would have heard Steinberg's drawing as well as seen it. Letters are small works of art for both men, to be looked at rather than merely to be read through. One would wish to see in addition a drawing never made: the visually inclined writer Nabokov embracing the literarily inclined artist Steinberg. Both men, after all, continually explored mirror images in their works.

Even the title, *The New World,* seems now almost a joint decision: such a world would have been for both Nabokov and Steinberg America, where they arrived after escaping the Old—Nabokov in 1940; Steinberg two years later. "When I arrived here," Steinberg tells Hilton Kramer, "—this whole nation was involved in painting like Cézanne. . . . I had such a joy to find these things that were untouched—the diners, the roads, the small towns—while the natives were painting like Rubens on Fourteenth Street and Rembrandt upstate." His closest artistic kinships are with "real immigrants—men like Bashevis Singer, Nabokov, de Kooning."[28] But it would also have been the world that every good artist creates by virtue of his imagination. Nabokov tells his students, "We should always remember that the work of art is invariably the creation of a new world . . . having no obvious connection with the worlds we already know" (*LL,* 1). The fantasies apparent in Steinberg's "New Worlds," however funny or puzzling, seem always to guide us toward something real and true, and they rhyme with Nabokov's fictional worlds in which real life and imagined life cannot be effectively sundered, even by the twentieth-century dictators and their henchmen whom both men knew all too well.

Steinberg drew and painted the iconic *View of the World from 9th Avenue,* a map/landscape of the continental United States as it rolls so far westward out of Manhattan that eventually the shores of Asia come into view, and in which geographical detail and scale diminish precipitously beyond the Hudson River. But if there is a second image associated with Steinberg, it is probably the man who draws himself (and sometimes also his double) into being (fig. 3). "This is how I do it," this repeated image implies. Steinberg comes into being by the very act of drawing: that is how, in a metaphysical bootstrap operation, he constitutes himself. As we'll see, he will continue across the years to draw the act of drawing as well as the implements of drawing, depicting pens, pencils, ink, brushes, paper, and various domestic items arrayed on tables.

Nabokov, too, writes frequently of the scenes of writing, and the mechanics of pen, ink, paper, and furniture. We learn, for example, how the poet John Shade of *Pale Fire* arranges himself in the bathtub so that he can shave, and while shaving, await literary inspiration. Both shaving cream and the "icy blaze" of sudden inspiration set his "little hairs" on end (*PF,* 67). Nabokov gives John Shade one of his own peculiarities—they both write on index cards. Their work proceeds spatially, as a picture: "I find now that index cards are really the best kind of paper that I can use for the purpose. I don't write consecutively from the beginning to the next chapter and so on to the end. I just fill in the gaps of the picture, of this jigsaw puzzle which is quite clear in my mind" (*SO,* 16). Nabokov also explicitly likens writing a novel to creating a painting. He waits patiently for inspiration to fill out the entire novel in his mind, and once it is complete, he writes it out, explaining that "since this entire structure, dimly illumined in one's mind, can be compared to a painting," he doesn't write it from beginning to end, instead "pick[ing] out a bit here and a bit there, till I have filled all the gaps on paper" (*SO,* 32).

Properly reading one of his novels, first presented to him like a "pic-

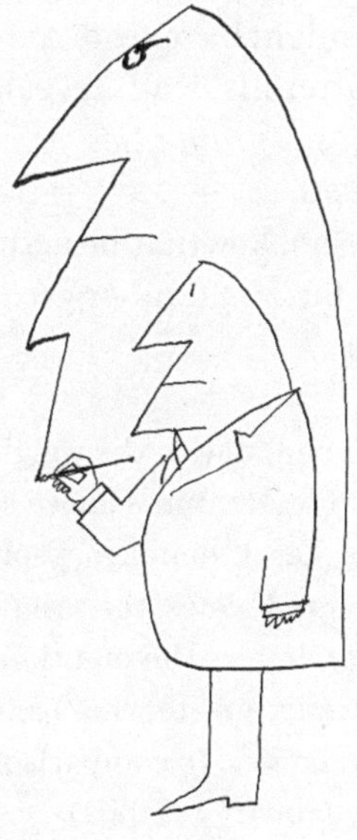

Fig. 3. Untitled, 1963. Ink on paper. Originally published in the *New Yorker,* February 16, 1963.

ture" in the mind, must involve the intellect: "A book of fiction appeals first of all to the mind. The mind, the brain, the top of the tingling spine, is, or should be, the only instrument used upon a book," but here a problem arises (*LL,* 3–4). Nabokov explains: "If the mind were constructed on optional lines and if a book could be read in the same way as a painting is taken in by the eye, that is without the bother of working from left to right and without the absurdity of beginnings and ends, this would be the ideal way of appreciating a novel, for thus the author saw it at the moment of its conception" (*LL,* 380). Rereading, then, becomes the only way to "see" an entire novel spatially: "Curiously enough, one cannot read a book: one can only reread it. A good reader, a major reader, an active and creative reader is a rereader. . . . At a second, or third, or fourth reading we do, in a sense, behave towards a book as we do towards a painting" (*LL,* 3).

Steinberg mentioned Nabokov from time to time in notes to himself (citing the latter's concept of *poshlust* or reminding himself, "Nabokov: In Afterlife—no privacy . . . Read Nabokov Speak Memory").[29] An inventory of Steinberg's library at the time of his death shows that he owned

Nabokov's *Ada or Ardor: A Family Chronicle, The Eye, Nabokov's Quartet, Nabokov's Dozen, Lectures on Literature, Selected Letters 1940–1977,* and *The Annotated Lolita.*[30] Such a list gives us only hints of his actual reading of Nabokov: he didn't necessarily read all of these works, nor does the list include other works by Nabokov that he might have read. At his Amagansett house, an inventory taken three years after his death reveals copies of *The Gift, Glory, Pnin, Look at the Harlequins, Tyrants Destroyed & Other Stories,* and *A Russian Beauty & Other Stories.*

But our best guides to the books by Nabokov that he actually read lie in his comments made to his friend Aldo Buzzi. Steinberg read Brian Boyd's biography of Nabokov, writing to Buzzi:

> I'm reading an enormous (not readable in bed, due to the weight) biography of Nabokov. In 1950, at age 50, all his teeth went, dentures above and below plus a long series of urinary and pulmonary woes, heart, lumbago, psoriasis, hospitals, clinics, sanatoria—his wife, too—plus fractured bones, the result of hunting butterflies, and meanwhile the work continues, letters (he mentions me only once: a marvelous visit with the marvelous St. in a letter—to who?) and struggles with editors, publishers, lawyers, biographers, relatives. In comparison I see myself as lazy, extremely lazy, my biggest flaw. (*LAB,* January 14, 1992)

In fact, when Steinberg decided to enter a clinic in Switzerland in order to quit smoking, he was inspired by Nabokov's own efforts to beat the nicotine habit (*SS: I,* 65).

In another letter to Buzzi: "I'm still reading the life of Nabokov (by Brian Boyd), almost finished: it's a crescendo, as in Dickens, from poverty to triumph—after Lolita success and enormous riches, cosmic fame, yet he remains down-to-earth and writes even more (and better). A fine example of a life administered with sound judgment" (*LAB,* January 25, 1992). Or again, tantalizingly, he tells Buzzi, "I read the Nabokov you mentioned, years ago. It's in the country [Amagansett], I'll reread it. A mind like his, serious and playful, is a rarity: he was the type who loved puns, rebus[es], nonsense" (*LAB,* February 27, 1995). So did Steinberg. Like Nabokov, who frequently punned on or anagrammatized his own name, he once referred to himself as "the Dominican author, el afamado Estémber." Here he indicates the way Spanish speakers pronounced his last name, and the way the Portuguese press referred to him, as *el afamado pintór,* that phrase itself suggesting a "found" interlingual pun—"a source of confusion for the Italian reader, given the dual cognates of famoso (famous) and affamato (starving)" (*LAB,* June 10, 1994).

Which specific works by Nabokov did Steinberg actually read? While we may never have a complete answer to this question, factual accounting will in any case get us only so far in thinking about the relations between these two artists. Their art testifies to the importance of illogic, of a playful but committed tampering with the facts, of riddles without answers, and of what Nabokov identifies as "the emphatically and unshakably illogical world which I am advertising as a home for the spirit" (*LL,* 373). Nabokov advised his students at Cornell to adopt the "irrational standards" beloved of his favored authors, "this capacity to wonder at trifles—no matter the imminent peril—these asides of the spirit, these footnotes in the volume of life are the highest forms of consciousness, and it is in this childishly speculative state of mind, so different from commonsense and its logic, that we know the world to be good" (*LL,* 374). It is in this spirit that I hope to look at Nabokov's and Joyce's prose and read Steinberg's drawings, although facts will figure prominently, too. For example, when Nabokov writes, "I remember a cartoon depicting a chimney sweep falling from the roof of a tall building and noticing on the way that a sign-board had one word spelled wrong" (*LL,* 373–74), I think of Steinberg's drawings in which people in motion do double takes at various printed signs.

Another example of Nabokov's and Steinberg's coincidental ideas appears when Nabokov writes in *Ada* of the "L disaster" as having comic results and likens it to "bric-à-Braques" (*Ada,* 17). Vivian Darkbloom—Nabokov's anagrammatic persona and writer of *Ada*'s endnotes—glosses the phrase as follows: "Braques: allusion to a bric-à-brac painter,"[31] thus making use of the very same pun that Steinberg gives the museumgoer daydreaming in front of a Braque-ish painting in a drawing of 1964, "Braque, bric-à-brac, break, bark" (fig. 4). Nabokov's name appears there. The result of a conversation between the two men? Pure coincidence? Appropriation/friendly theft? Mysteriously shared daydream? Both Nabokov and Steinberg would have been capable of seeing it as any of these phenomena. This drawing appears, with some changes, as a *New Yorker* cover for the October 18, 1969, issue (fig. 5), the same year that *Ada* appeared. In this later version "James Joyce" appears, as well as "Nabokov."

In contrast to Steinberg's actual acquaintance with Nabokov, his knowledge of Joyce came solely from the printed page. Steinberg read him for the first time after emigrating to the United States and didn't understand him—"he was a great puzzle to me"—until several readings later. Then Joyce gave him the nerve to overcome his own lack of confidence in himself and his art:

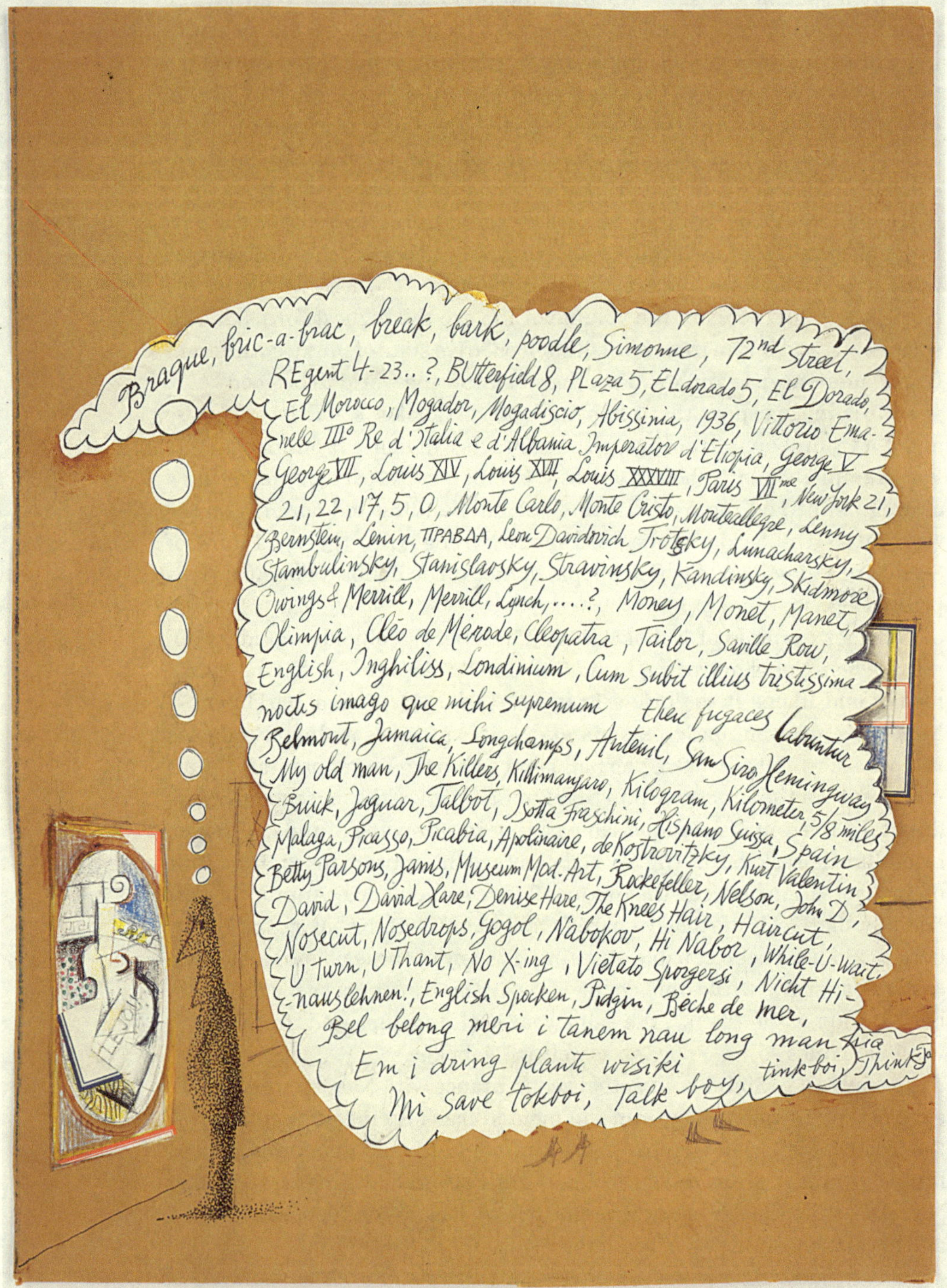

Fig. 4. Untitled, 1964. Ink, pencil, colored pencil, and collage on brown paper, 20¹⁄₁₆ × 14¾ in. (Art Institute of Chicago, gift of The Saul Steinberg Foundation; photograph by Ellen Page Wilson, courtesy Pace Gallery)

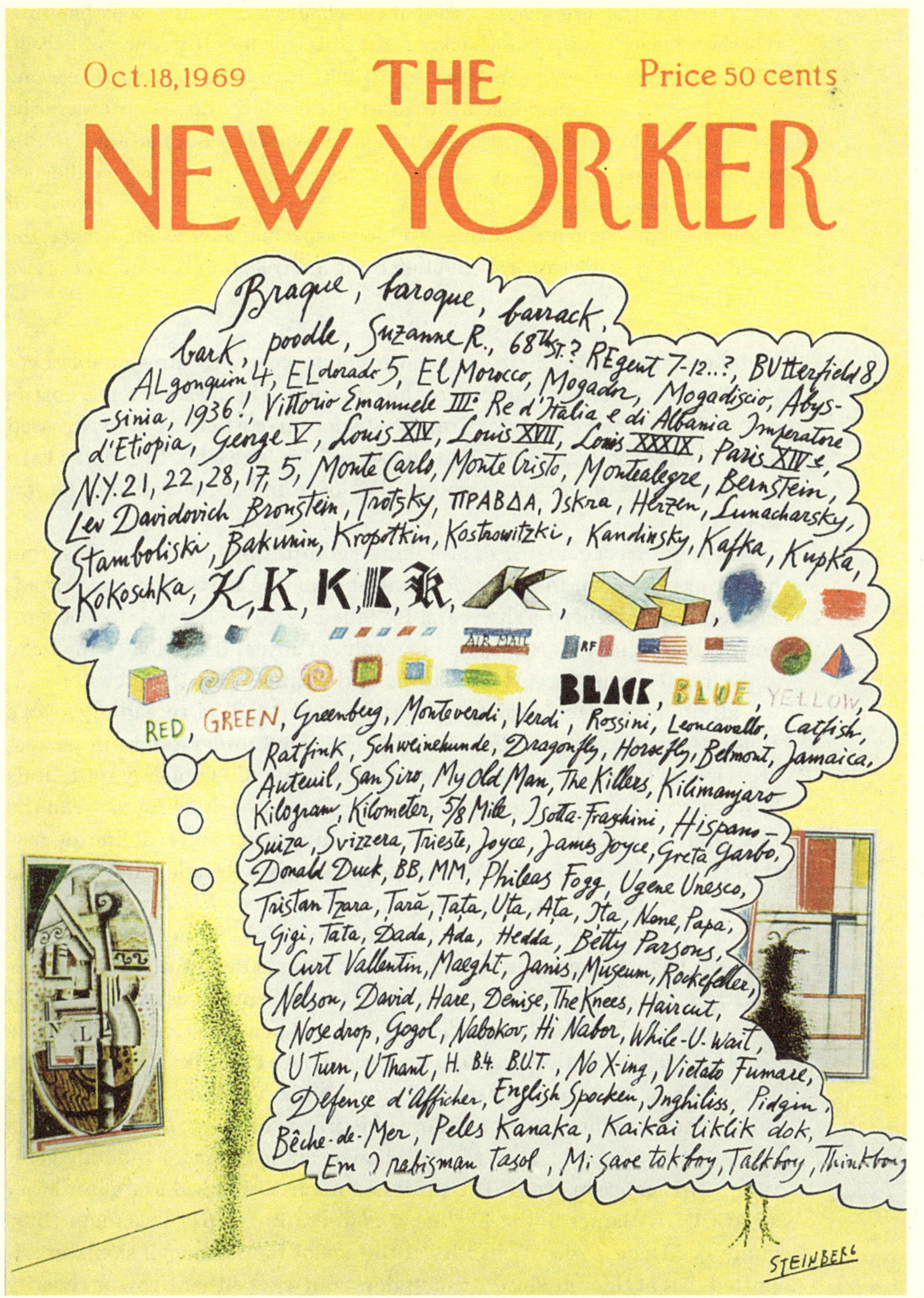

Fig. 5. Cover of the *New Yorker,* October 18, 1969. (Reprinted with permission of the *New Yorker* magazine; all rights reserved)

Well, it was the amazement to find that somebody could write a book like this, that there is such a thing like a book. . . . And this gave me great courage . . . well, confidence, something like this, to the possibility that one can do what he wants and still be great and magnificent, because there is a doubt that . . . in order to be good you have to do like the great—which is nonsense. . . . But I meant it in this way, that the [aspect?] of Joyce that pleases me and gave me so much confidence was that he used for his life, for his work, if I may put it this way, . . . the power of the microscopic elements, and one never has respect . . . for the importance, the genuine quality of microscopy. The other thing was true, the giantism. The praise of the hero.[32]

Steinberg goes on to discuss the nature of Joyce's hero (presumably Leopold Bloom), whom he connects to the situation of being Jewish in a hostile world. Rather than endorsing Steinberg's notion of a hero as "a guy dressed up on a horse fighting the dragon and so on," Joyce teaches him that a hero is one who lives *inside* the dragon, as do "Joyce and . . . myself and the Jew in general."[33]

The best direct evidence of Steinberg's admiration for Joyce comes from his letters to Buzzi, in which he mentions that he is reading and rereading Joyce's works across the years. He tells Buzzi in a letter dated December 15, 1959, that he's reading a biography of Joyce. It's "a life to my taste and surely to yours too." He mentions in the same letter that he's "rereading all of Joyce." On January 8, 1960, he reports, "I'm rereading Joyce's *Ulysses,* also *Finnegan's* [*sic*] *Wake,* which now I understand—in part. A great loss of time not to have understood it years ago." October 9, 1961, finds him congratulating Buzzi on reading Joyce and advising him to "read the biography of Joyce by Elman [*sic*]." "Rereading Joyce and still finding new things, hidden," he reports May 15, 1970. Nearly a decade later, on January 30, 1980, he reports, "I'm slowly rereading Joyce's *Ulysses*" (*LAB*).

For Steinberg, Joyce becomes a touchstone for valuing other writers, historical figures, and even things. He calls Manuel Puig, author of *The Buenos Aires Affair,* "Joyce's illegitimate son" (*LAB,* September 15, 1976). Difficult works, such as *Il calzolaio di Vigevano,* by Lucio Mastronardi, he reads "slowly (it's like reading Faulkner or Joyce, I have to think)" (*LAB,* June 15, 1964). When he drinks an especially good wine, Fendent de Sion, he tells Buzzi that it's mentioned in Ellmann's biography of Joyce. *Dubliners* comes up in a letter of April 1, 1983 (*LAB*), when he quotes from an annotated edition: "This concerns you: 'The promises made to Blessed Margaret Mary ALACOQUE' James Joyce *Eveline, Dubliners* Born 1647 in Janots (Burgundy)[. M]ade a vow of chastity at the age of four although she later admitted that at this age she did not understand what either a vow or chastity was. Etc., etc. [*sic*]." When Federico Fellini writes to Steinberg, comparing him to "great artists (if you allow me . . . : Kafka, Joyce, Picasso)," Steinberg forwards the letter three weeks later to Buzzi (*LAB,* February 26, 1993). He criticizes Joyce's "19th century Italian" but sends Buzzi a little book containing Joyce's essay/lecture on Defoe. Perhaps most telling of all, because most whimsical, Steinberg sends his friend a photocopy of his birth certificate with notations indicating that he was born at 11 p.m. on June 15: "One hour later and it would be June 16, Bloomsday, the Leopold Bloom day described by Joyce" (*LAB,* September 26, 1995).

Beyond such exact evidence, it is the "asides of the spirit" shared by Steinberg, Nabokov, and Joyce that this study will reveal. I will work with details of their individual works, finding the hints and nuances of those best kinds of companionship for artists—a shared artistic practice and a shared sensibility.

A note on critical method. Readers may hope that I discuss Steinberg as a figure who expressed attitudes toward key issues of our times such as race, class, and gender. Or they may hope for a discussion of, for example, the importance of the city to Steinberg's art, or the effect that market forces had on his career. In short, they will look for some approaches to literary study—"new historicist," "materialist," "cultural critique," or "cultural studies"—which furnish contexts of varying kinds to formalist analyses.

While my study is largely formalist in nature, it participates in what some are calling the "New Formalism," which Marjorie Levinson has analyzed in her essay "What Is New Formalism?"[34] This still loosely constituted movement "seek[s] to reinstate close reading . . . as the opening move, preliminary to any kind of critical consideration. Reading, understood in traditional terms as multilayered and integrative responsiveness to every element of the textual dimension, quite simply produces the basic materials that form the subject matter of even the most historical investigations" (560). This is an up-to-date formalism that is not blind to history and context but carefully informed by them, while keeping the work of art as the sum of aesthetic processes front and center. It is my hope that future, primarily contextual, studies of Steinberg's work will use my study as a foundation on which to build. The best cultural studies / materialist / new historicist critics begin with an understanding of the complexities and nuances of texts and images. Their arguments arise in part from paying close attention to what appears on the page or the canvas, rather than seeking conclusions that largely ignore aesthetic and formal matters.

As I discuss the particulars of works of art in this study, however, I *am* practicing a type of cultural critique. That is, I have chosen one context in particular: the biographical. In finding parallels and intersections among the life stories of Nabokov, Joyce, and Steinberg, I have gone beyond pure formalism to discuss how their experiences as emigrants amid unsettling historical conditions inflected their art. My discussion of Steinberg's *Library,* for example, yields information about what it means to be an intellectually inclined, cosmopolitan, émigré artist—one especially interested in the art of translation—in twentieth-century New York.

In the end, there can be no sharp distinction between the two "isms," contextualism and formalism, as Levinson demonstrates (562). Because looking, reading, and describing are active, interpretative practices, not simply passive mirrors held up to the art work, formalism is never without a contextual lens. Not only do formally and historically oriented critics need one another's insights, they also share approaches.

2

The "Springboard of Parody"

As I tease out the affinities among Steinberg, Nabokov, and Joyce, one will emerge most strongly: their shared fascination with parody. It is, after all, a rhetorical strategy we know to be common to both literature and visual art. The particulars of our three artists' parodic energies will appear in the following chapters, but to set the stage here, I want to focus on Steinberg's understanding of parody, with some initial help from Nabokov.

Parody has a rich history. When we consider it, a classical notion of the concept often comes to mind. The term *parodia* first appears in Aristotle's *Poetics,* where it refers to a poem written in the epic style but engaging in subjects and manners of expression foreign to the traditional epic genre. One thinks of a literary text that is repeated in another text with a satiric, comic, or generally deprecating twist. Standard literary definitions of parody long fell into this form: for example, "Parody imitates the distinctive style and thought of a literary text, author, or tradition for comic effect."[1] Mockery is seen as its characteristic quality because, from its beginnings, "parody was originally 'a song sung beside' (*parodia*), i.e., a comic imitation of a serious poem."[2]

There is, however, no accurate transhistorical definition of parody.[3] Theorists of modern parody have tended to emphasize a formal quality: its doubled structure in which a parodied text lying in the background lends some of its qualities to the foregrounded text. Parody is now discussed as "repetition with ironic critical difference, marking difference rather than similarity." "Ironic inversion" is regarded as the distinctive quality of parody, marking its difference from pastiche, hoax, plagiarism, or forgery. According to this view, allusion and quotation can be parodic if they aim at ironic inversion.[4] Other theorists, most notably Mikhail Bakhtin, have dropped the necessity of both form and irony, understanding parody more broadly as intertextuality or inter-art discourse, including echoing repetition and a "defining mix of repetition and difference."[5] They understand parody as a *process* or *function* rather than a form.[6] It is to this latter understanding that Steinberg, Nabokov, and Joyce implicitly subscribe, but of course definition isn't their goal. When they speak of parody directly, they tend to offer broad descriptions such as "Any repetition is parody"[7] or "Satire is a lesson; parody is a game" (*SO,* 75).

Perhaps the best way to think of modernist parody as practiced by our three artists is to begin with a statement about parody in *The Real Life of Sebastian Knight:* "As often was the way with Sebastian Knight he used parody as a kind of springboard for leaping into the highest region of serious emotion" (*RLSK,* 91). According to John Burt Foster, "once parody becomes a springboard for innovation, one's writing will no longer necessarily carry any clear trace of the source text."[8] Parody, then, accounts for some of the modernist difficulty that we experience in parsing works by Nabokov, Joyce, and Steinberg. The "game" of parody can be played for high stakes, and that "leap" from the fact of parodic repetition to serious emotion can leave the reader scrambling to descry the territory below.

To understand the mode of parody favored by these artists, we may turn to a passage from Nabokov's *Pale Fire.* In his autobiographical poem in that novel, the poet John Shade remembers seeing an "iridule," "one opal cloudlet" which "Reflects the rainbow of a thunderstorm / Which in a distant valley has been staged" (PF, 36–37). Nabokov coins the term "iridule" to depict the reflection (or repetition) of a rainbow in a slightly different form in the sky above another valley. The iridule is an emblem of Nabokovian parody. We might say that it parodies the "original" rainbow, showing it in an altered form. The notion of mockery of a specifically literary text is absent, as is ironic inversion; the idea of parody as *repetition in a different context* substitutes for them. What's equally important here, however, is the view that even "nature" is artificial, for Nabokov ends the passage with "we are most artistically caged." Nature, then, becomes a type of text or performance that can be reiterated (or here, reiterate itself) textually as parody. And since "reality" is itself staged and artistic, there is no absolute or degree zero of reality/text from which parody is a formal deviation—it's parodic energy through and through. Steinberg has said: "You can make a palm tree look funny—and it *is* funny, it's a strange thing. Nature has parodies."[9] From there Steinberg comes to believe, as we shall see, that nature itself *is* parodic.

Charles Kinbote of *Pale Fire* "translates" Shade's poem into a lengthy "Commentary" marked by madness, but a commentary nonetheless, "borrowing," as he says, "a kind of opalescent light from my poet's fiery orb" (*PF,* 81). His parasitic, parodic rendering of the poem's meaning is akin to the opalescent iridule or to the moon, which borrows the sun's light. From as early as the "Foreword" to the volume, Kinbote thinks along these lines. He describes John Shade as he stands on the terrace of his borrowed house and looks at a distant lake: "I am looking at him. I am witnessing a unique physiological phenomenon: John Shade perceiving and transforming the world, taking it in and taking it apart, re-combining its elements in the very process of storing them up so as to produce at some unspecified date an organic miracle, a fusion of image and music, a line of verse" (*PF,* 27).

Nabokov creates here the idea of "transformation," of repetition with a difference, that is, parody as the very process of making art. The passage establishes a corollary to modernist parody: it can be a way of repeating or re-creating natural phenomena, persons, ideas, things, even cities. It's not limited to literary texts, although it loves to play among them. That many things might already be parodies—or offer themselves as amenable to parody—are ideas that, as we shall see, enchanted Steinberg and his two "great teachers," Nabokov and Joyce.[10]

Saul Steinberg thought about and deliberately practiced the art of parody. At one moment he writes, "In a way artists like James Joyce and Jackson Pollock make giant clever frauds, like my passports,"[11] pointing to the parodic nature of his faux documents. But is a fraud a parody? For Steinberg it is. His own theory of parody includes but also takes him beyond his blatant mocking of official documents (fig. 6), one of which was probably the affidavit of travel that enabled him to leave Italy in 1941.[12]

He also reflects on parody as part of a family of concepts having to do with illicit doubling, as he writes out his thoughts (fig. 7). Parody appears twice, once in a list that includes the false, the fake, the copy, forgery. It appears again, grouped with epigones ("the less distinguished successors of an illustrious generation")[13] and with raisins, which might be considered parodies of grapes. Below, he lists Spinoza, an epigone or parody of Maimonides. With Walter Brennan, Steinberg might have been thinking of the midcentury actor who often played sidekicks and also "Grandpa" in *The Real McCoys*—a television comedy about an Appalachian family that moved to California. Cortizon (if not referring to a steroid) is a stumper, unless perhaps it's a pun on courtesan—puns being derivative, off-kilter repetitions.

In another, lengthier list in one of his sketchbooks entitled "Parody" (fig. 8) he notes, among other parodies, "Nose parody of face; Architecture parody of past . . . Styles: constructionist, Expressionist, Punk; Fortress, Palace, Farm, Palladian, Babylonian, Aztec, Norman . . . Geography as Parody: Europe is duplicated in Asia & America; Asia—Arabia (Spain) India (Italy) Indochine (Greece) . . . Australia plays the part of Africa." In fact, he insists upon the widest definition of parody: again, "Any repetition is parody."[14]

Deanna Petherbridge has created perhaps the most thoroughgoing account of such repetition: "Copying embraces an enormous range of

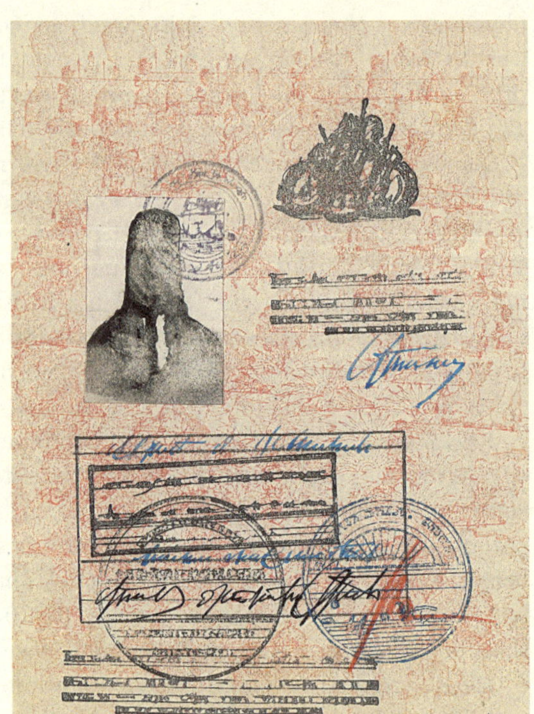

Fig. 6. Untitled, c. 1951. Ink, rubber stamp, crayon, and collaged paper on paper, 7½ × 5 ½ in. (Beinecke Rare Book and Manuscript Library, Yale University)

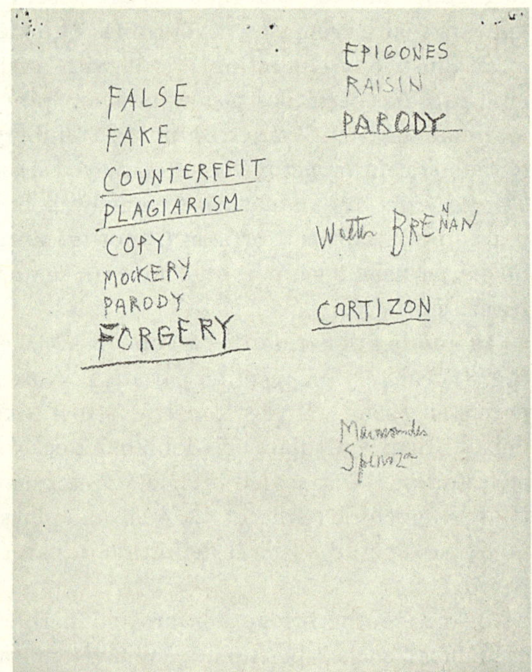

Fig. 7. Untitled, n.d. Pencil, ink, and colored pencil on paper, 11 × 8 ½ in. (Beinecke Rare Book and Manuscript Library, Yale University)

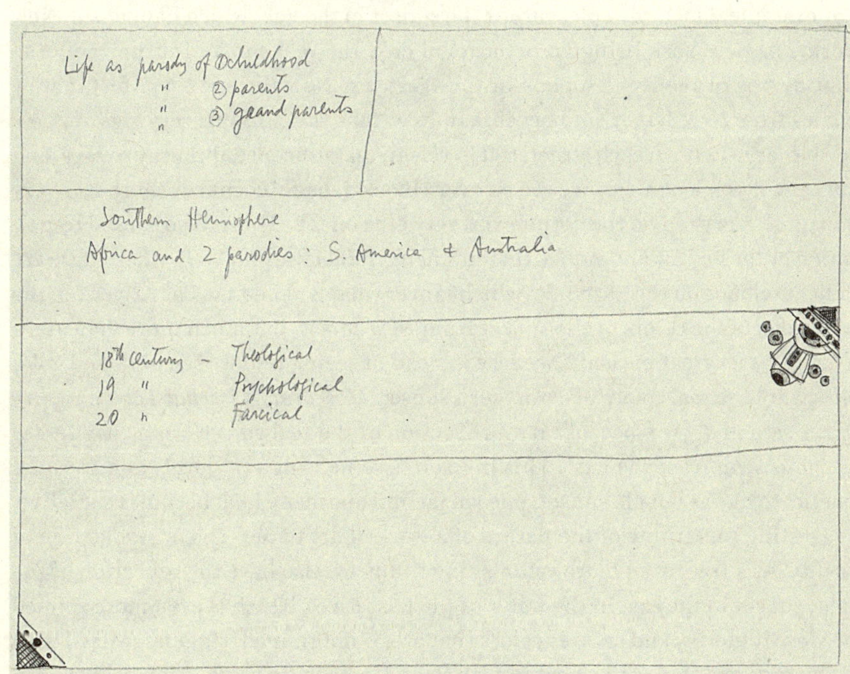

Fig. 8. Sketchbook page, 1984. Pencil on paper, 14 × 11 in. (Beinecke Rare Book and Manuscript Library, Yale University)

philosophical and semantic constellations around imitation and emulation, mimicry and mimesis; reproduction and representation; similarity, simulation, simulacrum and counterfeit; transcription, transformation, translation; authenticity, attribution, assimilation and dissimulation; prototype, paraphrase, pastiche and parody. All shades of intermediate states blur the dialectical space between original and copy."[15]

To understand the pervasiveness of parody in Steinberg's works, it helps to examine what he calls on several occasions "reality of the first, second, and third, etc. degree or the problem of reality moving towards illusion."[16] As he explains, "The thing that remains essential for me is the aspect of reality of the first, second, and third degrees. I don't really understand why this attracts me so much. It makes up part of the old family of things that I always did. A box inside a box inside a box, naturally. And also concentric circles of things that evolve from the center and expand toward the exterior, or things that start at the exterior centrifugally."[17]

He gives as an example of "situations of second and third degrees" the sunset in New York City. I quote at length in order to clarify the notion of repetition-parody that accompanies the idea of degrees of reality:

> For example, I look with pleasure at the sunset in the East which happens in New York. . . . New York being an orthogonal city, the real sunset [purportedly the first degree of reality] happens in the West. . . . Now the sunset unfortunately comes from New Jersey, and because in New York the sunset is very vigorous, we see it everywhere, in each street. If it is a clear, magnificent day there are very long sunsets, if you look west. We see on every block a magnificent sunset that is very Japanese. Very red on the bottom and very blue on top. This is also caused by pollution or the bad air and smoke that intensify the coloration. Well, when there are delicate clouds on the East Side, which is over what is called the East River . . . the east reflects the colors of the sunset from New Jersey, but much more delicately. That gives us great pleasure because instead of seeing red, we see pink and gold, which are the real colors of a northern sunset. *Moreover, it is what I call a reality of the second degree,* because it's a reflection of the real sunset from New Jersey which is seen from the East. This in itself is something very lovely and free and poetic: to have a double sunset, one vulgar and another which becomes secretive, suggesting something of the nature of a work of art to me. That's a reflection of reality. As a free, even more astonishing thing, we also have the reflection of the false sunset in the east in the water of the East River, which is even more refined because it moves, and creates colors that are, if not refined, singular. Mixed with tints from real things like boats which in reality seem to navigate on gold for me, but to pass in the reflection at third hand of a sunset. *So this mixture of things are at a third or fourth degree for me* [emphasis added].[18]

Like Nabokov's description of an iridule discussed above, Steinberg initially looks to nature for an example of multiple degrees of reality. Nature, however, acts *as an artist*—"suggesting something of the nature of a work of art to me"—and this suggestion links what nature does to what Steinberg believes his art to be, an artful repetition (second degree) of what he sees in the world around him. Just as the sunsets of the second, third, and fourth degrees take on different colorations, so his art is not a strictly mimetic activity, but rather something that changes as it passes through his imagination and intellect. "In general I no longer paint things I see. I know them. Instead, I paint things that have passed through my mind, so to speak. . . . In a certain sense, this is the method of the novelist, who tries to capture the essential of each situation."[19] He doesn't objectively record nature, he parodies it—repeats it with a difference.

However, such an explanation doesn't capture the full scope of parody in Steinberg's art. It still seems to depend on an originary and "real" first degree—"the problem of reality moving towards illusion," the sunset in New Jersey that nature makes. To explain his parody, it's necessary to understand that he parodies not just "real" objects in the world but already parodic objects, things that exist at what he would call (at least) the second degree of reality. He parodies what are already illusions, imagined things.

"Nature is an artist and, like all artists, is ruled by clichés. Nature repeats itself, with and without variations and in time the repeated image becomes an indelible sign." Even nature for him is already imagined before he takes up pen and brush: "For nature . . . and for whatever is untouched by people, I use a series of clichés."[20] Cliché captures cliché, and parody thrives in that action. "When I admire a scene in the country," he tells his friend Harold Rosenberg, "I look for a signature in the lower right-hand corner."[21] Nature has parodies, he insists, because "Nature *arts*—people, animals, skies get themselves up to look like objects in pictures. Trees try to resemble trees."[22] Like Nabokov, who said that "every great writer is a great deceiver, but so is that arch-cheat Nature" (*LL,* 5), Steinberg sees nature as artificial. He wants us to understand that, "like James Joyce," he "makes giant clever frauds," in the sense that "the real," the zero degree of reality, is absent not only from his art but also from "the world" or nature as he sees it.[23]

It would seem to follow—and it actually does—that Steinberg rarely worked "from life," but preferred to parody not just an already parodic nature but his own and other artists' second- or third-degree versions of things in the world. Anton van Dalen, Steinberg's friend and assistant toward the end of his career, tells us that he worked either from his imagination or from photographs: "Steinberg asked me to take pictures of the Empire State Building and pictures of taxis. He would draw a diagram of how he wanted to photograph it, at what angle."[24] He would then draw from the photograph.

Perhaps Steinberg's most useful reflection on his own work is "What I draw is drawing, [and] drawing derives from drawing. My line wants to remind constantly that it's made of ink."[25] He parodies not just already made things but also mediums, techniques, methods, even attitudes. "I like to make a parody of bravura. You have to think of a lot of my work as some sort of parody of talent. . . . I wish to create a fiction of skill in the same sense [that] my writing is an imitation of calligraphy: fine flourishes that can't be deciphered, official stamps no-one can read."[26]

At times he seems to speak of parody in the narrower sense, as a deliberate imitation of a model. When he parodies other painters, he does so to improve his painting techniques:

> I wanted to be able to paint like that [nineteenth-century country landscape painting]. When I move into unfamiliar territory, to educate myself, I have to make a—let's say a parody of that territory. When I moved into the territory of painting with oil, I could not consider myself free to paint until I had mastered a short hand of the various techniques. . . . I had painted an Expressionist canvas, and I had learned that before being able to paint with absolute freedom, one has to learn the technique very thoroughly. . . . After the Expressionist experiment, I did a Mondrian or two; that is, I covered the given surfaces with painting in order to learn how to cover a surface well.[27]

But he also parodies for the pleasure of making frauds, telling Buzzi that he has enjoyed making a collection "of Mondrians and a few cubist collages of Braque, Gris, etc., all done by me and well framed. Nobody suspects and so the country house [where he hangs them] has become a great luxury for me too" (*LAB,* July 20, 1963). He develops a special technique for parodying old photographs using "the same high-gloss enamels that are used on automobiles and refrigerators" and aging them "by crumpling them or scratching them with a razor blade. They become relics, parodies of autobiography, of self-adoration, of the family."[28]

Steinberg mines his parodies of painters' and architects' styles for his drawings. As Hilton Kramer points out, we can find in his works "Cubist and rococo characters, expressionist conversations, Renaissance objects, Gothic words, and Pointillist emotions."[29] When he parodies art historical styles in his drawings, the cultured viewer is called upon to understand them in new ways: a "pointillist" person seems to have a personality different from a person drawn in a style of twentieth-century magazine realism. Sometimes, as we'll see, he draws each member of a couple in a different art historical style; we need no other evidence to tease out the difficulty or pleasure of the relationship.

Parody plays several roles in Steinberg's world. It expresses his modernist rejection of naive mimeticism and underscores his insistence on the primacy of intellect and imagination. Even his simplest drawings can suggest undercurrents of thought that the viewer can almost, but not quite, articulate. The narrator of *Ada* says of the titular character that "the quality of her innate wit had deepened, strange 'metempirical' (as Van called them) undercurrents seemed to double internally, and thus enrich, the simplest expression of her simplest thoughts" (*Ada,* 219). Critics have spoken of decoding Nabokov's works; Joyce expected that professors would long want to work out the difficulties of *Ulysses*. One of Steinberg's liberally used rubber stamps is an inspector, a detective-like figure. Steinberg's is a cerebral art, drawing what we might call "a line around a think,"[30] and he tells Buzzi that the intellect is "the salvation of us all" (*LAB,* March 25, 1988). To the passionately cerebral works of Steinberg, Nabokov, and Joyce we now, in the guise of inspectors, shall turn.

Part II

Steinberg

Writing, Drawing, Reading

3

Steinberg

The Man-Pen

In a 1960 letter to Aldo Buzzi, Steinberg confesses, "I have a great temptation—but not the courage—to write, writing can be a nightmare because of the duplicity of means" (*LAB,* January 8, 1960). Six years later, in *Washington, D.C., 1967* (fig. 9), he draws, not for the first time, a man who simultaneously writes and draws. This image is a *pars pro toto,* the beginning of a horizontal array of images, a "Chinese-type scroll thirty feet long, on which I developed a continuous drawing, based on what I did each day: a diary in drawings. . . . A few feet survived" (*RS,* 49). In this work he chronicles his own unfamiliar situation of living and working temporarily in the nation's capital, "In Washington in 1966 [correct date 1967], as an artist-in-residence at the Smithsonian Institution, I spent perhaps the strangest three months of my life. It was as though I'd emigrated to a place where normally no one emigrates," Steinberg tells Buzzi (*RS,* 45). The vortex of lines entitled *Washington, D.C. 1967* gathers about the point where the artist's pen meets the surface on which he draws and writes, Steinberg's home away from home. While passages of something that looks like writing appear within this drawing, it actually presents us with the collapse of the categories of writing and drawing, because Steinberg here self-consciously writes drawing and draws writing.

It is the energy of this interplay between drawing and writing that fuels Steinberg's extraordinary oeuvre from beginning to end.[1] He frequently uses the terms *stenography* (a substitution of contractions or arbitrary signs or symbols) and *calligraphy* (elegant penmanship) to describe his work.[2] *Graphology* (the study of handwriting) is his preferred mode of interpretation: "for me, seeing a work of art is, to some extent, a matter of graphology."[3] He adds, "I am a writer who can't write . . . The line—let's call it graphology—is my real language . . . for me, the scale of my own handwriting is always the right scale."[4] This image of the artist at work at his drawing table, and the Steinberg self-portrait we half see, half imagine there, offers instances of the steno- and calli-graphic, while viewing it involves

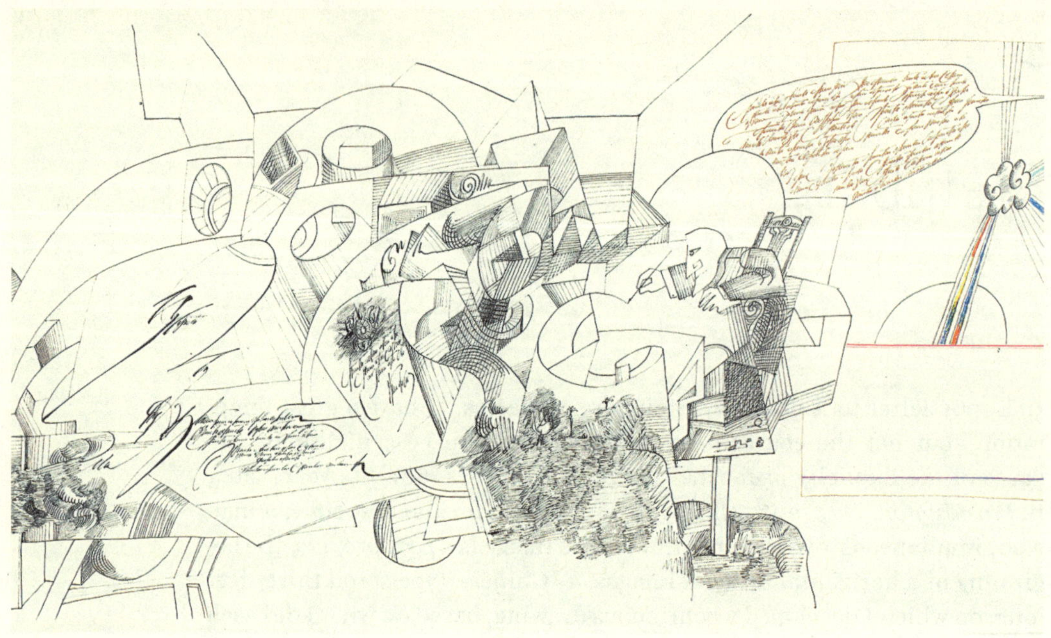

Fig. 9. *Washington, D.C. 1967* (detail), 1967. Screenprint on silk, 23 ¼ × 180 in. overall. (The Saul Steinberg Foundation, New York; photograph by Ellen Page Wilson, courtesy Pace Gallery)

us in graphology. As Joel Smith has written, "Millimeter for millimeter, Steinberg's line looked less like drawing than handwriting: an unpremeditated outpouring of personality that happened to take the form of articulate ideas and observations."[5] Roland Barthes has pointed out the rhetorical nature of Steinberg's drawings, their "great classification of forms of discourse that rhetoric called 'figures,'" noting there "figures of the signifier (metaphors, metonymies, repetitions, accumulations, antitheses, enumerations) and figures of meaning" such as deliberate slips and distortions.[6]

Let us then see whether, and what, we may read in *Washington, D.C. 1967.* Should we worry that acts of close reading will impose too heavy or tendentious a burden on the suggestiveness of the visual, Steinberg reassures us: "To honor a picture, you must tell it to yourself with every possible detail."[7] In "telling" his pictures, which are instances of drawing-writing, we will both discover and create narrative.

We may read first, perhaps, the drawing's parodic, artistic conventions. The drawing's largest area, an outpouring of geometrical forms, comes into focus as Cubist in nature. But here Cubism is subject matter as much as method: Steinberg presents stenographic Cubism, a sign for Cubist painting and drawing. Multiple shapes spreading with seemingly lax control to the edges of the page and beyond substitute for the early twentieth-century forms that Picasso and Braque carefully drew, painted, or pasted.

The ad hoc plenitude of this drawing seems at odds with the precision of Cubist forms. For all the seeming disorganization of *Washington, D.C. 1967,* the pictured man draws geometrical forms with utter concentration, while his multiplication of lines across the sheet also suggests an Abstract Expressionist energy that flirts with chaos. Yet, where Jackson Pollock, for example, pours paint on unprimed canvas, using his whole body as the vehicle for expressing something pre-verbal, this pictured artist, clothed in a business suit, writes in black pen and ink, carefully, even primly using his white-cuffed hand. The "allover" painting of Abstract Expressionism and the carefully balanced canvases of Cubism merge here to become "here, there, and everywhere" drawing.

Something's funny here, too. Steinberg says that he uses humor or satire "like a poetic stenography,"[8] and the humor of the image issues in part from the utter seriousness and control with which the artist has let himself lose control of his work. The drawing is stenographic, too, in its cartoonish character. It resembles a *New Yorker* cartoon, although Steinberg's drawings for the magazine early on outgrew that label. Nonetheless, we're looking for "the" joke. We want to decipher the situation, and that means accounting for the small scene located behind the artist's back. We see, apparently through a window, something that we come to make sense of as fireworks—colored rays zoom upward, exploding into a large puff of smoke and diffusing into rays of light. We decipher, too, that stenographic sign of speech, the balloon of comic strips, behind the artist. This one is filled with teasingly near-legible talk entering the artist's room from outdoors. Given the title of the piece and the fireworks, the calligraphic speech might represent official declamation upon the celebration of a national holiday. Given the year—1967—though, such "talk" may issue from Vietnam War protestors, who marched frequently in the capital.[9]

Calligraphy leaps to the viewer's eye in the mock handwriting that clusters in three areas before the artist. The entire drawing, however, issues calligraphically from elegant, if superabundant, penmanship. Steinberg's and the pictured artist's pens create lines that lead our eyes through a process of reading, as if they were so many sentences we try to parse. The syntactical units vary in size: the large outlines of what appears to be a room, the somewhat realistically portrayed artist in his chair, the smaller, unstably three-dimensional shapes that appear continuously to project from and recede back into the picture plane, and the surfaces of those shapes with their careful shading by way of cross-hatching and scumbling.

Deciding what the handwriting here tells us about the person who wrote it—both the artist in the picture and Steinberg, the artist "behind" the artist—requires what Steinberg calls "graphological" exploration. When he sees or makes a drawing through considering it as a kind of handwriting, Steinberg tells interviewers, "stylistic variations in line might serve to define distinctions among ideas, sounds, personalities, or frames of mind."[10] The doubled handwriting in *Washington, D.C. 1967* (both Steinberg's and that of his drawing man) belongs to someone with a desire to show the passage of time. The contrast between the small part of the image that the artist draws now, as we look, and the vast amount of artistic work that appears to have been made before this moment invites us to enter the world of narrative, to wonder how these shapes came to be and how they reflect their maker. It looks as if the artist in the picture has drawn them earlier, perhaps beginning by drawing the very room in which he sits. John Ashbery has aptly described Steinberg's images as "chronicle[s] of used time."[11] Perhaps he has, prior to the moment captured in the drawing, even drawn himself, as some of Steinberg's best-known images reveal.

And while he has drawn his room, his handwriting reveals that he has also drawn what is outside the room. Outside, then, we imagine crowds, explosions, and speeches, while inside, the artist, with his back to "out there," literally draws "in here." He doesn't appear to know or care about that world outside, even though it, too, seems to have issued from his own pen. Steinberg, speaking of Chekhov, might have been describing his own works: "The gifted ones gaze attentively at what they know, inside, while ordinary people try to replace it with the latest banalities" (*LAB,* July 28,1989). The banalities of the political games and public spectacles of the nation's capital, together with the protestors' desire to "bring the war home" outside the window, pale in comparison to the explosion of forms inside both the room and the artist's imagination. The artist recalls, too, one of the writers Steinberg revered and often mentioned, Charles Baudelaire. We can read this figure at a desk as an instance of Baudelaire's "Man of the Crowd," the artist who first immerses himself in the world outside and then retreats to his room to draw, through memory and imagination, the crowd scene he has absorbed.[12]

We especially want to know what Steinberg's penmanship tells us about the man who is always both drawing and drawn. We want to know, too, about the character and ideas of "Steinberg," the handwriter-draftsman of it all. Reading for personality and psychology doesn't at first yield much, and that fact, in itself, enables us to know him better—as a type of the modern artist. We learn only that the drawing man seems to possess both a formidable power of concentration and a passion for drawing. While his suit may mark him as a member of Washington's bureaucratic corps, he's equally a figure from literature. He's impersonal, like Joyce's artist who remains "within or behind or beyond or above his handiwork, invisible, refined out of existence, indifferent" (*P*, 233). Steinberg's artist is only half-present, his lower body dissolving into a Cubist rectangle or simply disappearing.

He resembles, too, Flaubert's view of himself: "I am a man-pen. I feel through the pen, because of it, according to it, and a lot more with it."[13] While Steinberg's man is the artist who comes to life only through drawing his black lines on white paper, he's also any man, the generic man or woman whom we see frequently in Steinberg's work: "For cartoons, I made myself a 'stenographic' character so that it would not be identifiable. It is a foundation that with a small modification can become something else. If I add high heels, it becomes a woman. The way one changes the sense of a sentence with a comma."[14] "If I add a table and a pen, it becomes an artist," we might add.

Steinberg's artist may be nondescript, but he quietly expends more—and longer-lived—energy than any fireworks. He is, to refer again to Baudelaire's study "The Painter of Modern Life," a cool, aloof man who hides volcanic energies within, "full of fire, passion, courage and restrained energy."[15] These energies take form, spreading across the page through his pen. The richness of his imagination defies the stenographic dome of the United States Capitol past which the fireworks shoot.

Self-created in shorthand, the draftsman has placed passages of documents written in mock traditional calligraphy over the surfaces of his geometrical shapes. A few sweeping, thick black lines enclose lines of smaller rhythmic handwriting. These documents (the one nearest the center of the picture appears to have a fancy letterhead) contain the abstraction of writing—shapes that partly represent and partly invent writing that we can almost—but never—read. Or, rather, we read them as pictures of an imagined alphabetic language. Extravagantly stylized in form, these mock calligraphic passages draw writing. For Steinberg they also carry literary meaning: Steinberg "took the inspiration for his feverish exercises in unintelligible penmanship" from Kafka, telling Dore Ashton, "'It amuses me to write with great facility nothing—which Kafka discovered in 'The Trial'—so many empty notions."[16] Just as the artist's lower body metamorphoses into Cubist shapes, so these letters and words disappear into an abstraction of the verbal.

Close readers will find, toward the bottom of the picture at the center, a passage that differs from the rest of the drawing in its lack of sharp edges. It consists of striated horizontal lines together forming a blob-like shape that gradually yields the image of a tree drawn atop a curved horizon with wavy parallel lines, and the striation seems to open, deep within the picture plane, into a fantastical, rocky promontory where a small, dark figure (a person, a tree?) stands. The leg of the desk in the lower right corner of the drawing stands on a rock that, with its parallel wavy lines, seems a continuation of this landscape. It's as if a small visual poem or short story has been inserted into the overall narrative of the artist at work, or as if we've been given a window into the artist's deeper psyche. We want to know where we are, what the weather is, who or what it is that stands in this tiny world.

Once we note this embedded landscape, the larger outpouring of shapes across the picture begins to suggest a story, too. The documents appear to bear witness to something that has happened. Strikingly, the geometrical forms begin to form a labyrinthine landscape themselves, one that reads as hills, caves, paths, ladders, leading to a horizon which is also the line where wall meets ceiling. We're now reading, if we're so inclined, a fictional world in which a confluence of questing travel, officialdom, and important missives alluding to unknowable events appears.

This is the man-pen in his worlds. But the drawing is a riddle, too: "I am all of these things. What do I show?" The answers are no less satisfying for remaining tentative: perhaps the images are about drawing one's surroundings into being in an alien land, especially when those surroundings are as strange as Washington, D.C., is to the New Yorker, as strange as New York is to Saul Steinberg, the immigrant from Eastern Europe, and, on the largest scale, as alien as the world outside is to the man who lives in his imagination. Perhaps they are about the drawing of oneself in relation to other artists. They suggest that an artist must both accept and question a variety of things: himself, officially stamped documents, crowds that prefer colorful spectacle, crowds that march in protest, and the mysterious dimensionality of shapes within shapes. "It's your choice to find meanings," Steinberg says of his drawings.[17] In our readings of this *mise en abyme*—the artist Steinberg at work depicting an artist at work—the best answer to the riddle of meaning must be "Keep reading, you'll find out."

4

Steinberg

Writing Drawing

"Up a trackless slope climbs the master artist, and at the top, on a windy ridge, whom do you think he meets? The panting and happy reader, and there they spontaneously embrace and are linked forever": thus Vladimir Nabokov, in his essay "Good Readers and Good Writers," describes artist and reader as companions in scaling aesthetic heights (*LL,* 2). How curious that Nabokov refers to the "master artist" (usually associated with the visual arts), not the master writer. Nabokov introduces this small ambiguity in English in order to preface a discussion of the difference between seeing a painting and reading a text, a difference he hopes to reduce. (In fact, "the Russian verb 'to write' (*pisat'*) may be applied to both writing and painting.")[1] When we first read a book, he tells us, we can't see it in its entirety, as we can when we first glimpse a painting. As mentioned above, the only true reading, then, is rereading, because that enables us to see the literary work whole—something like looking at an entire painting at once. Rereading renders a book more like a painting, and its writer more like a painter.

Steinberg was himself a serious reader and rereader of literature as well as a maker of visual art. To extend Nabokov's metaphor, climbing the mountain of visual work, Steinberg the visual artist roped himself securely to his other, Steinberg the writer. "Je est un autre" (I is an other), declares Arthur Rimbaud, another of the writers who figure powerfully in Steinberg's imagination. When we not only look at Steinberg's works but also read them, we too reach the top of the mountain where all four of us—Steinberg the writer and the visual artist, oneself the reader and the viewer—may at last embrace.

Throughout many interviews with journalists and critics Steinberg deliberately confuses writing and drawing. I must pause here for a necessary word about nomenclature. One might replace the word "drawing" with the phrase "drawing, painting, print, or assemblage," because Steinberg made all of those things. I shall at present use the words "draw" and "drawing" because Steinberg himself most often does when he describes his general artistic activities. He draws, applying ink and pencil to paper, but he also draws and paints on his assemblages, prints with rubber stamps on his drawings, draws on his paintings, paints on his drawings, draws faux "printed" forms—and the experimentation goes on. "Drawing," signaling the special sense of "Steinbergian visual-verbal creation," will have to do, at least as we begin to scale the mountain of Steinberg's many images, numbering roughly between eight and ten thousand.[2]

Steinberg self-consciously and simultaneously writes and draws, and he does so in a literary way.[3] He tells us as much. Taking a tour of the Louvre Museum with the art historian and critic Pierre Schneider in order to comment on works of art there, Steinberg states it simply: "I am a writer. I draw because the essence of a good piece of writing is precision. Drawing is a precise mode of expression."[4] Furthermore, he sees himself at work as a "literary man, who found this language of drawing. The essential thing about drawing with the fingers—the pencil, the pen—is that I think of the fingers themselves as being the continuation and part of the circumvolutions of the brain. The fingerprints themselves serve as a reminder of those circumvolutions."[5] "Drawing," he states, " is a kind of reasoning on paper."[6] As the words "language," "brain," and "reasoning," suggest, making art is for Steinberg an intellectual activity, with a direct connection between his fingers and his winding, folding, patterned brain, which thinks in yet other patterns, those he records.

"I decided to become a novelist when I was ten," he told the poet John Ashbery.[7] Although Steinberg never matured into a novelist per se, he evidently submitted a series of drawings based on the novel *Robinson Crusoe* to Farrar Straus & Cudahy. The only indication we have of its existence comes from the signed rejection letter dated June 15, 1962, which reads in part, "I have now had the opportunity to examine your manuscript, ROBINSON CRUSOE, with care. I am sorry to inform you that your material does not suit our editorial needs at present."[8] Steinberg offers a hint about this title when he tells an interviewer years later that the artist "in general" is Robinson Crusoe: "He must invent his stories, his pleasures; he succeeded in reconstructing a parody of civilization from scratch. He makes himself by education, by survival, by constantly paying attention to himself, but also by creating a world around himself that hadn't existed before."[9] We'll have occasion to explore the many ways in which Steinberg's work returns the reader-viewer repeatedly to the notions of parody and the invention of worlds, just as Nabokov's and Joyce's novels do.

Steinberg may not have written a novel—graphic or otherwise—but he nonetheless often compares his work to that of the novelist. His childhood, he believed, prepared him for fiction making. Coming from Romania, which he saw as a small, inferior nation lacking in "development," "literature," and "independence," he does attribute to his homeland two admirable traits. First, it instilled in its people an understanding of motive as a novelist comes to understand it. Faced with a questioning outsider, the native of a small, weak nation learns to "figure out what the outsider wants to know when he asks the question. He will not be told the truth but [the insider] will try to understand what [the outsider] wants—his motive" for asking the question. "This is the key to the novel—the motive. . . . Like psychoanalysis and historical understanding, a good novel grows out of a faceted truth dependent on figuring out the motives of people."[10] Second, Romania's people learn as children the intensities of life: "At five or ten you already have a full knowledge of human nature. You didn't have to be told the facts of life, you saw brutality, goodness, sex—all the human facets."[11] Adult self-protection through artfully sly invention and a vivid, unprotected childhood: here we begin to see the "novel" that Steinberg did create: the tessellated fictions he tells across time through the writing of many lines.

Steinberg's claim that "I am a writer," however, joins hands with another statement, "I don't write."[12] He explains the contradiction by emphasizing the categories between which his artistic practice falls: "I use this medium of drawing so I am on the fringes as a writer but I don't write, I'm not a painter. I draw, I'm a draftsman, I'm a cartoonist, I don't know, it's hard to say what I am. . . . I am in a region where I feel that I am alone and I don't need to explain myself so much . . . I feel that my work is of the nature of the artist if only because my work is often of a poetic nature."[13] Even as Steinberg creates a confusion of judgments (I'm a writer manqué, a writer, not a writer) and a confusion of categories (mind and brain, drawing and painting, I and Other, literature and art), he issues a simple directive: "My drawings have to be read."[14]

How are we to read them? Once again, helpful motifs appear in his interviews. "I appeal to the complicity of my reader who will transform (my line) into meaning by using our common background of culture, history, poetry. Contemporaneity in this sense is a complicity."[15] Here is an invitation to readers not only to view the fluidity of forms so frequent in Steinberg's images but also, actively, imaginatively, to transform those images themselves. However vexed the phrase "common cultural backgrounds" may be in the early twenty-first century, in 1965 Steinberg spoke to a community of shared interests, the readers of "The Magazine for People Who Read," the *New Yorker*, where, beginning in 1941, he published his way to fame and financial security. These readers likely had some college education and a taste for well-wrought prose. Their common background was one of respect for the world of "culture," a world both reproduced in and constituted by the pages of the magazine: advertisements for luxury goods, difficult poetry, lengthy—even book-length—essays on a wide variety of topics, contemporary fiction, cartoons and small drawings, and announcements and reviews of events in the cultural and financial capital of the United States. The magazine's editors stayed with Steinberg even after he gradually stopped drawing "funny" cartoons and began to draw the circumvolutions of his brain, to publish a Steinbergian world.

In addition to *New Yorker* readers, his audience consisted of two overlapping groups. There were those who attended his shows at galleries and museums, across the United States and the globe, where they could experience other images that he made simply to satisfy his own imagination, drawn "freely on my own" in contrast to those "I have to do for the *New Yorker.*"[16] Also, he gained an audience of people who read his ten published books: collections of his own drawings that, with one exception, he arranged, referring to himself as the "author" (*LAB,* June 2, 1978).[17] He expected his audiences "to move through sensation and perception to understanding,"[18] hoping that, like the man on the cover of the *New Yorker* (October 18, 1969) (see fig. 5; p. 17), they would have at least a passing familiarity with history, paintings, music, poetry, travel, foreign languages, finance, mass culture—along with the ability to be amused by their own foibles, wittily figured forth.

The viewer in this picture—cultured, playful, graphologically inclined (he thinks in handwriting, including all those "K's for example")— is a stand-in for cultivated viewer-readers of Steinberg's own images. According to him, we should read his works both closely and freely, as we would a poem, a brief narrative, or a tableau of symbols in the nineteenth-century Symbolist tradition—those reverberating images inviting us to feel, associate, and interpret as we will. Far from being a necessarily dulling response, as some critics have suggested in passing, close readings that involve detailed and imaginative looking are the readings Steinberg most hoped for. As Oscar Wilde said, "It is the spectator, and not life, that art really mirrors."[19]

In many cases, readers and viewers of his pictures feel initially at a loss. He draws sphinxes, but he also frequently draws images that are sphinx-like in their reticence. In fact, he claims, "Art is a sphinx. The beauty of the sphinx is that you yourself must do the interpreting. When you have found an interpretation, you are already cured. The mistake people make is to believe that the sphinx can give only one answer. Actually, it gives hundreds of answers, or maybe none at all. Interpretation probably does not give us the truth, but the act of interpretation saves us."[20] Interpretation saves us, not the work of art, which exists as a spur to human thought and feeling, first the artist's as he draws and edits, then ours.

Readers who are satisfied by lazy interpretations are a problem for Steinberg. For them "one must build attractive traps."[21] He wants to make us jittery by giving us ambiguous situations admitting of multiple interpretations:[22] once again, "To honor a picture, you must tell it to yourself with every possible detail." [23] Tell it to yourself, he counsels, make a survey that might become a story. Or, he muses, "The reader, by following my line with his eyes, becomes a draftsman."[24] Steinberg and we are writers and draftsmen, receivers and makers. To think of Steinberg as a cartoonist[25] is, in the twentieth-century meaning of the term, to understand him as a maker of a "humorous or topical drawing (of any size) in a newspaper, etc."[26] We might, however, also think of his picture as a "cartoon" in the Renaissance sense of the word, as something drawn on a *cartone,* a large sheet of paper, often meant as an underdrawing for a painting or textile. We would then take Steinberg's invitation to interpretation as a challenge to apply our mental paintbrush or shuttle to his underdrawings, to complete them as simply or intricately as we wish—so long as we pay attention. His pictures, often combining (fanciful) representation with abstraction,[27] can lead us to a spectrum of reading styles, from decipherment to dreaming.

We also find, in addition to the concept of drawing that is linked closely to reading and writing, plenty of actual letters, words, and numbers in Steinberg's works. For those who love literature, his world is reassuringly direct in its verbal marks, at least at first. These characters we recognize both as shapes on the page and as the contingent transporters of linguistic meaning—letters of the Roman and Slavic alphabets, recognizable words, numerals, even "captions" to a few of his drawings. Such verbal forms suggest the captions and speech balloons of comic books and newspaper funny pages as well as the depiction of word and number in Cubist paintings and in the works of artists such as Robert Rauschenberg, Jasper Johns, Andy Warhol, and Roy Lichtenstein.[28]

As we begin to parse the groups of images that form the nucleus of this study—Steinberg's maps, official documents, postcards, landscapes, portraits of the artist, mythological drawings, and assembled tabletops—we'll tell ourselves in detail of the appearances and activities of these verbal forms. A few general observations are in order, though, in discussing the drawing *of* writing, which is one particular form of Steinberg's widespread drawing as writing.

The presence of letters, words, and numbers in a work by Steinberg is never simply writing. Placing it in quotation marks as "writing" more accurately indicates its self-reflexive, derivative, or parodic nature, the changes in meaning that proliferate when what we think of as writing per se is included within a picture or assemblage that itself moves between the categories of writing and drawing. Just as he writes and draws pictures of objects, living beings, places, and ideas, so he also writes and draws—pictures—words and numbers, in different sizes and styles, in and against different colors.[29] Just as Steinberg "draw[s] drawing,"[30] rather than trying accurately to represent "reality" in his pictures, so, in parallel, he "writes writing," where writing refers to itself as well as to the thing or concept we take it to signify. Words in his pictures tend to raise questions about the act of writing: What do these words look like? Why, where, how, when have they been written? What is their relation to one another and to the other parts of the image? Letters, words, and punctuation marks appear in speech or thought balloons, in signs for businesses or motels, and they also stand on earth, process through the sky, or climb stairs or trees. They appear on documents: signs, maps, mock certificates, actual envelopes, drawn envelopes, or the covers of mock books constructed of wood. They create or impede narratives. Steinberg's verbal shapes can metamorphose into something else: buildings, humanoid characters, furniture, or abstract designs. They ask the viewer to decide how legible a series of lines must be before we feel comfortable calling them "writing."

In complicated works, such questions and variations can multiply so quickly, and the answers prove so complex and difficult to synthesize, that we may trip across the lexical and land vertiginously on a ledge of understanding. From this space of relative safety, viewers may survey other possible meanings of the writing and drawing we're looking at and the entire image of which they form a part. Yet, for all the depth and complexity of Steinberg's engagement with writing/drawing, his comic ability continues to bubble up. Simple reactions matter, too. Sometimes, looking at a drawing, we quickly smile and, voilà, the *fait* of interpretation is charmingly *accompli.*

5

Steinberg

Reading

From his teenage years Steinberg aspired to become an intellectual, and it is impossible to separate Steinberg the reader and intellectual from Steinberg the artist-writer.[1] To fully appreciate his interest in Joyce and Nabokov, it's helpful not only to look at *Library* (see fig. 1; p. 6) but also to survey briefly his reading across his adult life, noting his special interest in the nineteenth-century writers Flaubert, Baudelaire, and Tolstoy. We should remember that he was, in his own estimation, an intellectual who operated in the realms of reasoning, ideas, and, surprisingly, fantasy. Speaking in 1967 with an interviewer for German television, he offered his own version of "the child is father of the man": "I feel that the child in me, the child that I was is my origin, my . . . let's call it, my grandfather." The poetic quality of childhood, however, must be nurtured across the span of a lifetime through education: "[T]he only salvation that people have, is to become intellectuals, either through education or through some curious biography of adventures, of trouble and so on. The intellectuals—we confuse very often the intellectual with a scholar, I'm not a scholar but I became an intellectual slowly. . . . I don't quite know how to define 'intellectual.' I think it's a combination of general culture or interest in what's called culture and poetry and fantasy. It's impossible to be an intellectual without fantasy."[2]

He tells interviewers in a variety of ways that he thinks before he draws. "Basically, I work in the realm of ideas. Essentially the search for ideas is self-amazement."[3] The joining of thinking and fantasizing requires dedication and sacrifice. He explains, "I give up everything else and sit down, mornings, and I reason . . . about things. This sitting down and reasoning is one of the most difficult things to do. It requires a great loss of energy, physical and mental, it is exhausting. You have to purge yourself of all the clichés, and the commonplace. You have to eliminate everything that is probable and possible and reach something that is satisfying to you at the moment."[4] That work includes connection: "the important thing is that I am able to associate ideas in altogether unforeseeable ways."[5] Telling himself about something in words often precedes drawing it: "I draw because I want to explain to myself something I have seen. . . . And of course it helps to make verbal observations about it—to make a comparison and sometimes transform this comparison into a reality by drawing it."[6]

Evidence of such verbal ideas appears throughout his manuscripts, notebooks, diaries, and sketchbooks. One diary entry reads:

> For crimes of omission Surrender to guards of
> Museum of Modern Art
> Subway
> Brooks Brothers
> Zoo
> Chemical Bank
>
> ---
>
> or
> Elevator operators
> Doormen, Movie ushers
> Airline stewardesses
> People in black tie[7]

In Steinberg's mental world, one doesn't have to be a policeman or soldier in order to wear a uniform of authority; and one doesn't have to commit a crime in order to surrender to those in charge. Steinberg's city guards might have issued from Kafka's *Amerika,* or, for that matter, from any of his guilt-laden fiction.

Sometimes Steinberg's reading leads directly to his drawing, such as the picture of a hybrid dog/man wearing a tee shirt with the word "PAFNUTE" on it, this image itself drawn on an actual cotton tee shirt (fig. 10). He also labels a volume in *Library* "Pafnute." This word he takes from Dostoevsky's *The Idiot.* Like Joyce's and Nabokov's allusions, which upon examination open to ever-proliferating commentaries on the fiction in which they appear, "Pafnute" exemplifies the depth that a superficial reference can introduce.

Prince Myshkin of *The Idiot* refers to Pafnute:

> "The Abbot Pafnute lived in the fourteenth century," began the prince [Myshkin]; "he was in charge of one of the monasteries on the Volga, about where our present Kostroma government lies. He went to Oreol and helped in the great matters then going on in the religious world; he signed an edict there, and I have seen a print of his signature; it struck me, so I copied it. When the general asked me, in

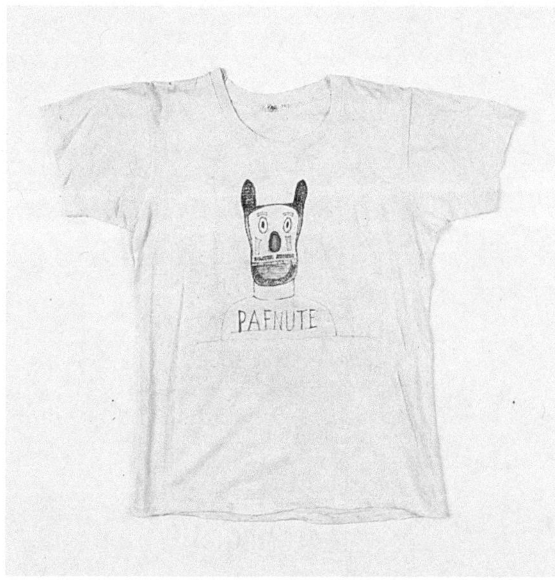

Fig. 10. *PAFNUTE,* 1970s. Cotton T-shirt with marker, 23¼ × 16 in. (The Saul Steinberg Foundation, New York; photograph by Jenny Gorman)

his study, to write something for him, to show my handwriting, I wrote 'The Abbot Pafnute signed this,' in the exact handwriting of the abbot. The general liked it very much, and that's why he recalled it just now."[8]

Prince Myshkin has earlier revealed himself as someone most learned in various historical scripts; and the mimetic chain of Prince Myshkin's calligraphy—a *copy,* in "medieval characters" of a *print* of the original signature of the Abbot Pafnute—has been added to (and sent up) in the "tee shirt Pafnute," by that other reader, parodist, calligrapher, and graphologist—the King of Steinbergia.

Writers' names and book titles appear repeatedly in his personal papers and sketchbooks: for example, in a list of writers born in 1821, the year of Napoleon's death: "Baudelaire, Dostoyevski, Flaubert" (fig. 11), and in another list in which Napoleon and Alexander lead a roll call of distinguished thinkers: Dante, Plato, Marx, Goethe, Kant" (fig. 12). In one of his drawings of a room the drawers of a desk bear the neat labels "Crime Punishment / Fear Trembling / Bouvard Pecuchet / Dante Mozart."[9]

A few portraits of writers appear, as well as portraits of literary characters, such as a series of Gogolian tram conductors with noses that have slipped out of place or wildly mutated (fig. 13). "Nosedrop, Gogol, Nabokov, Hi Nabor": so Steinberg's art appreciator daydreams on a *New Yorker* cover (see fig. 5; p. 17).

By far the richest and most accurate accounts we have of Steinberg's

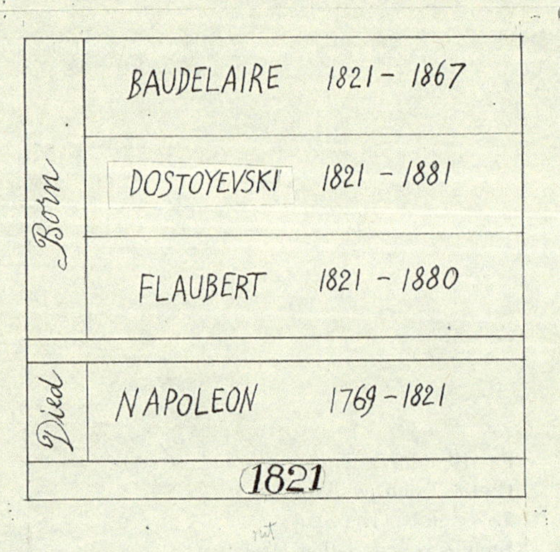

Napoleon Alexander
Dante
Plato
Marx
Goethe
Kant

OSCILOCOCCINUM

Fig. 11. Untitled, 1984. Pencil and ink on paper, 11 ½ × 12 in. Originally published in the *New Yorker* "Inventory" portfolio, January 14, 1985. (Beinecke Rare Book and Manuscript Library, Yale University)

Fig. 12. Sketchbook page, c. 1988. Pencil on paper, 14 × 11 in. (Beinecke Rare Book and Manuscript Library, Yale University)

Fig. 13. *Nose #5,* 1980. Pencil, crayon, varnish, marker, and colored pencil on wood panel, 22 × 16 in. (The Saul Steinberg Foundation, New York; photograph by Kerry Ryan McFate, courtesy Pace Gallery)

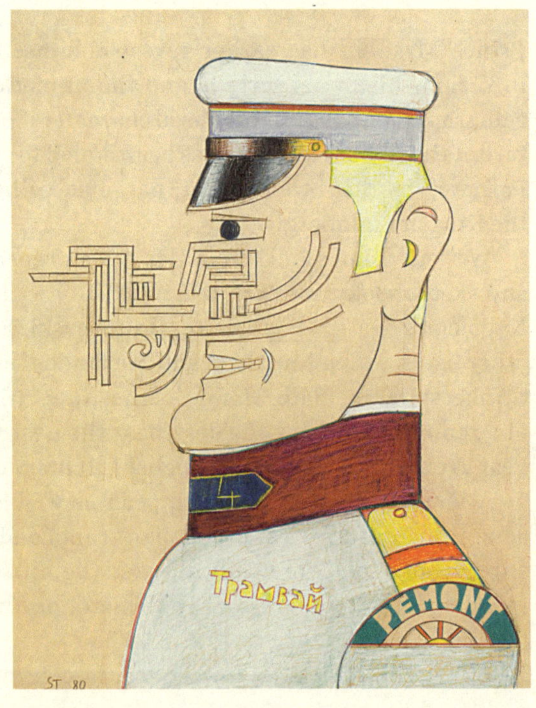

reading appear in the letters he wrote throughout his adult life to Aldo Buzzi, whom he met during his student days in Milan. There he lists books he's reading and also frequently comments on them. Buzzi, a travel and food writer, architect, filmmaker, and critic, saved many of Steinberg's letters. (As a bonus, and thanks to Buzzi's special interest in food, we find book titles interspersed with detailed accounts of Steinberg's meals.) *Reflections and Shadows,* a book in which Buzzi transcribes discussions he had with his friend (only Steinberg's side of the conversation appears) also mentions some of his reading.

Further, a detailed inventory of the books in his estate numbers over 1,200. As noted above, while we don't know how many of these he actually read, or the number of books he read that did not appear on this list, the number does at least demonstrate that he lived among books. The plentiful literary references in his works of art, along with his letters, brief manuscript memoirs, interviews, and the suggestive inventories of his books, provide us with more than a mere guess, but less than a certifiable or complete record, of Steinberg's reading.

Taken together, these sources suggest that, in addition to Nabokov and Joyce, Steinberg most admired Tolstoy and Flaubert. A study of the links between his oeuvre and these nineteenth-century authors (both of whom were also favorites of Nabokov's) remains to be written. "If anything, the writer I identify myself with is Joyce. For the rest, I wish I were Tolstoi; that was a magic thing. Nobody's like him."[10] He reports reading two biographies of Tolstoy, as well as rereading *War and Peace* and the short stories (*LAB,* June 15, 1946, and October 6, 1965). Tolstoy becomes a standard against which to judge other fiction: "as interesting as War and Peace" is the way he judges Thomas Mann's *Joseph and His Brothers* (*LAB,* March 11, 1980). Steinberg reports reading Tolstoy's "Family Happiness" in 1991, with a gloss of "Tears."[11] When an interviewer asks whether he's reading any Russian fiction, his answer is direct: "Some. The only witness we trust is the first-class novelist. We miss Tolstoy."[12] The inventory of books at Amagansett includes *Anna Karenina,* two collections of Tolstoy's short fiction, and another biography of him.

When Steinberg creates a list of writers (and painters) with date of birth and death, Flaubert, Freud, Rimbaud, Gogol, Goethe, Joyce, Manzoni, and Tolstoy appear. He adds the names of only two characters: Ivan Ilych and Charles Bovary.[13] Why Tolstoy? If nothing else, Steinberg aspired to a Tolstoyan breadth of knowledge and depiction. Like his Russian forebear, Steinberg draws a stunningly wide range of phenomena, including war, spiritual and metaphysical questioning, large cities and small towns, artistic creation and creations, plant and animal life, and, in the largest sense, the human tragicomedy. His family portraits and drawings of couples suggest Tolstoyan love refined to the size of a small sketch.

Steinberg mentions Flaubert in much the same way as he does Tolstoy—frequently, and with reverence. Toward the end of his life, he reports to Buzzi, "I have reread more than once the end of Charles Bovary. He was, I believe, about 33 years old" (*LAB,* June 12, 1998). He especially admires *Trois contes* and *Madame Bovary* (*LAB,* April 29, 1946). Indeed, he mentions rereading the latter across the decades: 1946, 1962, and 1984. The publication of the Flaubert-Sand correspondence adds to the pleasure: "Yesterday evening, supper at the home of Francis Steegmuller, perfect translator of *Mme Bovary* and the classic Flaubert specialist of the past 30 years. . . . He gave me his latest book, which is about to come out. It's the Flaubert-Sand correspondence. The excellent part is that the greetings, endearments, and other obvious things are left in French, making it a cult item" (*LAB,* February 15, 1993).

He also reads Steegmuller's *Flaubert and Madame Bovary,* "a kind of biography." Further excursions in Flaubert criticism led him to photocopy a page of a book by Roger Shattuck in which he quotes Flaubert. There Steinberg partially circles Flaubert's words, "Never, as long as I live, shall I allow anyone to illustrate me, because: the most beautiful literary description is eaten up by the most wretched drawing. As soon as a figure is fixed by the pencil, it loses that character of generality, that harmony with a thousand known objects which make the reader say: 'I've seen that' or 'That must be so.'"[14] On the occasions when Steinberg drew "illustrations" for books, he avoided anything that looked like a realistic rendering of the writer's characters or settings.

Although Flaubert makes an explicit appearance in only a few of Steinberg's drawings, his implicit presence is, like Flaubert's own artist-god, everywhere present. Steinberg's refining process, his perpetual paring down of his images, his continual editing of his thoughts and works, we might think of as a search for *la ligne juste*. Flaubert catalogues Mme Bovary's purchases, mocks her cultural education and her husband's professional abilities, and attacks with precision the political and social hypocrisies of mid- and later nineteenth-century France. Steinberg, too, tells the story of (twentieth-century) middle-class everymen and everywomen: their homes, life cycles, possessions, work, and travels, all colored by the local and national myths and abstractions (love, power, virtue, greed, fame, propriety, etc.) that structure their thinking and sometimes issue in thought balloons or documents of remarkable gibberish. Both artists lucidly depict muddles, and with special relish. "A good part of my mind is 19th century," he notes in a sketchbook;[15] Tolstoy and Flaubert together define that century for him.

And, perhaps most powerfully, Steinberg marks Flaubert's times as the usual limit of his historical comfort zone: "I've never been able to identify with a past any more remote than that of Flaubert, who is more or less our grandfather" (*LAB,* September 24, 1985). Steinberg often draws images of the past becoming the present—here, his words indicate that his personal past is best measured by this particular literary precursor.

Stendhal provides a welcome exception to the "Flaubert" time limit. "I'm reading *Henry Brulard* [Stendhal's *Life of Henri Brulard*] with pleasure," Steinberg writes, "slowly, noting not only the coincidental overlap with my life but also yours. It's the first time that I've read a free-thinking (which is to say, modern) book about the 18th century" (LAB, September 24, 1985). Stendhal's book is autobiographical—Henri Brulard is, like Stendhal, one of Marie-Henri Beyle's multiple pseudonyms. But the pleasure of reading its "coincidental overlap" with Steinberg's own life is surely heightened by the 170 diagrams, maps, and line drawings that Brulard/Beyle created for it, most of them a combination of image and text.[16] To Buzzi, Steinberg avows his own autobiographical impulse, "What I draw is part of a diary" (*LAB,* January 10, 1963).

Dore Ashton points out one important tendency in Steinberg's reading:

> Over the years I was struck by Steinberg's choices in his reading: many of the authors he chose had transferred out of their native tongues into others' languages. One summer, for instance, Steinberg spent all his free time reading a huge biography of Joseph Conrad and, after that, all of Conrad's works. Like him, Conrad had early in life abandoned his mother tongue and country. The other author that never ceased to intrigue Steinberg was Vladimir Nabokov. . . . Then there were Beckett and Steinberg's good friend Ionesco, and even Kafka, who lived in a place that habitually used two or more languages.[17]

While Steinberg mentions reading English[18] and American literature[19] he nourished his sensibilities by reading (and sometimes rereading) works by Russian, Eastern European, Irish, Italian, French, Scandinavian, and German writers.[20]

Steinberg more than once starts to read Proust, but "the truth is he sort of bores me" (*LAB,* July 23, 1947). Charles Baudelaire is another story. Steinberg owns two volumes of the essays in which Baudelaire describes Constantin Guys's drawings of city life as "poems."[21] "Here comes Baudelaire again!"[22] Steinberg writes in a notebook and explains that "like

Baudelaire, I have continued to draw even now preserving toward the external world the same attitude of the child who observes things as if he were seeing them for the first time."[23]

This is a reference to a chapter of *The Painter of Modern Life* entitled "The Artist, Man of the World, Man of the Crowd, and Child," in which Baudelaire writes that "the child sees everything in a state of newness; he is always *drunk.*"[24] In an appointment book, Steinberg lists Baudelairean images,[25] and when he reads a biography of Baudelaire writes "how sad" (*LAB,* July 30, 1959). His library contains Georges Poulet's *Baudelaire: The Artist and His World.* Baudelaire insisted, as Steinberg would a century later, that the visual artist must be a cosmopolitan man of letters, "a man of the world, . . . a man who understands the world and the mysterious and lawful reasons for all its uses" rather than an artist who is "a specialist, a man wedded to his palette like the serf to the soil. . . . His interest is the whole world; he wants to know, understand and appreciate everything that happens on the surface of our globe."[26] The artist as child, as world traveler, as "writer" of poems: Steinberg recognizes himself in that fountainhead of modernity, Baudelaire, for whom the actual painter of modern life, Constantine Guys, is a stand-in. In sum, Baudelaire writes, "the genius of the painter of manners is of a mixed nature, by which I mean that it contains a strong literary element."[27]

Steinberg frequently read biographies, autobiographies, letters, diaries, and memoirs. "I'm reading at random biographies of obscure people, and then also a life of Rimbaud (Starkie) with new details on the Abyssinian past," he tells Buzzi (*LAB,* April 25, 1963). As we'll see, he reimagines Rimbaud's life in some of his eeriest drawings. He likes "to see how people invented their professions and lives."[28] He reports reading biographies of writers: not only Tolstoy, Flaubert, Rimbaud, Stendhal, Joyce, and Nabokov, but also Prosper Mérimée, T. E. Lawrence, Chekhov, and Gogol (his letters). Steinberg's address books reveal contact with many contemporary writers, but he especially sought the company of William Gaddis, Saul Bellow, Harold Rosenberg, and Ian Frazier.

History, too, fascinates him in a personal way. As a foreign Jew in Italy during World War II, he was sent to an internment camp until official papers arrived that enabled him to leave Italy.[29] Across the years he would parody such documents. He writes, "As soon as I was put in [Tortoreto] prison I saw myself as an important character. In history, all important characters have gone to prison. . . . I wasn't just a reader of novels but a real hero, as I'd always wished. And I saw the moment come true when the dream becomes reality" (*RS,* 33). "I've read a few books on China and India, history books, wars and massacres" (*LAB,* December 7, 1949), he writes, mentioning "a history of the Turkish empire that tells me a lot about the history of Romania," "a couple of books on Mao's cultural revolution—to give myself a scare" (*LAB,* September 25, 1972), biographies of Lenin, Haile Selassie, and Maximilian Emperor of Mexico, memoirs of Herzen and Kropotkin, and the *War Diary* of Isaac Babel.[30] He also favored books of travel and exploration. Not all of his reading is "serious"—he confesses to reading "inconsequential stuff" (*LAB,* November 23, 1945) and "a lot of newspapers and magazines, which interferes with the reading of books" (*LAB,* January 26, 1946).

Books were, for Steinberg, mirrors, teachers, and muses. But they were also, importantly, vehicles, and in this sense they rhymed with his actual traveling, a centrally defining activity of his life and work to which the viewer-author may now turn.

Part III

The Artist Abroad

Steinberg and Nabokov

6

Steinberg

A Provisional Life

Before turning to Nabokov's works, some context: To understand Steinberg's fascination with him we must remember that both emigrated from their childhood homes and continued to travel widely thereafter. In 1932 Steinberg left Bucharest for Milan. From there a series of flights and journeys followed: from Fascist police in Milan; from a six-week internment in Tortoreto-Teramo, Italy, for lack of proper traveling documents; to Santo Domingo, Dominican Republic, in 1941 (via Ellis Island); and thence back to New York City in 1942. From there he traveled to Los Angeles and back, became a citizen in 1943, and accepted a commission in the US Naval Reserve, which sent him to India, China, Algeria, and Italy. Although he resided in New York City and Amagansett, Long Island, he took trips to all fifty states and every continent but Antarctica. His education continued through that "curious biography of adventures, of trouble and so on."[1]

Three months before he died, Steinberg wrote to Buzzi that his friend Prudence Crowther found in the public library "a 1938 map of Bucharest, with my past in little streets and houses, all of them now demolished. It's six o'clock, my streets have exhausted me" (*LAB,* February 4, 1999).[2] By then, Steinberg had created a large body of work that reflected his restless journeying, but the discovery of a mapped chronicle of childhood places, "little streets," gripped him. He found their fixity on paper, reversing their actual demolition, absorbing. As Harold Rosenberg has noted, "With the immigrant, the issue of 'Who am I/ What shall I become?' is sharpened by 'Where am I?' "[3]

That last question brings Steinberg's unpublished work *Robinson Crusoe* to mind. He underlines his interest in Daniel Defoe's *Robinson Crusoe* by mentioning it over the years to Buzzi (in 1971, for example, he tells him "I've been reading Robinson Crusoe—which I'd read only in the version for children"; *LAB,* May 23, 1971), and, after reading it, creating a wooden replica of the volume for his assemblage *Library* (see fig. 1; p. 6, lower left edge). On the cover of the faux book, Steinberg chooses to draw two ships and one small boat on a river, emphasizing the hero's travels rather than his homemaking activities or spiritual development.

Defoe's Crusoe leaves York, where he grew up, but he also leaves one home after another: England, Sallee (Rabat), where he is enslaved, the plantation he develops in Brazil, and eventually his island. Even during his lengthy sojourn there, where his thoughts and actions turn relentlessly on the creation of a safe and comfortable home, he takes a cross-country trip to the other side of the island, tries to travel around the island by boat, and eventually builds himself two other residences so that he might enjoy traveling among homes. What's more, Defoe's novel presents Crusoe as a writer; its reflexivity must have interested Steinberg, who often drew, crafted, and assembled artists' tools.

Steinberg traveled for a variety of reasons, but at base he considered travel, especially emigration, as a, perhaps *the* necessary condition for his life as an artist: "An artist *has* to run away from home. This is the premise. There is no modern artist who hasn't run away from home. . . . I would say for myself that I ran away from home through emigrations. I'm addicted to them: emigrations caused by school, persecution, war, and military service. Sometimes I was deported, sometimes I was ordered to report to this or that place. These were machinations made to keep me on the move. After that, I became addicted. I traveled for so many years! I couldn't stand still."[4] Steinberg's rationale for the addiction of travel lay in its necessity for the intellectual and the artist: "The fact is, travel or emigration forces you to start all over again. It's the essential element of progress and evolution. . . . An intellectual has to change and has to shake himself."[5]

As we've seen, Baudelaire describes the iconic "painter of modern life," Constantine Guys, as a much-traveled war correspondent who retained a child's playfulness, fresh perspective, and curiosity. Steinberg, too, associates travel with childhood: long before he was able actually to travel, he imagined himself as a man in motion across time and space. He remembers, "Even as a small child, I imagined I was an Invisible Man traveling throughout the Past. Today the Battle of Legnano, tomorrow Bucharest in 1940, a visit to Flaubert's house in Croisset in 1850 (he was 20, perhaps he was in Egypt, it doesn't matter), the year 1,000 in Rome, and so on—until, after 200 years, I'd get fed up, enough" (*LAB,* March 29, 1996).

"Traveling is not for picking up ideas," he tells an interviewer. "One travels in order to make some sort of intermission, a tabula rasa. And by putting oneself in the uncomfortable position of the immigrant, one is again like a child."[6] Travel is for him both chosen and forced; it frees and renews but also addicts and even causes regret. "[I u]se the USA map as an oracle," he tells Buzzi, and confides years later, "The way it always is, a provisional life" (*LAB,* May 28, 1986 and November 8, 1993).

A fundamental account of drawing in the Western tradition is also a story of travel. Appearing in Pliny the Elder's *Chapters on the History of Art,* it reads, "Modelling portraits from clay was first invented by Butades, a potter of Sicyon in Corinth. He did this owing to his daughter who was in love with a young man; and she, when he was going abroad, drew in outline on the wall the shadow of his face thrown by a lamp. Her father pressed clay on this and made a relief."[7] Drawing in this story functions as a way to remember one who is on the road. Like Butades's daughter, Steinberg draws in order to remember; like Butades he goes on to create, later in his career, versions of his earlier drawings in relief sculpture and assemblages. And many of his "self"-portraits appear not as images of his own face, but rather as a host of autobiographical images having to do with travel: landscapes, maps, and postcards among them.

Travel for Steinberg often involved, as it did for Nabokov the butterfly collector, lengthy car trips and flights abroad, but it also included artistic movement best understood by us as versions of travel. He moves through phases of various artistic media, into his memory, around his assembled drawing tables, and always across a variety of smooth surfaces, pen or brush in hand. Self-consciously analogizing his aesthetic, emotional, and physical voyages, Steinberg creates a visual autobiography, the shadow of his face traced by his own pen.

"Let's say that my geography and my psychology mingle in my biography," Steinberg proposes, thus elegantly linking questions that he implicitly asks in drawing after drawing: where am I now, where did I come from, and what is my state of mind?[8] "Autogeography" is another name he gives this mingling.

Autogeography (fig. 14) is at once a map, a landscape, and even a sort of postcard announcing many of his former destinations. Regarded as a map, its depiction of trees, rocks, and clouds seems anachronistic or absurd; regarded as a landscape, lettering grows strangely upon the land. *Autogeography* forces us to develop our own key to its complexities as landscape and map, drawing and text. One place to begin is the course of the unnamed river, on whose banks Râmnicul Sărat, Bucuresti, Springs, Amagansett, East Hampton, and New York have the largest lettering—that is, loom largest in his life story. That makes sense for a Romanian who was born in Râmnicul Sărat (a town situated on the river of that name eighty miles north of Bucharest), grew up in Bucharest, and became an American citizen, a New Yorker with a house in Amagansett, Long Island. The

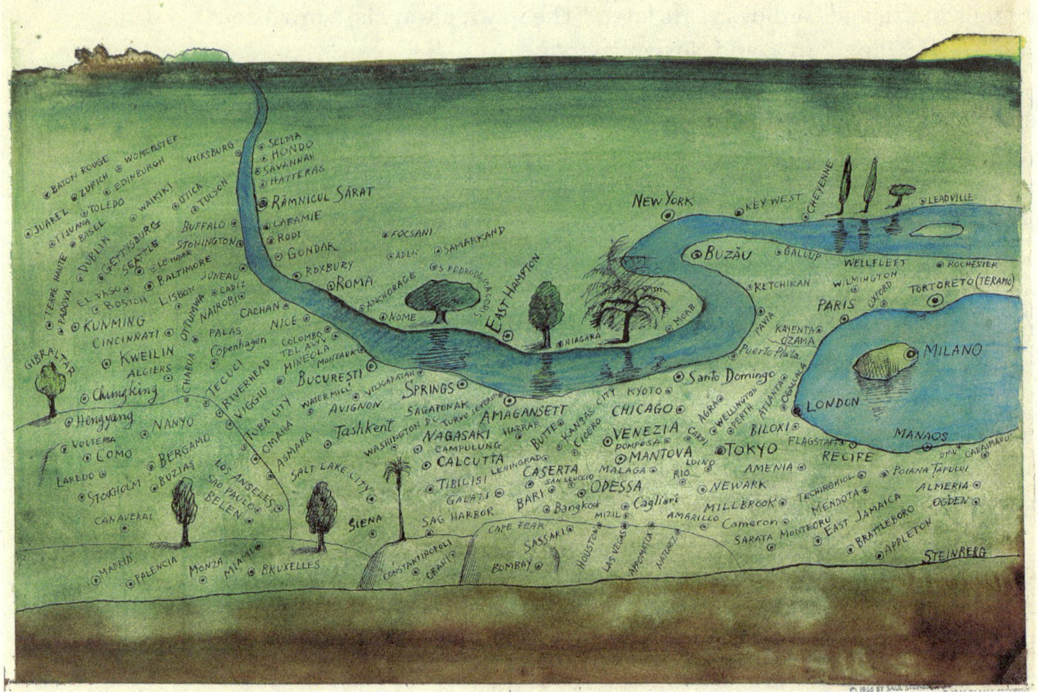

Fig. 14. *Autogeography,* detail, 1966. Ink, gouache, and watercolor on paper, 29½ × 20¾ in. (Centre Pompidou, Paris; gift of The Saul Steinberg Foundation)

other, densely packed place-names have no logical arrangement on the map or in the landscape, unless it be the logic of reverie, the way in which, for example, Sag Harbor, Orani (the Italian childhood village of the sculptor Costantino Nivola, his friend and neighbor on Long Island), and Constantinopoli, appearing as they do on a single hillock in the drawing, occur in proximity in his musings.

If we relax enough to forget the need for a conventional key to the map, what we find are the pleasures of inhabiting this strange bit of the world. Harrar (just south of Amagansett) is the ancient Ethiopian city where Rimbaud lived after he left the old world of Europe; Steinberg visited there in part because of his fascination with the poet, whose journal pages he would, as we'll see, parody. Harrar appears close by Butte (Montana), which he probably visited. Or it might be part of his own imagined frontier, or possibly just a name whose appearance of tall t's appealed to him as a visual pun, just as Harrar's repeated, low-slung r's and a's suggested its stony ruins. Tokyo, with its interior and final o's, isn't far from Biloxi, with its interior and final i's. And so on: Steinberg's *Autogeography* flows and pools, as much poem as map.

The interruption, the tabula rasa of travel, enables the artist to lose his personal bearings, including a fixed sense of his own identity. So many interruptions of space and time suggest a life of continual imaginative renewal and of an accompanying insecurity. When Defoe's Robinson Crusoe writes that he was "born to be my own destroyer," he alludes to the life-threatening situations his wanderlust places him in, but he comes to understand that another, more positive, aspect of his self-destruction involves the slow obliteration of his unbelieving, prideful self through his gradual rebirth as a Christian. Steinberg was a secular Jew, but he embraced the notion of personal change through travel and the making of art. This process can be painful; as Steinberg notes in a sketchbook, "tourist = homeless, insecure" (YCAL inv. no. 3067-001).

Steinberg's association with the *New Yorker* magazine has fixed him in the contemporary imagination as an Eastern European transplanted in postwar New York City, a cartoonist of mid-twentieth-century cityscape and city folk. From January 1944 to April 1945, the magazine ran a cycle of ten portfolios of his drawings of off-duty military life entitled "China," "India," "Italy," and "North Africa." "Republished in periodicals around the world" and partly reprinted in the best-selling book *All in Line,*[9] these sets of drawings helped to establish his cosmopolitan bona fides but also ironically underscored his identity as a New Yorker, since many of his local readers were—or aspired to become—world travelers. What is lost in a view of Steinberg as the settled émigré *New Yorker* "cartoonist" is the evidence of his restlessness. Orientations of familiarity gave way to deliberate disorientation and reorientation, a process that we as viewers are often called upon to rehearse as we find our way amid his complex images. Steinberg's exploration, not just of particular places, but also of the very acts of losing and finding his way, appears with particular clarity in his drawings of postcards, landscapes, and maps. All of them send us, the viewers, on interpretive trips that fascinate and frustrate, soothe and disturb. And in doing so, as we'll see, they correspond to Nabokov's and Joyce's own requirements that we assemble for ourselves the confounding fictional worlds they offer us.

How Nabokov would have icily repudiated that generality, "immigrant experience." Even in his novels of immigrant life that contain painfully awkward Russian-born characters such as the eponymous Professor Pnin and Victor Botkin[10] of *Pale Fire,* he invents indirections of rhetoric and style that, when carefully read, direct the reader to subtler imaginative truths of life lived in simultaneous location and dislocation. We'll watch Steinberg and Nabokov examine kitschy postcards, unfold odd maps, and fashion foreign landscapes out of words and paint. Such emblems of travel converge upon what these amended artists regarded as the saving truth of displacement: that it is the imagination that travels, creating locale as it goes. Places come into fuller existence as we read and reread Steinberg's and Nabokov's works, and they convey the paradoxical "inner truth" or "autogeography" of men who never confess, remaining half-hidden from even the most creative readers by fronting various personae. Behind all of his drawn people "Steinberg" lurks, a parody whose original cannot ever be captured. He confesses to Buzzi that it is "impossible to recount things, we'll see each other and in speaking of other things the story of the trip, including Abyssinia, the wild animals in Kenya, the Turkish baths in Japan etc.etc. will all gradually come out. As always I was more interested in myself (that is, trying to understand what sort of man I am) than in seeing outside things. It's a fine game and I imagine even explorers experience it. Also coming home and finding myself no longer the same" (*LAB,* February 19, 1964). He masks himself not just to hide from viewers, but also to enclose his identity, the better to view it from within. Traveling and masking are twinned activities, and drawing makes three.

Actual travel was for Steinberg even a means of clearing his life of remembered pain: "For some time I've been drawing up a balance sheet of lost years, mistakes, wrong paths, connivances, etc. etc., an endless list," he tells Buzzi. "Traveling has been for me a gift for avoiding solutions. I change space which looks like a tabula rasa, we start all over again, a neo-virgin. In fact—in all seriousness—I was traveling to forget! And I knew it but it was such a pleasure" (*LAB,* January 8, 1960). Because he drew thousands of images, each "tabula rasa," whether paper or canvas or wood, was an opportunity to avoid finality and even to remedy the regretted disproportions of his life's "balance sheet."

Steinberg's and Nabokov's (and later in this study, Joyce's) images of travelers, postcards, landscapes, and maps seem a useful collection to assemble in order to explore a central, shared element in the creation of their work: moving across the world as the hand moves across paper, making art and literature, line by line.

7

Steinberg and Nabokov

Wandering Men

Steinberg's insistence that his work resembles Nabokov's—"I am more a writer than an artist. . . . I have all the elements of a writer. I am most like Joyce or Nabokov."—lures us to find those similarities.[1] As we have seen, the visual-verbal arrow of comparison points in two directions. Visual art appears in Nabokov's writing in three central ways: ekphrasis; a rich field of reference to visual artists; and detailed figurings forth of the look of the world, his exquisitely acute word pictures.[2] Nabokov counsels readers to reread novels, because that enables them to see the literary work whole, with all its intricate patterns, as if it were a drawing or painting taken in at a glance.

Additionally, as Steinberg urges us to think of his drawings as texts to be read, Nabokov reciprocally hints that we might well regard words and letters as if they were drawings. When, for example, Clare Bishop, Sebastian Knight's lover in *The Real Life of Sebastian Knight,* types his manuscripts, "The words she typed were to her not so much the conveyors of their natural sense, but the curves and gaps and zigzags showing Sebastian's groping along a certain ideal line of existence" (*RLSK,* 84).

A fascination with motion itself—of the drawing or writing hand, of the viewer's eye, of the entire body—underlies Steinberg's and Nabokov's mutual interest in the convergence of the visual and verbal. Most simply observed, both are traveling men, first as exiles, then as perpetual explorers. Steinberg tells the *New Yorker* writer Brendan Gill: "It seems I have spent my life crossing from one boundary to the next, some of them real, some imaginary. In my day I have been a traveler by necessity, and now I am a traveler by choice. Frontiers and the showing of passports are as natural to me as a fixed abode is to most people."[3] Similarly, Nabokov's childhood travels, butterfly-collecting excursions, employment opportunities, and shifting house rentals kept him in motion until he settled in Switzerland, a location between the major poles of his life, Russia and America.

Steinberg's adult "fine game," traveling to discover "what sort of man I am" (*LAB,* February 19, 1964), together with his belief that true artists retain a childlike curiosity, are akin to a particular bedtime game that Nabokov played as a child and later developed into the fantasies of Kinbote in *Pale Fire.* It went as follows. During his travels, he pleasurably imagined the state of exile which was later to be his lot: "In the first decade of our dwindling [twentieth] century, during trips with my family to Southern Europe, I imagined in bedtime reveries what it would be like to become an exile who longed for a remote, sad and (right epithet coming) unquenchable Russia under the eucalypti of exotic resorts. Lenin and his police neatly arranged the realization of *that* fantasy" (*SO,* 177–78). Nabokov was, like Steinberg, an artist whose thoughts about travel and exile found form in his art, an autogeography that appears explicitly in *Speak, Memory* and implicitly in every work of fiction he wrote.

Nabokov and Steinberg also shared a taste for writers whose characters traveled across the unmappable lands of absurdity. Nabokov lectured on *Don Quixote,* arguably the first work of literature to chronicle travel for travel's sake, and Steinberg drew many a version of a Don Quixote-like knight tilting at a pineapple—for example, the *New Yorker* cover of March 4, 1967. Steinberg read *Don Quixote* in an effort to learn Spanish while he was in Santo Domingo, waiting to gain entry to the United States, and he wrote to Buzzi of Sancho Panza's glorious silliness (*LAB,* February 11, 1982). Steinberg and Nabokov both treasured Gogol's absurd travelers, among them Chichikov of *Dead Souls* and Khlestakov of *The Government Inspector,* not to mention the roving organ of "The Nose" and Akaky Akakyevich of "The Overcoat," both of whom travel the dream streets of St. Petersburg. Steinberg read and reread Nabokov's study *Nikolai Gogol* (*LAB,* October 29, 1993). Both turned to the same two nineteenth-century chroniclers of aesthetic and spiritual travel, Baudelaire and Rimbaud.

We might say that Saul Steinberg traveled not only to know himself but also to escape, during the intermission that travel afforded him, the very self he had been busy inhabiting. In *The Real Life of Sebastian Knight* Nabokov wrote an almost allegorical novel on this very subject—the self in search of the not-self, the urge to explore the mystery of identity rather than to grasp its simple fulfillment. V. seeks who he is not (Sebastian, he mistakenly thinks), and that search involves traveling in order to gather and decipher clues. The solution, to skip to the end of the novel, is more mystery.

The Real Life of Sebastian Knight (1941), the first novel Nabokov wrote in English, can be schematized as a series of journeys taken by its two principal characters to, from, or within Russia, France, England, Germany,

Finland, and Switzerland. In parallel, it presents, as I'll trace, a flickering, textural movement between those two characters themselves, suggesting that they share an identity. As the narrative moves across Europe it also travels across the sometimes bordered, sometimes borderless land of V.'s and Knight's identities. It is with a pair of half brothers who are both kin and strangers to each other that we begin, and it is to the Nabokovian and Steinbergian mysteries of identity, plumbed through travel, that we shall advance.

At first reading the novel seems to take the form of a first-person biographical account, by a businessman we know only as "V.," of the writer Sebastian Knight. Yet just as Steinberg says that he "draws drawing," Nabokov in this novel writes writing in at least two important ways. First, he quotes texts supposedly written by both V. and Sebastian. Second, to the extent that Nabokov parodies literary forms—biography, memoir, mystery novel, detective story, *Künstlerroman*—he pushes the "already written" quality of his prose upon observant readers who can both lose themselves in the story and look at it, in all its derivative glory. More on this in a moment. Although the narrative moves erratically forward and backward through time, the story it most obviously tells is easy enough to reconstruct. Sebastian has already died as the novel opens, and V., feeling that he never really knew his half brother, sets out to explore (and thereby close) the gaps in their relationship as they developed over the years. Through memory and detective work, V. reconstructs Sebastian's childhood, including the death of his mother after she abandoned him and his father, that father's subsequent marriage to V.'s mother, and Sebastian's (and V.'s) father's subsequent death. The family of three—Sebastian, V., and V.'s mother—flees Russia in 1918. Sebastian, a writer from his childhood days, goes up to Cambridge, settles in London, publishes novels and stories, and conducts a six-year relationship with Clare Bishop. He leaves her for a femme fatale, Nina Rechnoy, who then rejects him, and he eventually dies, in 1936, at the age of 36, of the heart disease he has suffered from for several years.

While recounting his brother's life, V. gives us a few facts about his own. He studies at the Sorbonne, settles in Paris, becomes a businessman, meets Clare and Sebastian by chance when they visit Paris, interviews several witnesses to Sebastian's life, examines his papers and his lodgings, and both paraphrases and quotes from Sebastian's fiction. Toward the end of this "novel-as" elegy, V. travels to visit the gravely ill, sleeping Sebastian. Hospital personnel allow him a short bedside visit, during which he thinks about Sebastian and hopes that he will eventually awaken so that they might have an intimate conversation. However, a mistake has been made; in the darkness he has been sitting by the side of a stranger while Sebastian is already dead. V. always fails to make what he believes to be meaningful contact with his brother.

The novel's last sentence confirms what careful readers have suspected, that the real plot of the novel has less to do with the episodes of these men's lives than with the related mysteries of human identity, travel, and artistic creation. V. and Sebastian have all along been intermingling characters who travel in tandem. For example, V. meets along the way characters who seem to have issued from Sebastian's works, and the patterns detected in Sebastian's fiction can also be found in V.'s narrative.[4] Our initial, naive reading teeters as we read, "I am Sebastian, or Sebastian is I, or perhaps we are both someone whom neither of us knows." All the other characters are dismissed from "the masquerade," only "the hero remains," and V. cannot step from the stage because "Sebastian's mask clings to my face, the likeness will not be washed off" (RLSK 205). V.-and-Sebastian's travels have come to an end, but finding clues as to their "real" identities requires rereading the novel. Because V. and Sebastian are caught together as one ("the hero"), inside a drama in which they might be, not only one another, but also "someone whom neither of us knows," the notion of a character's discrete identity, of an "I" distinct from other characters, is a presumption that Nabokov challenges.

A second presumption—that characters in a novel do not know of their own fictionality—also fails at novel's end, as it will go on to fail in metafictions by many subsequent writers. For most of the narrative, V./Sebastian seems analogous to Steinberg's landscape painter (fig. 15) who is oblivious or aware (impossible to say) of the fact that the landscape in which he is seated has itself been drawn and painted by another—i.e., Steinberg. However, as the novel ends, V./Sebastian possesses just this kind of knowledge. Perhaps this "someone whom neither of us knows" is the artificial someone we as rereaders have come to know, the covariant characters V. and Sebastian now collapsed into one. Throughout the seemingly "actual" circumstances of their fictional lives, V. and Sebastian retain their distant relation to each other. They are, however, also always close, as they continuously appear and disappear, one into the other, through Nabokov's sleights of pen. For all his dogged travels and detective work (again, Steinberg travels to discover "what sort of man I am"), V. can never arrive at the real life of Sebastian Knight, which is also his own real life.

Perhaps this mystery man might also be "Nabokov" the author, who has disappeared into these characters, only to appear (and disappear) again in his other books, or even Vladimir Vladimirovich Nabokov, the historical person (1899–1977) who created this labyrinthine tour of identity—unless we take into account the fact that his wife, Véra, often read and criticized

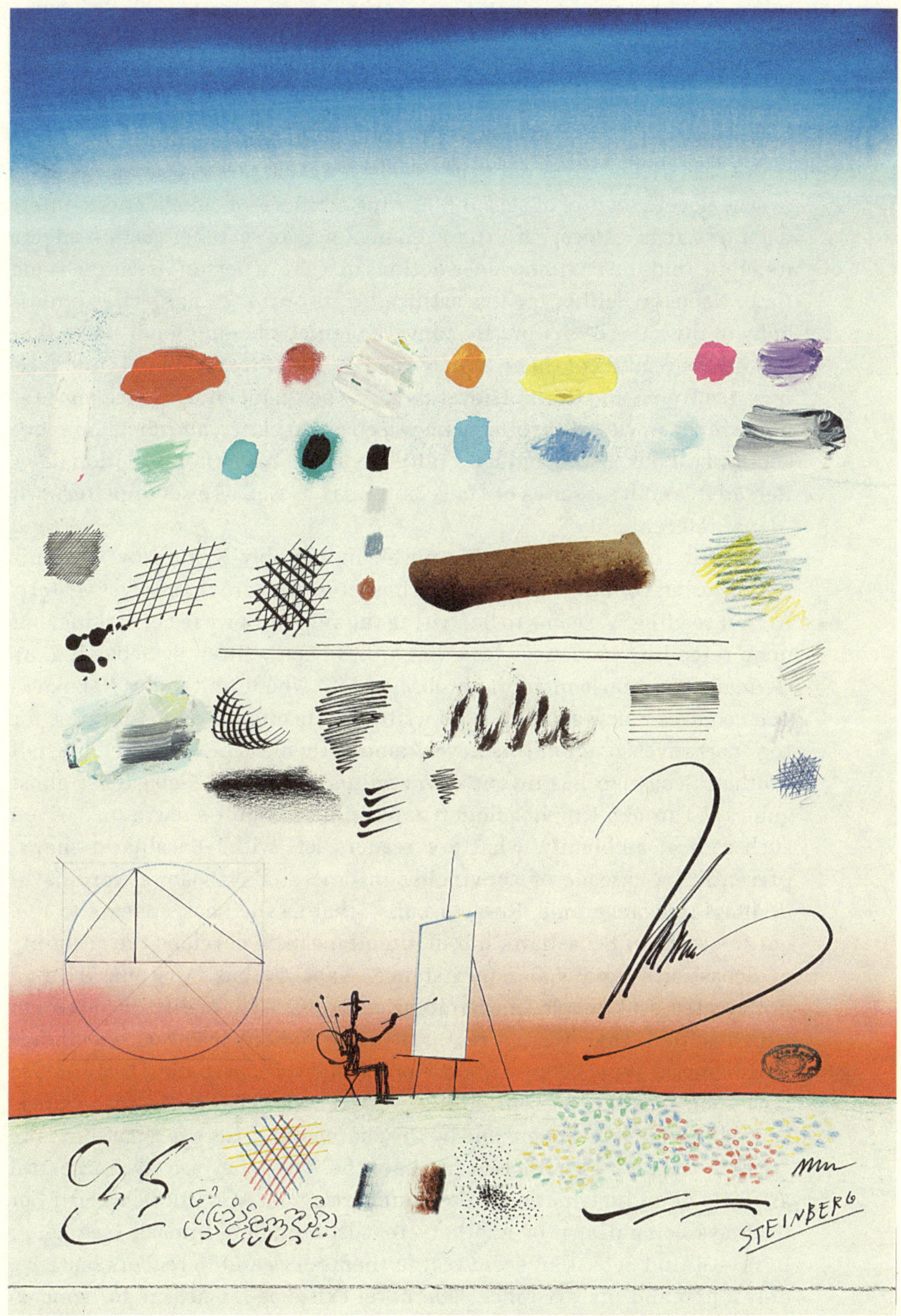

Fig. 15. Untitled, 1968. Watercolor, ink, oil, colored pencil, and rubber stamp on paper, 18½ × 12 ½ in. Cover drawing for the *New Yorker,* January 11, 1969. (Beinecke Rare Book and Manuscript Library, Yale University)

his work in progress, and thus contributed to the work's creation.[5] The someone might be, then: an implied creator of the novel standing behind the first-person narrator V.; the historical Nabokov "himself" (although there are as many of the latter as there are critics, biographers, and readers who consider him); or even the composite figure Véra-Vladimir. The identity of "the writer" turns out to be as elusive as that of a character.

The novel's texture of self-announcing artifice—of coincidences, internal mirrorings, games, patterns, even instances of seeming magic—effects its subtle raids on commonsense notions of what "a person" is. At the same time, Nabokov neither creates artifice for its own sake nor writes philosophy in the guise of fiction. He conveys mental and emotional states that feel, in the reading of them, akin to readers' own "real" thoughts and feelings. Look now, and this is a novel about V.'s poignant efforts to feel more at home in the world by learning to know Sebastian better, and about how love goes awry. Look again, and it's a novel about what a writer of fiction does. Reread it, and it's a series of "false bottoms," as well as a set of patterns of "dense referentiality."[6]

Shifting frames enclose this novel, indubitably written by Vladimir Nabokov, but containing two major characters who are themselves writers. At first reading, V. seems to be writing the very work we're construing, but upon rereading we notice clues that V. has been written by Sebastian. As Gennady Barabtarlo memorably observed, "A whodunnit under Nabokov's pen acquires a new sense of 'who writtit.'"[7] He offers five possibilities for the "narrative agency of this novel," among them: V. has invented his half brother, Sebastian has invented V. and his story, and "Sebastian's ghost guides V. through Knight's fiction as Virgil does Dante's narrator."[8] Given such radical ambiguity, what are readers left with? Barabtarlo shows, presenting a cascade of convincing instances of Nabokov's wordplay—cryptograms, anagrams, Russian puns—that as the book appears to reel out the story of Sebastian's life, it simultaneously develops the certainty of Sebastian's (and V.'s) nonexistence. Nabokov has "written writing," not created real people. As Barabtarlo writes, "The reality of Sebastian Knight's life is that it is not real. . . . In the end one is left with a vibrant nothingness, a special kind of post-processed void: Sebastian is absent, so is V. Their maker is present, filling every cell and fiber of the text, imperceptible and incomprehensible by the characters."[9] Here is a paradox: the "realer" Nabokov's characters become, the more they are the successful artifacts of an imagination. Like Steinberg's man who draws himself but is always being drawn by another—that is, Steinberg himself (see fig. 3; p. 13)—V. and Sebastian seem real to themselves and to readers but have only a pen and ink existence. The novel exists as a machine for concurrently creating and de-creating what we think of as human identity. Steinberg has explained the "man drawing a man" genre of his drawings in this way: "The first man has the illusion that he is creating something. . . . He thinks he is creating some thing. I let him have the illusion he is a creator. He is a puppet creator."[10] In parallel, V. thinks he's writing a memoir when all along it's possibly Sebastian at work, and certainly "Vladimir Nabokov" who writes it.

Steinberg, too, mused on mysterious people encountered in his travels, his memory, and his collection of photographs: "I have in front of me a family photograph, taken in 1924, in Solca, a small vacation resort in the mts. of Bukovina. . . . There are mysterious areas in this photo. There's a man who can barely be seen—it looks like he's wearing a top hat. For a long time I didn't notice him, and I don't really know what he's doing there: an invisible man who popped out only in the photograph" (*RS,* 21–23). Travel to a resort, "mysterious areas," visible-invisible man: Steinberg's phrases coincidentally describe the ghostly presence of the "someone" in Nabokov's novel.

Orders of reality intriguingly vex all of Nabokov's fictions, what Steinberg calls "the problem of objects of first, second, and third, etc. degrees or the problem of reality moving towards illusion," before adding, "One of the things that has always attracted me is, for example, shadow and reflections."[11] Sebastian Knight and V. are simultaneously second-degree or realistic imitations of real or "first-degree" people, reflections of each other, and men made out of words. The characters of the novel are as alphabetical or written as they are human. They are also parodies—repetitions with a difference—of each other. As we have seen, V. himself writes of Sebastian that he "used parody as a kind of springboard for leaping into the highest region of serious emotion" (*RLSK,* 91). We need not choose any single solution listed by Barabtarlo in order to appreciate Nabokov's "combinational magic" (*PF,* 253). Indeed, it is in part the sheer pleasure of playing the game *and* feeling the joy and pain of human life that Nabokov has set out for us, rather than arriving at a single victorious explanation, that keeps us rereading the novel. A novel in the end is not a chess puzzle; we're not aiming for checkmate against the text.

The albinos of "Albinos in Black," the title of one of Sebastian's stories, can be thought of as characters who rise from the white page to take shape and color only within the blackness of print. As such, the title is one of many markers that remind readers of the artificial nature of the novel. "Albinos in Black" also describes, coincidentally, the pen and ink drawing of a person on a white sheet of paper. In his compilation of previously made drawings entitled *The New World,* Steinberg includes the picture of a man drawing a picture of another man who is a version of himself—say, his double, twin, or half-brother (see fig. 3; p. 13). But the delineation of character is not the only goal—the man issuing from Steinberg's or Nabokov's pen goes on to create within the frame of the drawing or the novel (in Steinberg's words) "amusements . . . games . . . his life."[12] Over time, the drawn man, in Steinberg's fantasy, claims his independence. But then, artists drawing artists just *are* engaging simultaneously in those three things.

Perhaps most closely apposite to *The Real Life of Sebastian Knight* is Steinberg's drawing of a small man (fig. 16) (like V.) who carries through space and across a sheet of paper a huge hand with pen (like his mental notion of Sebastian as a writer whose full identity eludes him). Because the scale is impossible to determine—is this a tiny man holding a normally sized hand, or a normally sized man holding a gigantic hand?—and because the relation between the pictured man and the larger arm suggests an artist's tongue-in-cheek depiction of the heroism of supporting a drawing habit or talent, the viewer is at sea in trying to determine the drawing's message. The man is not just everyman toting a strange burden, but also the image of an invisible presence, "Steinberg" or Steinberg, who, with his drawing arm well-connected to his body, has created him.

Could it be that Steinberg had in mind Nabokov, the expert who traveled across the United States in search of butterflies, when he drew a man with a butterfly net trying to capture a question mark (fig. 17)?[13] The drawing is,

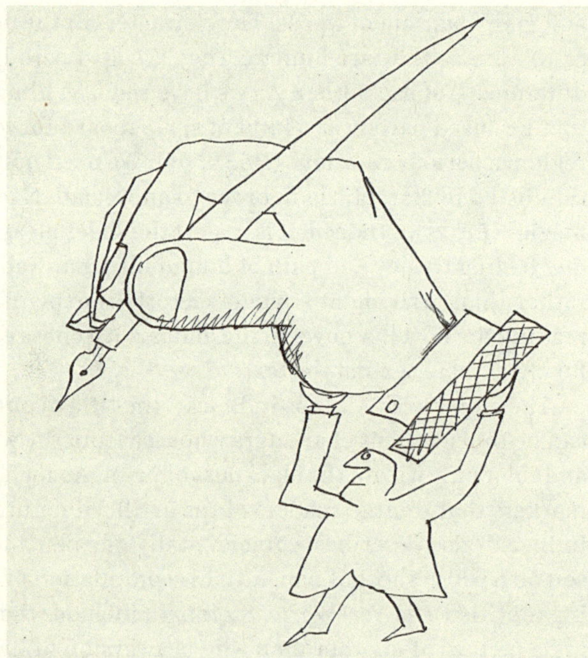

Fig. 16. Untitled, c. 1949–54. Ink on paper, 7½ × 10 ½ in. (Beinecke Rare Book and Manuscript Library, Yale University)

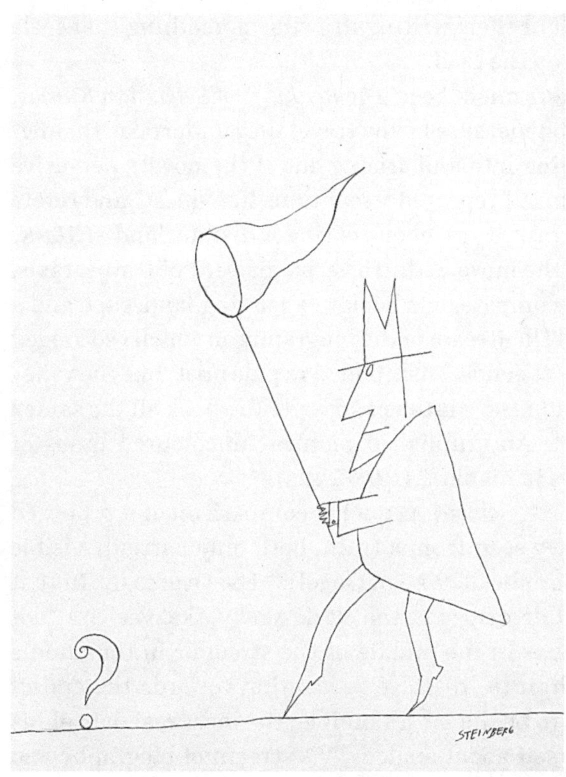

Fig. 17. Untitled, 1965. Ink on paper, 22⅞ × 28⅞ in. Originally published in the *New Yorker,* January 30, 1965. (The Saul Steinberg Foundation, New York; photograph by Jenny Gorman)

however coincidentally, as valid a work of interpretation of *The Real Life of Sebastian Knight* as those in print. It suggests V.'s attempts to answer the always flitting question that is Sebastian, to catch him in a net only to discover that the specimen is always an absence. Steinberg's sketched man pouncing on a question mark is, as it were, half brother to Nabokov's V., but also to Sebastian, who is better at presenting mysteries than solving them. The novel's net of words turns out to be, at the end, as much interstice as solid thread. Steinberg's net is made of lines, and drawn lines are for him a net with which to catch, not the beautiful thing itself, but the multitude of possibilities circulating about through air or mind. In short, Steinberg and Nabokov always invite us to trap within the grid of logic a work of art that must remain a question mark, eluding us as it moves, fluttering beautifully, frustratingly by. While some would argue that any artist issues the same invitation, that any work of art, as Wallace Stevens would say, must be almost successful in defying the intelligence, Steinberg and Nabokov belong to the elite club of twentieth-century artists who share something more. Their art issues in paradox: in depicting elusiveness they also manage to capture, through the precise detail of their writing-drawing, something that feels like reality on the wing or on the road.

Whoever these characters might be in *The Real Life of Sebastian Knight,* they are constituted in good measure by the travel they undertake, that figure of travel itself dissolving into and arising out of the novel's pervasive currents of identity. V. himself repeatedly mentions his "quest" and refers to himself as "the embarrassed traveller visiting a distant land" (*RLSK,* 52). All characters are on the move within a verbal pattern of trains, taxis, and foot travel. V. in fact compares his book to a passing landscape and a black-and-white picture, "The stream of the biography on which I so longed to start, was, at one of its last bends, enshrouded in pale mist; like the valley I was contemplating. Could I leave it thus and write the book all the same? A book with a blind spot. An unfinished picture—uncoloured limbs of the martyr with the arrows in his side" (*RLSK,* 125).

Beyond the allusion to St. Sebastian, such a comparison of a proposed literary stream and a valley seen from a train, both only partially visible through a mist, is itself parodic of Nikolai Gogol's "The Overcoat." In that work, as Nabokov himself describes it, the clerk Akaky Akakyevich's "not quite knowing whether he is in the middle of the street or in the middle of the sentence" causes him to "dissolve . . . so that towards the end of the story his ghost seems to be the most tangible, the most real part of his being."[14] This parody is itself about analogy, V.'s stream of biography and valley outside the window resembling Akaky Akakyevich's middle of the sentence and middle of the street. At this moment, the "blind spot" in V.'s book, its immaterial ghost, is the unfinished portrait of Sebastian "himself," whose "uncoloured" or black-and-white limbs will exist only through the black-and-white print in which V. hopes to bring his half brother to a new life. By novel's end, however, the blind spot has grown to encompass the entire work.

The images and metaphors of travel infusing *The Real Life of Sebastian Knight* always raise questions of destination. V. deliberately seeks Sebastian, but Sebastian tends to seek higher destinations, the answers to questions about beauty, being, last things, higher realms. As V. listens in the dark to what he thinks is Sebastian's breath, that breath itself takes a trip: "the soft sound was there, following a thin trail which seemed to skirt time itself, now dipping into a hollow, now appearing again,—steadily travelling across a landscape formed of the symbols of silence—darkness, and curtains, and a glow of blue light at my elbow" (RLSK 203). Steady traveling, traveling memorialized: it is to Nabokov's and Steinberg's postcards and landscapes that we now turn.

8

Steinberg's Postcards

"Short Stories"

When Steinberg drew postcards, he traveled, memorialized, parodied, and invented. In short, postcards are for Steinberg artifacts in which he entangles his experiences of travel and exile, visual and literary art, and memory, all of which combine in shifting patterns.[1] In his parodic postcards he synthesizes cliché and experimentation, mass-market and upmarket tastes. A postcard for him could be as delectably banal as an American motel advertisement or as delicate as a "haiku of geography" through which a miniature world shines forth.[2] Steinberg's delight in postcards began during his childhood, according to Hedda Sterne. An opera singer, one Mme Stibal, lived in his Bucharest neighborhood, and her housebound invalid son played with postcards. Saul loved to visit the boy and play with them, too.[3] As an adult he collected Romanian postcards (among many others) through an agent in Queens and an art dealer in Amsterdam, according to the writer Norman Manea, a Jewish Austrian-Romanian friend of Steinberg's who managed both to survive the Nazis and to flee the Communists, eventually settling in New York. These postcards were, Manea writes, "picturesque views from the interwar years of Romanian towns and villages and spas. As I looked with amusement at a market sequence with halva sellers . . . I was inevitably reminded that when Saul first came to our house, he arrived not with the usual bottle or the even more usual box of bottles, as he would later, but with an old colored postcard of interwar Buzău, the town of his grandparents and parents and his early childhood."[4]

Throughout his half-century-long correspondence with Buzzi, Steinberg sent him numerous postcards. Late in life he told Buzzi that "I found a good collection of Romanian postcards here, from the period around 1912 . . . Now I'm passing the time with a magnifying glass, reading the signs and watching the people walk with the kind of grace and style that will never be repeated. Vehicles, dreshke, briska, dogcarts, caleshe, with their horses, dogs, kids in school uniforms" (*LAB,* November 23, 1995). "Greetings from the horse on the left," he writes of a Russian postcard from 1905,

"I hope you have a good magnifying glass" (*LAB,* November 7, 1998). With a magnifying glass in one hand and a small printed postcard in the other, Steinberg can return to pre–World War I Eastern Europe. Postcards invite his memory to speak.

Steinberg reads them freely, too, bringing his adult experience to bear: "I'm sending you an excellent gift: the actual postcard of Rybinsk with the dog . . . Look at the man walking with the same gait as the Rimbaud portrait. And the other one in the middle! And the troika, a kind of samurai (*LAB,* February 3, 1992).[5] Of a second postcard of Rybinsk in his collection, he writes, "The date is the same as the other one, 1913, a few months older than I am. Again, there is much to discover if one studies it with a magnifying glass: a fat dog (or perhaps a skinny pig), lamps, balls, excavations, what chaos! What could have moved the photographer to make a postcard of this marvel, which certainly isn't a view?" (*LAB,* January 24, 1992). Not a "view," i.e., a well-known site or point of touristic interest, these Rybinsk postcards instead speak to him about the times and places of his life, the latter broadly construed as Eastern Europe, not just Romania.

After enlarging to a meter across some old Russian postcards, he tells Buzzi, "When you look at them you enter into that world, shortly before our birth—which is a more attractive and comprehensible era. People in uniform, soldiers or students or civil servants, dogs, horses, a caffè . . . a print shop on the 2nd floor, a man in a long overcoat walking with his hands clasped behind him" (*LAB,* April 11, 1981). Setting and characters (has the man escaped from Gogol's "The Overcoat"?) are there—and, in Steinberg's imagination, a narrative as well. Like Nabokov, who discovered the small made large at the "radiant bottom of a microscope's magic shaft" (*SM,* 166), Steinberg uses a magnifying glass and photographic enlargements to examine postcards, these enlargements themselves magnifying his memories of childhood.

Given his early love of the genre, almost any postcard will speak of his childhood, even those picturing other times and places. Engaging in the linked processes of travel and art often involved for Steinberg an exploration of popular forms related to travel—maps, advertisements, postcards—by calling attention to their conventional, commercial artifice. In this taste he resembles Nabokov's and Joyce's characters who are both roving aesthetes and connoisseurs of mass-produced commercial art: think of Humbert Humbert's careful recording of motel names in *Lolita* and Leopold Bloom's job selling newspaper advertising in *Ulysses.*

Steinberg not only paid attention to commercial art but also made it himself, including greeting cards and desk calendars for Hallmark and drawings for advertising agencies such as Foote, Cone & Belding.[6] No bright line can be drawn between his advertisements and his nonpromotional works appearing in such periodicals as the *New Yorker, Life, Flair, Fortune, Harper's, Town & Country, Harper's Bazaar,* and *Vogue.*[7] He did a series of ads for d'Orsay, Jones & Lamson, Noilly-Prat, Simplicity, Emerson, and Morton Salt, among many other companies.[8] All of it helped him pay the bills. But he also thought about the artistic conventions and clichés he encountered there, especially in postcards, as did Nabokov: "I am going to pass around in a minute some lovely, glossy-blue picture-postcards," Humbert Humbert promises (*AnL,* 11). Most such glossy postcards contain identifying titles printed near or even over the picture, but Nabokov parodies in Humbert's own mass-produced diction, "lovely, glossy-blue," the same banality of verbal and visual message.

Steinberg drew picture postcards, copying the conventions closely and then applying the torque of his imagination to pass through banality to something new. The *New Yorker* issues of January 16, 1978, and February 25, 1980, for example, contain portfolios of postcards with views of cities, postcards that, he said, "*strike me as the equivalent of short stories*" (*LAB,* August 13, 1979; emphasis added). The narrative must arise as viewers "tell themselves" his postcards in detailed ways. Moreover, as we'll see, he created montages of individual postcards—those "short stories"—that gave rise to extended and interwoven narrative possibilities, visual novellas as it were.

Postcards of landscape and cityscape "views" are messages we receive from places we can't actually visit, and not because the things and places they depict are prohibitively distant from us in time or space. We can't get there because these views hold reality suspended in a peculiar little box that often measures 4 x 6 x .016 inches, a container that, in Steinberg's hands, resembles the fantasy space of Joseph Cornell's boxes. What we *can* do is visit them imaginatively. Rather than merely documenting the world, Steinberg's postcards invite our double engagement with them as both conventions and free-form fantasies. Because we understand the conventional pictorial postcard, we don't actually have to look at the specific view it presents or read its reverse side to know the sender's clichéd message, paraphrasable as "thinking of you, but not in a very detailed way." Successful advertising postcards, a subgenre which Steinberg parodied, play the less enchanting game of creating and sustaining consumer desire.[9]

Municipalities, for example, actually advertised their achievements and points of interest, as in the postcard of "The Airport Terminal Bldg., Fort Worth, Texas—65" (fig. 18).[10] Steinberg made many "postcard drawings" that self-consciously parody this genre (and this particular postcard), itself dependent on reproduction. Over a Bauhausy Fort Worth Airport ter-

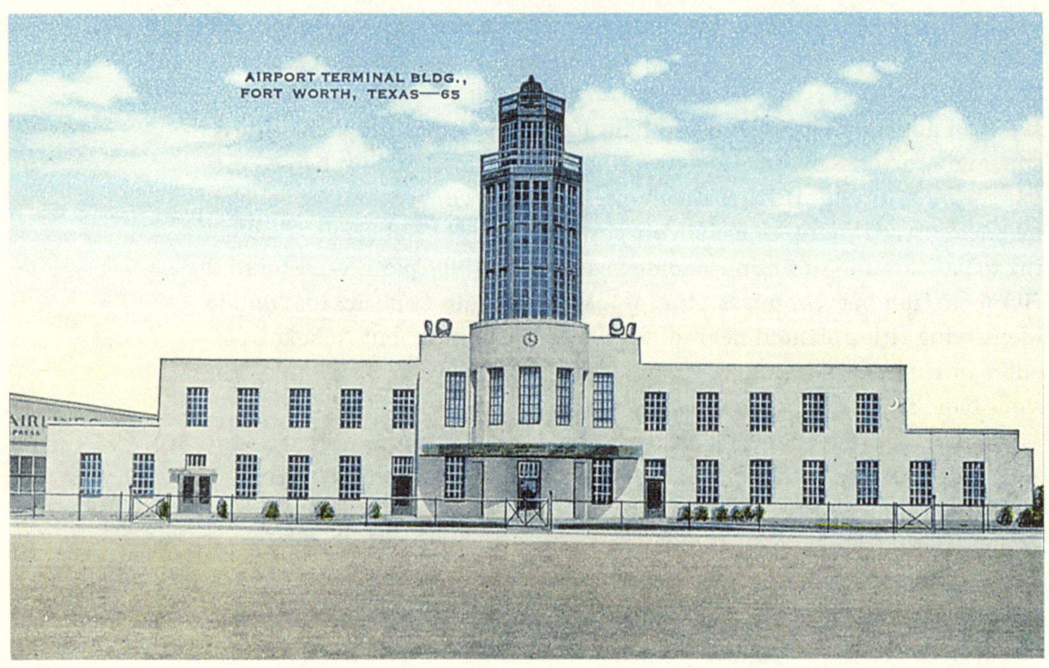

Fig. 18. *The Airport Terminal Bldg., Fort Worth, Texas—65*, postcard. (Collection of the author)

minal building (fig. 19) rises a glass tower akin to an art deco skyscraper, and over it flies Steinberg's addition to the "original" postcard (itself a reproduction): that commercial jetliner, a plump but streamlined cartoonish creature with rainbow contrails and forward-looking, identical passengers neatly framed by its portholes. Building and airplane alike soar against a background of abstract clouds that seem to have blown in from a Dalí painting. Steinberg here parodies the subgenre of postcards we might call "regional sites of interest," a hybrid of art card, view card, and advertisement. As we read it, we come to understand that Steinberg has transformed his travels, his continuously self-generated exile, into emblems of a wittily derivative and always ambiguous journey. Questions arise if we stop to think about this miniaturized scene. Are these passengers headed out of Texas toward another geographical state of the Union? Or is the plane circling before landing? Are the passengers emigrating for good, entering the psychological state of tourism, or suffering temporary business-travel exile? Who are those air passengers anyway, and how will they feel if the plane decides to fly through the donut hole of a cloud that turns out to be made of cardboard? Possible narratives multiply, each tinged with uncertainty, and perhaps the only narrative we can be sure of is the story of possibilities. Even when views are meant to be historically accurate, the frame of the

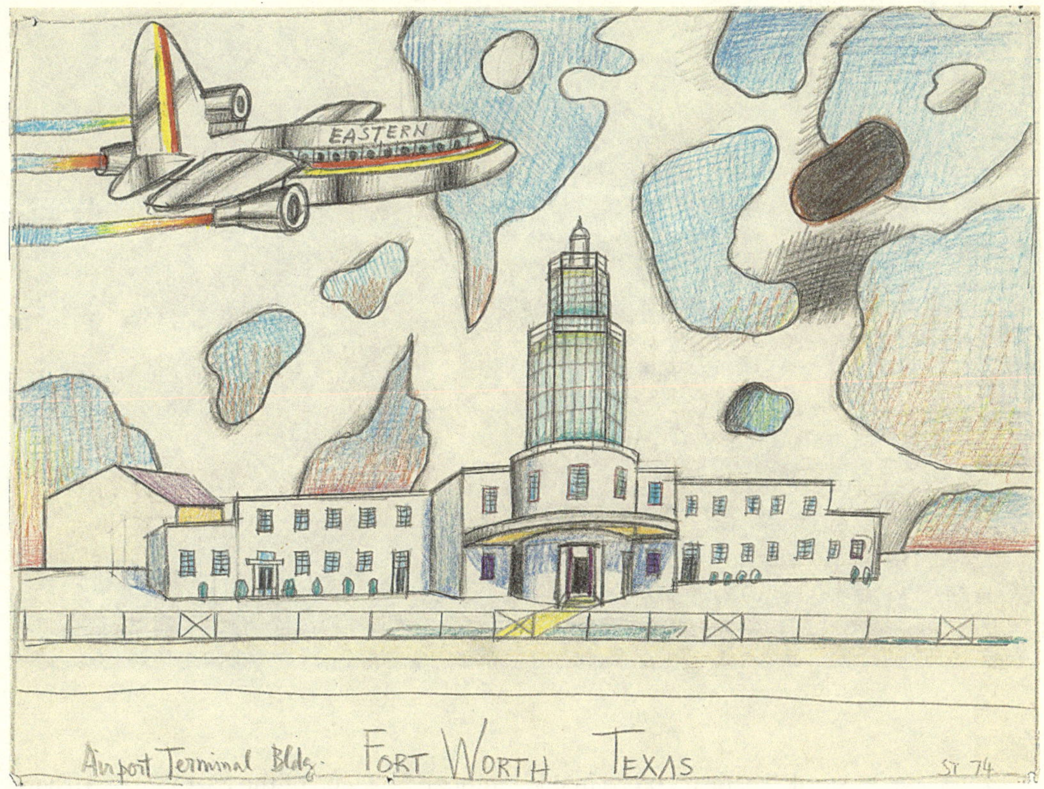

Fig. 19. *Airport Terminal Bldg. Fort Worth, Texas,* 1974. Crayon and black pencil on paper, 11 × 14 in. (Beinecke Rare Book and Manuscript Library, Yale University)

sketched postcard becomes a stage where Steinberg may add or subtract actors and shift scenery around at will.

The postcard genre implies another order of narrative that arises when we contemplate the postcard as an object in the world. Steinberg parodically draws a picture of something that is already a picture, a thing that people send, receive, and collect. During the pre-Internet days of the twentieth century, such postcards not only chronicled travel but traveled themselves. Just as tellingly, postcards also spin the tale of their own creation. Drawn, painted, engraved, or photographed images are printed by a variety of techniques on, typically, cardboard or rag paper. Once printed, these images may themselves be painted upon, embossed, spread with glitter, even embroidered. What results are versions of the real world captured, miniaturized, replicated—and tinkered with. Within that huge world made small, words can stretch across the night sky, undergird city blocks, or drip from trees. Captions that are "outside" the view, typically along a border at the bottom of the card, speak to words that appear within the view. The

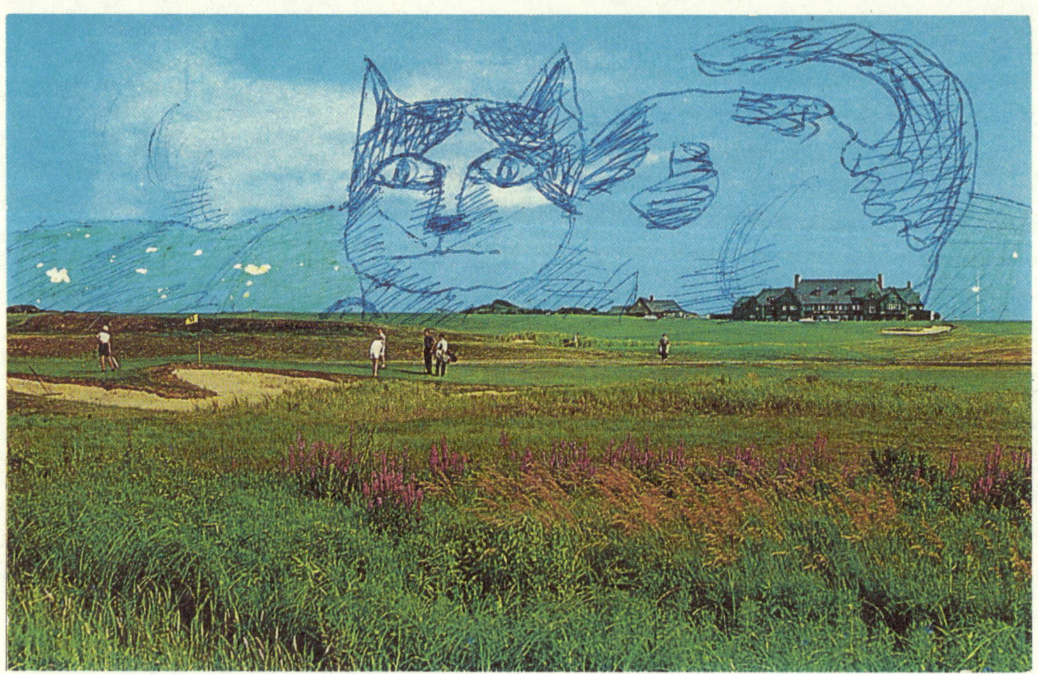

Fig. 20. Untitled, n.d. Blue ink on postcard, 3½ × 5½ in. (Beinecke Rare Book and Manuscript Library, Yale University)

word "Eastern" exists inside Steinberg's "view" of the Fort Worth Airport, while the words at the bottom, "Terminal Bldg.," etc., exist outside it; both exist within the sketch. What Steinberg calls our attention to, more than the "view," are frames, worlds within worlds, degrees of reality, within a single card.

Lest we miss the message of orders of reality, Steinberg delights in playing with frame and scale in obvious ways (fig. 20). By embellishing a postcard view, complete with "glossy-blue" sky, Steinberg asks us to ponder the meaning of the human form as it shrinks to fit within an artistic frame. Are we perhaps tiny beings in the eyes of a giant cat-god? If the cat is drawn to actual scale, then the rest of the image becomes a model of a tiny golf course, complete with players and clubhouse, a visual pun on the twentieth-century invention of "miniature golf." And, as Joel Smith has discussed, Steinberg also blew up postcards from his collection and "tacked the enlargements to his studio wall. Then he sat and watched them, like a cinema of stills. . . . In this way he took historical core samples of 'the world just before I was born,' in a range of locales such as Bucharest, Buzau, Moscow, Brest, Heidelberg, Lille, and Avignon" (*SS: I,* 79).

At times Steinberg even imported images from actual postcards for

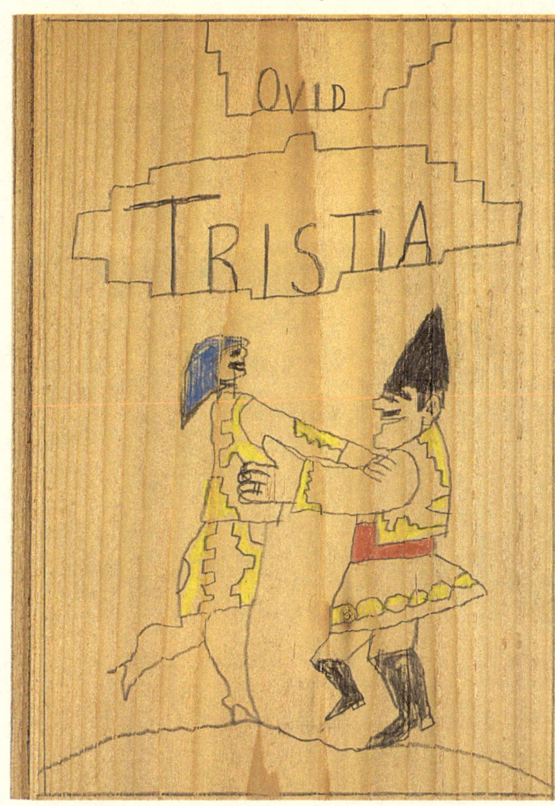

Fig. 21. *Ovid TRISTIA*, c. 1988–98. Pencil, crayon, and pastel on wood, 9¾ × 6¾ × ⅝ in. (The Saul Steinberg Foundation, New York; photograph by Teresa Christiansen)

their literary resonances. When Steinberg created a wooden book of Ovid's *Tristia* (fig. 21), an account of the poet's exile, he made use of an image from a postcard of dancers from northeast Romania (fig. 22). Ovid was banished to the Black Sea port of Tomis—what was to become Romanian Constanța. In a 1988 letter to Eugen Campus, a friend from school days in Bucharest, Steinberg includes a copy of Ovid's "Third Elegy" from *Tristia* in the original Latin and English translation, telling him that "all of a sudden I was very interested in re-reading Ovid."[11] Ovid's elegy begins, "I'm an exile's book. He sent me. I'm tired. I feel trepidation / approaching his city—kind reader, lend a hand!"[12] Canto 1 of the elegy is "spoken" by a personified book (*Tristia* itself) who is also a traveler and an advocate for Ovid, who remains hidden behind that mask.

Steinberg, exiled from Romania, rereads Ovid's poetry written from exile in what was to become Romania, and several years later constructs a wooden book to memorialize the connection. The image of dancers on the book's cover is not an exact copy of the postcard, which presents a photograph of folkloric dancers who pose, somewhat grotesquely, against a back-

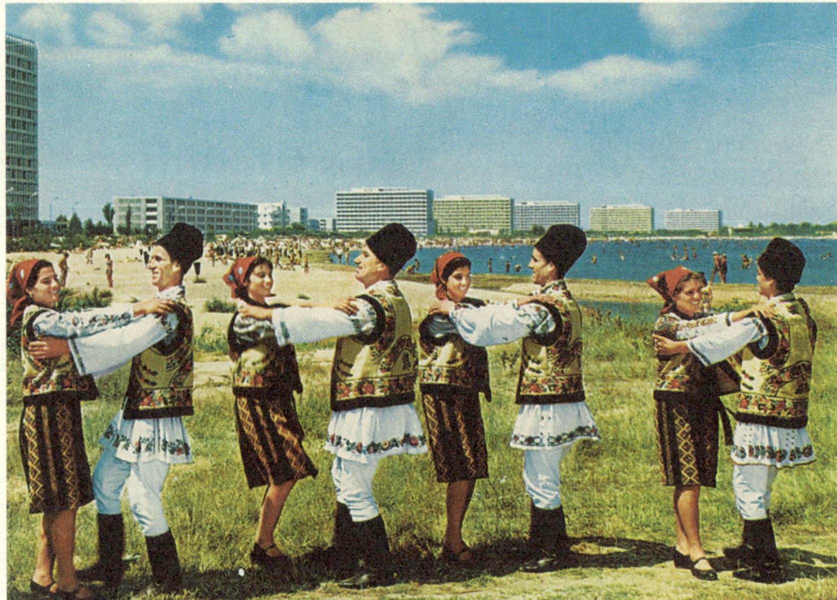

Fig. 22. *Dancers of Northern Moldavia,* postcard, c. 1970, from Steinberg's collection. (Beinecke Rare Book and Manuscript Library, Yale University)

ground of bleak high-rise buildings, a coincidental visual pun on Communist "blocs." Instead, Steinberg draws a deliberately primitive, "folk" rendering of two dancers from the postcard photograph. Ovid worries that his Latin has been barbarized during his exile; Steinberg chooses to draw a crude, childlike version of the postcard image.[13]

Tracing the parodic image chain, we see that an anonymous photographer takes a picture that is then reproduced on a postcard, meant to be sent (as is Ovid's book of exile) to another place, that picture received by Steinberg and redrawn on wood so as to write the story of *Tristia,* the sorrows of the artist-exile-personified book who never feels at home. Postcards, books, elegies, travel, and exile: how suitable that Ovid, the genius of metamorphosis, should speak through the words and images that Steinberg reads, writes, and draws anew.

Beyond mirroring his own life, postcards mirror one another and, to his delight, contain mirrors as subjects. He asks Buzzi, "Do you remember my collection of picture postcards? A few years ago I discovered that this collection, with its groupings of railroads, monuments, etc., harbored a whole additional collection of reflections in water and in mirrors (nude women)" (*LAB,* May 1, 980). Mirrors within mirrors—we're once again suspended in Steinberg's "degrees of reality" or "boxes within boxes." Like the multiple sunsets over Manhattan, postcards of views issue for Steinberg from an unavailable original, presumably the physical place they document. He seems to escort them through a series of metamorphoses, from drawing his own images upon actual postcards, to using them in his collages, to mounting them on his assemblages. At times he photocopies them and adds some color, imitating the hand-coloring of postcards before the era of cheap color reproductions called "chromes" (*SS: I,* 72). Or he simply makes a drawing of an existing postcard. His photocopied, colored version of an actual postcard of "Tortoreto Stazione-Via Roma" refers to the place of his 1941 internment before his flight from Italy (fig. 23).

When he makes drawings that, while much larger than actual postcards, observe their conventions, he favors local views, such as a block or two of a humble downtown area: "San Pedro California" (SSF 01610), "Cheyenne, Wyo." (SSF 01709), or, as pictured here (fig. 24), "Charlotte N.C." There

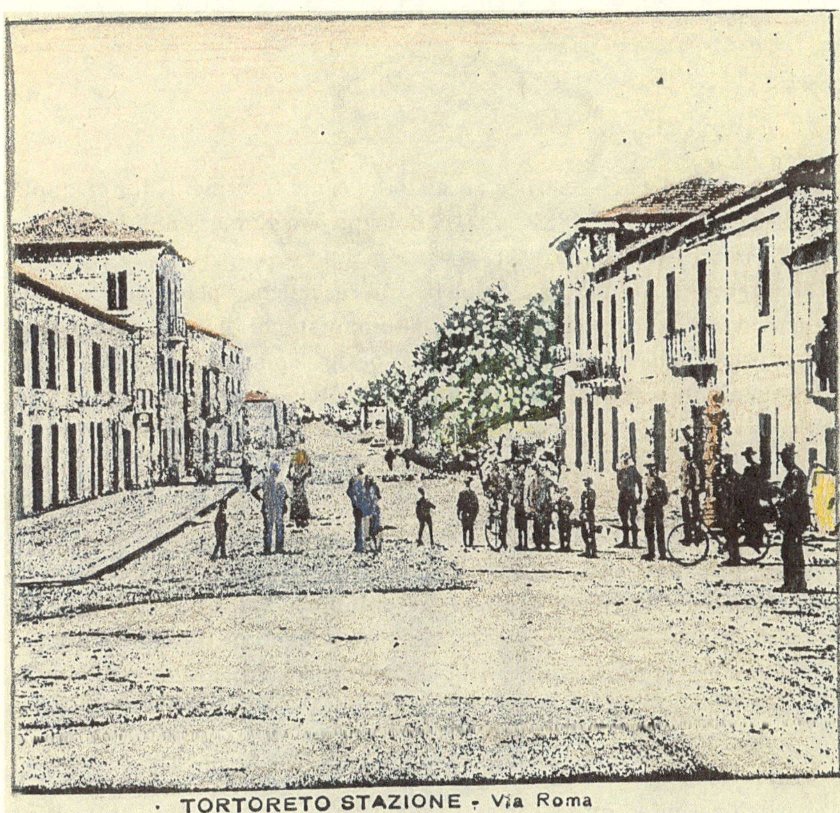

Fig. 23. *Tortoreto Stazione—Via Roma,* sketchbook page with Steinberg's hand-colored photocopy of an old postcard, c. 1985–90. (Beinecke Rare Book and Manuscript Library, Yale University)

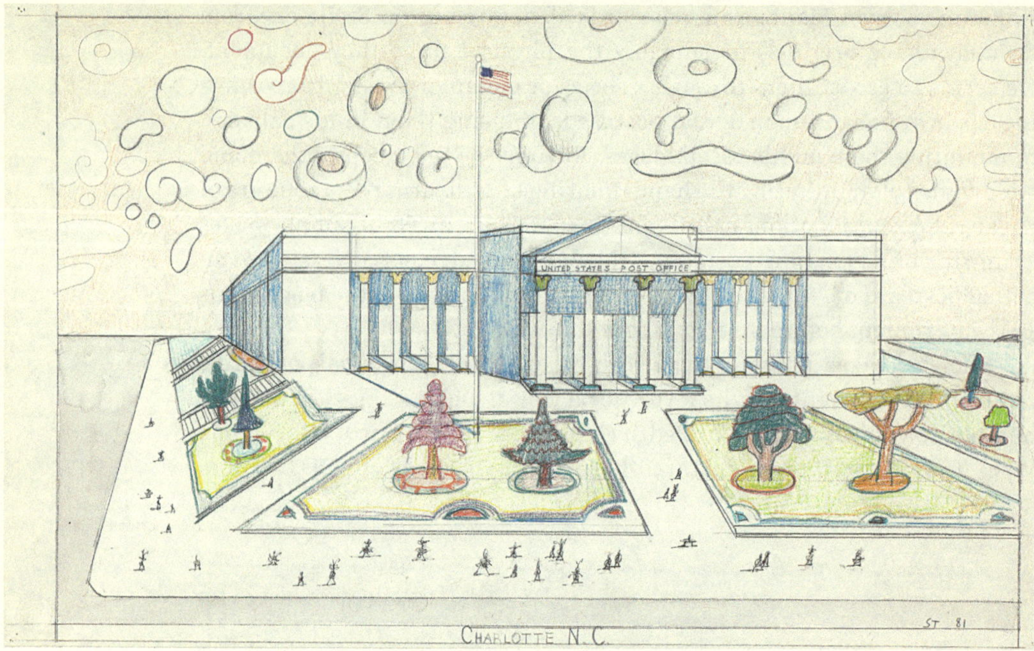

Fig. 24. *Charlotte N.C.*, 1981. Pencil, colored pencil, watercolor, crayon, and ink on paper, 14 ½ × 23 in. (The Saul Steinberg Foundation, New York; photograph by Teresa Christiansen)

are many others. Cities abroad receive the same treatment, for example, sketches of "Tel Aviv" (SSF 1732), "Bologna Via Roma" (SSF 03628), or "Paris, France" (SSF 05150).[14]

For Steinberg, postcards emphasize time as much as place, because they are narratives of memory. Just as his Romanian childhood can be recaptured through looking at postcards, each of these places visited as an adult can become, by virtue of its postcard view, a flowering of that childhood. The very conventional nature of their composition, combined with local architectural details captured in a faux photorealistic style, their often-stylized clouds, and their implicit invitation to enter them as one would a dollhouse or a model train set landscape with its trees on little stands: all these suggest that even "Charlotte N.C." has become a part of Steinberg's adult past, which is itself a version of childhood lost and regained. The postcard "views" he draws are the émigré's version of the miniature Romanian worlds of his memory. And postcards as artifacts—remember the postcard collection of his childhood—regardless of what they picture, carry emotional import for Steinberg.

While "view" postcards imply a traveling from place to place, they may also, when gathered into a series, drawn or printed upon, and affixed to a board, become small, stay-at-home collections. In contrast to sending and receiving, collecting postcards gives the advantage to an active receiver. Brought to rest in collections, postcards—like coins and stamps—allow the collector to make an order of his own devising, to care for assembled bits of the world, even to pose as an enlightened leader of lands and minions.

Nine Postcards (fig. 25) is an image of a collection. Here, Steinberg creates frames within frames using "found" art. From the outside in, we see: the frame of the cream-colored board, within it nine rectangles, within each of these a cropped view of a distant place on earth. Within six of these postcards—those in the left-hand and middle columns, we can read "framed" signs, e.g., "Monte Carlo Commercial Hotel," some of them easily legible, others, as is the case with the incised letters above the two tunnels or distant commercial signs, requiring a magnifying glass. The two postcards with titles (superimposed on the sky) carry another, verbal frame; those without labels presumably carry them on the verso. The images themselves have interiors: the depths of that ocean, those dark tunnels, the interiors of those buildings. To these multiplying layers or degrees of reality, Steinberg has added one more, the rubber-stamped figures (he designed and had produced a variety of rubber stamps) copied from Jean-François Millet's *Angelus* (fig. 26).

Here, then, are nine "short stories," as Steinberg has called postcards, a novella, chapters from a novel, or haikus. They initially seem to form groups: two of them are set in identified places, "Railroad Station, New London, Con." and "View of 41st Street and Sheridan Ave., Miami Beach, Florida"; three are small-town main streets; one is a divided highway leading into and out of a tunnel; and three are varied landscapes (seaside, rolling plains, and verdant fields and hills). These divisions, however, begin to waver as we read more closely: the landscape on the bottom right has just the suggestion of a building among the swath of trees, perhaps at the edge of town. All nine of the pictures have blue skies. The exterior of the tunneled mountain displays a rather wild landscape. The small-town main streets extend to what must be the plains, and if you drive far enough east on 41st Street in Miami Beach, you'll approach the ocean. If these are poems or short stories, they form a cycle; if chapters, they form a modernist novel of discontinuities and gaps that nonetheless manages alternating centrifugal and centripetal forces, like so many of the novels Steinberg read, including, as we'll see in detail, those by Joyce and Nabokov.

We can read characters and plot here as well. Examining the cards as a cartoon strip that we read from left to right, top to bottom, we can watch these Millet peasants traveling from town or city to landscape, three times over, as if they insistently end up far from the modern, concrete world to which they can never belong. By the last frame, they're back on the farm.

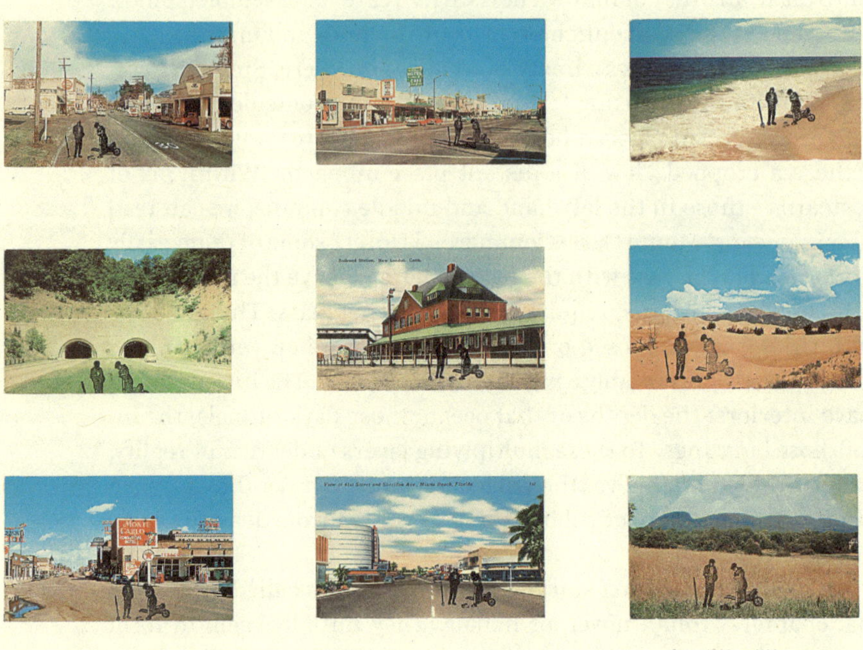

Fig. 25. *Nine Postcards,* 1969. 20 × 24⅝ in. (Museum of Fine Arts, Boston; photograph by Teresa Christiansen)

The rubber-stamped *Angelus* figures carry a special message for those familiar with Steinberg's biography. "Nothing that has been deposited in the memory is lost," he writes. "Memory is a computer that all one's life goes on accumulating data which are not always used, since man is often like an ocean liner that sets sail with only a single cabin occupied. We ought to be able to use this huge accumulation of data continually, keep it functioning, combine and multiply its elements and reintroduce them into the circuit of our thoughts" (*RS,* 5). *Nine Postcards* is a work of memory, possibly of places he has visited, but certainly, in the rubber stamp he has applied to each postcard, of his childhood.

His father was first a book printer and binder and later, at the bidding of his wife, a manufacturer of cardboard boxes, "Victoria, Fabrica de Cartonaje." "He made cardboard boxes, a profession he didn't like, near the flower market on Strada Soarelui (the street of the sun), a narrow, rat-

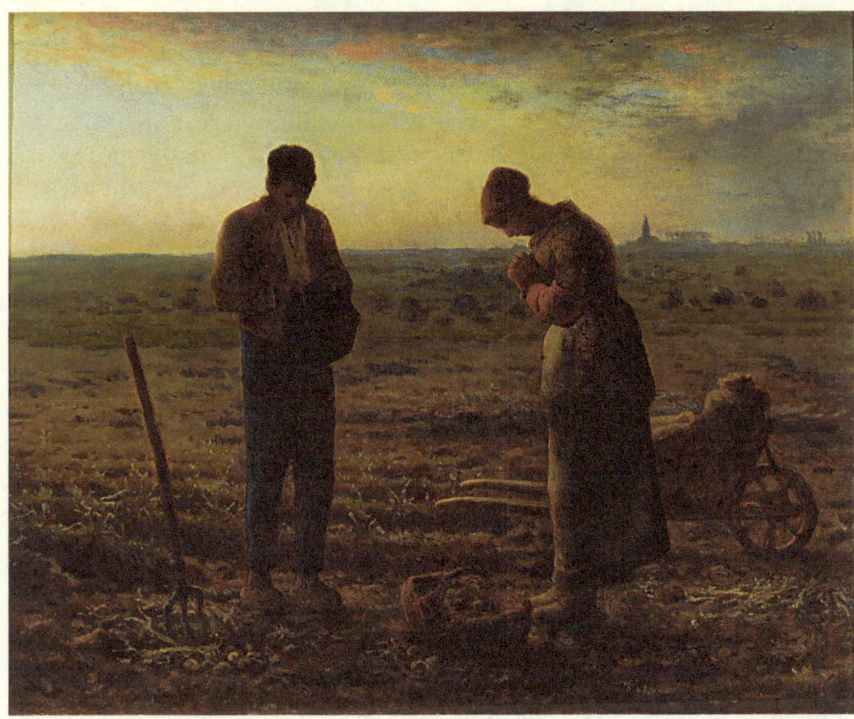

Fig. 26. *The Angelus*, Jean-François Millet, c. 1857–59. Oil on canvas, 22 × 26 in. (Musée d'Orsay)

infested lane." Perhaps boxes within boxes, frames within frames, began here, in memory: "These horses pulled a lightweight pagoda of boxes, but you had to factor in the wind, an adventurous life" (*LAB,* October 2, 1988). He adds, "The factory also produced boxes for chocolates, bonbons, and sugar-coated almonds—deluxe boxes on whose glossy covers was an artistic reproduction in chromolithography, the imitation or reproduction of an oil painting" (*RS,* 7–8). "Millet," he told Buzzi, "was ideal for chocolate boxes because he combined the classicism of the Renaissance with socialism, which at that time was not only popular but also virginal (no one yet knew of the horrors that might come, and did come)" (*RS,* 12).

Steinberg first knew Millet and other painters through reproductions of their work: "Actually, when I really want to look at art, reproductions are a blessing. It's like going to the opera. I wouldn't dream of going to an opera unless I first knew it by heart. It's the only way to enjoy an opera. . . . And so it is with certain paintings. I first look at reproductions for a long time, then I go to see the originals. Of course, it's a great emotion to see them. It's a strange emotion, because it's like encountering a fictitious personage.

And so it goes for cities. I first study the map of a town and then I go to see it, and it turns out to be perfectly true."[15]

Seeing the original of Millet's *Angelus* was evidently a moving experience for him, because he sketched viewers standing before the painting and noted, "Seeing the Angelus of Millet—the original, the real painting at a large and melancholy retrospective of Millet at the Grand Palais in Paris."[16] Millet's painting had been transformed over the years into what he called "bondieuserie" (similar to "kitsch" or the Nabokovian *poshlust*). But by having a rubber stamp of Millet's peasants made to order and then printing them atop these nine postcards, Steinberg creates one of those "circuits of memory" he mentions to Buzzi, rehearsing not only the child's pleasure in looking at chocolate-box images but also his father's pain, an urban "peasant" forced to run a business he didn't care for in a dirty back street.

The story he tells in *Nine Postcards,* then, is one that juxtaposes eras and geographies of his life, and looking at those images, we see "found" allusions to the Millet painting. Instead of Millet's church in the background, the postcard shows the edge of a house; instead of a sentimental and didactic work of peasant piety and persistence, the bleached-out towns of the American interior; instead of lives bound to the soil, lives lived in transit; and instead of cultivated potato fields, engineered roads and streets, lush and sere landscapes of rolling hills, and a seascape.

These rubber-stamped parodies of Millet also refer to Steinberg's reading. "I admire the essay on art by Isaiah Berlin, 'On the Naiveté of Verdi.'[17] In every one of us there is an innocent. As I get older, I realize that the beautiful according to the naïve, is the best." He then lists seven artists whom he judges to be naive, Millet among them.[18] In this essay Berlin discusses Friedrich Schiller's "On Naïve and Sentimental Poetry" (1795–96): sentimentalists are, in Berlin's retelling, nervous, self-conscious, and decadent, while naïfs are direct, positive, serene, and clear. Berlin classifies Baudelaire, Dostoevsky, and Flaubert as sentimentalists, and these were some of Steinberg's favorite writers.

It's surprising, then, that Steinberg mentions a preference for naïveté in art. We have to reflect on the possibility that, in rubber-stamping the peasants and farming implements on these postcards, Steinberg's parody is not purely satiric, nor does he feel contempt for candy-box art. Millet matters to him, not just because *Angelus* brings back his childhood, but also because the painter speaks to Steinberg's admiration for naïveté—aesthetic simplicity and authenticity in tension with his parodic energy. The apparent simplicity of his works, *Nine Postcards* included, may belie their complexity and sophistication, but we should never explain away that simplicity. Steinberg, the eternal wanderer, admires those who know where they belong. Yet he has exiled Millet's naive peasants, no longer bound to the land, to the sentimental spaces of America. Within his "always provisional" life, Steinberg is of two minds.

Narrative in quality, born of parody, physically thin but thick with memory, Steinberg's postcards also prefigure his painted, drawn, and engraved landscapes. To them we now turn.

9

Steinberg's Landscapes

"Miles of Voyages"

Steinberg frequently painted (in addition to drawing) landscapes during the 1970s and '80s.[1] When Grace Glueck, an art critic, asked him about this change in medium, he explained: "This is the first time in my life that I've been working standing. I've been a sitting man all my life, comfortable, I sat making a drawing, then I sat reading a book or went to bed reading a book. . . . Now I make miles of voyages every day, backing up, looking at the picture, backing up, advancing, brooding about it, going around it in circles, looking at it from this side and that side, so there is a whole physical activity that will probably change my metabolism."[2] Painting elicited a kind of travel for him, a movement around his studio, and, in a typically reflexive move, he also painted places he had seen during both actual and imagined trips.

Painting landscapes enabled Steinberg to enter a simpler world than that of his drawings. As he comments to Buzzi, to whom he sends a portrait of Courbet that he has drawn after a Nadar photograph, "Courbet is somebody I admire, it's clear from the photo that he's one of the last pure peasants, like those that Tolstoy was in time to see. He understood the landscape as a companion, colleague, cousin . . ." (*LAB,* March 27, 1994). Steinberg's own lost naïveté can perhaps be temporarily reclaimed through the very ease and pleasure with which he paints landscapes—as if he, too, can know them intimately. "When I paint landscapes," he muses, "I feel as if I have been doing them always, that I know them by heart. They are my stock-in-trade; to paint them is as simple as breathing and causes me no difficulty."[3]

The challenge of drawing, of posing a problem and then solving it, offers the pleasures and rewards of discovery, of "stumbling onto something that will lead me into territory never seen before," but this can involve "the torture of finding an idea and then representing it in a less personal way, since otherwise you spoil the clarity of the idea" (*RS,* 86). Painting landscapes, in contrast, allows him to enter into a more relaxed state, in which he has "the satisfaction of finding exactly what I am familiar with and what I know."[4] The act of painting offers rewards of serene pleasure: "the happiness of knowing that you have in front of you a peaceful day of filling a canvas full of color is heaven."[5] "Painting of the simple Color combinations," he notes, delivers him into a world of "Harmony (Equilibrium, Justice etc.). These are only the means or proper tools."[6] It's unusual to see words such as happiness, peaceful, heaven, and harmony in Steinberg's reflections on his work, and odder still when we first look at his landscape paintings. Placing colors in combination may deliver him into a world of harmony, but the experience for the viewer can be different. Steinberg's painted landscapes with human figures can evoke loneliness as well as the pleasure of solitude.

Steinberg's landscapes bear a family resemblance to his postcards.[7] "View" postcards, with their printed references to actual places, imply landscapes, the contexts for the limited sites they represent. In fact, landscapes in Steinberg's work metamorphose from postcard views to painted landscapes and back again; and, as he has done in his collages of postcards, he sometimes arranges two or three landscapes on one sheet or canvas. We might say that, in parallel to Renaissance landscape painting, which gradually emerged as a genre of its own from the backgrounds of religious paintings, Steinberg's landscapes at times emerge from the backgrounds of his postcards. We can see him, for example, experimenting with painting his own backgrounds for imitation view postcards, as in *Garden State Pkwy Toll Plaza, Asbury, N.J.* (fig. 27). Steinberg takes the often bland "fill" in postcards and turns it into landscapes that are mysterious, sensuous, and eerie, suggesting an immanence of unidentifiable power.

Steinberg was well aware of the parodic nature of his postcard/landscapes. He tells an interviewer:

> Now, to go further on this thing, we have here masks of postcards. [Shows a wall with several of the multiple-panel postcard landscapes.] Masks of landscapes. These postcards represent not the reality, not the truth—they represent our convention and our idea of what nature looks like. So in a sense, the greatest influence of a landscape has been Poussin, let's say, the inventors of landscapes, who have also been the inventors of the postcards. So that now nature looks to us like imitating art, of course, and imitate either Poussin, the good sense and the good cases, or it imitates the slapstick of the sunset, all the histrionics of nature and light and sun. Now, the way I do it is to solve this thing with just two or three brushstrokes. I then cut them and mail them sometimes, or I . . . I enjoy making them, it's some sort of obsession, obsession that came recently. I'll get rid of it fast, I hope.[8]

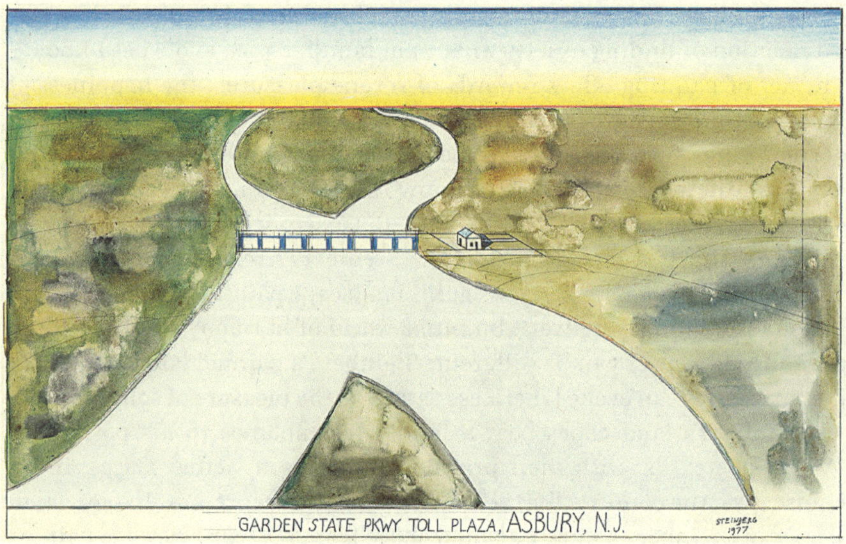

Fig. 27. *Garden State Pkwy Toll Plaza, Asbury, N.J.*, 1977. Watercolor, ink, colored pencil, pencil, and collage on paper, 13¾ × 21⅝ in. Originally published in the *New Yorker*, January 16, 1978. (The Saul Steinberg Foundation, New York)

While postcards of "views" are meant to show us where we are or might go, Steinberg's landscapes, even those in postcard form, often leave us disoriented. He relishes the unidentifiable landscape, and his painted works reflect not so much a place as a memory or a state of mind: "In general, I no longer paint things I see. I know them. Instead, I paint things that have passed through my mind, so to speak. In order to keep only the essential . . . In a certain sense, this is the method of the novelist, who tries to capture the essential of each situation."[9] I'll come back to the issue of "novel writing" in his landscapes, but for the moment I would just observe that "essential" is a strange word to appear in accounts of his landscape painting, since the activity for him often involves parodic play, an acknowledgment of the derivative and multiplying rather than the essential quality of the nature he paints. When he places within a single work a collection of possible landscapes "that have passed through [his] mind," as in *Three Landscapes* (fig. 28) and *Four Landscapes* (fig. 29), our sense of their mystery increases.

The print series *Three Landscapes* shows each one in a different medium, from the top: screen-print in color, lithograph, drypoint on Dutch etching paper. But all show a single figure in the foreground. Steinberg chooses to emphasize medium here, and what's striking is his decision to present a continuum, from top to bottom, of color to line, thus suggesting that the act of painting landscape may be a pleasure, but the subject of landscape itself might be conveyed through both the intellectual quality of line and

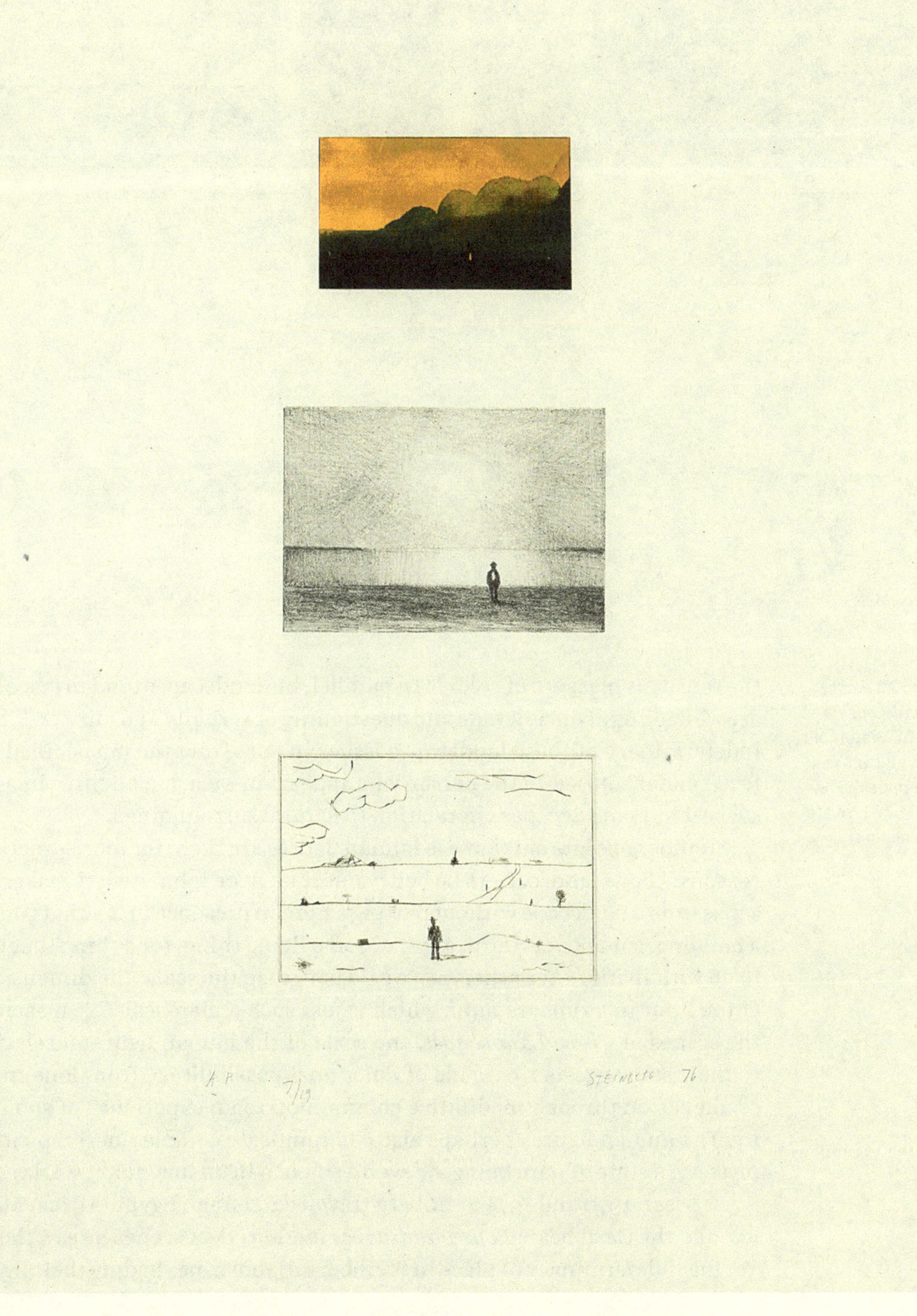

Fig. 28. *Three Landscapes,* 1976. Screenprint in colors, lithograph, and drypoint on paper, 20 × 21½ in. (The Saul Steinberg Foundation, New York; photograph by Jenny Gorman)

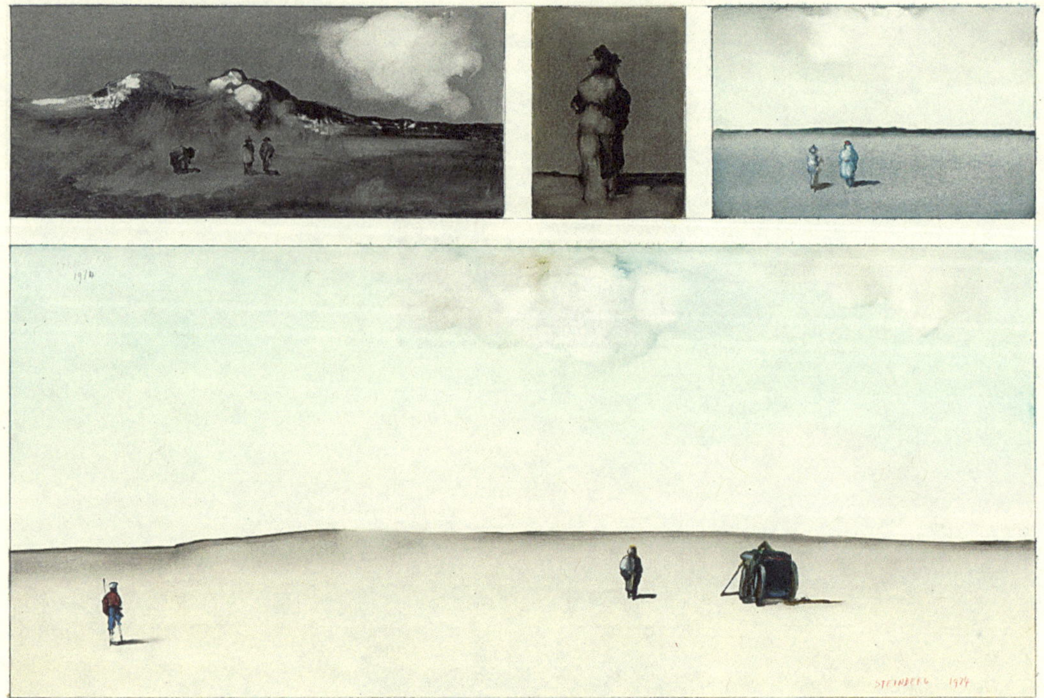

Fig. 29. *Four Landscapes,* 1974. Watercolor, oil, and varnish on paper, 18⅞ × 27⅝ in. (Private collection)

the sensuous pleasure of color.[10] In parallel, his landscapes tend to tease us: are we looking at disquietude and questioning or serenity and answers? The indeterminacy of these landscapes issues in part from the unspecified affect, gender, and age of the person who appears in each, but all three images suggest human slightness in relation to natural surroundings.

Steinberg points out that the human figures are there for more practical reasons: "For a landscape to be believable it must be inhabited. It makes no sense to do a landscape without putting a human presence in it—that can be a building, a man, or even an animal: some living thing, (or a thing that has to do with living)—for otherwise we do not grasp the scale, the dimension. Often I put in a rubberstamp, which is just such a man-scale."[11] In each of the scenes of *Three Landscapes,* the scale of the human figure in relation to the vista suggests a cascade of emotional possibilities, from loneliness or alienation through meditative communion to an experience of sublimity. The human figures perhaps also communicate completeness, spiritual mystery, a state of pure being, or even a sojourn in an imaginary world.

Between 1970 and 1974 Steinberg traveled to Israel, Egypt, Africa, Mexico, and the Caribbean. *Four Landscapes* might reflect scenes he saw there. Yet the indeterminacy of place in Steinberg's landscapes haunts their light-filled and many-hued depictions of land, water, and sky. We don't know where we are or even, at times, what we're looking at—the middle landscape of the three might be a seascape. In some of Steinberg's landscapes, a single strip of blue green may be read as a body of water, the sky, and even a field. Perhaps their vagueness is the point. Any landscape requires the artist to frame a bit of the earth's surface and bring its details into relation with one another. The strong horizontals in Steinberg's landscapes, however, suggest a movement out past the edges of the work, as if it has been framed by chance, a "still" in a film in which the camera just keeps panning horizontally the interminable meeting of sky and land or water. What might they be hinting at? Perhaps, as Steinberg commented himself, it's mystery: "I'm in love with sunsets, I love to look at them, paint them. The place where the sky and the earth meet is the most beautiful thing, the most mysterious in the world. The essence of the world. So, I paint them."[12]

The notion of miracles surprises us in his explanation of watercolor: "I believe that the painter has in him an infantile desire to create miracles. Now, miracles in art are created out of nothing. What is it the painter does? He uses water, color and paper to make clouds, almost re-doing the work of the creator who made clouds by means of the evaporation and condensation of water. In fact, in the act of drying, the damp colored spots on the paper follow quite closely the physical process of cloud creation."[13] The very notions of creation ex nihilo, miracles, or spiritual experience might seem antithetical to Steinberg's sensibility, a passing fancy communicated during an interview, until we look at his paintings. Landscape painting implies travel—"I've come just here," or "Here is the land for your eye to cross"—and travel for him suggests wonderment. His phrase "infantile desire," easily read as self-deprecation, instead signals the childlike curiosity that he valued highly.

Four Landscapes (fig. 29; p. 92), for example, reminds us of Rothko's luminous rectangles of color both in its frontality and its pulsating tactility of land and air—and that air we might experience "as an actual substance rather than an emptiness."[14] Steinberg describes the act of painting as not only serenely escapist but also mysterious to himself, surging from beyond the limits of his intellect: "Maybe I make them as antidote to the bitterness that's in my drawings. It's my drug. The great painters often lived during rather violent times, and their work was a manner of escaping them. My paintings, my 'trompe-trompe-l'oeil' are a way of escaping my drawings—in other words: my times. I don't understand them truly myself. What leads me to do them, that remains obscure for me. It's like a sensuous or poetical part, that makes me uneasy, because I've been for a long time used to understanding everything in my drawings. Here, that becomes inexplicable."[15]

Escaping one's times may take one beyond the horizon of rationality: painting that is a "drug" may open the doors of perception.

The word "essence," which appears repeatedly in Steinberg's comments on his paintings, gestures toward what is *sine materia,* thus relating his work to, for example, Proust's understanding of the "little phrase" of music that is Swann's anthem of his transient love for Odette or Baudelaire's Symbolism as he announces it in "Correspondences." In that poem, "mankind" crosses a landscape "As vast as midnight and as vast as clarity," a synaesthetic mingling of "scent and hue and sound." The poem speaks of "the expansion of infinite things," just as Steinberg's *Four Landscapes* seems to vibrate forth an atmosphere of color, chiaroscuro, texture, and silence. The feeling of correspondences between earthly and spiritual realms involves for Baudelaire "the transports of the mind and every sense," just as Steinberg's landscape paintings, through the sensuous beauty of paint, record a journey toward an undeterminable "beyond" even as—perhaps because—they depict static figures.[16]

But we might also explore Steinberg's statement that "my paintings, my 'trompe-trompe-l'oeil' are a way of escaping my drawings—in other words: my times." Since trompe l'oeil is a type of illusionism in painting in which "the intention is that something should seem not so much represented as substantially present,"[17] a trompe-trompe-l'oeil would mean that such illusionism is at first experienced, then negated, reminding the viewer that there is a real thing here. The effect in Steinberg is potentially twofold. First, it can urge the viewer to realize that the painting itself is primarily a thing in the world, not a representation of the world. Second, that painting can itself be understood as a painting of a (already painted) landscape painting—he has painted painting—and we recall his insistence that "the thing that remains essential for me is the aspect of reality of the first, second, and third degrees."[18]

As such a "trompe-trompe-l'oeil," landscape painting points to a place outside "my times." That place is enigmatic even to Steinberg: once again, "I don't understand them [landscapes] truly myself," and why he makes them "remains obscure for me;" the part of him involved in their creation is "inexplicable." Mysterious in origin, his landscape paintings themselves appear cryptic. For all their light-filled scenes, they feel shadowy.

Consider *Four Landscapes.* Where are we and where are those human presences: in a remembered landscape of an actual trip? In a tableau of dream-travel? The landscape occupying the bottom section depicts two men on a plain with their backs to us, perhaps standing guard near what might be a four-wheeled cart unhitched from a beast of burden that we do not see. Certain actions seem to have preceded this scene, although we aren't given enough information to infer it. The harsh emptiness of the terrain suggests a lonely outpost, but the sky is oddly reassuring, a pale greenish blue with tinges of pink and gold, and those cottony clouds just might be promising rain. Whatever meaning we can glean from this landscape must eventually be understood in relation to the other three landscapes, and here the unanswered questions multiply.

Certainly, in *Four Landscapes* Steinberg indulges his taste for degrees of reality: the horizontal line that creates the white "frames" between the rows of paintings roughly parallels the dark horizon lines of the paintings (even the mountain range tapers down to a flatness). Thus Steinberg suggests a framing *within* each individual image that echoes the framing of each of the four images, that frame echoing the drawn line enclosing the whole montage. Perhaps what we see here are four realities within the reality of the painting itself, that reality enclosed by Steinberg's and our imaginations. Viewed as a whole, the work suggests an altarpiece reversed, with the predella on top, the imagery not specifically religious but perhaps broadly spiritual.

Thinking about groupings might help. The painting at the top right most closely resembles the large picture at the bottom—both depict two shadowed figures alone on a plain. The other two paintings, top left and center, most closely resemble each other in tone and technique, although either their scale is entirely different or the lone figure in the central painting is gigantic. Attempts to create a narrative that reads from top left, clockwise, seem tendentious; one can create a story that brings all four together, but easily (or even more convincingly) each painting seems finally to insist on its independence from the others. If these images have a "novelistic essence," they suggest the constellations of incident and character within modernist fiction, the texture of gaps that we feel, for example, when reading *Ulysses.* Using formalist tools, we might look for repeating patterns, and we do find them in clouds. Focusing on them, the whole might read as three scenes of holy figures under a cloudy sky—these three scenes then surrounding the Virgin Mary or Venus placed against a dark and cloudless sky. Steinberg claims to paint such scenes easily, with his internal censors turned off, and he's showing us thought revolving into paradox: companionship that is loneliness, stillness in movement, "natives" who are visitors.

"Multitude, solitude: equal and interchangeable terms for the active and productive poet. The man who's unable to people his solitude is also unable to be alone in a busy crowd"—thus Baudelaire states a goal of artistic self-involvement that shuts out actual people.[19] When Steinberg puts it this way, "The only genuine thing is man alone. When you are alone you tell yourself. Otherwise it's a lie," he is, in the context of an interview, railing against politicians.[20] But these landscapes with figures, for all their hints of a "beyond," also convey the solitude of the post-Romantic artist who desires to engage the world anew—even if that "new" engagement turns out to require a fresh figuring forth of a natural scene already pre-formed through cliché. The single large figure then might suggest a personification of the imagination. The figures are also reminiscent of Nabokov's loners such as Charles Kinbote, Sebastian Knight, Humbert Humbert, those figures themselves suggestive of the Nabokov who prided himself on being a soccer goalkeeper: "'He is the lone eagle, the man of mystery, the last defender" (*SM,* 267).

To entertain such suggestions is not to state a fact about Baudelaire or Nabokov as source, but rather to suggest that each viewer who seeks even a temporary resolution of this complex work might bring to it a different literary background with which to create meaning from Steinberg's hints and feints. The montage doesn't demand literary framing, but it certainly rewards it. And for the many viewers who first came across Steinberg in the *New Yorker,* literary associations seem natural. The painting, with its lack of specific references, opens readily into the private occasions of our viewing, and that is certainly an idea which Steinberg, with his love of mental association figured forth in the *New Yorker* cover "Braque, baroque" (see fig. 5; p. 17) would endorse.

The pleasure associated with Steinberg's landscape paintings; their relation to travel and to postcards; their gesturing toward the essential, the indeterminate, the mysterious; their exploration of what Steinberg called "degrees of reality"; their celebration of the person who stands apart from other people and from the vagaries of historical situation: these qualities we will also find in Nabokov's fiction. To pursue these notions, we'll return to *The Real Life of Sebastian Knight* and eventually progress to *Ada, or Ardor: A Family Chronicle.*

10

Nabokov's Postcards and Landscapes

Leaves in a Book

In thinking about his own work, Nabokov emphasized the visual. "I think in images," Nabokov asserts (*SO,* 14), even going so far as to maintain that literature, rather than relying primarily on ideas, depends on a "pattern of images" along with some "magic."[1] Nabokov thought of his own writing as similar to a painting: again, "[the] entire structure, dimly illuminated in one's mind, can be compared to a painting" (*SO,* 32).[2] In *The Real Life of Sebastian Knight,* he analyzes Knight's final novel in which, as we've seen, "One thought-image, then another, then another, breaks upon the shore of consciousness" (*RLSK,* 175). Nabokov uses the verb "picture" more often than "describe," and he asserts, "All the great writers have good eyes."[3]

Visual to verbal: Saul Steinberg's picture postcards and landscapes seduce viewers, who, in telling themselves the narratives that each depicted scene suggests, enter into the realm of the verbal. In a mirror image—verbal to visual—the scene that Nabokov creates in words in the second paragraph of *Sebastian Knight* delivers the reader to the visual pleasures of a wintry St. Petersburg scene, complete with shape, color, texture, and composition. This imagined visual little world, complete with ambient sound, is presented just as it metamorphoses into an "old picture postcard" with "a dream-wide street" (*RLSK,* 6). For both Nabokov and Steinberg, postcards act as miniaturizations, re-creating in a small rectangle their views of the wider world.

Nabokov's narrator, V., introduces his world with a display of texts—a calendar, a diary, a picture postcard—indicating that it is the very artificial quality of this novelistic world that matters, its insistence on inhabiting what Steinberg would call a "reality of the third degree": for example, V.'s written account of both "first-degree" actual weather and a "second-degree" recording of that weather in a diary. After establishing Sebastian's initial location in space and time—"Sebastian Knight was born on the thirty-first of December, 1899, in the former capital of my country"—V. turns briskly to the kind of character that Nabokov so enjoyed in Gogol's work, one who appears for the scantiest of reasons and then rapidly disappears forever. An elderly Russian woman diarist is brought onstage, but we begin to wonder why, when her diary entry for that day yields next to no information—just the weather on the day of Sebastian's birth in St. Petersburg. Like the narrator, her name is not to be divulged, so that two clues immediately appear—this book is going to be about pairs of people who have things in common, and there will be plenty of ciphers where information might be. But thoughts come in pairs, too, and "on second thought" the narrator decides to reveal her name, which is itself a study in ciphers: Olga Olegovna Orlova, "an egg-like alliteration which it would have been a pity to withhold" (*RLSK,* 5). The visual quality of this name, with its three initial Os (and three ultimate a's), is so striking that it takes a moment to realize that the weather on Sebastian's birth day, "twelve degrees below Reaumur zero," presents "zero," a word that both refers to the notion of cipher and contains the numerical image of its own meaning in its last letter. Os are eggs, Os are letters, Os are zeroes, and, for the moment, Os reign. Look at and listen to the marks on the page, don't just read through them, Nabokov silently instructs.[4]

But in paragraph 2 the narrator immediately fills emptiness with rich details of a wintry St. Petersburg scene. At first, we don't know what it is we're looking at, exactly (a memory? a painting? an actual scene outside his window?), but whatever it is, it appears to change, "by the way," into a postcard:

> the pure luxury of a cloudless sky designed not to warm the flesh, but solely to please the eye; the sheen of sledge-cuts on the hard-beaten snow of spacious streets with a tawny tinge about the middle tracks due to a rich mixture of horse-dung; the brightly coloured bunch of toy balloons hawked by an aproned pedlar; the soft curve of a cupola, its gold dimmed by the bloom of powdery frost; the birch trees, in the public gardens, every tiniest twig outlined in white; the rasp and tinkle of winter traffic . . . and by the way how queer it is when you look at an old picture postcard (like the one I have placed on my desk to keep the child of memory amused for a moment) to consider the haphazard way Russian cabs had of turning whenever they liked, anywhere and anyhow, so that instead of the straight, self-conscious stream of modern traffic one sees—on this painted photograph—a dream-wide street with droshkies all awry under incredibly blue skies, which, farther away, melt automatically into a pink flush of mnemonic banality. (*RLSK,* 5–6)

We're in St. Petersburg, in a dreamy world where everything pleases the senses and engages the memory. The "hard-beaten snow of spacious streets" is almost legible, like a line of print, with its "sheen of sledge-cuts" forming patterns complemented by a pattern of birch twigs—small curved lines like so many dark forms "outlined in white." V.'s postcard contains, like some of Steinberg's postcards, a mixture of media. It is a "painted photograph," in which the black-and-white prose of street and page is ushered into color by imagination: bright balloons, the snow-dimmed golden curve of a cupola, the "tawny tinge of horse-dung," blue skies that melt into "a pink flush of mnemonic banality." Banal, conventional, intense, imaginative—we have entered, as we read and visualize the second paragraph of the novel, postcard land.

Like Steinberg's postcards, this one implies a complex of aesthetic ideas. It is both realistically of the earth (dung and rasp), and ideal ("pure," "incredibly blue skies"). It is an emblem of the large world made small; and V. embraces it for its very conventionality while making use of memory like a microscope, letting the small live large again in the reader's mind. He reveals a possible source for the postcard when he writes in chapter 8, "Two years had elapsed after my mother's death before I saw Sebastian again. One picture postcard was all I had had from him during that time, except the cheques he insisted on sending me" (*RLSK,* 71). Perhaps this is the postcard that V. only now, after Sebastian's death, describes. Perhaps not, but either way, it embodies the only roads that he and Sebastian can travel together—those of dream, memory, text, and their printed, painted, parodic reproductions—the final, always artificial, landscape of quest.

Within the description a second kind of visuality appears, initially signaled by the Os of the disappearing diarist. Nabokov distributes patterns of alliteration throughout the two opening paragraphs: daily/details/delights/day; tawny/tinge; brightly/bunch/balloons; curve/cupola; and tiniest/twig, among others. V. seems to be in control, the maker of artifice here, and Nabokov lets us know that this writer of alliterative prose is, like his half brother, a writer of patterned playfulness, even though he often writes disparagingly of his own literary talents, confessing that he has taken up "a 'be-an-author' course buoyantly advertised in an English magazine" (*RLSK,* 34). His near twinning of Sebastian's prose, like the near twinning of a postcard and a memory of city streets, suggests alliteration as a way of describing the relation between V. and Sebastian, as they slowly travel toward their final shared identity, which means their utter disappearance into their maker's prose composed of "thought-images" (*RLSK,* 175).

This postcard's invitation to dream and reverie includes its banality, and in the little world that it offers our exiled Russian narrator it appears as an icon of aesthetic worlds—like the magic lantern slides of his childhood—a "neat little world of hushed luminous hues" (*SM,* 166). It's the image of a place the narrator can't or won't return to, and in dreaming within it, he exemplifies what Nabokov himself achieves in his fiction: anatomizing in order to mock the hackneyed and the vulgar, caressing the particular, recapturing the past through reverie and dream, and enticing others to enter the verbal word-pictures of his prose.

With even more virtuosity, Nabokov has his postcard epitomize the novel as a whole. V. can no longer travel to this place, the St. Petersburg of tsarist Russia, nor can he travel to Sebastian's bedside in time, nor can Sebastian reach his dead mother through a visit to what he believes to be her place of death, nor can we as readers bypass the novel's artifice to step into this fictional world as if it were real, to enter the visual text of the novel as a portal to its world. "Wish you were here," the picture postcard generically tells us. For V., postcards are more a matter of "Wish *I* were there," there being Sebastian's heart and mind. Looking at a postcard's view and message, we are always, alas, somewhere else.

Landscape, too, emerges in painterly fashion in *Sebastian Knight.* Exile (Sebastian and V. have been forced out of Russia) implies geography, and geography implies, in the world of visual and literary art, landscape. Sebastian's writings, like Steinberg's works, circle through landscape and travel. His memoir, *Lost Property,* details "his literary journey of discovery." Only a bit of "Albinos in Black" is quoted or paraphrased, but what we do hear of is the description of a hotel room and of train travel. All we learn of "The Back of the Moon" is that a "meek little man waiting for a train" helps three needy travelers in three different ways. The main character of *Success* is a business traveler, and its plot traces the course of two lives to the point in space and time at which they intersect for the first time. Only *The Prismatic Bezel* has apparently little to do with travel—it takes place in one location, inside a boardinghouse—but V. tries to explain its unusual methods of composition by likening it to landscape painting.

Nor must one board a train or cab in order to travel. V. also quotes a long passage from Sebastian's work (*RLSK,* 67–68) in which the narrator describes the unusual qualities of his mind, which he calls "the dangerous vagrancies of my consciousness." Not only does the main character wander throughout the novel, but even when he's not on the move, his mind itself is always taking trips that make normal social relations with others difficult. His "endless vague wanderings" around London seems to describe body and mind in one trip to and from nowhere in particular.

While explicitly described landscapes are few in *Sebastian Knight,* the entire novel, with its incessant journeying, aspires to the condition of landscape: "I daresay Sebastian and I also had some kind of common rhythm; this might explain the curious 'it-has-happened-before-feeling' which seizes me when following the bends of his life" (*RLSK,* 34). V.'s lengthy description of Sebastian's last novel portrays it as having been written during his travels, and containing "grey seas" with waves and shore, followed by "hideous landscapes" as death draws nearer.

A face, for example, can metamorphose into a place in nature, such as when V. sees in a painted portrait of Sebastian a version of Narcissus. As Steinberg's small postcards transform into landscapes, so metamorphosis rules here, and the portrait expands to include a landscape, complete with pond and clouds: "But as I look at the portrait Roy Carswell painted I seem to see a slight twinkle in Sebastian's eyes, for all the sadness of their expression. . . . These eyes and the face itself are painted in such a manner as to convey the impression that they are mirrored Narcissus-like in clear water—with a very slight ripple on the hollow cheek, owing to the presence of a water-spider which has just stopped and is floating backward" (*RLSK,* 119). A fallen leaf and ripples of painted water, shadow and "glint" transform brow, hair, and lips. The head dominates the painting as a shadow seems to make the body fall away. The ekphrasis ends: "The general background is a mysterious blueness with a delicate trellis of twigs in one corner. Thus Sebastian peers into a pool at himself" (*RLSK,* 119).

Reflections abound here: remember Steinberg's special interest in "reflections and shadows" as well as parody, repetition with a difference. V. reflects in prose Carswell's painted reflection of Sebastian as a man who sees his own reflection. But V. also more directly reflects or embraces Sebastian, because this ekphrastic passage, verbally rich, could not have been written alone by the unimaginative V. V./Sebastian must have had a hand in it. The written portrait itself provides a visual reflection of water, sky, leaf, insect, sunlight, shade, twig—an implied landscape. Sebastian-as-Narcissus has become, in V./Sebastian's words, simultaneously a portrait of a man, a painting of landscape, an Ovidian figure of yearning, and a being inhabiting what Steinberg would call "boxes within boxes" or reality of the third (or fourth, or fifth) degree.

Furthermore, this passage of portrait-landscape "word painting" (a term that Nabokov liked) includes what Steinberg has mentioned as the mystery he experiences in seeing and painting landscape. A Wordsworthian "sense sublime / Of something far more deeply interfused, / Whose dwelling is the light of setting suns, / And the round ocean and the living air, / And the blue sky, and in the mind of man"[5] prevails in Carswell's painted "mysterious blueness," which gestures toward Wordsworth and beyond to that French literary notion of an ideal realm, *l'azure.* Sebastian's dying man in his novel *The Doubtful Asphodel,* V.'s Sebastian, Nabokov's game with V. and Sebastian: all bring to the foreground "the mind of man" and the framed and reframed, staged, riddling, and artificial quality of *Sebastian Knight.*

Sebastian's "own" fiction depends, as I've noted above, on travel, both actual and metaphorical. Significantly, he considers landscape as a doorway to, or a text of, an ideal realm. As we've seen, Steinberg's landscapes and cityscapes suggest mystery; Nabokov's often gesture more explicitly toward an ideal realm. Here is V.'s description of Sebastian's novel *The Doubtful Asphodel,* which V. regards as his masterpiece. Nabokov devotes an entire chapter to it. Its dominant theme is "a man is dying," but after great suffering and questioning, V. tells us that Sebastian has had a revelation "which had nothing to do with any of the thoughts or feelings, or experiences he might have had in the kindergarten of life" (*RLSK,* 178). The passages in quotation marks below include both words V. has quoted directly from *The Doubtful Asphodel* and V.'s paraphrase of the work. The traveler (by sea, train, foot) who is the novel's main character learns—like the "reader" of Steinberg's images—that the landscape is meant to be read as if it were a verbal text yielding every answer that one could want: "The answer to all questions of life and death, *'the absolute solution'* [emphasis added] was written all over the world he had known: it was like a traveller realising that the wild country he surveys is not an accidental assembly of natural phenomena, but the page in a book where these mountains and forests, and fields, and rivers are disposed in such a way as to form a coherent sentence, the vowel of a lake fusing with the consonant of a sibilant slope; the windings of a road writing its message in a round hand." The voyager "spells the landscape" to fathom its meaning, and also learns, similarly, that "human life" is read through its "interwoven letters." The passage concludes: "Remodelled and re-combined, the world yielded its sense to the soul as naturally as both breathed" (*RLSK,* 178–79).

V's summary sounds like Sebastian's "own" or "quoted" words. Perhaps, Nabokov suggests, there is a reality that encompasses all three—V., Sebastian, and "Nabokov." And Steinbergian "degrees of reality" intermingle—worldly landscape, visual landscape, and verbal landscape are all told and retold by V., by Sebastian, and by Nabokov. "The man is the book," V. writes (*RLSK,* 175), and at novel's end the three of them disappear into—die into—the whiteness of the page stretching beneath Nabokov's last two words, "The End."

Beyond this kind of textual death, however, Nabokov here hints at what William James called a perception of "*something there* . . . more deep and more general than any of the special and particular 'senses' by which the current psychology supposes existent realities to be originally revealed."[6] This is a realm that lies beyond, and Nabokov refers to such a "there" from time to time.[7] To the creative reader (and re-creator of nature in his own text), the "beyond" is graspable here in the landscapes of our lives—something like Steinberg's mysterious landscapes. Those landscapes are at once visual and verbal; a landscape is "a page in a book," and the one who travels does so by spelling the landscape. The "soul" learns the answers. Nabokov, like his friend Steinberg, images a visual-verbal involute, a compound experience. Not only do the "authors" and texts of the quoted passage nest one within another, but the passage itself suggests that the elements of a landscape nest within something greater than themselves, the "absolute solution" to the puzzle. Having graduated from the "kindergarten of life" (*RLSK,* 178), the traveler stops to define that "*something there,*" reading its messages from beyond *and* within himself. Further, the parodist—describer of the already verbal landscape—becomes the type of the enlightened man.

From the postcard/cityscape of tsarist St. Petersburg with which the novel opens, Nabokov creates the larger and later landscapes through which his characters rove, but he seldom describes them directly. Rather, the landscape "background" to the initial postcard, which the narrator V. examines through the lens of all his experience to date, including his unsuccessful attempts to know Sebastian, appears in narrative complexity: the representational account of one man's attempt to write a biography and to be reunited with his half brother; the parodies of quest romance, detective fiction, Künstlerroman, biography, and memoir; the autonomous fictional artifact created by Nabokov-the-world-maker. However complex these layers or "leaves" in a book may be, the traveler learns that "the intricate pattern of human life" turns out to be, once again, "monogrammatic, now quite clear to the inner eye disentangling the interwoven letters" (*RLSK,* 179). That intricate pattern made simple and whole is, as it were, the message written on the verso of the novel's originating postcard in which the vast world is made small. Now, with the simple truth revealed, the small world of the postcard and the book become as vast as the mysterious landscapes of imagination, akin to those of Steinberg.

11

Steinberg's Maps

Projection Unmoored

Steinberg drew maps throughout his career, but their language and visual forms chart psychological experience or imaginative forays such as fiction writers capture more than they accurately chart geographical or political space. They are narrative maps, an occasion for "writing" about human experience. As Joel Smith has observed, "The map was an ideal format for Steinberg's imagination: a three-way marriage of diagram, picture, and text, loaded with covert opinions and irrefutable trivia."[1] Just as he drew drawing, he mapped (supposedly objective) maps. No map is ever wholly objective, of course, but Steinberg's maps flaunt their biases and send their viewers into reverie. What's more, they're related to his postcards and landscapes in compelling ways. The brief survey of his maps that follows shows us parodies of landscapes which, as we've seen, leave us in indeterminate and mysterious places, while his postcards tend to tell us decidedly where we are. His maps oscillate between the mysterious and the known. "Knowledge of maps made me see more than what I physically see," he explained,[2] and, as mentioned above, at the time of his death a street map of Bucharest lay on his desk next to a drawing of his Bucharest neighborhood.[3]

Daniel Defoe placed a world map on the frontispiece of the fourth edition of *The Life and Surprizing Adventures of Robinson Crusoe* (1719). On it he drew Crusoe's route and shipwreck.[4] Judging by the sheer number of maps Steinberg drew, we can happily imagine that he supplied maps for his own *Robinson Crusoe.* He liked to consult city maps of his childhood neighborhood, the "magic circle" in Bucharest, because they, like postcards, provided him with a passage to his past through word and image.[5]

Steinberg drew maps of varying scale, from rooms to buildings, city blocks, roads, interstate highways, continents, and even the cosmos. Along the way, he expanded the notion of what counts as a modern road map or a political-geographical map by adding representational figures to his map's more diagrammatic information—think of the trees, river, and sunset of *Autogeography* (see fig. 14; p. 60). He didn't invent this technique:

Renaissance mapmakers, for example, drew maps of cities from an imagined aerial view and included perhaps a big-cheeked Aeolus, a conquering hero astride the city's streets, or ships sailing its rivers or seas. Uncharted areas, blank spaces on the map, were often filled with figurative drawings, too. The cars, people, plants, furniture, weather, etc., of Steinberg's maps suggest that familiar places have been partially cleansed of the information we've accepted about them. Terra incognita can be, unexpectedly, anywhere, even a room in your Manhattan apartment.

While presenting some information diagrammatically, his maps also giddily depart from commonsense notions of space and place, requiring us to supply the map "key." Or keys. Space tends to occupy a wavering or discontinuous grid and sometimes is translated into time. One inch in *Autogeography*, for example, represents thousands of miles here, in one bit of the map, and there, the space of a few years. Steinberg's maps can best be grasped through close and imaginative rereading.

Geographical mapmakers, however seriously they view themselves as deliberate and rational in their methods, have long carried out the central sleight of hand of any representational painter or draftsman: taking the three-dimensional, physical reality of a part of the observed world and transforming it into a two-dimensional document, complete with lines, colors, shapes, and even words. If the mapmaker is thus always akin to an artist, the typical reader of maps has been trained as an anti-artist. He or she learns to looks through or past the abstract magic that has transformed three dimensions into two in favor of "accurately" reading those two dimensions back into the three dimensions of the "real" world. The quest is for accuracy and predictability of orientation: turn north here to reach the capital city. By deliberately surprising, amusing, and disorienting us with his maps, Steinberg disrupts such decoding and encourages map readers to enter mapland for renewing imaginative journeys of their own. Steinberg leads us to read these maps as parodies of "accurate" maps.

Because maps present the story of their own creation, they are easily absorbed into modernist traditions of creating autonomous worlds, texts that do not rely on precise imitation of so-called reality. Oscar Wilde expressed this notion when he decried "careless habits of accuracy"[6] and asserted the freedom that art must claim: "Art finds her own perfection within, and not outside of, herself. She is not to be judged by any external standard of resemblance. She is a veil, rather than a mirror. . . . She makes and unmakes many worlds."[7] Steinberg, in a Wildean moment, avers, "I first study the map of a town and then I go to see it, and it turns out to be perfectly true."[8] In one reading of this statement, the map is for him the basis, the truth against which the physical reality of a place must be measured. In contrast, professional cartographers hew to a notion that the primary reality is the surface of the earth, and making a good map involves what we might call a correspondence theory of map truth, in which each point in the map corresponds to an actual place on the surface of the earth, "according to a fixed scale or projection."[9]

While cartographers may regard themselves as unbiased and their creations as objective, scholars have of late devoted themselves to teasing out the preconceptions and ideological slants always to be found within these supposedly objective maps.[10] What interests Steinberg, however, is the freedom from (supposedly) accurate cartographical projections. His maps may have a referential element—this map diagrams this part of reality—but they also enact or present a reality of their own, skewing reference, unmooring projections, counting on our ability to recognize their distance from the norm of accuracy. Steinberg's own maps deliberately deviate from "common reality": they are often simplistic, fantastic, riddle-like, confused with other visual genres such as landscapes, portraits, or domestic scenes, or just plain wacky. What they correspond to are Steinberg's and our moods, memories, and sensibilities—they chart our interior states by finding spatial correlatives. "Found" maps especially delight him: observing Sigrid Spaeth's (his longtime companion's) cat, Steinberg jots in a notebook that it leaped from the rooftop to an oak tree "using the oak as a city map, each branch a street uphill & downhill."[11] Each of his maps offers a portrait of his own mind as it leaps to the found maps that he teasingly reveals to us in ink and color wash. He delights, for example, in the whimsy of a face that reminds him of the Eastern Seaboard ("map" is a colloquial term for face) (fig. 30). Or a domestic interior map built up of states' names that partially rhyme—e.g., Nebraska/Alaska—complete with a New Mexico cat seated on a New York/New Jersey/New Hampshire chair (fig. 31).[12] Anything can be taken as the basis for a map: Steinberg "finds" them in unexpected places: a dog (fig. 32), or a portion of cubistic desktop clutter (fig. 33.) Steinberg playfully muddles the distinctions between "official" maps and "found" maps, as in an actual zip code map of Manhattan that, with a little doctoring, becomes a map of Manhattan-Israel in a rearranged Middle East (fig. 34).

Yet Steinberg depends on the conventions of mapping in order to code one "reality," the boredom and anxiety of jet travel, by charting a journey from New York to Paris as he does in a flight map (fig. 35). The jet's flight pattern is, to say the least, odd: here is a painted and inked world in which an implied traveler eats at intervals and experiences the mental turmoil of hypochondria, paranoia, and hallucination, only to settle into catalepsy. This is a world in which continents exist as forms evenly dispersed around

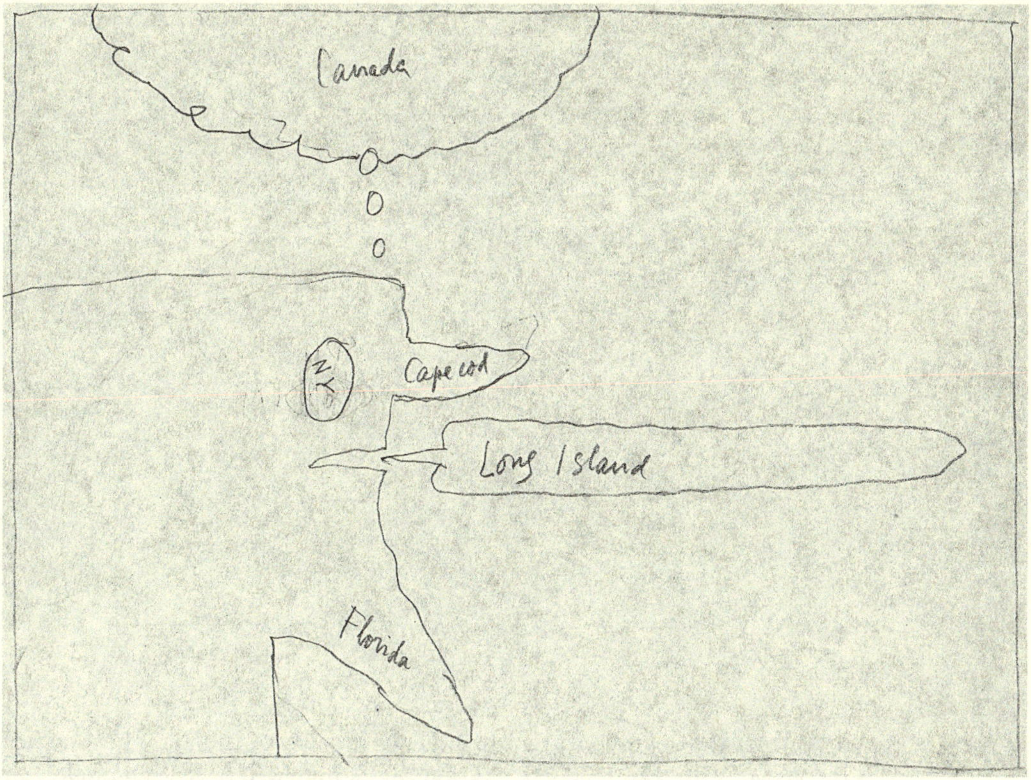

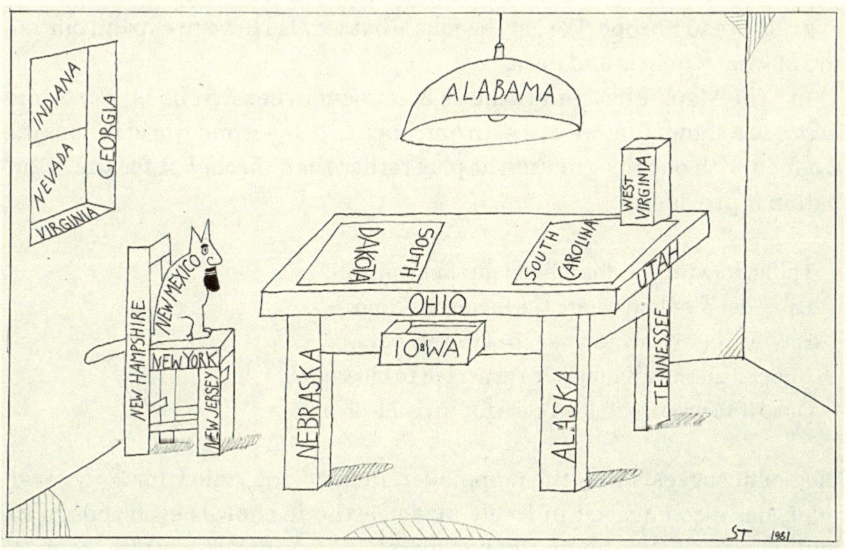

Fig. 30. Untitled, c. 1985–95. Pencil on paper, torn from sketchbook, 11 × 14 in. (Beinecke Rare Book and Manuscript Library, Yale University)

Fig. 31. Untitled, 1981. Ink over pencil and colored pencil on paper, 14½ × 23 in. (The Saul Steinberg Foundation, New York; photograph by Jenny Gorman)

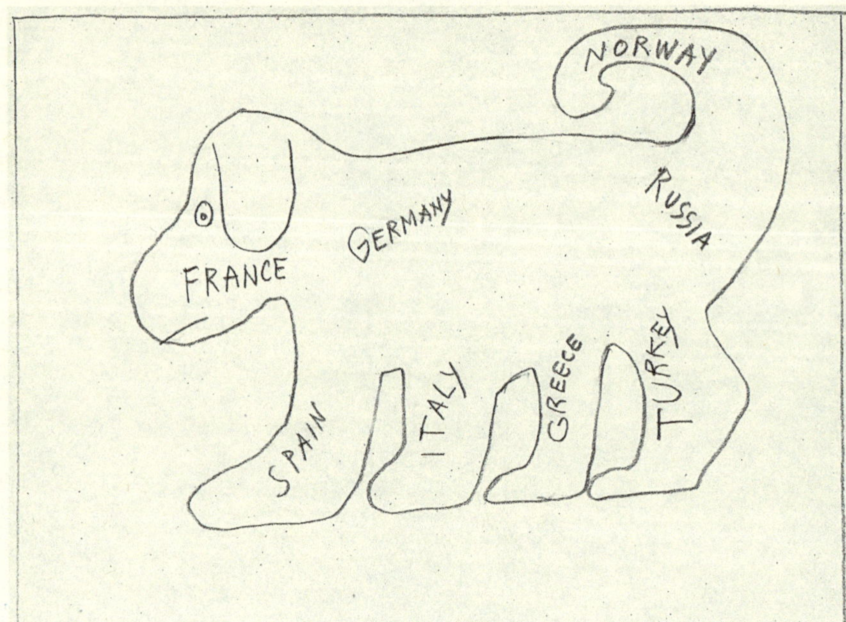

Fig. 32. Sketchbook page, c. 1980–94. (Beinecke Rare Book and Manuscript Library, Yale University)

a central sky. To create this "second level" reality of the map, he troubles the viewer's unexamined expectation that a map will be a scale model, an accurate version of part of an authorized original, the planet Earth. The map is experientially accurate to anyone who has been wedged into a seat on a red-eye to Europe. We get the joke—but we also have to expand our notion of what a map is and does.

In "The Map," Elizabeth Bishop's first poem in her first book, *North and South,* she shows that we can gain entrance to this second world by looking *at* a map with our imagination at play rather than *through* it for the information it provides:

> The shadow of Newfoundland lies flat and still.
> Labrador's yellow, where the moony Eskimo
> Has oiled it. We can stroke these lovely bays,
> Under a glass as if they were expected to blossom,
> Or as if to provide a clean cage for invisible fish.[13]

The poem suggests that the mapmaker, in choosing yellow for "oily" Labrador, has also engaged in freely made aesthetic choices even though we tend to believe that he or she has merely followed cartographic conven-

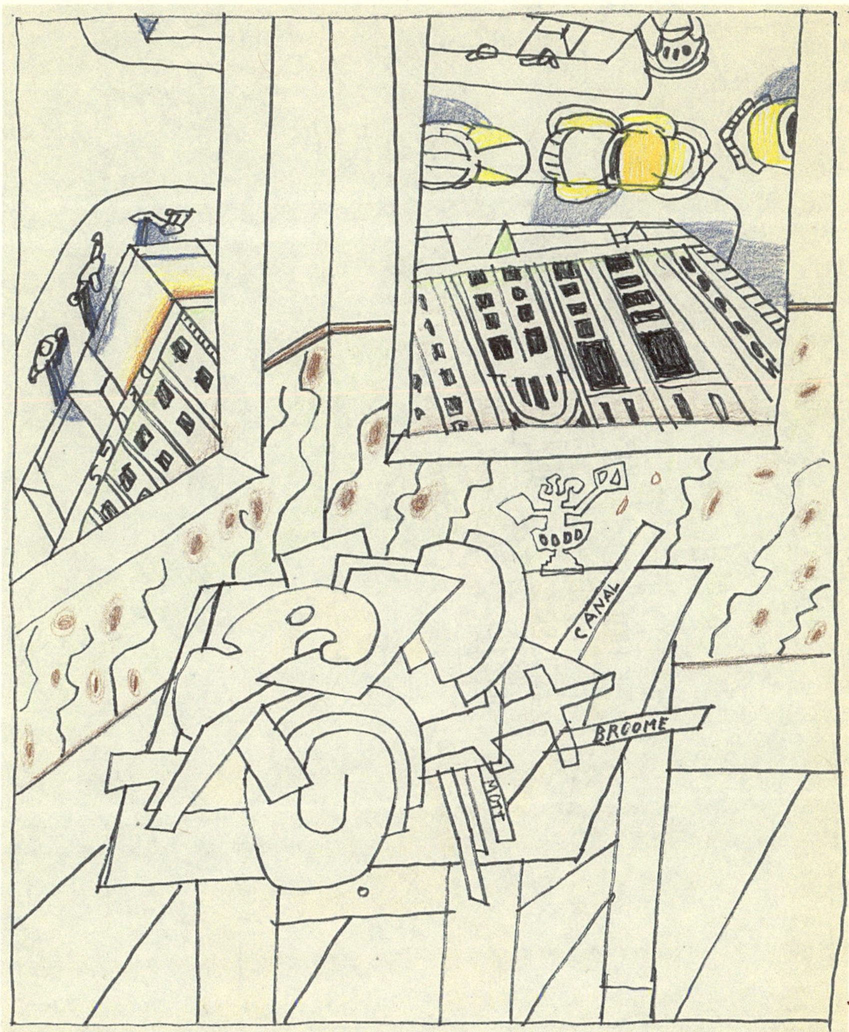

Fig. 33. Untitled, c. 1989–90. Felt marker and crayon on paper torn from sketchbook, 17 × 14 in. (Beinecke Rare Book and Manuscript Library, Yale University)

tions. Bishop sees mapping as aesthetic play, in Friedrich Schiller's sense, as that which combines feeling and reason.[14] Steinberg—and Nabokov, as we shall see—both follow conventions and alter them, making up rules as they go, inviting us to worlds that teasingly track "reality" and then flip us into imagined worlds with their own cartographic logic. When Botkin, the pathetically lonely, émigré academic of *Pale Fire,* creates the imaginary world of Zembla (which is and isn't Greenland's or Alexander Pope's Nova Zembla, which is and isn't revolutionary Russia), its location on the face of the earth and its geography accurately convey his states of mind,

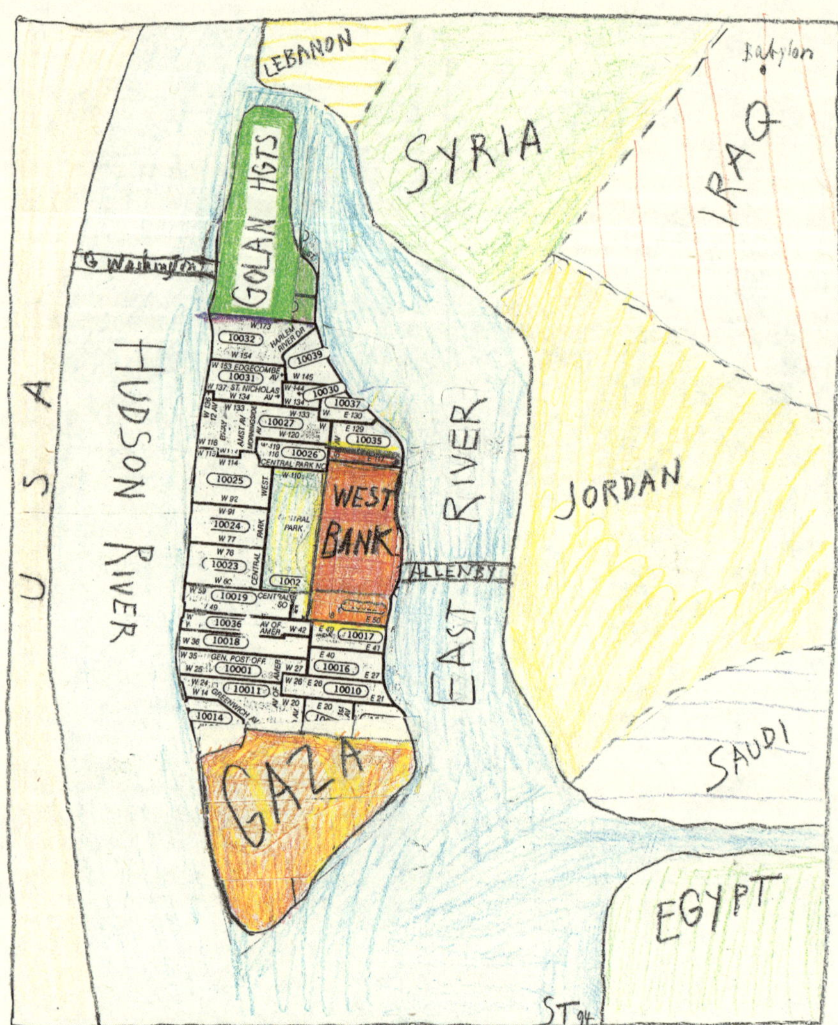

Fig. 34. *Zip Code Map,* 1994. Pencil, crayon, colored pencil, and collage on paper, 13½ × 11 in. (Beinecke Rare Book and Manuscript Library, Yale University)

even though it is unlocatable on any standard maps of the Northern Hemisphere. He's a troubled man who has fantasized a land where he was a happy king, but he has also mapped an exile's sad experience. To the extent that we feel our own unbridgeable distance from an intangible home, his imagined map is accurate. Latitude and longitude, we see, give way to attitude and longing.

Maps figure among the jokiest of Steinberg's drawings—but the laugh is often pitched to readers who can see themselves, their own emotional home territory, in the witticisms, anxieties, and even cynicisms of a Stein-

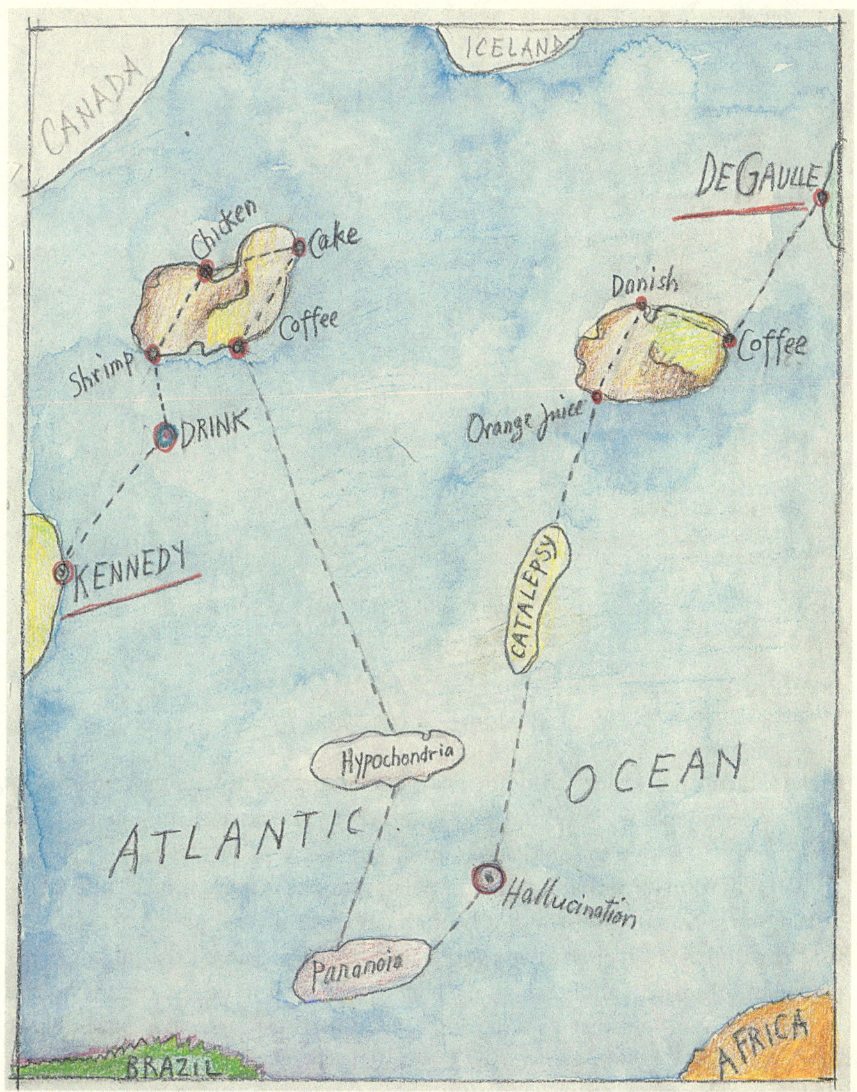

Fig. 35. Untitled, c. 1980–90. Pencil, crayon, and watercolor on paper, torn from sketchbook, 14 × 11 in. (Beinecke Rare Book and Manuscript Library, Yale University)

berg map. "Per aspera ad astra" (Through difficulties to the stars) is a Latin phrase that now turns up widely in popular culture—and was, coincidentally, Vladimir Nabokov's father's motto.[15] On a map he draws and entitles thus (fig. 36), Steinberg shows us that a route ends in the Stars only if one turns off onto a secondary road. And the small town of Difficulty (Aspera) lies close to Astra—only a small part of the map addresses the motto directly. The map's stippling and scumbling seems to represent height, as in a topographical map, and the route repeatedly turns as it negotiates

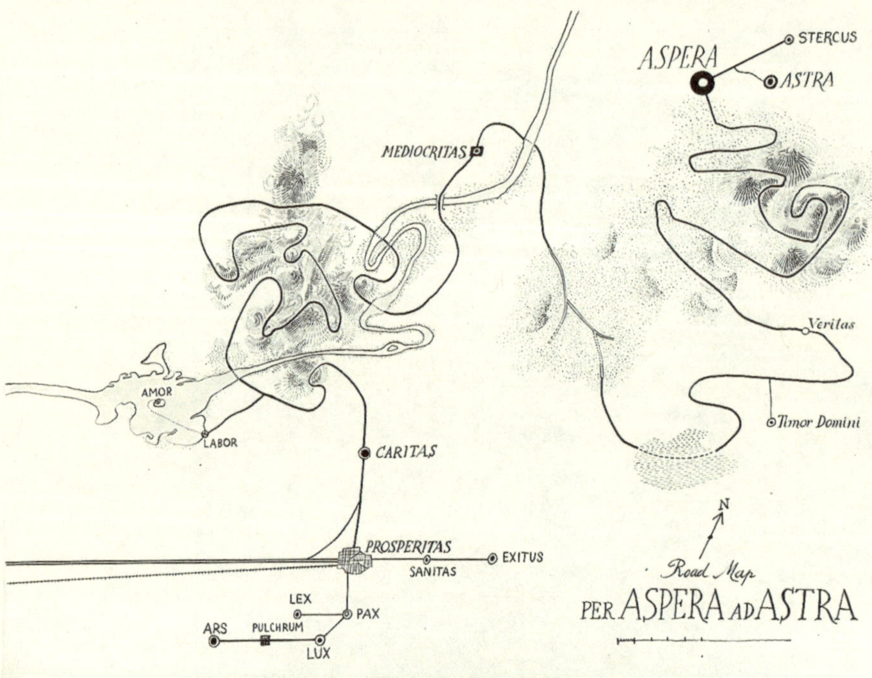

Fig. 36. *Road Map Per Aspera ad Astra,* c. 1959. Ink and watercolor on board, 20 × 30 in. (The Saul Steinberg Foundation, New York)

these mountains—more difficulties. Even such good towns and villages as Caritas, Prosperitas, Pulchrum, Pax, Lex, etc., are part of the journey that Steinberg has added to the titular route.

This cartoon cum road map or itinerary mocks official mottos and seals, but it also shows us that ways of human aspirations will progress, pilgrim-like, through a landscape of attractive possibilities. Such is the plot of many a novel, including Nabokov's *Ada,* a parody of the nineteenth-century novel as family romance, just as this map parodies the paper road map of the sort once dispensed by gas stations as well as the work of fiction that might end in love (see "Amor" midriver).

For all the desirable stops along the way, however, the main route moves between Art (Ars) and Dung (Stercus), so that this imaginary place's implied motto is "From Dung to Art" or "From Art to Dung." Here are the preferred motto and feared anti-motto of every artist who has struggled to transform the heavy mass of what is into art. Further, we all know that every human story must take us all the way to the mold of the grave, ourselves decaying to dung in the earth. Perhaps the route through Timor Domini (*Proverbs* 14:27: "The fear of the Lord is the fountain of life [*fons vitae*]") will provide some passing relief. What at first seems humorous, a visual play on Latin and pseudo-Latinate words, gradually reveals itself as existentially threatening. It all depends on the route we choose, and whether we decide to settle down in Mediocritas along the way, an option Steinberg took pains to avoid.

Orientation, disorientation, reorientation:[16] Norman Manea aptly called his friend Steinberg a "juggler with reality."[17] For those who once navigated the highways of a pre-GPS America by opening large, unwieldy paper road maps, the refolding of their accordioned sections was a traveler's rite of passage. Steinberg's road maps seem to flutter open and shut in the breeze from the car window, because they simultaneously diagram possible journeys in conventional ways, flaunt their invented patterns, and promise enfolded mysteries.

The deep pleasure of roadside relaxation on a sunny day is one such mystery (fig. 37). We see in profile a man sitting on a porch, drink in hand and dog at his feet, looking out at the landscape, which first appears to be the road map of a section of a New England state blown up to something larger than an actual road map but smaller than life-sized roads would appear. The humor of the image has in part to do with our double take at Steinberg's dissonant systems of representation, a visual banana skin. Yet there's no implied punch line here, and the more time we spend pondering the image, the stranger and more interesting it becomes. The upright columns of the porch can also be read as part of the grid of roads; they are at right angles to Route 92 and roughly the same width, so that these two systems of representation begin to merge into one. Similarly, the parallel, diagonal lines of the porch floor echo the single diagonal line running from the back end of the automobile over routes 92 and 6, and disappearing into the horizon. The curved lines of the rocker crossing the parallel floor boards echo the curved lines of the river crossing the map's grid formed by both Routes 92 and 2 and the porch columns.

Just as the figurative porch rhymes visually with the diagrammatic map, so the more diagrammatic map contains figurative passages akin to those of the porch. We see a river with sandbars and agricultural fields of differing colors. A railroad appears in conventional map-ese as a line with short, repetitive cross lines, but this indication of a railroad reads also as realistically portrayed barbed wire edging one of the fields. Blue colored pencil shades the plant on the porch, car windows, river, lake, interstate sign, and eventually the sky—or is that the ocean or a lake?—into a continuity that mingles the conventions of figural porch and diagrammatic map. Dozing dog and drinking man seem delightfully unperplexed by the visual riddles before them.

US Route 92 (now in Florida) locates us somewhere in an imagined New

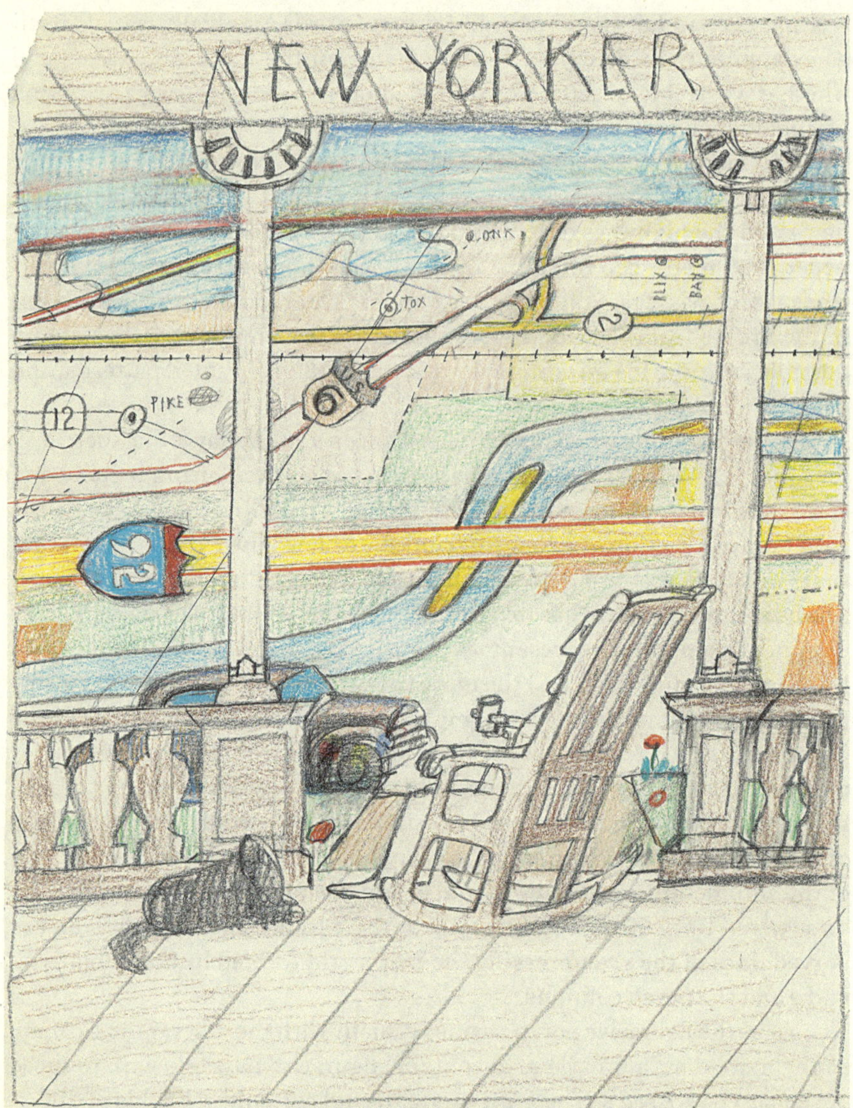

Fig. 37. Untitled, c. 1980. Crayon and pencil on paper, 14¼ × 10½ in. (Beinecke Rare Book and Manuscript Library, Yale University)

England. It was proposed early in the twentieth century as a highway to run from east to west through northern New England, parallel to the old Route 2 (as it is in the picture), but it was never built. In Steinberg's drawing, then, it's a possible highway among actual highways, the subtle creation of another degree of reality. US Route 6, it turns out, crosses Steinberg country as well; it's an actual interstate highway pieced together from other roads. It "runs uncertainly from nowhere to nowhere, scarcely to be followed from one end to the other, except by some devoted eccentric."[18] Such a meandering and inefficient route perfectly sums up Steinberg's own, actual travels along the back roads and hamlets of the United States, like the intriguingly named towns of Pike, Tox, and Bay lettered on this map.

For all its charming wit, this drawing also escorts us into an eerie map-become-reality, reality-become-map. It disarmingly disposes of the notion that a place and a map of that place are two different things, the latter in service of the former. If a map becomes increasingly accurate as it includes more and more of the territory it surveys, then its logical endpoint would be a map coterminous with that territory, and Steinberg hints at this very outcome. The difference between tourist and native dissolves too. Not only can we not identify the figure as one or the other, but we also must ask, native or tourist of which land: imagined (US Route 92) or actual (US Route 6)? As an artist of travel, Steinberg seems both to mock and to sympathize with the common need to locate ourselves in space, especially the big open spaces of America, in order to gain self-knowledge and a series of toeholds, however temporary. Manea reports that Steinberg told him "more than once," "We can't be Americans."[19] Nor, we might add, is America wholly foreign to Steinberg—he traveled it mile by mile, porch by porch.

If every immigrant has to reorient his mind in order to cope with a world whose center has changed, why not, Steinberg seems to ask, press back by rearranging the world itself to correspond with his fantasies about it? In a series of maps exemplified by *Europe Year 3000* (fig. 38), he wittily redraws the political map of a Europe which had been tragically reshuffled by actual nineteenth- and twentieth-century events. This is a map that might well have been inspired by Steinberg's reading of *Ada;* even if that isn't the case, the affinity between the Steinberg's and Nabokov's mappings is strong. I will return to this subject. Steinberg considered entitling one of his books "The Wrong Century" (*LAB*, June 1, 1949); here he imagines not just a new century, but a new millennium.

To chronicle the mock historical (and geological) events that might have resulted in just this constellation of nation states would seem to require shelves of novels. In addition, the viewer's reading experience of the map itself involves the recognition of multiple allusions to literature: the nation of Kafka, Ibsen, (Ovid's) Tristia, the cities of Lux and Kalma (the "luxe, calme, et volupté" of Baudelaire's "L'invitation au voyage") on the coast of Paris-Fwans, and the nation of Armida, a character from Torquato Tasso's *Gerusalemme liberata.* Such identifications might also be taken as mere jumping-off points for meditations on the ways in which the works of these writers shed light on the map itself—for example, will Americans have to liberate their sacred soil, their New Jerusalem, from global incursions?

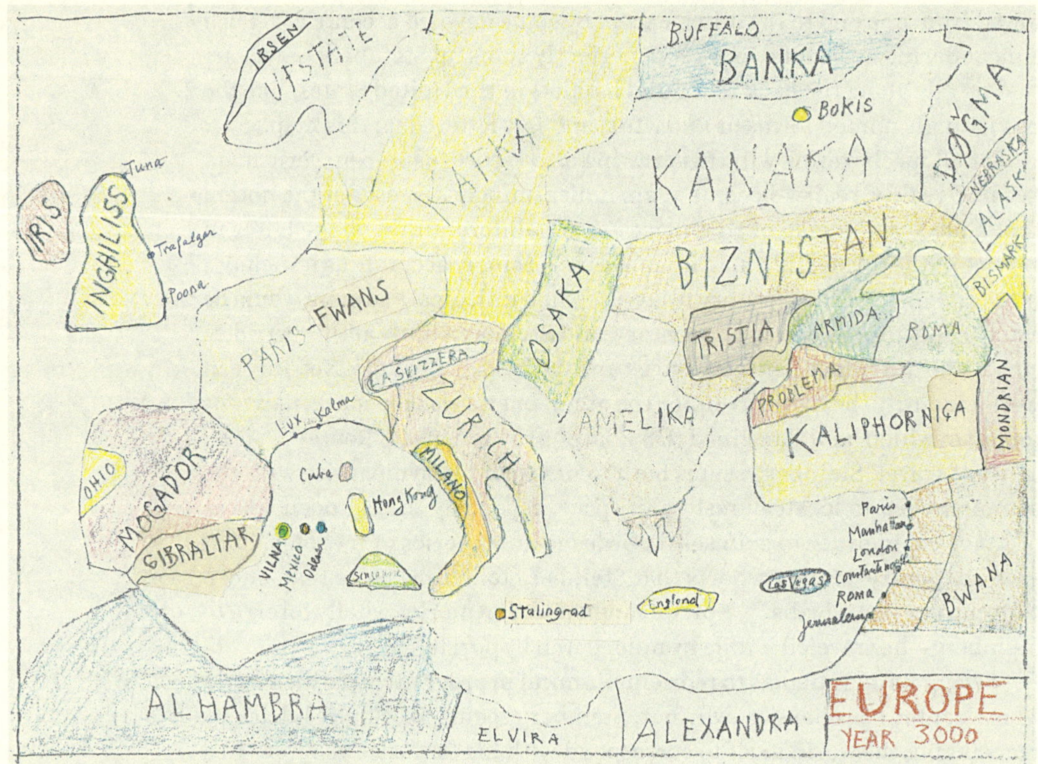

Fig. 38. *Europe Year 3000*, c. 1990. Color photocopy with correction tape, pencil, pen, marker, crayon, and colored pencil, 11 × 17 in. (Beinecke Rare Book and Manuscript Library, Yale University)

Political and economic unrest have evidently led to Asia's establishing of a foothold throughout Europe: Osaka, Amelika, Hong Kong, and Singapore have moved toward the coast of Italy. Not just Europe, but bits and pieces of several continents appear here. Capitalism has overrun parts of Europe, establishing the nations of Banka and Biznistan, while the banking center of Zurich has overtaken most of Italy. Some of the United States have arrived as if by magic carpet: Upstate and Buffalo are now northern European nations, Ohio lurks in what used to be Portugal; Manhattan is now a city in an unidentified Gulf state; and Alaska and Nebraska are countries bordering what used to be Ukraine. Stalingrad and Las Vegas join many other "islands" that seem to have floated in from around the world as we used to know it. Part of Russia has become Kanaka, a name that suggests Canada, since Kanaka is both a railroad point in British Columbia and the name given workers from the Pacific Islands who labored in North America. Then there are the countries whose borders have been established by euphony. The North African countries ending in "ra"—Elvira, Alexandra, even the lovely Alhambra—might be women's states or simply, like one's motherland, gendered female.

Anyone can play with the map of Europe, but Steinberg gives us a choice of intertwining narratives. Perhaps he maps the tale of American imperialism, capitalist power, and sinister Kafkaesque nonsense. Perhaps the "third world" is now, in fantasy, integrated with the "first world," terms that were in play during the decade that Steinberg drew the map, and all these nations constitute a more egalitarian second world. Or perhaps Europe in 3000 is part of a world ruled by a poet who simply likes words ending in the same letters, political geography delightfully giving way to rhyme. Sobering historical and political readings of the map emerge from and melt back into a drawing that seems not to take any of this quite seriously. And—however strangely—the map shows us our own world, in which, however active the professional projectionists, the future must remain a fictional projection of here and now, an extrapolation into the unmappable.

Steinberg's maps may feature the local, built environment, such as the Manhattanite Canal Street and the Holland Tunnel that lead west to the rest of America (fig. 39). But for the same New Yorker, more than the western states beckon. The thoroughfares of New York metamorphose into a grid-like United States, itself surrounded by the grids of other continents and oceans, and beyond it, through a Holland Tunnelesque rainbow, lie the planets, the universe, the cosmos, and the farthest reaches of chaos, beyond which space becomes time (fig. 40). Lest we take too seriously the sense of mystery evoked here, the banners of "Law" and "Order" surmount the cosmos.

The microcosm of our selves, too, can be mapped: Steinberg's everyman deciphers his location on the bit of earth where he stands, just off center: the intersection of latitude and longitude, and of hour, day, and week (fig. 41). It's 4:15 p.m. on a Sunday in February, he's far from town, the wintry tree shows no signs of life, and the little man stands, wondering. The only vectors toward the heavens are labeled Doubt and Duty. The mapped life is the limited life, the one we all must face.

Steinberg's maps, however visually enchanting, are more graphological and typographical than topographical or geographical. They are instances of Steinberg's "handwriting" that chart human experience, recapture the past, and imagine the future in much the same way as did nineteenth- and twentieth-century literary texts. Narrative and poetic, Steinberg's maps invite us to stand before them and tell ourselves their stories, and, like much of modern literature, they are made for disorientation as well as orientation. Nabokov's novel *Ada* performs the same visual-verbal magic in

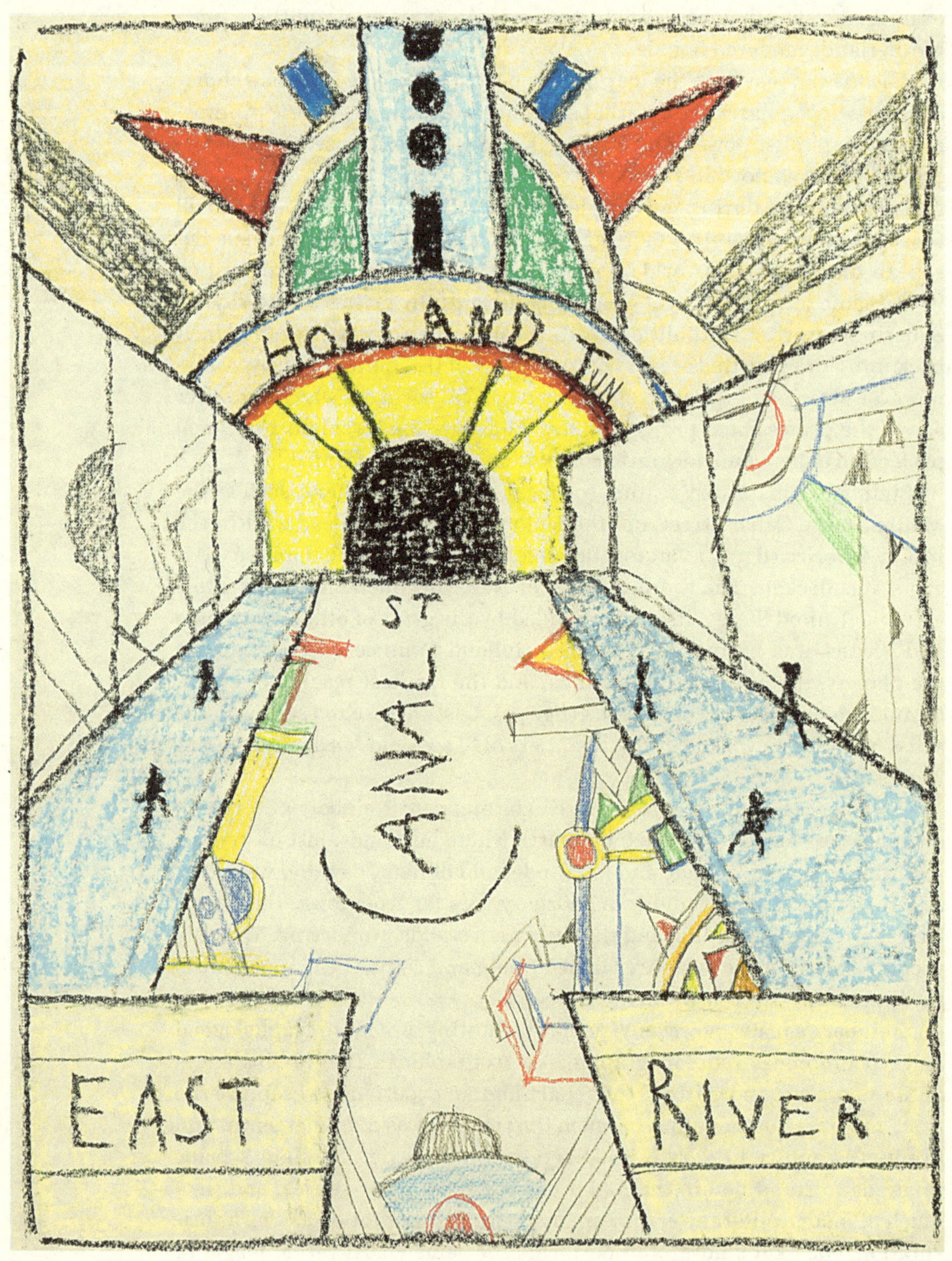

Fig. 39. Untitled, c. 1988–90. Oil crayon, pencil, and colored pencil on paper, 24 × 17⅞ in. (The Saul Steinberg Foundation, New York; photograph by Jenny Gorman)

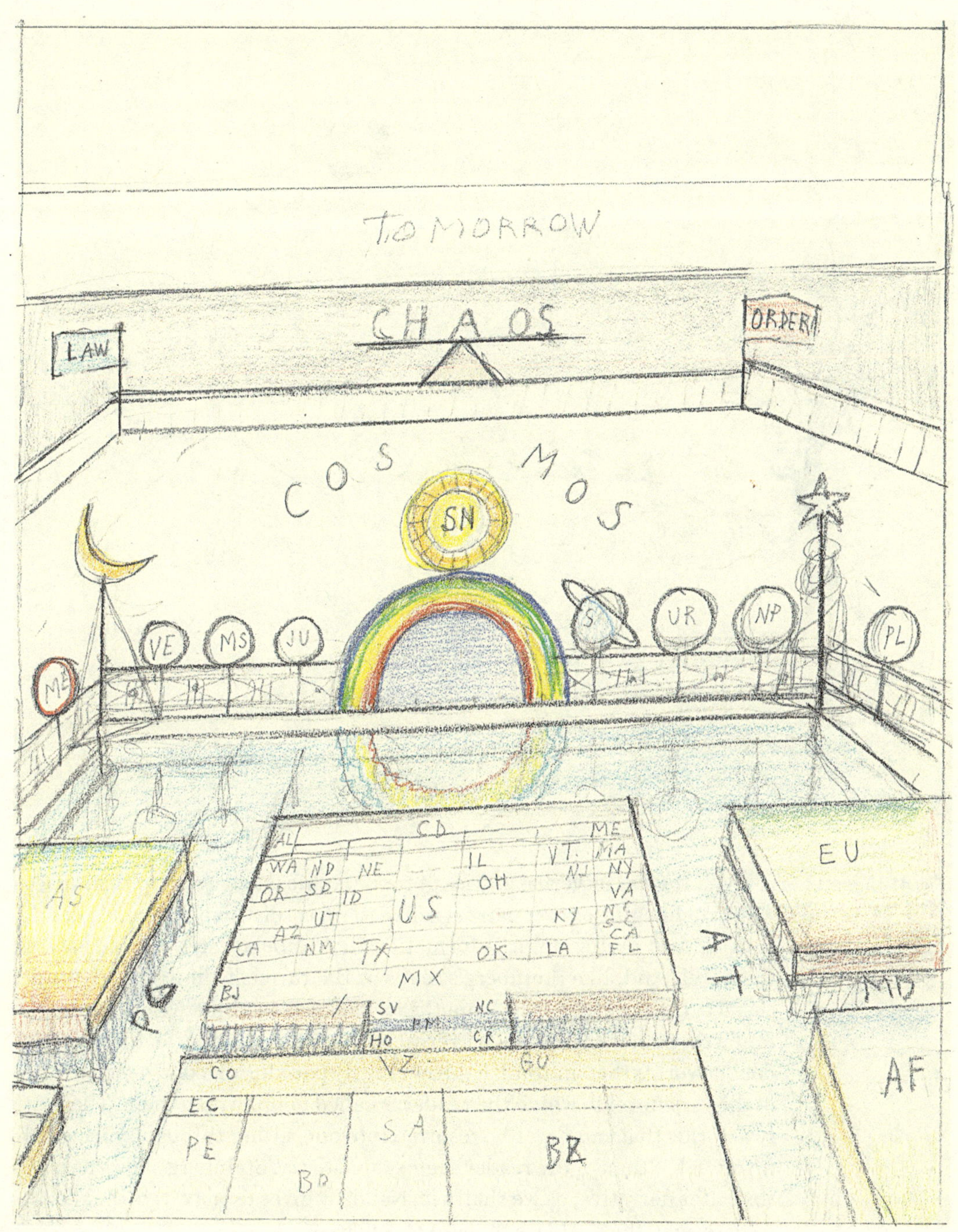

Fig. 40. Untitled (*Chaos/Cosmos*), c. 1990. Pencil and crayon on paper, torn from sketchbook, 14 × 11 in. (Beinecke Rare Book and Manuscript Library, Yale University)

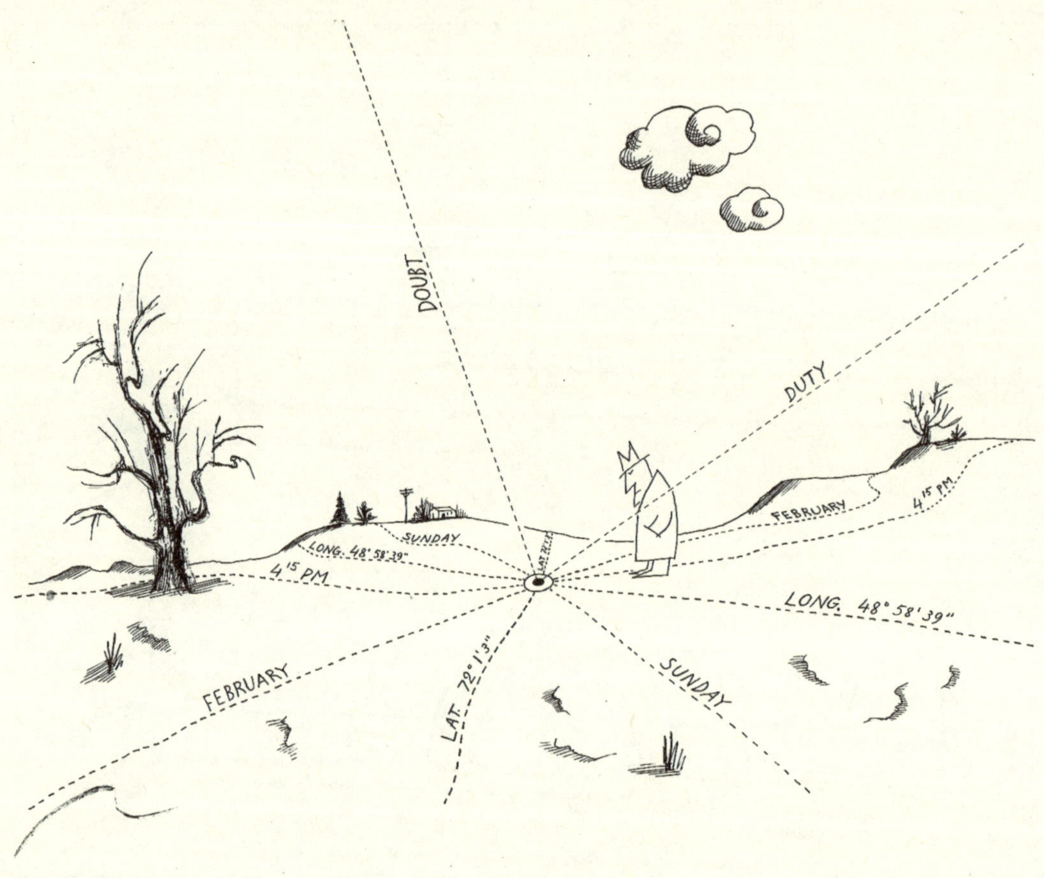

Fig. 41. Untitled, 1968. Ink on paper, 23⅛ × 29⅛ in. (Private collection)

reverse. It gives us verbal stories of topographical and geographical spaces while challenging us to construct a mental image of a map that combines the many bits of cartographic information that Nabokov slyly spreads across the novel. And, like Steinberg's maps of the through-the-Holland-Tunnel cosmos, the novel sends us from the local places we think we know into the fantastic planetary realms of Terra and Antiterra, imperfectly reflective double worlds that epitomize the nervously parodic, discontinuous texture of the very novel in which the reader is called upon to map them. These are two worlds that can never be resolved into one, either through synthesis or dismissal, although the reader seems fated to try. Steinberg shows us maps that offer narrative; as we shall see, Nabokov gives us narrative that causes us to re-map the world we thought we knew.

12

Nabokov's Maps

"Whereabouts and Whenabouts"

Vladimir Nabokov's *Ada, or Ardor: A Family Chronicle* (1969) is a novel about orientation in and across space in which deeply allusive, punning, and riddling sentences unfurl, one after another, their exotic colorations. Complicated family trees grow along literary rivers; fields, woods, and poems overlap; and a physical love affair blossoms, withers, and blooms again across the territories of "'French,' Estoty," which is akin to both the Russia of Nabokov's childhood and the nineteenth-century French texts that it absorbs and refigures.[1] The novel deliberately confuses physical geography with an allegorical geography of love, and also with the geography of a textual world: the whole can be thought of as an antic map. Nabokov orients the text before us in parodic relation to selected literary texts by other authors, most prominently François-René de Chateaubriand and (as we'll see in a later chapter) Arthur Rimbaud.[2]

Ada seems at first to resemble the massive nineteenth-century European novels of private life played out against backdrops of historical events. Its opening sentence teases us with a reminder of that literary world—"'All happy families are more or less dissimilar; all unhappy ones are more or less alike,' says a great Russian writer in the beginning of a famous novel (*Anna Arkadievitch Karenina,* transfigured into English by R. G. Stonelower, Mount Tabor Ltd., 1880)." Such mocking parody, however, escorts us from the beginning into a fantastic world, and then proceeds to map that world verbally. *Ada,* we learn, is set on Antiterra (also known as Demonia), a planet that is both like and unlike our earth. Antiterra exists in relation to Terra, another planet, of which Antiterrans know little for sure, and about which they hold a variety of opinions, even as to its very existence. This is science fiction of a sort, but *Ada,* as we shall see, contains parodies of many kinds of literature and visual arts. The love story that dominates the narrative requires that we acknowledge as well a story of craft, the assembling of a novel by using other works of art.

Ada is a novel of transportation: horseback, carriage, airplane, train, bicycle, ship, sports car. Because the family it chronicles is wealthy in the grand nineteenth-century European manner, its members move between city homes and country estates, but they also dash across the globe toward scenes of sexual pleasure, or pass sadly from one mental asylum to another (Van's putative mother Aqua), or around the neighborhood of Ardis. The skeleton of the plot consists of Van and Ada's incestuous love affair, stretching from childhood to old age, and Van anxiously chronicles Ada's "whereabouts and whenabouts" (*Ada,* 164) during their lengthy, periodic separations.

For all the simplicity of its plot, this is a notoriously difficult novel. Its "manic shifts in space and time, subject, reference and tone, within one centrifugal sentence after another," renders it for many readers merely puzzling and irritating.[3] Of all Nabokov's novels, this one most tests its readers' patience. Deciphering its difficult, sometimes nearly illegible, prose has required the work of dedicated scholars and Nabokov aficionados ever since its publication.[4]

Its plot unfolds as follows. In the summer of 1884 the "cousins" fourteen-year-old Van Veen and eleven-year-old Ada Veen first embark on a love affair that yields an abundance of physical bliss. They discover through their own sleuthing skills that they are actually brother and sister. During this summer of love, the younger Lucette, Ada's "sister," who is actually her half sister, becomes an unwelcome companion to the always randy older children. She is at first bodily removed from the scenes of lovemaking but she eventually sees and knows all, or all that an eight-year-old can understand. In this way Van and Ada corrupt a little girl, the indefensible crime (along with the taboo of incest) at the center of this novel.

At the end of the summer, Van and Ada return to their respective schools, communicate in coded letters, meet twice, briefly, and travel to differing destinations. Jealousy of Ada's lovers—some actual, some only imagined by Van—is the worm that tunnels through his years at "Chose University" in England and takes on renewed force during his second stay at Ardis, in 1888. Although Ada reminds him that they cannot marry and makes little attempt to hide her current lover, Percy de Prey, she and Van continue their "ardencies" and from time to time even include Lucette in a three-way "cuddl[ing]and cosset[ing]" (*Ada,* 225). However, as evidence of Ada's inconstancy gathers, Van leaves Ardis, planning to reject Ada forever. Memories of her torture him nonetheless.

Ada sends him letters of pleading apology, which he doesn't open. He writes "a philosophical novel," *Letters from Terra,* which appears in 1891, and he commences medical studies. When morally monstrous sex with very young girls at a private club doesn't assuage Van's longing for Ada, he turns to intellectual pursuits at Kingston University's "Department of Terrapy," writing a work on the "Idea of Dimension & Dementia." His father has bought a Manhattan apartment, and there Van works while fending off Lucette, who has arrived suddenly. It's 1892, and she is now a chic young woman. Still a virgin, she desires Van more than ever. Van and Ada reunite briefly in 1893 and 1905.

Van and Ada voluntarily separate, she to marry a boring man, become a second-rate movie actress, and take up residence in Arizona, he to become Professor Veen and study, teach, and write books such as *Illegible Signatures,* 1895; *Clairvoyeurism,* 1903; *Furnished Space,* 1913; and The *Texture of Time,* begun 1922. In 1901 he sails from France to America, and it is on this journey that Lucette, still in pursuit of Van but spurned by him yet again, kills herself by jumping overboard. It isn't until 1922, when Ada's husband dies, that Van and Ada reunite for good and start "a new life" (*Ada,* 609) together.

As the novel closes, Van and Ada remain together, never punished for their corruption of Lucette or for their appalling arrogance. He is ninety-seven years old and still writing his memoirs, to which Ada has added editorial comments from time to time. This is the book we hold in our hands: "One can even surmise that if our time-racked, flat-lying couple ever intended to die they would die, as it were, *into* the finished book, into Eden or Hades, into the prose of the book or the poetry of its blurb" (*Ada,* 587). They're flat-lying perhaps because they're diminishing with age, perhaps in order to "die" sexually, but Nabokov also alludes here to what he elsewhere calls "stereographic" representation. In geometrical terms that means the projection of a sphere onto a plane, and in novelistic terms it would, by analogy, mean the projection of a three-dimensional "real" world onto the flat, written page.[5]

Van Veen relegates space ("the imposter . . . his trial will take place at a later stage of our investigation") (*Ada,* 541) to a secondary role in the drama of time he explores in his philosophical work *The Texture of Time.* Yet he actually thinks as much, or more, about space during the course of his life. It is, after all, space that achingly intervenes between his body and Ada's during the years of their exile from each other. Antiterran Van writes a novel about Terra with the help of mental patients who seem to have knowledge of that planet that everyone else lacks, even while realizing he doesn't know his own planet at all well. He then imagines travels he might, and eventually does, take, mapping even more of the strange political geography of Antiterra. He plans, after medical school, to travel through South America, Africa, and India, and across America by train, whose schedules he has been consulting since his teenage years. The list of imaged travels by "dark-red New World Express" includes passage through Manhattan, Mephisto, el Paso, Meksikansk, the Panama Chunnel, Brazilia, and Witch.

"There it split into two parts, the eastern one continuing to Grant's Horn, and the western returning north through Valparaiso and Bogota" (*Ada,* 345). His imaginary travels continue, through Nigero, Rodosia and Ethiopia, London, Ceylon, Sydney, Turkey, and several more Chunnels. "It is not clear," he observes, "when you are falling asleep, why all continents except you begin with an A" (*Ada,* 345). You *are* the continent, Van notices, indicating that at the edge of sleep mind extends through space in a confusion of identity, geography, and orthography that would do Steinberg proud.

While the very young Ada and Van are still enjoying a glorious love at Ardis, they discern that "it was not impossible that [in the past] somewhere along a winding Riviera road they passed each other in rented victorias . . . or perhaps in two different trains, going perhaps the same way, the little girl at the window of one sleeping car looking at the brown sleeper of a parallel train which gradually diverged toward sparkling sketches of sea," and it is in thinking about such matters that "he found himself tackling, in still vague and ideal fashion, the science that was to obsess his mature years—problems of space and time" (*Ada,* 153). Van lacks a home because his widowed father doesn't establish one, but also because his true home, created by Nabokov's parodic forays into sentimentalism, seems to be Ada's body and soul. He travels in the novel away from her, and toward the void he believes death to be. It's no wonder that he wants a better map, one that will show him how to travel toward Ada after they take diverging routes, so that their parallel or mirror version childhood selves may meet again. Time exists primarily to reveal the route to fulfilled love.

Nabokov loves coincidences, so why not mention a few as we begin our travels in *Ada?* We have already seen the coincidence of "bric-à-Braques" (*Ada,* 17), and Steinberg's drawing of 1964 (see fig. 4; p. 16) "Braque, bric-à-brac, break, bark."[6] But there's more than one coincidence here: in *Ada,* Nabokov writes of the "L-disaster," "The details of the L disaster (*and I do not mean Elevated*) [emphasis added] in the beau milieu of last century" (17). Here Van introduces the "electricity disaster" that resulted in the banning of electricity on Antiterra. In 1994, Steinberg writes a letter to Buzzi in which he remembers that "[i]n 1942—June 28—arrived in NY from Santo Domingo and, speaking little English, I saw the following headline in the *Daily News:* TAXI HITS EL PILLAR. El Pillar? Perhaps he was a famous bullfighter, Spanish dancer, perhaps a transvestite. It was, as you can see on the reverse, a pillar of the Elevated [train] which you'll remember, on 3rd ave . . ." (*LAB,* June 10, 1994). Steinberg suddenly remembers a punning El/Elevated disaster long dormant. This is what Nabokov would call "topsy-turvy coincidence"—evidence that these two artists share not necessarily "text, but texture" (*PF,* 63).

Nabokov created an image worthy of Steinberg when he wrote in "The Art of Literature and Commonsense" that "by digging a little deeper somewhere near the waistline of South America a lucky geologist may one day discover, as his spade rings against metal, the solid barrel hoop of the equator" (*LL,* 374). In advocating for the "divinely absurd world of the mind," a world in which geometrical projections no longer rule the world of maps, he was utterly serious. Orienting ourselves by art and imagination intrigued him: "All poetry is positional: to try to express one's position in regard to the universe embraced by consciousness, is an immemorial urge" (*SM,* 218). As we have seen, Steinberg's *Autogeography* (see fig. 14; p. 60) expresses position in three modes—map, landscape, and visual autobiography or memoir. Together they capture Steinberg's self-orienting act, his embrace through consciousness of a world that cannot be captured by one mode alone. In a similar way Nabokov's text positions a multitude, perhaps even an excess, of place-names in verbal relation to one another, that is, on a map that readers, not just fictional characters, must construct in their minds.

Against the novel's dense texture of geographical-verbal fiddling (e.g., Panama Chunnel, Grant's Horn) Nabokov places a series of landscapes (more about these later) and a memoir of a long-lived affair conducted by the novel's peripatetic lovers, Ada and Van. A visual example might help us begin. We read Steinberg's *Autogeography* as autobiography that runs allegorically and temporally along life's river only to swerve to space, the stasis of fields covered with place-names like so many rocks and plants. We continually cycle through the related, but still perplexingly distinct, orders of mapping that *Ada* calls for—topographical or geographical, political, autobiographical, allegorical, allusive, typographic. Like Steinberg's rocking-chaired man who participates in a work that is simultaneously map, landscape, and portraiture (see fig. 37; p. 114), Nabokov's characters move among multiple kinds of fictional space. Every reader is an immigrant in this new world, and even after many explorations of the terrain, we can never hope to orient ourselves wholly. The novel is not a puzzle to be solved, but an ongoing match of our wit and heart with those of its author.

Reading *Ada* involves mentally creating maps that bear a family resemblance to Steinberg's playful chartings of space. The February 21–28, 2000, issue of the *New Yorker* contained the posthumously published portfolio "Maps." (Nabokov coincidentally had a short piece in the same issue: "Butterflies," dated June 12, 1948, about a collecting trip that begins in the marshes of a Russian river and magically ends in Colorado.) The map entitled *Europe Year 3000* (see fig. 38; p. 116) is perhaps most germane to *Ada.* A visual chronicle of political change and aesthetic incursion, it encourages us, as we've seen, to imagine that cities, states, and countries have, by 3000, alighted on unexpected continents, some with slightly altered names: Upstate, Buffalo, Nebraska, Alaska, Bismark, Kaliphornia, Amelika, Ohio, Miami, and New York now inhabit Europe—much as Nabokov's remembered and invented Russian places inhabit North America in *Ada.*

Steinberg drew most of his maps during the 1970s and '80s, although he began in the 1960s. The as yet unanswered question becomes: did he do so before or after reading *Ada,* if indeed he read it at all? Whether Steinberg took his inspiration directly from the shuffled geography of *Ada,* looked at fantasy maps appearing in other novels, or developed on his own the notion of a fantasized political world map, the fact remains that both Nabokov and Steinberg created imaginary geographies by playing with the map of the world as they knew it in the second half of the twentieth century. Both expressed through their art the unsettling political changes in the Europe in which they were born, and both experimented with the notion of changing, through fictions of mapping, the commonly accepted depictions of the face of the earth. Nabokov and Steinberg map bodies, rooms, continents, worlds, and even the cosmos freely, outrageously, delightfully.

In interviews, Nabokov advised mapping and diagramming the places mentioned in novels, and he did so, too, in his lectures at Cornell. When teaching Joyce's *Ulysses,* "Instead of perpetuating the pretentious nonsense of Homeric, chromatic, and visceral chapter headings," one should, he advised, "prepare maps of Dublin with Bloom's and Stephen's intertwining itineraries clearly traced" (*SO,* 157).

Don Quixote makes an appearance in *Ada* as *Don Juan's Last Fling,* Ada's film "with its absurd echoes of Don Quixote and Pushkin's Don Juan minidrama, *The Stone Guest.*"[7] The actual work, though, presented him with a problem as he prepared to teach it in 1951. When Nabokov tries to map Cervantes's Spain for the benefit of his class, he describes it as "a ghastly muddle."[8] However damning this might sound, we should remember that Nabokov begins his introduction to *Lectures on Don Quixote* by advising strongly against looking for "for so-called 'real life' in novels. "Let us not try and reconcile the fiction of facts with the facts of fiction. *Don Quixote* is a fairy tale . . . but without [this] fairy tale the world would not be real."[9] Decades later, Nabokov would create a wildly imaginary geography and topography in *Ada.* Thus Cervantes's "ignorance" is a state that Nabokov both excoriates and adopts. As we have seen, Steinberg, too, imagines maps that freely chart the "whereabouts and whenabouts" of people (*Ada,* 164).

Like Cervantes's places, the cluster of towns in Ladore where much of the action of *Ada* occurs defies exact geographical location. *Ada* contains no visual map, because Nabokov expects his careful readers (the only ones that matter to him) to create their own mental maps of Antiterra. Thanks to Dieter E. Zimmer, we now have the outlines of a geopolitical map of North America on Antiterra (fig. 42).[10] Early in the novel Nabokov begins to train readers in visualizing his shuffled world. It's as if in *Ada* a map underlies or extends from everything that characters do, feel, and think—such a map made semivisible in our imaginations by Nabokov's continual references to travel and place-names.

The narrator begins with Terra, that world which exists in the novel (set in Antiterra) only as an untested hypothesis. Terra's geopolitical arrangements resemble those of the Earth circa 1969, although their description reads as a hectic performance. Van asks us to image that Russia,

> instead of being a quaint synonym of Estoty, the American province extending from the Arctic no-longer-vicious Circle to the United States proper, [as it does on Anti-Terra] was on Terra the name of a country, transferred as if by some sleight

Fig. 42. *North America on Antiterra,* Dieter E. Zimmer. From Vladimir Nabokov, *Ada oder Das Verlangen—Eine Familienchronik,* Reinbek: Rowohlt Verlag, 2010, p. 134.

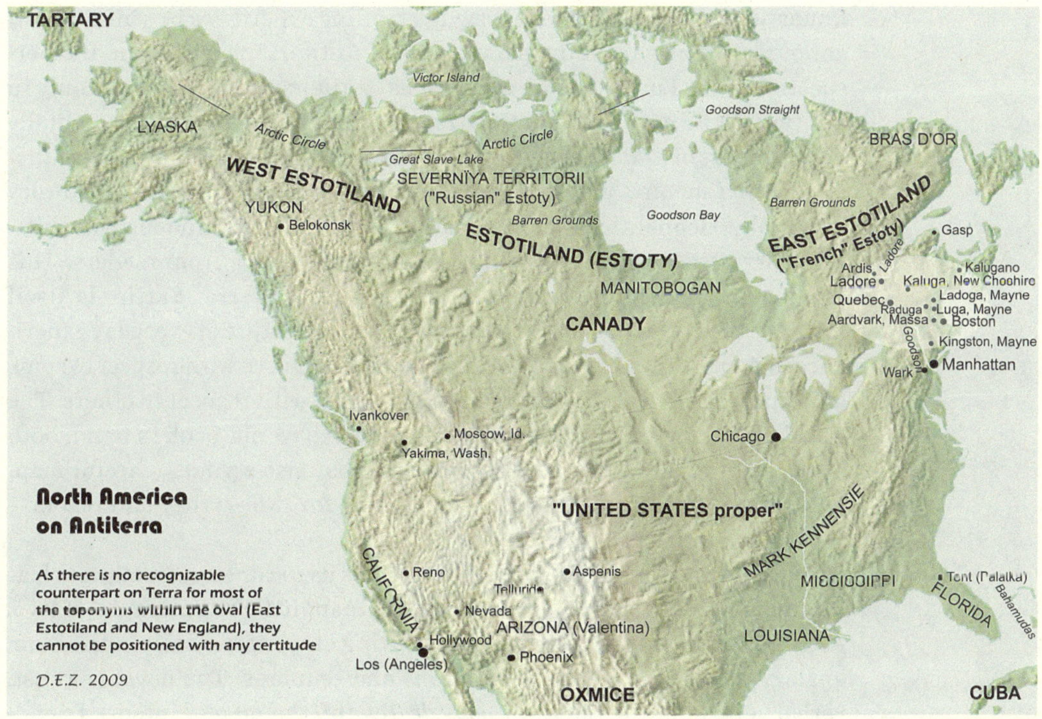

of *land* across the ha-ha of a doubled ocean to the opposite hemisphere where it sprawled over all of today's Tartary, from Kurland to the Kuriles! . . . in Terrestrial spatial terms, the Amerussia of Abraham Milton was split into its components, with tangible water and ice separating the political, rather than poetical, notions of "America" and "Russia." (*Ada,* 17–18)

What? Here Nabokov asks us to imagine partial maps of three planets, Antiterra, Terra, and Earth. "Russia's" location on a "ludicrous" map of Terra resembles Russia's location on Earth, separated from its original other half, "Amer," that division inflected by "Abraham Milton" recalling Lincoln and the American Civil War and John Milton's *A Brief History of Moscovia: And Other Less-known Countries Lying Eastward of Russia as Far as Cathay.*[11] On Antiterra, the principal setting of the novel, Russia has become "Russian" Estoty, and it's an American province.

From the point of view of the novel's characters, the less likely, even "laughable," map is that of Terra, whose existence many rational Antiterrans doubt while "deranged [Antiterran] minds . . . accepted it in support and token of their own irrationality" (*Ada,* 20). From the limited information we're given, Terra tracks Earth's nineteenth- and twentieth-century geography more closely than does Antiterra, but it's also strikingly fantastic. Nabokov launches a dizzying reading experience in which we orient ourselves now from the perspective of Antiterrans, now from the perspective of the Earthlings we are. Just as Antiterrans meet Terrans only in a fiction (Van's novel, *Letters from Terra*) or in the accounts of the mentally ill, so readers of *Ada* meet Antiterrans only in a fiction, itself playfully lunatic, another moony "pale fire" reflecting the sun of mid-twentieth-century geography. Geopolitical fictions and facts exhibit a continuous and shifting topsy-turvyness that demands mental gymnastics from readers. This tripling of geographical possibilities—Antiterra, Terra, Earth—is itself raised to the power of two when we reflect on the texture of everyday experience in *Ada.* Life on Antiterra sounds like life on Earth with respect to some of its day-to-day realities, but intriguingly sci-fi with respect to others. The world of the novel and the "real" world in which we sit, book in hand, both attract and repel each other. *Ada* rewards, but also stymies, careful mapping. Mapping in *Ada* turns out to be a game for two—writer and reader—that Nabokov will always win.

While *Ada* offers information that invites us to construct a map such as Zimmer's, it also requires a second kind of mapping: the geography of love. After all, that confusing splitting and roving of territories also exists as an analogy of Ada's and Van's separations and reunions. The novel is a vast, verbal version of the *Carte du pays de Tendre,* the map of intense friend-

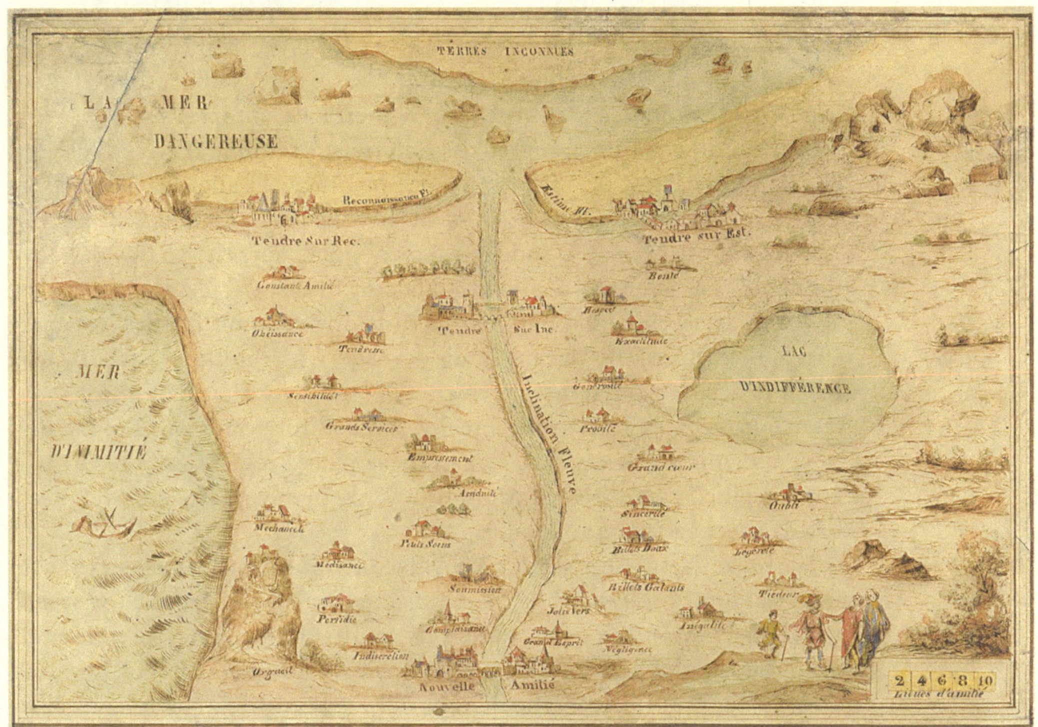

Fig. 43. *Le Pays de tendre.* (P. J. Mode Collection of Persuasive Cartography, Cornell University Library)

ship and even love, imagined as a land called "Tendre" (fig. 43). Created by members of Madeleine de Scudéry's *salon,* it first appeared in her 1654–61 novel *Clélie.*

Conceived as a type of board game as well as a map, it challenged viewers/ players to proceed through an allegory of the ideal love affair or the ideal communal friendship by sailing along rivers to three destinations: *Tendre-sur-Estime, Tendre-sur-Reconnaissance, Tendre-sur-Inclination* while avoiding villages such as *Négligence, Oubli, Perfidie, Orgueil,* and staying as far as possible from *La Mer Dangereuse* and *Lac D'Indifférence. Dévotion, persévérance,* and *ardeur* were required.[12] And so it is in Nabokov's *Ada, or Ardor:* Van and Ada must journey through emotionally dangerous terrain before they can be reunited in a lasting tender embrace. Mme Scudéry drew on a conventional literary conceit: Tasso, Spenser, and Bunyan, among others, also mapped the heart or soul on its journey toward the highest good. Her drawing of an actual map so caught the imagination of its readers that imitations followed apace.[13] Reading *Ada* involves a process of tracing possible reorganizations of the political world map as we have known it and, at the same time, discerning the progress of Van and Ada's love affair.

The novel consists of a verbal version of a visual map that readers may construct, much as Zimmer has, but with an added layer of allegorical geography: a map of the Nabokovian Land of *Ardeur*/Ardor, as much their "homeland" as the country estate, Ardis, where their love commences.[14]

Like Steinberg's mapping of the emotions of an air traveler between New York and Paris (see fig. 35; p. 111) or his quasi-allegorical mapping of life's difficulties and rewards, *Per Aspera ad Astra* (see fig. 36; p. 112), Nabokov maps the places and emotions of a journey: the course of a love affair between sister and brother that begins in ecstasy, festers in jealousy, infidelity, and pride, and culminates in loving reunion for the last forty years of their lives. The affair at Ardis develops with reference to the nearby area of Ladore (situated in what we think of as Quebec), which seems to include topographically, typographically, and auditorily the towns of Ladore, Ladoga, Laguna, Lugano, and Luga. These places register autobiographically as well: Vyra, the Nabokov family's estate in the province of St. Petersburg, lay between Luga and Ladoga.[15]

The novel's sentences skitter from place-name to erotic imagery to entomological lore, swelling with interconnected allusions. One such sentence unfolds as follows: "Chateaubriand's mosquito," he explains, "is characterized by an insatiable and reckless appetite for Ada's and Ardelia's, Lucette's and Lucile's (multiplied by the itch) blood" (*Ada,* 106). Nabokov here refers to some of his own itches. First, his incessant urge toward literary allusion, for the mosquito actually or figuratively bites Van's sister Ada, his half sister Lucette, his cousin Ardelia (bringing to mind Anne Finch, Countess of Winchelsea, who used that pseudonym in her poetry), and the writer François-René Chateaubriand's sister Lucile. Second, Nabokov itches to insert entomological lore and word games into his sentences: the precise mosquito is *Culex chateaubriand Brown* (an insect invented by Nabokov), "insect" tracks "incest," and *cousin* in French means "gnat" or mosquito."[16] The Chateaubriand who found the mosquito is, Nabokov tells us, "Charles," not François-René, the writer whose works will, as we'll see, appear prominently in the novel.

After describing their (and his) voluptuous fits of scratching, he notes that this insect approaches extinction because of a cooler climate and "the moronic draining of the lovely rich marshes in the Ladore region, as well as near Kaluga, Conn., and Lugano, Pa." (*Ada,* 108). On Earth, Kaluga is an industrial city ninety miles southwest of Moscow; on Antiterra, it is a city in "New Cheshire, U.S.A," about fifty miles from Ladore.[17] In *Ada* cities as well as characters exist in familial relations: Kaluga, Kalugano, and Raduga. Van, Ada, and their family members spend time further afield in Antiterra's North America, where some places track closely the names and locations of North America as we know it, while others send them up (e.g., Vancouver is Ivankover, Mexico anagrammatically metamorphoses to Oxmice). Nabokov also redraws the political map of the continents: Russia and swaths of Asia are part of the Tartary Empire, while the British Empire claims Europe and Africa.[18]

Nabokov infuses the personalities and circumstances of his characters with the odd names of places they inhabit, and those places complete a circle by taking on the characteristics of their inhabitants. Ardis the place, in "French" Estoty, is a rural seat in North America, not far from Boston, Mayne, or the town of Quebec, but "ardis" is also the tip of an arrow—time's arrow—which moves unerringly toward the ends of lives and stories. But Ardis is also punningly made of Van and Ada's ardor, their par-ardis.[19] During their first summer together, the estate is not just the backdrop for their romance but also the sum of their honeyed, sun-dappled, shaded, and shady encounters as well as the scene of a barn fire that seems to have been ignited by their own (at first) repressed desire.

Even the supporting actors of this romance are made of place-names written across the Antiterran globe. Consider Aqua, supposedly Van's mother. Aqua's sister Marina is his biological mother; he is "given" to Aqua during one of her periods of mental incapacity to replace her stillborn son and to hide the secret of his paternity. Aqua has an unspecified mental affliction for which she is treated at places across the globe: Scoto-Scandinavia, the Riviera, Altar, Palermontovia, Canady, the Indias. Nabokov launches another rich list of places that reorganizes twentieth-century nation states as we know them, but concludes that Aqua's "real destination was Terra the Fair and thither she trusted she would fly on libellula [dragonfly] long wings when she died" (*Ada,* 21–22). Mentally ill, Aqua embodies the "War of the Worlds," which is not just Van's obvious allusion to H. G. Wells's work, but also to the tension between sanity and insanity, the latter obliquely related to Terra. Nabokov packs the passage with geographical information that is infused with the sadness of Aqua's "solid black" life. Her travels suggest a sadder version of Nabokov's own anger: "I propelled myself out of Russia so vigorously, with such indignant force, that I have been rolling on and on ever since" (*SO,* 27).

Maps need not be geographic in nature; any graphic representation "that facilitate[s] a spatial understanding of things, concepts, conditions, processes, events in the human world" can serve as a map.[20] Mapping a novel in its widest sense is coterminous with reading it for various clues, and in this sense almost any novel rewards mapping. Rereading *Ada,* though, results in a specific layering of maps that move from the *actual,* if parodic—"Equally fascinating was a five-fold screen with bright paintings on its black panels reproducing the first maps of four and a half continents" (*Ada,* 43)—to the *metaphorical,* as Ada learns to read Van's genitals—" 'Relief map,' " said the primrose prig, 'the rivers of Africa.' Her index traced the blue Nile down into its jungle and traveled up again" (*Ada,* 126)—and on to the constant *verbal sketches* hinting at Antiterra's political geography. We "see" not just places with proper names but also a verbal and visual web of spatial clues. Like Steinberg, Nabokov can see maps in the most unlikely of places. Even down to coincidental details: like Steinberg, Nabokov refers to a "tree's intricate map" (*Ada,* 94).

Nabokov and Steinberg adopt a specific cartographical art: they write and draw maps that playfully announce their fictionality while retaining just enough of the verisimilitude we expect to make them legible. They deviate from the accuracy we expect not for fantasy's sake itself, but for the sake of truths we can develop only through fantasy's freedoms. We decode Nabokov's capricious maps in order to discover where we are, not just on Antiterra, but on Earth. Nabokov leads us on in our mental mapmaking, teases us for our orientational desires, and rewards us, as we close the volume, with a clearer vision of our own Earth, our ways and places of being that are visible from Antiterra. Yet that is not the end of the story for him: landscapes beckon.

In *Ada,* Nabokov, like Steinberg, creates abstract landscapes, and for some of the same reasons. In the Russian version of *Speak, Memory* (*Drugie berega*), Nabokov confesses: "Longing for home. It has its clutches, that longing, in a small corner of the world, and it can be pulled away only by killing it. . . . Give me, on any continent, a forest, meadow, and air that resemble the province of Saint Petersburg, and my soul gets turned inside out."[21] Nabokov actually painted landscapes at the Vyra family estate in Russia, none of which has been found, but we do have a drawing entitled "Autumn in Sans Souci" that he made during his exile in Berlin—a view of King Frederick the Great's summer residence in Potsdam. He has chosen a pastoral scene of woods and pond, complete with classical statuary.[22] In fact, Van first meets Ardis in a landscape painting: "Van immediately recognized Ardis hall as depicted in the two-hundred-year-old aquarelle that hung in his father's dressing room: the mansion sat on a rise overlooking an abstract meadow with two tiny people in cocked hats conversing not far from a stylized cow" (*Ada,* 35). In Van's written account of Ardis's woods, streams, and meadows, he will reproduce this mixture of the figural and the abstract.

The landscapes of *Ada* are for the most part as abstracted as they are in Steinberg's paintings. Nabokov is more interested in details of domestic scenes (genre paintings of rooms, people engaged in conversation, sexual couplings), psychological and physical portraits, and what we might call Nabokovian "history paintings" depicting a character in an extremity of emotional action: Van, as he charges across the countryside to defeat his sexual rivals, or Lucette as she makes her final attempt to bed Van.

Descriptions of Ardis's grounds and the surrounding countryside appear most frequently as brief descriptions of Van and Ada's trysting places and of family gatherings. Panoramic landscapes are few, but strategically placed. On Van's first visit to Ardis we're given one of them, as he is driven through a countryside of pine trees, ravines, and animals in the undergrowth: "Sunflecks and lacy shadows skimmed over his legs and lent a green twinkle to the brass button deprived of its twin on the back of the coachman's coat. They passed through Torfyanka, a dreamy hamlet consisting of three or four log izbas [small houses], a milkpail repair shop and a smithy smothered in jasmine. . . . They were now spinning along a dusty country road between fields. The road dipped and humped again" (*Ada,* 34–35).

Part panorama, part travelogue, the passage insistently pulls our eye from the landscape back to the "old calèche" and its driver; and such a vacillation of focus between landscape and portrait, outdoor setting and character, is typical of this novel. Like Steinberg, who insists, "It makes no sense to do a landscape without putting a human presence in it,"[23] and often provides tiny figures within his vast landscapes, Nabokov peoples this landscape. What makes it distinctive, however, is its multiple orders of patterning. The sun patterns the landscape, "Sunflecks and lacy shadows . . . lent a green twinkle," and the passage in prose is itself flecked with alliteration and its half siblings assonance and consonance: green/twinkle, brass/button, smithy/smothered, dusty/country. Nabokov asks us to look *at* words, not just through them, and he expects us to listen to them as well.

In place of expected landscape tableaux, Nabokov most often offers a verbal texture of light, shade, color, and sound, a few verbal brushstrokes akin to Impressionist images that point to an always elusive and changing landscape. Consider, for example, the description of the trip to Ada's twelfth birthday party, held in the woods: "The forest road remained reasonably smooth if you kept to its middle run (still sticky and dark after a rainy dawn) between the sky-blue ruts, speckled with the reflections of the same birch leaves whose shadows sped over the taut nacrine silk of Mlle Larivière's open sunshade and the wide brim of Ada's rather rakishly donned white hat" (*Ada,* 78). Beyond offering a play of visual and tactile images that are heightened by the internal rhymes of its sentences, this characteristic description of landscape also encourages readers to imagine the larger landscapes of which they are a part, "sky-blue ruts." "Larivière"—this time a male physician—is a character in a novel prized by both Steinberg and Nabokov, *Madame Bovary,* and the landscapes of that novel hover in ghostly presence in this description of a forest road. Those same ruts, for example, parody Flaubert's description of Charles Bovary on his way to meet Emma for the first time, "The ruts were getting deeper. They were nearly at Les Bertaux."[24]

Landscape appears in even more abstract ways. Nabokov likes to mention it without describing it at all, that is, folding it wholly into character: from his seat on a train, fourteen-year-old Van "surveys the capable landscape capably skimming by," such capability a mirror of his own feeling that he is "very much a man of the world" (*Ada,* 33). More common, though, is what we might term synecdochic landscape, because Nabokov implies whole landscapes through a few intense details. Ada, editing Van's memoir later in life, describes their preferred method of capturing a landscape. She calls it "unnatural history" in which "the detail is all: The song of a Tuscan Firecrest or a Sitka Kinglet in a cemetery cypress; a minty whiff of Summer Savory or Yerba Buena on a coastal slope; the dancing flitter of a Holly Blue or an Echo Azure—combined with other birds, flowers and butterflies: that has to be heard, smelled and seen through the transparency of death and ardent beauty" (*Ada,* 71). Steinberg paints abstracted landscapes with a few details; Nabokov writes details that suggest entire landscapes. Both associate landscape with an ideal realm, "the transparency of death and ardent beauty."

Nearly hidden "landscapes" abound, and these we need help in seeing. For example, when we learn that Van's last name, Veen, means peat bog or marsh in Dutch, and that Nabokov learned this when reading a novel by Nicolas Freeling, *Double Barrel,*[25] the glimmer of a landscape flits across the novel, as it has with the allusion to *Madame Bovary.* The landscapes of Arcady appear as well, drawing upon Sir Philip Sidney's *The Countess of Pembroke's Arcadia* (1590), with its theme of brother-sister (Philip/Mary) incest, and *Astrophel and Stella,* a sonnet sequence of 1591.[26] Andrew Marvell's "The Garden" (1681) also appears, here in direct quotation, there in Van and Ada's secret code, and nearly everywhere, through the pastoral eroticism and sensual wit that Nabokov borrows from the poem.[27]

For Steinberg, painting imagined or remembered countryside provides an escape from cerebral drawing into pleasurable painting and neo-Symbolist mystery. For Nabokov, the fields, forests, and bogs of erotic and emotional intimacy, alluded to rather than described, spell pleasure that approaches paradise. With the beautiful details of the natural world at Ardis and the lineaments of love (Ardor), he draws and redraws the portal of paradise, of a "*something there* . . . more deep and more general"[28] that infuses his writing from his earliest poems to his final novel.

Allusions to works by Chateaubriand account for the most pervasive, abstracted, and parodic landscapes of the novel.[29] Through Nabokov's appropriation of three of Chateaubriand's tales—*Atala* (1801), *René* (1805), and *The Last of the Abencerrajes* (1826), along with his autobiography, *Memoirs from Beyond the Grave* (1848–50)—*Ada* offers landscapes everywhere present but nowhere wholly visible.[30] The frequency and clarity of his clues, however, ensure that we will eventually notice them and tease out their meanings. As Steinberg plays with the internal mirror or *mise en abyme* of a landscape painter seated within a landscape (see fig. 15; p. 67), so Nabokov, in parallel, encloses within the text of Van's memoir Chateaubriand's troubling accounts of love, including those of his own memoir. Ardis is not just a fictional estate in a fictional country located on a fantastical planet, but it is also artificial in another way: it is made in part of the Chateaubriand family seat, the Château de Combourg in Brittany, as well as the forests, plains, and aristocratic estates that Chateaubriand encountered in his travels to North America and Spain.

In each of the four works, Chateaubriand features a passionate but forbidden love affair between a sensitive young man and an adamantly virtuous young woman—tabooed for reasons of consanguinity but also because of religious, social, or political differences. Chateaubriand, then, stamps his works almost obsessively with a pair of doomed lovers, but he employs the convention with the intense sincerity characteristic of French romanticism. Nabokov imitates such sincerity as he parodies Chateaubriand's fiction. Nabokov invites us to read his lovers doubly: as passionately, innocently in love and as arrogant, self-involved, even precious; as realistic figures of lovers and as parodic versions of lovers from another's works. Every allusion to Chateaubriand's works in *Ada* verbally imprints his lovers' outsize emotions of joy and despair on the narrative surface of Van and Ada's relationship. Yet every such allusion also calls attention to the very artificiality of that emotional intensity, its borrowed quality. The more heartfelt, the more contrived. Nabokov never feared a paradox.

Chateaubriand's landscapes matter as much to Nabokov as the characters themselves. The plentiful and detailed landscapes of Chateaubriand's Romantic wanderings hover implicitly, for the careful reader, throughout Nabokov's novel. He appropriates Chateaubriand's Romantic settings of outdoor earth, air, fire and water that half create, half express his characters' adolescent sexual passion. As Chateaubriand chronicles in *Memoirs*, his beloved sister Lucile and he together roam the woods and gardens of the family seat of Combourg.

Nabokov sometimes appropriates Chateaubriand's Romantic landscape image by image, for example parodying Chateaubriand's evening star with "the golden globes of the new garden lamps that glowed here and there in the sudden greenery" (*Ada,* 211). At every hint of Chateaubriand in *Ada,* and there are many, Nabokov suggests a Romantic landscape that is nowhere fully visible, an aura of the ideal, akin to Steinberg's idealized landscapes, that hovers above the all-too-Antiterran scenes of Van and Ada's love affair.

Nabokov's every mention of the amorous siblings and Lucette, his every mention of "Ladore" (the Chateaubriand chateau is bathed by the [la] Dore river) carries with it just such a whiff of the French romantic swoon into nature. What Van experiences, the perch in the tree where through Ada's "fortunate fall" he is able to make contact with her "pantyless crotch,"[31] Chateaubriand has pursued only in fantasy: "I had made a seat, like a nest, in one of these willows: there, alone between heaven and earth, I spent hours with the warblers; my nymph was at my side."[32] Nabokov constructs the sylvan settings for Ada and Van's lovemaking from his memories of family estates in Russia, his wide reading in French literature, and the "nocturna" (Chateaubriand's night wind) of his insomniac imagination. Like Steinberg, he explores degrees of reality.

Chateaubriand also offers Nabokov a trove of specifically *geographical* fantasies, inseparable from sexual fantasies, that enable readers to map sites of sexual and emotional exploration. René describes his emotional states in places ranging from "the paternal chateau, situated among forests, beside a lake, in a remote province" to landscapes of ruins in Greece and Italy. But, like Nabokov, Chateaubriand also creates a New World frame for his Old World narratives. A royalist who exiled himself to America in 1791 (and later to London), Chateaubriand created a character, René, who, to escape his sorrows, has likewise fled to North America. René tells his story to the Indian Chactas and the priest Père Souël during the time that he sojourns among the Natchez Indians. Chateaubriand layers the French landscapes of Amélie and René's childhood days, the New World "small space" in which Indians, "Negroes," and whites live together in the French colony, and the sublime, open landscape of the New World mountains, river, and sky.

Nabokov's tale of incest tracks the complexity of such a "picture," beginning at a Russianesque estate that is framed by the North American continent, including the wilds of "Canady" and "Lyaska" (*Ada,* 3, 102), and eventually extending across the Antiterran globe and into the sublimities of space where the planet Terra perhaps spins. He retains Chateaubriand's pleasure in layering maps of various scales, boundaries to the picture that can shift in the space of a sentence from a hidden perch by a river, measured in feet and inches, to the neighborhood of Ladore, measured in miles, to countries across the Antiterran globe, to the universe, and even, Nabokov hints, to an ideal realm that cannot be measured.

Wherever they travel, apart and together, Van and Ada inhabit specifically literary landscapes. Sometimes they consciously make the connection to Chateaubriand themselves, quoting and misquoting his perhaps most famous poem, "Le Montagnard émigré" (The Emigré Highlander), also known as "Romance à Hélène." Through his endnotes to *Ada,* Nabokov/"Darkbloom" takes care to mark the importance of this poem.[33] Nabokov makes the poem the anthem of Van and Ada's love and, according to a manuscript note to himself, turns it back to pleasure: "an exile's lament turns into pastoral high spirits,"[34] thereby paralleling the plot, in which frustration gives way to peaceful love. More often Van and Ada are unaware of their own parodic natures, because it is not they, but Nabokov, who has appropriated Chateaubriand's work and stamped Ada and Van as creatures made of French literature. Like Steinberg, Nabokov loves a good hall of mirrors.

In *Speak, Memory* Nabokov associates Chateaubriand's poem with his own exile from Russia: "Tamara, Russia, the wildwood grading into old gardens, my northern birches and firs . . . *et la montagne et le grand chêne* [and the mountain, and the great oak]—these are things that fate one day bundled up pell-mell and tossed into the sea, completely severing me from my boyhood" (*SM,* 249–50).[35] Indeed, "Du château que baignait la Dore" (Of the castle bathed by the Dore) was Nabokov's suggestion for the French title of his autobiography.[36]

My aim is not to catalogue every hint of Chateaubriand's works in *Ada.* But in addition to landscape, two more principal links must be mentioned. The first is characterization. For Chateaubriand, there are no characters apart from notions of travel, nation, or exile. Blanca is of Grenada, Atala is of the North American woods, Amélie is of the sad grounds of the Château de Combourg. All the brother-sister pairs are one pair written in different geographical styles. We know first the landscapes in which they dwell, and through descriptions of those places we come to know their emotions of frustrated longing. In *Ada,* Nabokov reverses the process. It's Ada and Van who first show us the Romantic fire and wind of sexual ecstasy; their feelings create the *Carte du pays de Tendre*—the map of the country of love—and the landscapes of the nation of two that they constitute.

Second, Nabokov's novel derives in important ways from Chateaubriand's fiction and poetry, but that fiction and poetry are themselves openly appropriative. Nabokov parodies Chateaubriand's own parodic method. Unattributed passages from several different authors often appear in a single paragraph of Chateaubriand's seemingly disordered prose.[37] His lushly appropriative and associative prose (recognizable to readers schooled in the discontinuities of literary works by high modernists), add to the already richly multiplying Steinbergian "degrees of reality" in *Ada.*

Steinberg and Nabokov freely and parodically create their imagined worlds by mapping them, and they provide landscapes—original and borrowed from other literary works—within which author, reader, and characters (painter, viewer, and human figures) may dwell together. Both of them, as we'll see, practice their "blue magic" (*PF,* 289) through rewriting the places that the poet and merchant Arthur Rimbaud inhabited, both at home in France and in exile in Africa. Once again, coincidence will show us the way.

13

Steinberg and Nabokov

Rimbaud's Memories

With his notions of what an artist must do and be, his ecstasies and despairs, his life in exile, and his mysterious poetry, Rimbaud offers both Steinberg and Nabokov a repertoire of visual and literary possibilities that it is the aim of this chapter to reveal. Both Nabokov and Steinberg directly engage with Arthur Rimbaud's works and with the mythic figure that he gradually became for modern artists. Their shared and widespread interest in French culture finds especially acute demonstration in *Ada,* where Nabokov quotes and hints at Rimbaud's poem "Mémoire," and in Steinberg's imagining of an advertisement for stores where Rimbaud worked in Ethiopia, along with several of Steinberg's imagined versions of Rimbaud's diaries from his African adventures. Steinberg's and Nabokov's works are often assembled, complete with gaps, from bits of their own earlier works and from the texts and images of others. Rimbaud's life events and works are both prominently and subtly displayed there.

Jean Nicolas Arthur Rimbaud left France in 1875 and, after traveling widely (Egypt, Cyprus, Java), moved in 1880 to Harar, an ancient Ethiopian city. By this time in his life he was no longer writing poetry. There, he opened a trading station that exchanged European merchandise for local resources such as coffee beans, hides, gum, ivory, and musk.[1] In 1946 Steinberg drew a mock advertisement for two African trading posts, imagining "Monsieur J. A. Rimbaud" as a bourgeois shopkeeper and gentleman-hero, complete with medals (fig. 44). Rimbaud himself acted, notoriously, as an arms merchant, and his poster version sells locally reconstituted shotguns, "Fusils à piston (reformés)." He also acted as "Fournisseur breveté de Plusieurs Cours Étrangères," perhaps best translated as "official supplier for several foreign courts." The image appeared as part of a three-page spread in the May 15, 1947, issue of *Vogue* magazine entitled "Monsieur Steinberg's French Notebook." The satire is obvious: what if Rimbaud advertised his business in a premier magazine of French and American style and consumerism? But the feature also demonstrates Steinberg's interest in the poet,

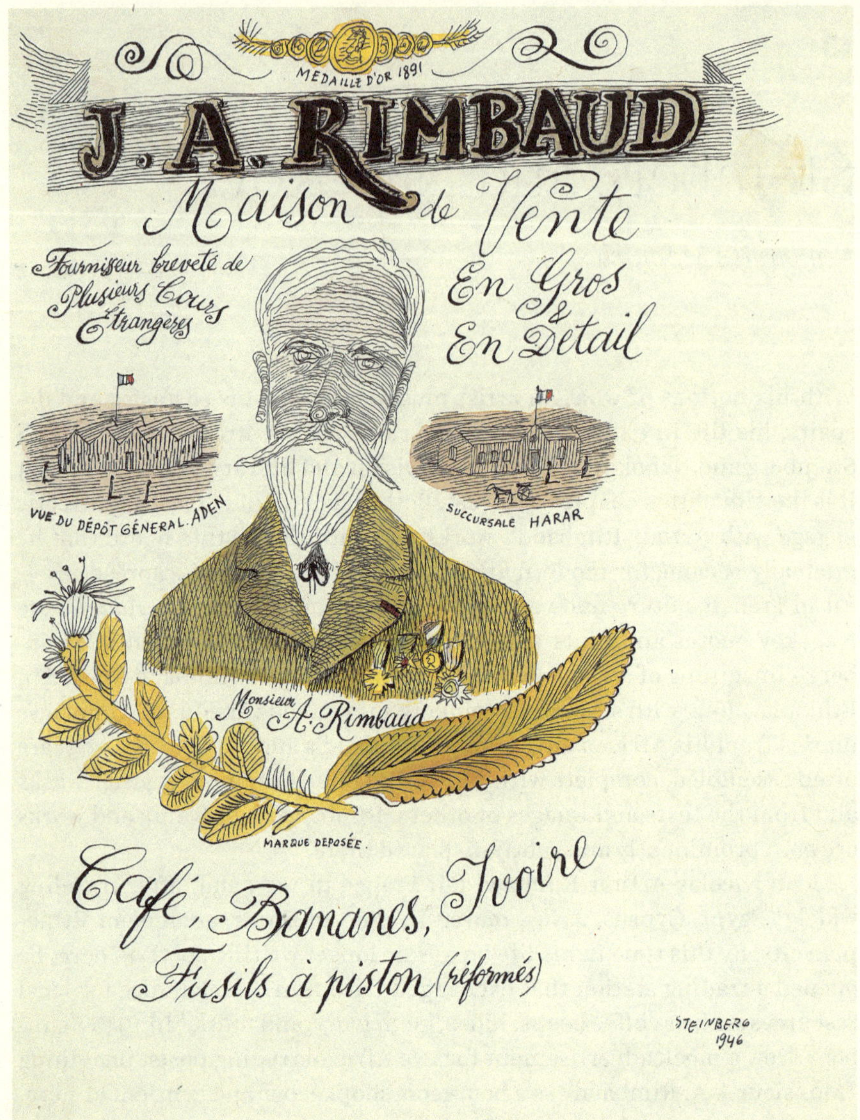

Fig. 44. *J. A. Rimbaud,* 1946. Ink and watercolor on paper, 11 7/16 × 8 11/16 in. (Private collection)

and in French culture more widely. In the same series he shows himself as "Monsieur Steinberg," clad in a nineteenth-century frock coat and drawing at an easel. He has in effect imported himself as a Frenchman for a foreign market. An image of a camel with a painted hump advertising the shop where Rimbaud worked in Aden also appears in the magazine.

Steinberg's oeuvre contains a trove of drawings about advertising, as well as actual advertisements he did for various companies, and this subject we'll take up later. For now, though, it is another subgenre of Steinberg's drawings that must occupy us: parodies of documents, often "official" documents, especially those related to travel (*SS: I,* 112–15). Steinberg's mock diaries of Rimbaud, like his other "documents," present drawings of handwriting that continually urge the viewer to acts of decipherment, only to stymie the effort. The variety and richness of the "hands" in which these documents are written provide the lure; the viewer is the prey, delighted to be caught in a world in which writing is neither wholly illegible (we do identify it as writing) nor legible. Near legibility turns out to be both a joke and a pleasure. Steinberg, the owner, as we have seen, of several books on handwriting, transmutes the alphabet into a texture of mysterious writing that short-circuits our ability to crack its code, to penetrate the alphabet-like shapes in order to get at meaning. Instead, we look *at* writing. Steinberg shows us the delight of seeing handwriting as part of the picture, inviting us to invent meanings for those marks on the page that comport with the seals, stamps, and figurative sketches that accompany them.

Steinberg read Enid Starkie's biography of Rimbaud and admired the famous portrait of him by Verlaine that appears there.[2] In 1968 he created a collage, crayon and watercolor work entitled *Luna Park,* a view of an amusement park with a "Rimbaud" booth or sideshow.[3] The visual appropriation of Rimbaud's name links his own memories of life in Eastern Europe to the legend of the French adolescent poet and rebel—both of them emigrants from their native countries. Steinberg's drawings of Rimbaud's diaries involve an even richer imaginative identification. How much of Rimbaud's poetry he read, and how closely, we don't know. What should interest us, though, are the *means* by which he figured forth his fantasies of Rimbaud.

Because the *Vogue* mock advertisement associates Rimbaud with the world of commerce and propriety, its parody deflates the myth of Rimbaud *le poète maudit.* Steinberg's Rimbaud "documents" (figs. 45, 46, 47), in contrast, seem to consist of attempts by Steinberg to inhabit the imagination of the gifted and cursed poet. In addition, when we easily "read" these drawings as documents but also find them illegible as to content, we experience a parody of nineteenth-century Mallarméan Symbolism in which the marks on the page vibrate with suggestions of mysterious truths that can never be fully deciphered.[4] These documents hint but never state, creating a fiction of Rimbaud's communication with us from an imagined beyond that is not just exotic Harar, but also a realm beyond death. It is as if Steinberg channels Rimbaud. As such, the Rimbaud documents resemble the hints that Nabokov's intensely imaginative characters such as Hazel Shade in *Pale Fire* receive in the form of fleeting visitations from supernatural

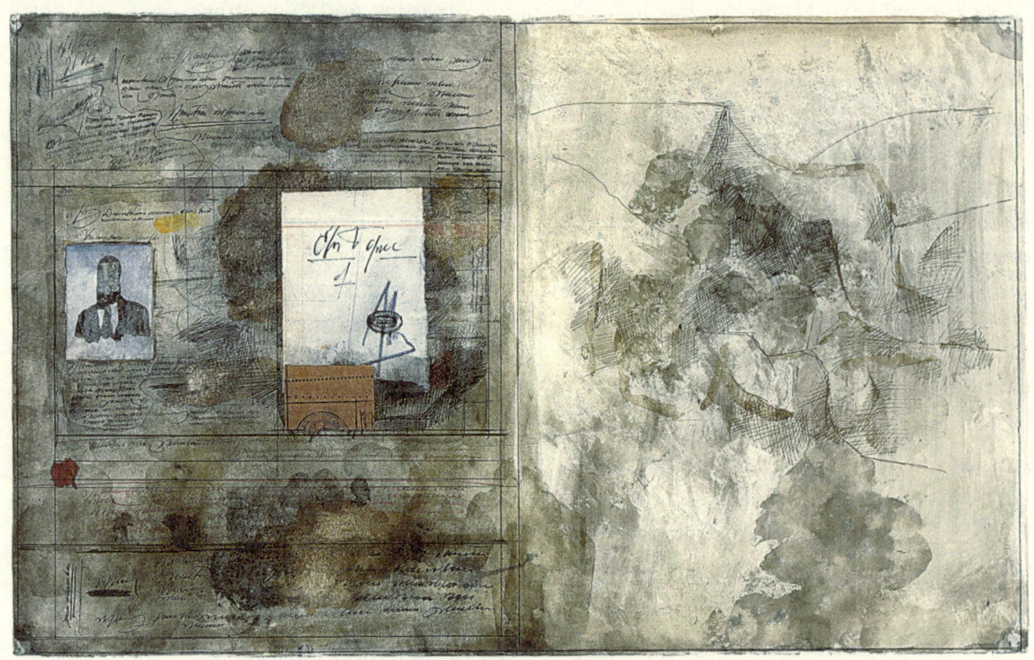

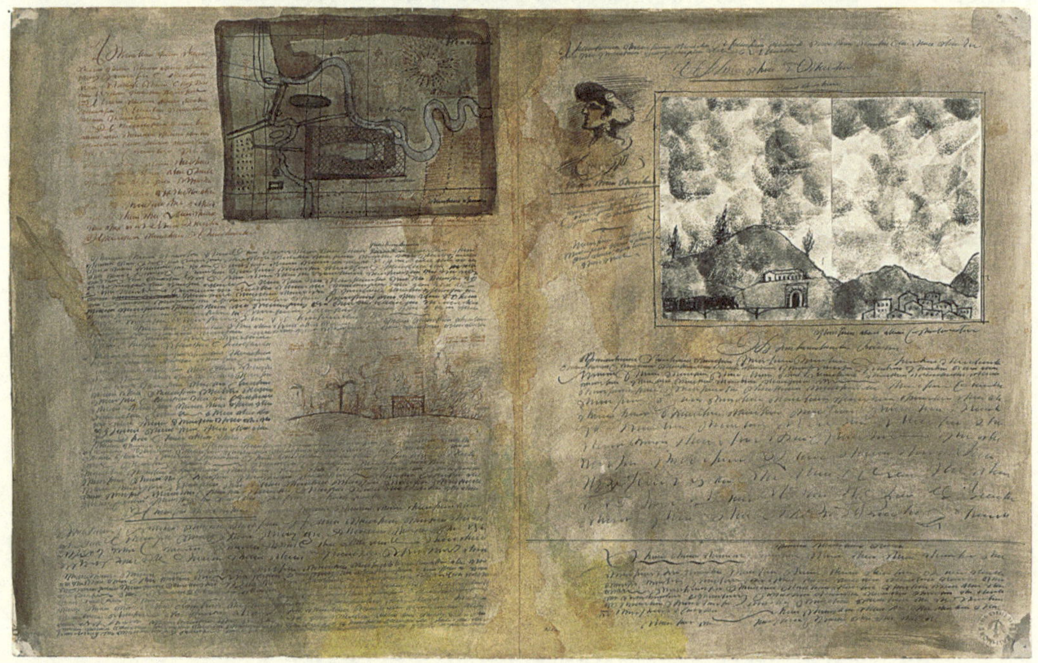

Fig. 45. *Rimbaud Document,* 1953. Ink, watercolor, rubber stamps, crayon, and marker on paper, 14½ × 22⅞ in. (Centre Pompidou, Paris; gift of The Saul Steinberg Foundation)

Fig. 46. *Harrar Diary I,* 1951. Watercolor, ink, and collage on paper, 14½ × 12 in. (Private collection)

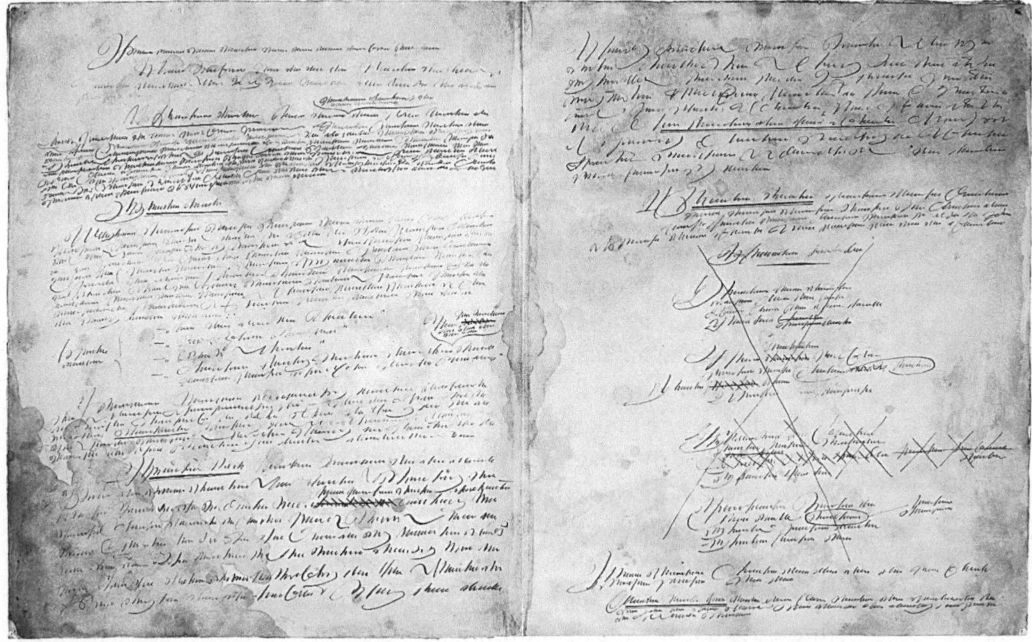

Fig. 47. *Harrar Diary II*, 1951. Ink and watercolor on paper, 14⅜ × 27 in. (Collection of Daniela Roman)

dimensions. Lucette in *Ada* also might be speaking from beyond the grave. Steinberg imagines Rimbaud as a thinking, writing, and drawing man who exists in the texts he wrote as well as in the works of art that he has inspired in other artists. That is, these diary pages are about Rimbaud's life as a textual being after his actual death. Steinberg has translated the "real" Rimbaud and the already storied Rimbaud into further texts—the "degrees of reality" multiply—just as Nabokov's narrator V. in *The Real Life of Sebastian Knight* has almost captured Sebastian Knight as a series of texts, a man made of words.

When Steinberg creates "Rimbaud's" diaries, there's never a question of plagiarism or of passing off bogus works as the real things. These drawings of documents call attention to their falsity. Yet, true to Steinberg's interest in trompe-trompe-l'oeil, they seem for a split second to be real pages written by Rimbaud (trompe-l'oeil); then we realize that they are imagined pages (trompe-trompe-l'oeil); and in the end we understand that they aren't wholly imaginary either, but are real things, real paper covered with real forms. Through making them, Steinberg realizes his own fantasies—and encourages the viewer's fantasies, too—that gather about the notion of "Arthur Rimbaud."

Steinberg directly likens himself to Rimbaud when he writes that he has "disdain for work, like Rimbaud," explaining that he doesn't like work for which one must manually prepare, like lithography or scenography: "I mean work that is not amusing, work as it is done by so many people, by employees and so on."[5] To this he contrasts the kind of work one can do with imaginative intensity, cousin to a Rimbaudian ecstasy of poetry writing.

Steinberg's documents explore Rimbaud's profound notion, expressed in his "Seer's Letters" to Paul Demeny, that "Je est un autre": "I is an other."[6] Rimbaud counsels artists to escape Romantic subjectivity by taking on a paradoxically impersonal persona and to escape a belief in the unitary self in favor of "me" as a set of possible selves. Steinberg tells an interviewer in 1973, "Art for me is a mask. . . . I'm in the tradition of the artist: to be himself, it's necessary first to be another."[7] When Steinberg imagines Rimbaud's diaries, he makes use of the notion that one can play with the idea of simultaneously imagining an other and creating oneself. The point is not that Steinberg sets out to become a Rimbaudian poet, adventurer, mystic, or rebel, but that when he imagines Rimbaud's diaries, he plays meaningfully with auras of those types, and invites viewers to detect them, too. These documents are fictions that convey truths. Nor does Steinberg limit himself to documents about Rimbaud. Creating across the years his many mock documents, Steinberg becomes a variety of "others": the powerful giver or humble recipient of traveling papers and diplomas, the American, Kafkaesque, or Gogolian bureaucrat, and any official possessing embossed letterhead, official rubber stamps, and a large swirl of a signature.

Rimbaud Document (fig. 45) presents itself as a fake document, perhaps Rimbaud's open passport with a few items scattered across it. It's a picture of an imagined document, drawn and painted to look weathered by time and circumstance. Since everything about it is contrived, we might call it a document that proves its own unreliability, a gathering of disinformation rather than information, a lesson about the contingent quality of all documents, including drawings. The actual Strathmore paper on which Steinberg has drawn it has been made to resemble a time-blotched background, and the marks he has made on it, one remove from the Strathmore, present another layer, that of inscription. As we look, layers multiply: fingerprints, a ruled black grid, lots of writing, and patches of black cross-hatching join the faux collage of a passport-like photograph, a ticket stub, and a piece of faint red- and blue-ruled paper with writing and a stamp layered on it. We're in a two-dimensional world giving rise to a trompe-l'oeil third dimension, the ersatz "collaged" photograph bits. The subjects at hand in *Rimbaud Document* seem to be travel or identification, but they are joined by the subjects of fiction, lie, surface, depth, and play.

Steinberg parodies a real travel document, but that observation is only a springboard to further meditation. "Real" travel documents are themselves artful, conventional documents of pictures and marks meant to show social facts—this is who you are, this is where you can go—by virtue of their artifice. A passport photo is, as many of us have observed, a strangely distasteful parody of "me" in my mind's eye, but it's also a parody of the portrait genre in its insistence on only one correct interpretation, that of official authorization. Steinberg and the other refugees of wartime Europe, including Nabokov, had good reason to see such documents as the infernal creations of those in power. That one sometimes needed them in order to stay alive only heightened their through-the-looking-glass quality.

The illegible handwriting reminds us that Rimbaud himself was a writer, and that learning to read his poetry requires the reader to celebrate his breach of the realist contract among writer, world, and reader. As *voyant* (seer), Rimbaud tended to see the "actual" world as a series of pictures of an illogical world with strangely metamorphosing objects, a mingling of real and imaginary things.[8] But where Rimbaud creates a proto-Surrealism, complete with fleeting strivings toward transcendence, Steinberg creates an intellectual commentary on such activity. His illegible handwriting becomes legible by our very acts of meditating on what illegibility itself might mean. We read these strokes of the pen and brush as a parody of handwriting, retaining something of the form of alphabetical marks but changing their meaning to paradox: "here is surface as depth," or "here is nonsense as sense."

Steinberg provides the scumbled face of an indeterminate man, perhaps Rimbaud, in *Rimbaud Document*—a vague mark of identity. But in *Harrar Diary I* (fig. 46) Steinberg marks the landscape with multiplying thumbprints that become a series of scudding clouds over a landscape of Harar. His mark of identity appears abstractly, in the sky and not in a face. "Harrar," we may remember, appears just south of Amagansett in Steinberg's *Autogeography* (see fig. 14; p. 60). Steinberg didn't travel there until 1963, but the mock "J. A. Rimbaud" advertisement in *Vogue* indicates that by 1947 he associated the place with the poet. In those pre-DNA-testing days, a thumbprint was regarded as the most personal mark of identity; by using it as a stamp to create clouds, Steinberg emphasizes its impersonality. I is not just Rimbaud; I is also Rimbaud's Harar skies, his very surroundings. Self and landscape actually merge. *Harrar Diary I* tells the tale of its own making and calls attention to artifice as a way to get to the truth of experience through memory.

Steinberg here "remembers" Rimbaud's days in Africa, with the damaged look of the paper suggesting the age of this "found" document, found, of course, in Steinberg's imagination. The work offers a characteristic mixture of words, figures, drawing, painting, as well as an assemblage of genres: manuscript, landscape, map, and quick sketch. Its very heterogeneity, echoed by the different colors, sizes, and styles of handwriting, also suggests the breakdown of the unitary person into a series of selves. Perhaps the writing is "Rimbaud's," but the collaged landscape and the faux-collaged map might, Steinberg suggests, have been done by "someone else," that Rimbaudian other. Just as "Nabokov," V., and Sebastian Knight are facets of one person, so too are "Steinberg," Rimbaud, and the putative mapmaker of *Harrar Diary I.* Steinberg, as we've seen, insisted that he drew drawing, and the meaning of the phrase, its insistence on the already artificial basis for what he drew, isn't difficult to grasp here. The collaged landscape indicates that it was first drawn, then attached to the drawing, and the map is made to appear as if it were glued on. The faux stamped seal at bottom right wittily authenticates an other's diary which is one's own. Or perhaps it's a drawing of a watermark, a pattern *in* paper that here sits mockingly on its surface. We can discern what might be lakes, towns, rivers, and fields on the map. The portrait might be of a woman Rimbaud lived with in Harar. Decoding is never the way, Steinberg implies. Far better to play, surmise, and add to the documents of travel rather than to extract the truth from them.

Focused as they are on the by-now familiar congeries of legibility, exile, identity, work, and travel, these Rimbaud documents can be read collectively as Steinberg's *The Real Life of Arthur Rimbaud.* As we'll see, Rimbaud's poem "Mémoire" is used in *Ada* as a code when Van and Ada wish to hide their correspondence from the eyes of others. This code exists within a coded book; that is, much of what we read in *Ada* is itself encoded, something to be deciphered, and thus we appreciate the discoveries of the many scholarly commentators who have "ma[d]e the plunge" and discovered "the limpid depths" under its often-confusing surface (*PF,* 14). Such meaning, however, remains wonderfully elusive. *Ada,* as one of Nabokov's latest and most difficult works, hovers always between legibility (I think I know what's going on) and illegibility (what could that sentence possibly mean?). Nabokov has Van entitle one of his own books (the Steinbergian) *Illegible Signatures* (*Ada,* 450). Let us move from Steinberg's legible-illegible Rimbaud to Nabokov's fascination with that artist.

In *Harrar Diary II* (fig. 47), Steinberg presents a poem, which, given its editorial deletions and emendations, seems to be by "Rimbaud" the diarist himself. Thus, Steinberg alludes to the pre-African phase of Rimbaud's life, when he was still writing poetry. Early in *Ada,* Nabokov directly refers to Arthur Rimbaud's poem "Mémoire" by title and author. He, too, reimagines the life and works of the poet. Like the landscapes of Chateaubriand's prose—those sites of forbidden love that provide shadow settings for *Ada*—the shifting landscape of "Mémoire" depicts a love relationship gone wrong. Nabokov quotes and parodies this poem, gathering up and multiplying its words and images across the span of the novel and weaving them into the places, people, and events he presents. Nabokov's appropriation of Rimbaud's poem (along of course with his many other intertextual forays) renders *Ada* a work that seems to call out for decipherment.

"Mémoire" ("Memory"), dated to the early 1870s, unfolds a human and natural drama at river's edge. At least two rivers, then, flow past Ardis—Chateaubriand's "La Dore," as we have seen, and Rimbaud's poetic river, which is simultaneously the flow of time and memory, the water of metamorphosis, and a series of beautiful, impressionistic riverine scenes that are also human emotions. Rimbaud's subtitle for *Illuminations,* the volume in which "Mémoire" first appeared, was "gravures coloriées" (colored plates), according to Rimbaud's friend and lover Paul Verlaine.[9] The poem is undeniably visual in its effects, as each of its five sections seems a tableau containing water (a golden current and clear water that eventually trickle to a standstill), the sky (source of a powerful sun and hosts of angels), and a group of people (a woman, a man, and children who are never distinct from the natural scene around them). It helps to know that Rimbaud entitled a slightly different version of the poem "Famille maudite" ("Cursed Family"). A few of the stanzas will convey the aura of the whole:

> Purer than a louis, a yellow and warm eyelid:
> the marsh marigold—your conjugal faith, O Spouse—
> At prompt noon from its dim mirror, vies
> with the dear rose Sphere in the sky grey with heat.
>
> . . . .
>
> Madame stands too straight in the field
> nearby where the filaments from the work snow down; the parasol
> in her fingers; stepping on the white flower, too proud for her;
> children reading in the flowering grass
>
> their book of red morocco. Alas, he, like
> a thousand white angels separating on the road,
> goes off beyond the mountain! She, all
> cold and dark, runs! after the departing man![10]

The poem's implied speaker sees with the intensity and acuity of an imaginative child, and what he sees is a drama of purity assaulted, of a marriage gone wrong, while children linger nearby on the riverbank. Through images of flowers Rimbaud creates at first a warmth and blossoming, then a scouring pain. What begins as a flowing river ends in final, muddy immobility.

To paraphrase the poem in this way is, however, to miss the ineffable channels by which it conducts the reader to a realm of dreamlike meaning, as if each image were a pointer to a silent world that lies beyond the changing scene and the mere words on the page. Words work as alchemical forces continuously making and unmaking, transforming a human drama into a drama of nature, a flow of energy into static, spatial moments, and meaning into feeling. And back again.

Nabokov doesn't simply quote the poem; instead he creates a repertoire of responses to it. Perhaps the most heart-rending of these is the creation of a motif issuing from two of its lines: "The green faded dresses of girls / make willows out of which hop unbridled birds." Nabokov gives Lucette a green nightgown and, later, "willow-green shorts," and he sets one scene of Van and Ada's lovemaking beside a brook where they tie Lucette to a willow so that she won't follow them. She's linked to water to the very end—she commits suicide by drowning. Although Van and Ada's feelings for each other triumph in the plot of the novel, the presence of "Mémoire," with its despairing final stanza, reminds us that such a triumph of love involves Van's brutality toward those who get in its way, including (among other acts) the blinding of one man, the crippling of another, and the buying of little girls in deluxe prostitution "clubs." In this aspect of his character he resembles Rimbaud, "le grand criminel, le grand maudit—et le suprême Savant," who believes that "the soul must be made monstrous: in the fashion of the *comprachicos* [kidnappers of children who mutilate them in order to exhibit them for profit as monsters], if you will!"[11] *Ada* is both a love story and the tale of a man who "makes himself a seer by a long, gigantic and rational derangement of all the senses. All forms of love, suffering, and madness."[12]

In addition to creating the motif of green, water, and willow, Nabokov also makes an emblem of the entire poem. Because Van and Ada know it while others around them do not, each time they refer to it they emphasize their own sense of intellectual and aesthetic superiority. Akin to the knowledge of good and evil which their tabooed lovemaking forces upon them (they taste, not an apple, but bread and honey), knowledge of "Mémoire" links them to the reading children of the poem. That it is the governess, Mlle Larivière, "the river," who requires Ada to memorize Rimbaud's poem about a river is a passing witticism. But that Dr. Larivière is an admirable professional in Flaubert's *Madame Bovary* is a detail that allows Nabokov to satirize by contrast the governess, a writer of hack fiction who channels

Guy de Maupassant, prominent on Nabokov's list of second-rate writers. Only Van and Ada may claim the preeminence of knowing the best French poetry.

Van and Ada understand anachronistically that Wallace Fowlie, an actual American translator of Rimbaud, has committed a howler in rendering the poem's "souci d'eau" as "care of the water" rather than (the correct) "marsh marigold" in the passage "Plus pure qu'un louis, jaune et chaude paupière / le souci d'eau—ta foi conjugale, ô l'Epouse." Nabokov's prose thus makes use of the poem, whenever it is mentioned, as a gloss on the subject of translation, which is itself a version of metamorphosis, the transformation of form and substance so vital to all of his works.[13] He ventriloquizes his two characters with his own characteristic disgust at those who profess to know a foreign language but don't, or those who translate too freely.

Nabokov's prose, which is characterized by seeming discontinuities from sentence to sentence, *also* portrays gradual, imperceptible change from one state to another.[14] The disorienting "Mémoire" (note, for example, its lack of the initial article *la* or *une*) also presents water, light, flowers, and human beings that seem to change, one into the other. *Ada,* too, is a work of flow. Its settings and its characters circle one into the other: we can't, for example, think of Ada and Van's first "summer of love" apart from the sun-dappled woods and lawns of Ardis, nor can we know what those landscapes look like apart from the exaltations of the randy adolescents.

Any reader of "Mémoire" learns that disorientation and orientation mutually vibrate there, that the different orders of space it presents disturb our footing. Its formal and typographical space (ten neat quatrains of classical alexandrines, its abba rhyme scheme); its visual, natural space (a landscape of a river running through fields, from day to evening); its symbolic space (the ardors and inconstancies of love, the yearning for wholeness that devolves to despair, its myth of the fall): all of these spaces overlap, interact, and flow, one to another, in our reading of the poem. This is the poem itself as a landscape, a vista viewable from multiple perspectives.

Just as Steinberg plays with legibility and illegibility in his Rimbaud documents, so disorientation tending to orientation provides the energy of *Ada.* The novel, too, calls upon the reader to travel through orders of space—fantasy planets; politically and historically bounded cities, countries, regions; the five unequal parts of a very long text that leads always to other texts; the space of Eros, as compact as the body and as diffuse as interplanetary distances. Like Rimbaud, who gestures toward—although fails to reach—a transcendent state, Nabokov, too, as we have seen, entertains the notion of a dwelling place, bordered by this life in time, that is a "more" or a "beyond."[15] Perhaps Lucette's messages from beyond the tomb point to a state beyond life as we know it, an ongoing, metamorphic transcendence.

To all these perspectives, Nabokov adds one more: that of parody. He appropriates not just Rimbaud's images of the cursed man and the intense love affair, but also his method, for Rimbaud, too, is a *bricoleur,* assembling within "Le bateau ivre" images from works by Edgar Allen Poe, Louis Figuier, and Jules Michelet.[16] Here we are back in Steinberg's and Nabokov's shared land, one that calls attention to its energetic construction from bits of other works: postcards, advertisements, handwriting manuals, roadmaps, multiple national literatures, and the works of visual artists. What Rimbaud and Chateaubriand, themselves parodists, began, Nabokov and Steinberg develop through allusion, quotation, misquotation, free translation, and more. When Ada refers to the paper on which she writes a letter to Van as a landscape—"against a background of snow, even the blue snow of this notepaper, the blunders are red and final" (*Ada,* 332)—her metaphor reveals not just her own habit of mind, but that of the text in which Nabokov has placed her. As we read this text into which other works have migrated, it reveals a significant achievement: the continuous flow within which the multiple landscapes of reality, fantasy, and printed words on actual paper merge. For example, "Mémoire" filters in for a moment as Ada writes of blunders. The finality of one of the novel's most serious blunders, Van and Ada's sexual abuse of Lucette, calls to mind the close of the poem. Rimbaud's lines "My boat still stationary, and its chain caught / In the bottom of this rimless eye of water—in what mud?"[17] suggest Van and Ada's inescapable moral disgrace. Like the brutal family drama in Rimbaud's "Mémoire," *Ada*'s unhappy family is one of pain: a mentally ill mother, a distant and corrupt father (Rimbaud's "he" who "goes off beyond the mountain"), a suicidal daughter, and a taboo love affair. Both novel and poem set these human difficulties within lovely but strangely threatening landscapes. One can move from almost any phrase in "Mémoire" to the particulars of *Ada*'s characters and plot: "the walls a maiden once defended," "children reading in the flowering grass," "body of woman," "your conjugal faith, O Spouse—," and especially (we're back now to the tragic arc of Lucette's life) "tears of childhood," "prey / to August nights which made rotting things germinate," and "She, all cold and dark, runs! after the departing man!"

As we register tacit and explicit references throughout a novel that "could serve as a one-text course in intertextuality,"[18] our imaginative pursuit of texts within texts can apply centrifugal force to our own reading self, for there are at least four of us. One of us can treasure the textual pyrotechnics from phrase to phrase, another explores the literary and visual allusions, another condemns Van and Ada, while yet another, however guiltily, savors the early passions and eventual triumph of their love. “I” is a group of “others.” Readers, not just writers, Nabokov shows us, can be Rimbaudian.

Steinberg’s and Nabokov’s interests in Rimbaud’s life and works resound with the methods, themes, leitmotifs, that have been the subject of “The Artist Abroad: Steinberg and Nabokov.” Reprised here are travel and exile; complexities of identity, parody, translation, and metamorphosis; the rhetorical exploration of orientation and disorientation; hints of Mystery; and, above all, the entwined verbal and visual life of the eye and mind. It is time to turn to Steinberg’s other avowed twentieth-century literary influence, James Joyce.

Part IV

Assembling Steinberg and Joyce

14

Steinberg and Joyce

Impermanent Sojourners

We can be certain that Steinberg read and absorbed James Joyce's *Ulysses* (1922), for, as we've seen, he twice writes to his friend Aldo Buzzi that he's rereading it (*LAB,* January 8, 1960; January 30, 1981). "Joyce is no mystery or puzzle," he declares. "All he wants from you is to be alert and intelligent."[1] Another day, another interview, finds Steinberg celebrating Joyce's mystery: like Leonardo da Vinci, "a man who amused himself greatly by being aware of his ability and mystery . . . James Joyce played with all his abilities . . . entered into the territory of madness like a tourist and later left."[2] Across some of his most fertile decades as an artist, Steinberg kept *Ulysses* in mind. Why, and to what effect? Answers will begin in biographical similarities—the subject here—but we will need to look in the following chapters at some of Steinberg's works themselves as they reveal Joycean echoes, parallels, and analogies: shared techniques and themes, shared aesthetic experiments.

Unlike Saul Steinberg and Vladimir Nabokov, whose exiles were precipitated by historical events—the rise of Bolshevism, Nazism, and Fascism—James Joyce voluntarily emigrated from Ireland, leaving Dublin for Paris on December 1, 1902, but returning to Dublin five times over the years, his last visit taking place in 1912. He tells his brother Stanislaus on February 28, 1905, "I have come to accept my present situation as a voluntary exile—is it not so? This seems to me important both because I am likely to generate out of it a sufficiently personal future . . . and also because it supplies me with the note on which I propose to bring my novel to a close."[3] Joyce speaks here of *A Portrait of the Artist as a Young Man,* but he might as well have been speaking of *Ulysses,* which famously closes with the acknowledgment "*Trieste-Zürich-Paris,* 1914–1921." In *Ulysses* itself, Leopold Bloom thinks about "departure (change of place)" as a way to escape possible "reverses of fortune," acknowledging "The necessity to counteract by impermanent sojourn the permanence of arrest." (*U,* 726).

Mapping movement mattered to Joyce as it did to the wanderers

Nabokov and Steinberg. Maps allowed Joyce to return, in mind only, to Dublin. In 1906 he asked Stanislaus to send him a map of Dublin in order to inspire his exilic imagination, to aid him in transmuting the sites of his home city into fiction.[4] The maps he consulted were for him sources of accuracy; he told his friend Frank Budgen, "I want to give a picture of Dublin so complete that if the city one day disappeared from the earth it could be reconstructed out of my book."[5] Joyce's studying of the British Ordnance Survey maps, the official maps of Ireland until after independence, which were appended to the 1904 edition of Alexander Thom's *Irish Almanac and Official Directory,* enabled much of the topographical detail of Ulysses.[6] "What considerations rendered [departure] desirable?" asks the voice in the "Ithaca" episode; the answer: "The attractive character of certain localities in Ireland and abroad, as represented in general geographical maps of polychrome design or in special ordnance survey charts by employment of scale numerals and hachures" (*U,* 726).

Perhaps Joyce's adult exile stemmed in part from the involuntary banishments of his childhood. Because of his family's straitened circumstances, he was, from an early age, transferred from one abode to another. Between 1894 and 1903, for example, the family moved nine times.[7] Like Steinberg and Nabokov, who after their initial flight to the safety of the United States continued to roam, he also became a wandering man, most often by choice—from Paris to London, Trieste, Pola, Rome, and Zurich—preferring to resolve complications in his life by moving from place to place.[8]

Resentment toward institutions such as the family, the Catholic Church, nationalist movements, and the British colonial administration sent Joyce to the Continent. Yet Ireland fascinated him from abroad and became the center of his art. Joyce the émigré, however, was of two minds, both researching the smallest details of Irish life, particularly Dublin life, and feeling bitterness toward his native land.[9] Steinberg certainly shared such divided feelings toward his homeland. Norman Manea wrote that, after looking at "a map of interwar Bucharest that Prudence [Crowther] had found in the New York Public Library,"

> [Steinberg] also spoke to me on the phone about that map, in which he had located the magical Palas district of his childhood. He seemed deeply affected by the past—by the sonority of the old street names, to which his rumbling voice and wonder-filled annotations indeed restored a degree of exoticism and fascination. His voice took on musical inflections as he kept repeating the name *Gentilă, Gentilă,* a street close to the market that we both remembered well. Then more street names: *Fetitelor* (Young Girls), *Gîndului* (Thought), *Gratioasa* (Gracious),

Zefirului (Zephyr), *Visinelor* (Sour Cherries), *Parfumului* (Perfume), *Trifoiului* (Clover). He said *Gratioasa* several times and continued with *Diminetií* (Morning), *Stùpinei* (Apiary), *Turturelelor* (Turtle Doves).[10]

Like Joyce, whose many references in *Ulysses* to Dublin's actual streets amount to a celebration of the city, Steinberg fondly remembered his childhood district. Yet, thinking of Romanian anti-Semitism, he also writes to Buzzi of "the hatred I feel for my homeland. . . . This hatred, which I encounter over and over in Céline and also in Thomas Bernhard, must be ignored, must not be nourished" (*LAB,* January 23, 1995).

Steinberg could easily have seen himself in both Joyce and Joyce's characters in *Ulysses.* Joyce makes Bloom the son of an Eastern European voyaging Jew, Rudolf Virag, whose name has been translated from Hungarian into English: "Rudolph Bloom (deceased) narrated to his son Leopold Bloom (aged 6) a retrospective arrangement of migrations and settlements in and between Dublin, London, Florence, Milan, Vienna, Budapest, Szombathely. . . . Leopold Bloom (aged 6) had accompanied these narrations by constant consultation of a geographical map of Europe (political)" (*U,* 724). Similarly, Steinberg was not only an emigrant but also the grandson of an emigrant: "My own grandfather emigrated to Romania from Tiraspol, near Odessa, in Russia" (*LAB,* March 18, 1988).

Molly Bloom, who travels for singing engagements, is herself identified with a Middle-Eastern travel motif in the novel. The "melonfields north of Jaffa" (60) that Bloom finds in a newspaper advertisement for "Agendath Netaim: planter's company" become, in the "Penelope" section, the "mellow yellow smellow melons" of her rump (*U,* 734). Marion/Molly Bloom is the daughter of a perhaps Spanish, Jewish, or Moorish mother named Lunita Laredo (according to Molly's untrustworthy father, Major Tweedy). She was reared in colonial Gibraltar and would also be something of a foreigner in Dublin.[11] Stephen Dedalus, who believes his strongest tactics to be "silence, exile, and cunning" (*P,* 269), has returned in *Ulysses* from his exile to the Continent because his mother is dying, and he feels deeply alien in Dublin. At novel's end, having rejected what Bloom has to offer, as he has rejected his teaching job, his family members, and his friends, he seems poised to leave Ireland once more.[12]

Beyond the characters who have come as immigrants to Dublin or exiled themselves from it, Joyce, beginning with *Dubliners* and continuing through *Portrait* and *Ulysses,* invites us to see his Irish city dwellers one and all as colonial subjects who are internally exiled in their own homeland. As Declan Kiberd reminds us, "Even in 1904 the Irish were still learning to master English." Because the reader's own experience of parsing the often-obscure references of the novel is akin to that of making sense of a non-native tongue, "decoding" the novel's language puts us all in the position of tentative foreigners.[13]

With emigration come foreign languages, and both Steinberg and Joyce were polyglot. Abroad, Joyce experienced multiple languages, especially in Zurich, which was a multilingual city where one heard and read High German, Swiss German, French, Italian, and even English. Indeed, "It was in Zürich that Joyce undertook 'the radical experiments in style and form that mark the intermediate chapters of *Ulysses.*'"[14] In addition, he collected words and phrases from multiple languages and displayed some of them in *Ulysses,* and many more—sixty to seventy languages—in *Finnegans Wake,* another of Joyce's works that Steinberg noted he was reading (*LAB,* January 8, 1960).[15]

Joyce's interest in Jews and Judaism (and associated exile) certainly resonated with Steinberg, an assimilated Jew who nonetheless fasted on Yom Kippur, helped to support an extended family thrust into flight by the Nazi and Communist anti-Semitisms of the twentieth century, and attended the Nuremberg trials. "Joyce was for me a . . . Jewish influence," he told two interviewers for the American Jewish Committee.[16] Steinberg regarded his own art as a version of communication among Jews: "It's all . . . the sort of intimate pleasure that usually disappears with school and military service that goes on among the Jews for the rest of their lives because of this sense of intimacy, of belonging, of using a stenography among themselves. This is, in the end, the greatest achievement of the human race, . . . the ability of understanding each other through the briefest amount of communication and so on, few words. That's my pride in drawing, that I can communicate with drawings."[17]

Is Bloom a Jew? The short, but incomplete, answer is no. Leopold Bloom's father, Rudolf Virag, is born an Orthodox Jew but converts to Protestantism; his mother, Ellen Higgins Bloom, has a Protestant mother and a Jewish father, so by Jewish law she is Gentile. Bloom, uncircumcised, has been baptized three times, as both a Protestant and a Catholic. Yet Bloom isn't wholly Gentile, either. In "Hades," he reveals himself as an outsider to Catholic ritual; he's the victim of anti-Semitism; a drawer in his desk, we're told in "Ithaca," contains the "hagadah book where a pair of horn spectacles folded still showed the prayer for seder night" (*U,* 723). Bloom even recites "fragments of verse from the ancient Hebrew" to Stephen: "*Kifeloch, harimon rakatejch m'baad l'zamatejch* (thy temple amid thy hair is as a slice of pomegranate)" (*U,* 687–88). In "Aeolus," inspired by a typesetter who must learn to read type from right to left, as in Hebrew, Bloom begins to recite the holiest prayer in Judaism, the Shema, but doesn't finish it. Only in the Nighttown of "Circe" will the Shema reach its conclusion. "Poor papa with his hagadah book, reading backwards with his finger to me. Pessach" (*U*, 122).

Bloom refers to the Exodus as "All that long business about that brought us out of the land of Egypt and into the house of bondage alleluia," characteristically flubbing the outcome of it all (*U*,122). Further, the Bloom of "Circe" "reads solemnly. . . . 'Aleph Beth Ghimel Daleth Hagadah Tephilim Kosher Yom Kippur Hanukah Roschaschana Beni Brith Bar Mitzvah Mazzoth Askenazim Meshuggah Talith,'" as if his father's Judaism metaphorically lives on in him, although reduced to a farrago (*U*, 487).[18] Steinberg, too, had noted that Romanian Jews "went through the rigmarole of praying and so on, but they didn't know [what] they were saying."[19] Bloom is also Jewish because Gentiles in Dublin consider him to be so. Steinberg reported the same phenomenon: "We were Jews not because . . . we were Jewish but because . . . of the goyim who had decided that we were Jews."[20]

While Bloom may be Gentile by birth and vague about Jewish law and ritual, Joyce takes care to associate him repeatedly with Judaism. Joyce himself was not only sympathetic to Jews he knew but also fascinated by Judaism. He can be regarded as a man living a Jewish life in the sense that he was deeply dedicated to textuality in the way that Jews of the Diaspora have clung to the Torah, Talmud, and Midrash as "portable sanctuaries."[21] Along with the Greek mythology of Odysseus, Joyce adopted the Hebrew mythology of the Jews as wandering exiles in the desert; Joyce himself wandered, as Steinberg would have known after reading a biography of Joyce, for thirty-seven—close to the biblical forty—years.

Steinberg specifically relates Joyce to his own Jewish victimhood, a state that is inseparable from his heroism: "The hero was always for me a guy dressed up on a horse fighting the dragon and so on. Now, I see Joyce and I see myself and the Jew in general as living inside the dragon and being literally inside. If necessary, you eat his liver and kill him, but that's the last resort because you have to live in the dragon, that's your house. It's warm inside, it's comfortable and you're transported, and there's a peephole you look out you see marvelous things . . . but you stay there."[22]

While it has become a critical commonplace to regard Leopold Bloom as an instance of the Wandering Jew figure, we might take Bloom-as-almost-Jew to be a type of the modern Everyman, the modern Ulysses, because, as Joyce writes, "Jewgreek is greekjew" (*U*, 504).[23] Bloom is modern in the Enlightenment sense: as Joyce tells us at length in "Ithaca," he prefers reason and science to superstition. If not wholly Jewish, Bloom is at least clearly philo-Semitic, believing that Aristotle "had been a pupil of a rabbinical philosopher," favorably comparing the Irish language to Hebrew, and likening Zionist and Irish hopes for "political autonomy or devolution" (*U,* 687–89). Like many twentieth-century assimilated Jews, Bloom admires multiple Jewish figures from history but "treat[s] with disrespect" the laws and mysteries of Judaism: "The prohibition of the use of fleshmeat and milk at one meal . . . the circumcision of male infants: the supernatural character of Judaic scripture: the ineffability of the tetragrammaron: the sanctity of the sabbath" (*U,* 724).

Steinberg, who mentions that "[s]ometimes I treat myself to a little Talmudic revery,"[24] is also an artist of seemingly endless commentary, creating thousands of textual drawings (as he thought of them) in response to his experience. Having been hounded out of Italy for his Jewishness, he meditates on anti-Semitism in a 1971 drawing of a woman with a banner that reads "No Jews" (fig. 48). As we shall see below, his many drawings treating the subject of "power and glory" can be related to Fascism, as can the lethal crocodile he frequently drew. "Essentially I am moralist, I must come from a long line of rabbis—anyway, my drawings have to be read."[25] He, like Joyce, links textuality with Judaism.

But it is perhaps the very ambiguity of Bloom's Jewishness that most reminds one of Steinberg's sense of himself as a Jew. Steinberg takes his Judaism as a fact, but his responses to it range from superficial acknowledgment to painful remembrance. He may be a "member of the tribe," but he values his isolation from it. Across the years of his correspondence with Buzzi he mentions, for example, that the Jewish New Year falls in autumn, that Cervantes "came from a family of conversos (Jews)," that he has called out to approaching Mormon missionaries, *"You haven't got a chance, we are Jewish"* (*LAB,* August 29, 1971; September 9, 1986; June 3, 1995). From 1985 onward, his comments on Judaism darken, and he writes more often of his childhood in Romania. His diploma from architecture school, the Regio Politecnico in Milan, includes the anti-Semitic phrase "of the Hebrew race," and he sent it to Primo Levi, mentioning that its elegant typeface "rendered it even more sinister" (*LAB,* August 12, 1985). He fasts on Yom Kippur, he explains, because it is "my way of showing respect for my tribe, but it's for me alone, I never go to temple, in fact I'm glad to be able to avoid it. Yet I haven't made peace with the memory of my childhood. During that period I witnessed not only national horrors but Jewish superstitions, the temple, still painful to recall. What a burden, this childhood" (*LAB,* September 29, 1990). The anti-Semites are to blame for the horrors of his early years, but Judaism also created its own troubling experiences. In the last decade of his life he's still hoping to make peace with it. He notices that, of late, "[t]here's a constant exchange of insults between women, Christians, *allegri* (gay), Arabs, Jews, *liberals* etc. There's a sense of rage in the air, as

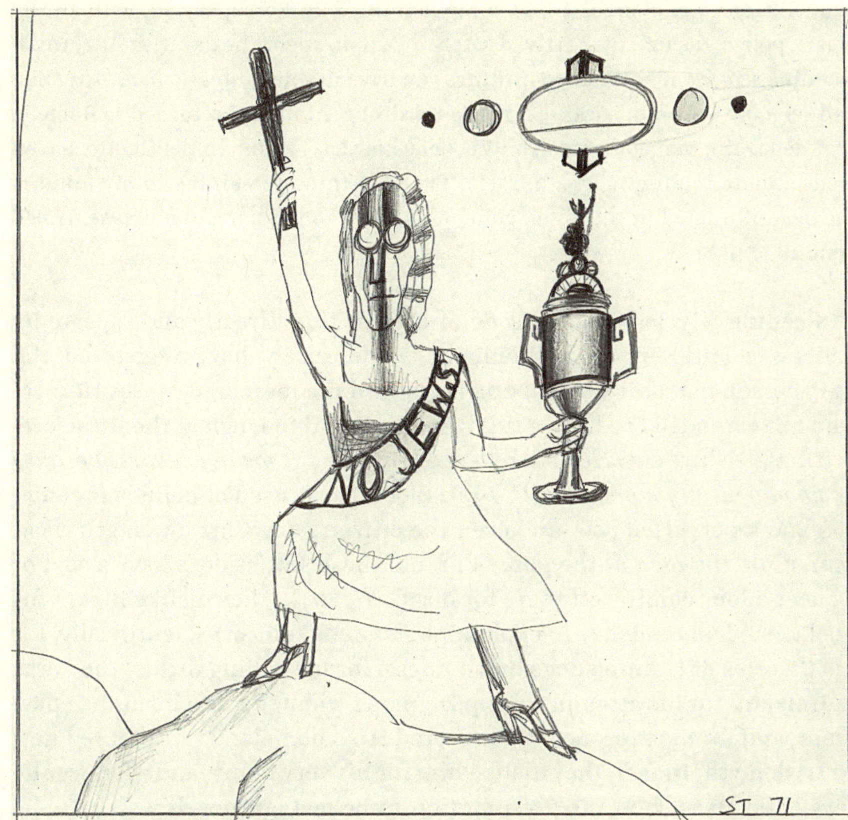

Fig. 48. Untitled, 1971. Pencil, marker, crayon, gold and silver markers, and colored pencil on paper, 10½ × 10 ⅞ in. (Beinecke Rare Book and Manuscript Library, Yale University)

there was during the days of fascism, in 36 37 38, rage that wants to prove its virility. . . . The Romanians, too, always offended, low foreheads, beady little eyes gazing out beneath their eyebrows, tiny, lipless mouths" (*LAB,* March 12, 1994).

Reading a book by Alexander Stille (son of his friend Ugo Stille) entitled *Benevolence and Betrayal: Five Italian Jewish Families under Fascism* brings back "the Italian Jews, the war, the intensity of those days, tragic but with the consoling happiness of being young" (*LAB,* June 19, 1995). A week later, he returns to the subject, the book eliciting detailed memories of his flight from Italy:

Sandro Stille's book took me back to the cruel days of 39 40 41 and, luckily, the courage shown by you, Ada, Donizetti. I don't forget. But other details [are] lost, because I didn't want to accept the reality, the betrayal—the way dearest Italy turned into Romania, hellish homeland. How lucky I was to be saved. Departing from Tortoreto on June 6, I took a night train from Rome, seated, with all the perils, police, documents. Arrived safely in Milan, spent the day with Ada, while Natalina scolded me: What poor things you have in your suitcase, *ingegnere!* She had seen my worn-out socks etc. in the wardrobe. At night I returned to Rome, a crowded train, nameless hotel, on Via dei Chiavari, I think, in the Ghetto. Saved from minute to minute by a miracle. The only thing remaining in my mind is the beautiful maid in the hotel, going up and down the narrow staircase. (*LAB,* June 26, 1995)

Reading "Cyclops," an episode of *Ulysses* that directly and repeatedly addresses anti-Semitism, Steinberg would surely have registered the first-person narrator's casual cruelty toward the merchant Moses Herzog, who has extended credit to a thief: "Jesus, I had to laugh at the little jewy getting his shirt out. *He drink me my teas. He eat me my sugars. Because he no pay me my moneys?*" (*U,* 292). Bloom is accused of being a Freemason and a perverted Jew, and even the citizen's dog Garryowen growls at him, as do the men at the pub: "I'm told those Jewies does have a sort of a queer odour coming off them for dogs" (*U,* 304). They dislike Bloom for his know-it-all tendency to explain phenomena (quasi-) scientifically, for his theories of training dogs by kindness, for his calling drink "the curse of Ireland," for his attempt to help Dignam's widow get life insurance payment, and for his presence in the sacred Irish homeland represented now by Irish myth. In fact, they dislike him for his very being, and whatever he says is taken to show his presumption in believing himself worthy to be part of the conversation:

> —What is your nation if I may ask, says the citizen.
> —Ireland, says Bloom. I was born here. Ireland.
> The citizen said nothing only cleared the spit out of his gullet and, gob, he spat a Red bank oyster out of him right in the corner. (*U,* 331)

That gob carries with it the poison of anti-Semitism, and Bloom responds bravely: "And I belong to a race too, says Bloom, that is hated and persecuted. Also now. This very moment. This very instant. . . . Robbed, says he. Plundered. Insulted. Persecuted" (*U,* 332).

Bloom unwittingly brings the episode full circle, to the tale of the robbing of Moses Herzog. Undaunted, he tells the group that "Love . . . the opposite of hatred" is what he stands for. "God save Ireland from the likes of that bloody mouseabout" is the typical response (*U,* 336). Nor is Joyce's study of anti-Semitism limited to the denizens of Kiernan's pub; the character Buck Mulligan parodies the actual Oliver St. John Gogarty, a notorious anti-Semite, and the unpleasantness of Mulligan's character stems in part from Joyce's dislike of this prejudice.[26] Bloom is his answer to it.

Beyond the "Cyclops" narrator's accounts of anti-Semitic talk, the very form of the chapter is double, divided between the "I" narrator's account of events and interpolations of lengthy passages parodic of Irish epic and newspaper items, blocks of prose that speak through Irish patriotism, romanticism, and sentimentality.[27] Joyce balances the high tide of Irish blarney that flows through the chapter with the insulting responses to Bloom. Such doubleness embodies in rhetorical form Bloom's doubleness as Jew and Gentile, and it also resonates with Steinberg's own embrace and rejection of Judaism.

Beyond its anti-Semitism, Joyce's Dublin in *Ulysses* is a place of swarming, realistic detail, and indeed Joyce, like Steinberg, greatly admired Defoe, one of the four writers Joyce claimed to have read in toto (the others are Flaubert, Ben Jonson, and Ibsen).[28] He called *Robinson Crusoe* the English *Ulysses.* But when Joyce was asked to give two lectures in Trieste at the Università Popolare he chose Blake in addition to Defoe. The miracle of the novel is its ability to give the commonplace (as in Defoe) almost sacred status (as in Blake), as if Stephen's decision in *Portrait* to make of art a faith, a transmuted Catholicism as it were, is here writ large. For *Ulysses* also asserts the mystery of Blakean symbol—enabling the reader to see the world and the cosmos not just in a single grain of sand but in a particular pub, or in the badinage of this person and that, or in the many grains of sand and points of light in scenes on the strand.

Ulysses is a novel of travel and movement, much as Steinberg's life and works. Its title alone makes the case, and even those who have not read it tend to know that it features the movements of Stephen Dedalus, Leopold Bloom, and a large cast of minor characters across Dublin and environs on June 16, 1904. The shape of the novel in three parts is clearly Homeric: Telemachus/Stephen's adventures; the meeting of Stephen and Ulysses/Bloom; and the journey of both to Bloom's home, the Homeric *nostos.* But this movement goes beyond the Homeric. By "Ithaca," the wanderers are moving through boundless space and time, "wanderers like the stars at which they gaze."[29] Each of its eighteen chapters or episodes features its own type of movement; and the changes in style across the novel's chapters present a movement of their own.[30]

Thinking about Joyce in relation to Steinberg raises an important difficulty: unlike Nabokov, Joyce himself was far more interested in music than he was in visual art. It is a truism of *Ulysses* criticism, perhaps inspired by Frank Budgen's book *James Joyce and the Making of Ulysses,* that Joyce knew little about visual art. Budgen was a painter, and he reports Joyce's comment that "I don't understand and can't talk about painting."[31] Joyce tells Stanislaus that he knows nothing of painting.[32]

"I have seen him take pictures, when their size allowed him to do so, and look at them close up near a window like a myope reading small print," Budgen reports, and this view, seemingly consistent with the eye trouble that Joyce suffered from, has led some to rule out any important presence of visual art in *Ulysses.*[33] That would be a mistake. Certainly, his choice of details did not often extend to word paintings of streets or buildings and their interiors: naming places was more important to Joyce in *Ulysses* than closely describing them.[34] The novel can more easily be read as an itinerary, even a quasi-cartographic document.[35] As we'll see when we examine the "Wandering Rocks" episode of the novel, Joyce "invokes the precision of cartography to draw attention to its absences, opacities, and representational failures."[36]

Ulysses nonetheless presents visuality in multiple forms, often in relation to textuality. Stephen combines the word with the visible in his early, overarching statement, "Ineluctable modality of the visible: at least that if no more, though through my eyes. Signatures of all things I am here to read, seaspawn and seawrack, the nearing tide, that rusty boot" (*U,* 37). He simply cannot escape from reading these fusions of form and matter. What Stephen, and therefore we, read is the signature of the very wheel of existence in its life-giving (seaspawn) and life-destroying (seawrack) powers. The music of the sentence is undeniable, but the repetition of "sea" catches the eye as well. Human imagination has played into the very physical images of the material world that Stephen emphasizes.

Joyce himself struggles to express this mingling of word and image when he discusses *The Book of Kells:* "In all the places I have been to, Rome, Zurich, Trieste, I have taken it about with me, and have pored over its workmanship for hours. It is the most purely Irish thing we have, and some of the big initial letters which swing right across a page have the essential quality of a chapter of *Ulysses.* Indeed, you can compare much of my work to the intricate illuminations. I would like it to be possible to pick up any page of my book and know at once what book it is."[37] As Joyce works over his manuscripts, adding words and phrases, he's creating—illuminating—a work that has spatial, as much as linear, narrative, form. The process of interlinking episodes continued into 1922, through many sets of proofs.[38] Nabokov would say that we must reread *Ulysses* in order to read it fully, to catch these details and echoes of what came before. The book has a simple sequence of events, but it needs a chance to spread out before our eyes in a vast moment of figuration and fragmentation which we can only ever begin to mend when we look at the text across space as well as time.[39]

Characterization can have a visual aspect in the novel as well. We come to know its minor characters primarily by what they say; the central actions of the novel are drinking, talking, and walking, with stops for more talking. Some figures take on the quality of quickly sketched caricatures, such as the Citizen in the "Cyclops" episode or that foppish grabber of the main chance, Blazes Boylan.[40] This is a novel of drawing—quick sketches—rather than painting, of the snapshot rather than the slow study. Joyce speaks of "the bounding line" in his lecture on Blake, "on the importance of the pure, clean line that evokes and creates the figure on the background of the uncreated void."[41] Joyce alludes here to a passage from Blake's "Descriptive Catalogue": "How do we distinguish one face or countenance from another, but by the bounding line and its infinite inflexions and movement? . . . What is it that distinguishes honesty from knavery, but the hard and wirey [*sic*] line of rectitude and certainty . . . in the actions and intentions? Leave out this line and you leave out life itself; all is chaos again."[42] Joyce treasures the words of the engraver; with his pen he hopes first to delineate character with a few strokes, as a verbal draftsman.

In *Portrait,* Stephen Dedalus adopts an Aristotelian aesthetic notion of the necessary *integritas* of the work of art: "The first phase of apprehension is a bounding line drawn about the object to be apprehended." He adds that "the esthetic image is first luminously apprehended as selfbounded and selfcontained upon the immeasurable background of space or time which is not it. You apprehend it as one thing. . . . That is *integritas.*" Such an apprehension is followed, according to Stephen's account of Aristotle, by the viewer's analysis of parts: "You apprehend it as complex, multiple, divisible. . . . That is *consonantia.*" "*Claritas,*" the feeling of "that supreme quality of beauty" experienced in "the luminous silent stasis of esthetic pleasure," may follow (*P,* 229–31). It is as if Joyce, in *Ulysses,* has created some of his minor characters so that readers may apprehend them in the quick visuality of *integritas,* seeing their "bounding lines."

Buck Mulligan, for example, appears visually in the opening paragraphs of the novel. He is himself "stately," or walks in a stately manner—that stateliness shown visually with a giant S—followed by a large-font "plump." Here is a sketch of a young man "bearing a bowl of lather on which a mirror and a razor lay crossed" and wearing "a yellow dressinggown, ungirdled" which is "sustained gently behind him by the mild morning air." He has "even white teeth glistening here and there with gold points." Bowing and making "rapid crosses in the air, gurgling in his throat and shaking his head," he begins to conducts a mock mass (*U,* 2–3). This visual portrait remains throughout the novel the *integritas* of Mulligan; he will never again be so visually presented. We learn more about him later primarily through his talk, that is, audibly, both further in "Telemachus" and later in the novel. Thus Joyce delivers to us his character's *consonantia.* Whether the aesthetic image of Buck Mulligan reaches a state of *claritas* is a matter for each reader to decide. Aristotelian aesthetics are, as it were, acted out by Joyce's methods of characterization, and visual *integritas* is the beginning of it all.

In contrast, Stephen in "Telemachus" appears before us from the first audibly, both in what he says and what we "overhear" him "saying" in his thoughts. Rather than beginning with *integritas,* Joyce begins his portrayal of Stephen with a bitter conversation he has with Mulligan, but that gives way to a collection of thought fragments that contain multiple, brief sketches, and paintings of one subject after another. Stephen is composed of a series of complexities marked by gaps rather than wholeness.

He thinks, however, in scenes and images, and these are often visual in nature. Joyce's first significant foray into Stephen's consciousness presents a grisly scene in which all the senses are appealed to, but sight and smell take precedence:

> Silently, in a dream she [his mother] had come to him after her death, her wasted body within its loose brown grave-clothes giving off an odour of wax and rosewood, her breath, that had bent upon him, mute, reproachful, a faint odour of wetted ashes. Across the threadbare cuffedge he saw the sea hailed as a great sweet mother by the wellfed voice beside him. The ring of bay and skyline held a dull green mass of liquid. A Bowl of white china had stood beside her deathbed holding the green sluggish bile which she had torn up from her rotting liver by fits of loud groaning vomiting. (*U,* 5)

Stephen here changes visual focus, from his memory of a dream—to his "cuffedge," to the sea and skyline—and back to a vivid white-and-green bowl from his mother's sickroom. Throughout "Telemachus," images from his mother's life and final illness haunt him, for example, "Her shapely fingernails reddened by the blood of squashed lice from the children's shirts" (*U,* 10). He sees himself in a mirror "cleft by a crooked crack, hair on end. As he and others see me. Who chose this face for me. This dogsbody to rid of vermin? It asks me too" (*U,* 6).

He not only sees but also thinks about seeing. Mulligan mentions Clive Kempthorpe, evidently a student in England, and Stephen immediately "sees" a scene in his mind's eye: "Young shouts of moneyed voices in Clive

Kempthorpe's rooms. Palefaces: they hold their ribs with laughter, one clasping another, O, I shall expire! Break the news to her gently, Aubrey! I shall die! With slit ribbons of his shirt whipping the air he hops and hobbles round the table, with trousers down at heels, chased by Ades of Magdalen with the tailor's shears. A scared calf's face gilded with marmalade. I don't want to be debagged! Don't you play the giddy ox with me!" (*U,* 7). The rhetoric of "Telemachus," then, contrasts the narrator's integrated visual description of Mulligan with Stephen's cyclical visions of his mother, which are accessible to him through dream, memory, and his own acute sense of color and shape, not to mention texture, smell, and taste. If Mulligan is a sketch, Stephen is a word painting, even though Joyce does not directly describe him. We come to know him through the richness of his visual imagination.

It's important to note, here, that in each episode of *Ulysses* Joyce plays with the visual imagination in different ways. "Telemachus" does not supply a template for visuality and its relation to characterization in *Ulysses,* but only an opening instance. This is a novel filled with spoken language, musical lyrics, and the nonlinguistic sounds that people, animals, and things make. Joyce's love of music is felt here. Yet visual it is.

We register the actual appearance of words on the page as a source of visuality. The style of each chapter issues in a particular look on the page, most obviously the drama script of "Circe," or the headlines and captions of "Aeolus," but also the "grey unbroken paragraphs that numb the mind by tiring the eye" of "Eumaeus,"[43] or the question-and-answer format of "Ithaca" with blank spaces between each pair. This is a book whose look changes in the increments of episodes, and sometimes within them. Conversations elicit em dash after em dash rather than quotation marks; when a character retreats to the language within his own consciousness, those dashes disappear.

Steinberg, then, would have found in *Ulysses* connections to his own life of exile, travel, and troubled Jewishness. The visual qualities of the novel, arising from its signifying language as well as inhering in its very black-and-white textuality, might well have caught his attention. But Joyce's fascination with multiple styles, and those styles' participation in meaning, is a topic we must explore further.

15

Steinberg and Joyce

Playing with Styles

Once again: "James Joyce played with all his abilities," Steinberg said.[1] One ability shared by the two men was a fluency in creating multiple styles, that very multiplicity becoming a prime subject of their works, not merely a technical facility. We will come to see, too, that the multiplying of styles represents a freeing movement that speaks to Joyce's and Steinberg's shared interest in depicting the contradictions and ambivalences that characterize the union—usually marriage—of two people. For both, too, playing with popular culture and the notion of a middle-class "everyman" represented an escape from the all-too-static standards of high culture.

Most serious studies of *Ulysses* address the fact that Joyce wrote it, chapter by chapter, in differing styles. As he wrote to Harriet Shaw Weaver on June 24, 1921, "The task I set myself technically [is] writing a book from eighteen different points of view and in as many styles, all apparently unknown or undiscovered by my fellow tradesmen."[2] Even without knowledge of the "Linati Scheme," which Joyce produced to help his friend Carl Linati comprehend the novel's structure, we can see that the novel begins in a largely traditional way with a comfortable third-person narration.[3] Its first nine chapters for the most part seem to imitate straightforwardly the thoughts and actions of characters in specific settings, albeit in slightly differing ways. The passages of stream of consciousness create no problems for most readers.

However, the strange appearance of the headlines or picture captions that appear in the seventh chapter, "Aeolus," alerts us to the difficulties that will characterize the second half of the novel.[4] With the tenth chapter, the trustworthy narrative voice seems to disappear, to be replaced, chapter by chapter, with a series of differing stylistic and rhetorical experiments. Joyce's rhetorical masks sever the "umbilical cord between writer and writing." Style is no longer the expressive signature of the writer, "James Joyce," but instead becomes a vast field of citation and of "revelation and disguise" by which the text seems to be "as it were cut off from any single creating consciousness."[5] Simply put, the notion of an author's "personal" style no longer applies. Nor are these styles for styles' sake—Joyce manages, throughout his experiments, to move forward the action of the plot and the development of characters in a comprehensible way.

Saul Steinberg, too, creates art in a variety of styles. He deliberately schools himself in and repeats art historical styles such as Cubism in his work (see, e.g., fig. 9; p. 34). Like Joyce in "Oxen of the Sun," he blatantly raids the past and celebrates the contemporary in the very act of creating modernist art. But multiple styles displayed within a single image fascinate him. They render style itself as important a subject of the work as the figures he inscribes, just as Joyce chooses to emphasize the drama of his writing in various styles alongside, and equal in importance to, plot, characterization, and setting.

Certainly, Steinberg's lithograph *Blue Pagoda* (fig. 49) asks us to contemplate multiple styles. Steinberg connects two blue pagodas, like those on blue-and-white porcelain, to a cartoon ladder that leads to a cartoon's speech balloon. There, a faux calligraphy of freely multiplying curves suggests the style of speech and therefore the style of being of the absent speaker. The rectangular Bauhaus architecture drawn within the balloon seems to be a subject of the speech, and it rhymes with the pagodas in their vertically layered construction. Both pagoda scene and speech balloon con-

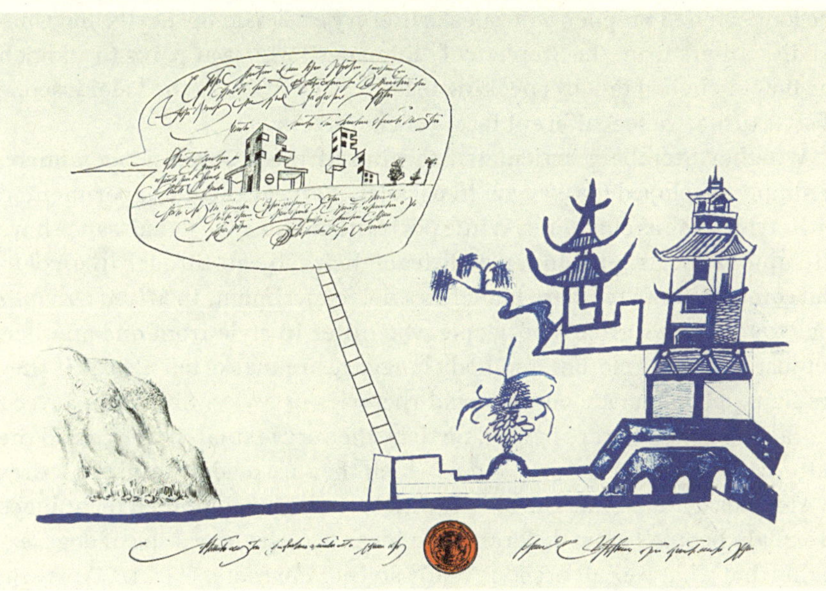

Fig. 49. *Blue Pagoda,* c. 1966. Lithograph in colors on paper, 22 × 30 in. (The Saul Steinberg Foundation, New York; photograph by Kristine Larsen)

tain plants that grow in differing styles. At the far left, rocks or mountains (we can't know the scale to which they're drawn) appear in the careful shadings of realistic drawing. A red or bronze-colored seal and more nonsense writing marks the whole as official, but the very idea of a whole has been sent up. The image speaks to us of the contingency and relativity of styles; it is about both the interruptions of viewing, the vagaries of landscape, and the reproduction of what is already artful.

Steinberg likes to think on paper about styles of people as indications of human character. In this he is very much like Joyce, for one of the effects of Joyce's different styles and rhetorics in *Ulysses* is the sketching of character. While it is true that Joyce's shifting styles and rhetorics tend to move readers' attention away from characterization to language and modes of narration themselves, it is also true that in the later chapters such "rhetorical performances" have been anticipated by characters earlier in the novel.[6] Thus, for example, Bloom's interest in popular science early on burgeons into the mechanical, scientistic rhetoric of "Ithaca." Stephen's interest in the "ineluctable modality of the visible. . . . signatures of all things I am here to read, thought through my eyes" (*U,* 37) develops into the dry precisions of "Wandering Rocks" and the visible metaphors of "Circe."

In *Ulysses,* style gives rise to character as well as imitating it. While we may generalize from the novel as a whole the personality of Bloom or Stephen, the experience of reading across multiple styles that call attention to themselves gives us complex versions of Bloom and Stephen. For example, the long-winded Stephen who speaks literary criticism in "Scylla and Charybdis" differs from the Stephen of "Eumaeus," who is at pains to staunch the flow of clichéd talk by speaking briefly and wittily. As the kaleidoscope of style turns, we see different facets of characters.

Whether Steinberg articulated to himself these Joycean phenomena or simply developed his own art in parallel, it's clear that he experimented with style per se as character. While portraitists since the Renaissance have attempted to portray the inner qualities of their subjects through line, color, and composition, Steinberg launches a new experiment. In *Mixed Group II* (fig. 50) he draws groups of people who differ in style from one another, not just as if their clothes and body language are masks but also as if they are living people made out of visual rhetorics or styles. Similarly, Joyce's characters in *Ulysses* are figured forth by the very textual rhetorics and the patterns of words on the page out of which they are made. Steinberg writes to Aldo Buzzi, "I too like the old drawings in which I combined techniques to explain people's great differences in ideas (Colette, speaking of dogs, explains that what we call breed is really style or character)" (*LAB,* April 29, 1964). In its pluralism of styles of people, we might well read *Mixed Group*

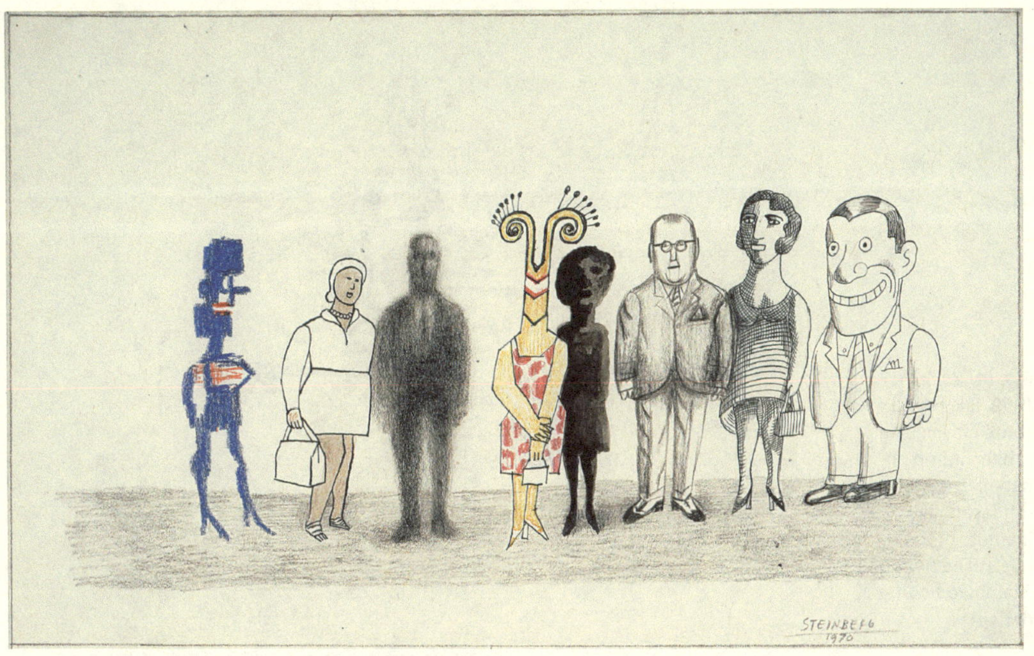

Fig. 50. *Mixed Group II*, 1970. Colored pencil, ink and graphite on paper, 14½ × 23⅛ in. (Private collection)

II as a parody of Picasso's *Demoiselles d'Avignon,* but it's equally reminiscent of the divergent qualities of people as they appear, made out of words, across the episodes of *Ulysses.*

From early on, Steinberg visually characterizes people's speech in both style and content, as in *Speech* (fig. 51). The (now unfunny) joke, of course, is that men speak logically, women emotionally, but the significance of the image surpasses tired stereotype. It's a step on the way to imagining the personality itself as a wholly received style.

Steinberg also experiments, in an untitled work (fig. 52), with people as various figures—circles, spirals, labyrinths, squares. Steinberg explains this image:

> A conversation between people is represented here in a stenographic way. A very hard outside with a soft inside sits on a straight-backed chair talking to a fuzzy spiral. On the sofa there is a boring labyrinth speaking to a hysterical line, a giggling, jittery bit of calligraphy. Then there is a dialogue between concentric circles and a spiral. The concentric circles represent the frozen, prudent people, the porcupine and turtle people. The spiral can look like a series of concentric circles. Therefore, these two people could seem similar in aspect. But actually the essence of spirals is different from the essence of concentric circles.[7]

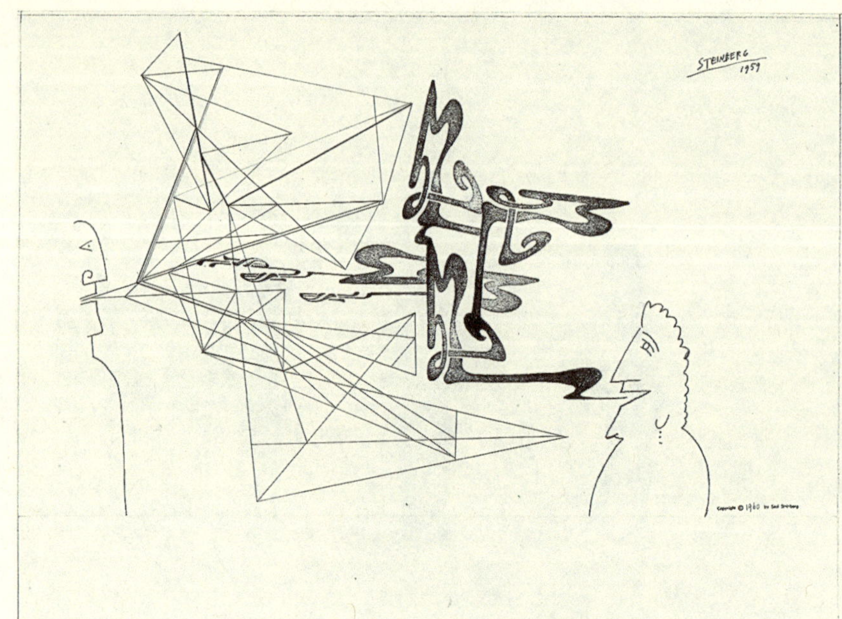

Fig. 51. *Speech,* 1959. Ink, pencil, conté crayon, and rubber stamp on paper, 15 × 20 in. (Minneapolis Institute of Art; gift of The Saul Steinberg Foundation)

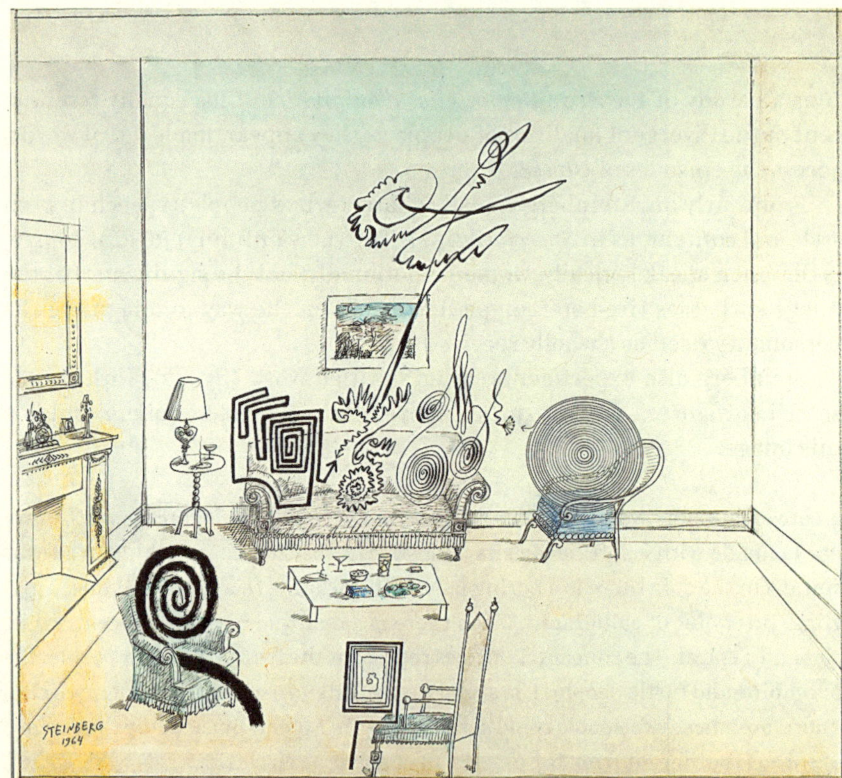

Fig. 52. Untitled, 1964. Ink, pencil, and watercolor on paper, 22 x 23 in. Originally published in the *New Yorker,* August 11, 1962. (National Gallery of Art, Washington DC; gift of The Saul Steinberg Foundation))

Similarly, Steinberg has imagined another cocktail party (fig. 53) in which, among others, a pointillist woman speaks to a cartoon man, a child's drawing of a woman stands between a soigné man and a Surrealist-headed fop in yellow. Two figures fade almost into invisibility, and only the clown, at lower right, casts a shadow. Joyce shows Dubliners at the pub; Steinberg introduces sophisticates in a living room and invites us to imagine their conversations, cigarettes, and cocktails.

It is in his later productions of people in various styles, when he lines them up in galleries or arrays them in orderly collages, that Steinberg's works take on a rectilinear quality or readability, where the page itself, not a living room or a conversation, accounts for their presence (fig. 54). Media differ as well as techniques. Like Joyce, Steinberg has lined up his experiments, invited us to read them from left to right, and then to reread them in any order that occurs to us. In a meditation on the theme of power (fig. 55), Steinberg offers four lineups of differing orders of creatures—animal-men, skeletons, military men in the uniforms of different countries. At the same time, he draws them in differing techniques—camouflage/abstract, Braque-Cubist, realist, cartoonish.

Joyce—and also Steinberg, as we'll see—thinks frequently about couples. Both men imagine intimate relationships as a power struggle, and one that limits mobility. The speaker of "Ithaca" asks, "Which domestic problem as much as, if not more than, any other frequently engaged his mind?" And

Fig. 53. *Techniques at a Party I,* 1953. Ink, watercolor, pencil, and crayon on paper, 14½ x 23 in. (Morgan Library & Museum; gift of The Saul Steinberg Foundation; photograph by Teresa Christiansen)

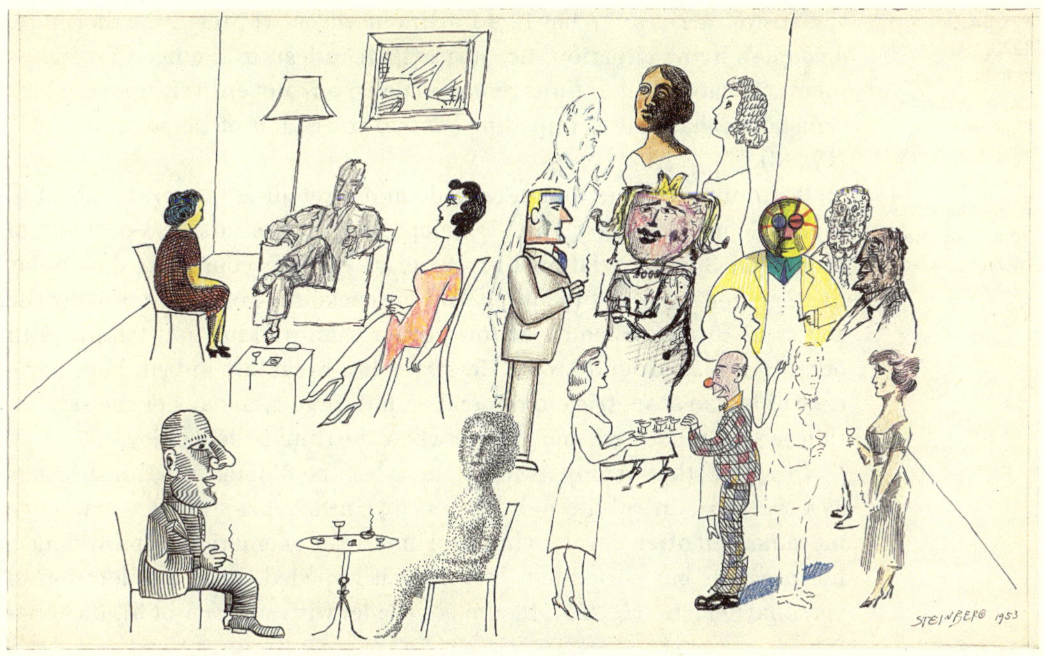

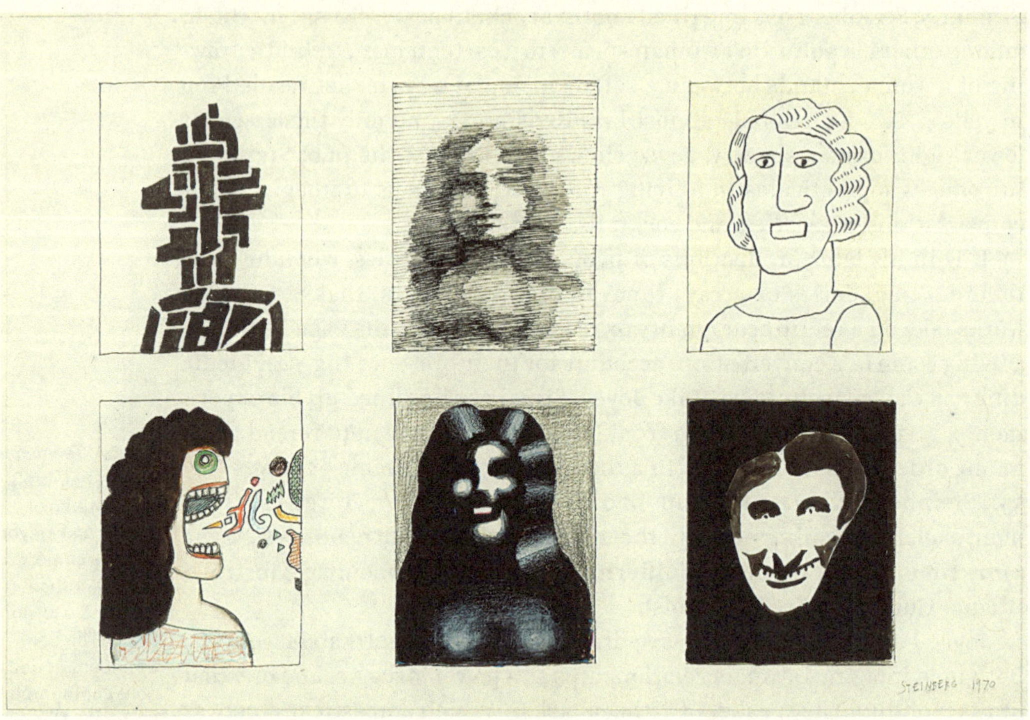

Fig. 54. Untitled, 1970. Ink, crayon, colored pencil, pencil, and collage on paper, 16 × 23 in. (The Saul Steinberg Foundation, New York; photograph by Jenny Gorman)

the answer arrives: "What to do with our wives" (*U,* 685). Furthermore, a couple's living situation, not just exile, can lead to the need for movement: "What considerations rendered departure not entirely undesirable? Constant cohabitation impeding mutual toleration of personal defects" (*U,* 726).

Beginning with its fourth episode and stretching across the novel to Molly Bloom's monologue in "Penelope," Joyce reminds us repeatedly of Molly and Bloom's relationship. We learn of their courtship, day-to-day life together, marital difficulties, and the cuckolding of Bloom. During the course of the day, Bloom's actions, other than walking and talking with others, revolve around Molly. He serves her breakfast in bed, buys her a cake of lemon soap, tries to remember, but forgets, to buy her the skin lotion she has requested, and obtains a book he thinks she'll enjoy.

In a novel that flaunts its multiple styles, the Blooms' relationship acts as a narrative thread through Joyce's labyrinth. Yet as a guide to narrative movement, it often devolves into vicious circles of emotional ambivalence, not progress but permanent "arrest," an impeded "mutual toleration of personal defects" (*U,* 726). Bloom is a reader with a library of his own that

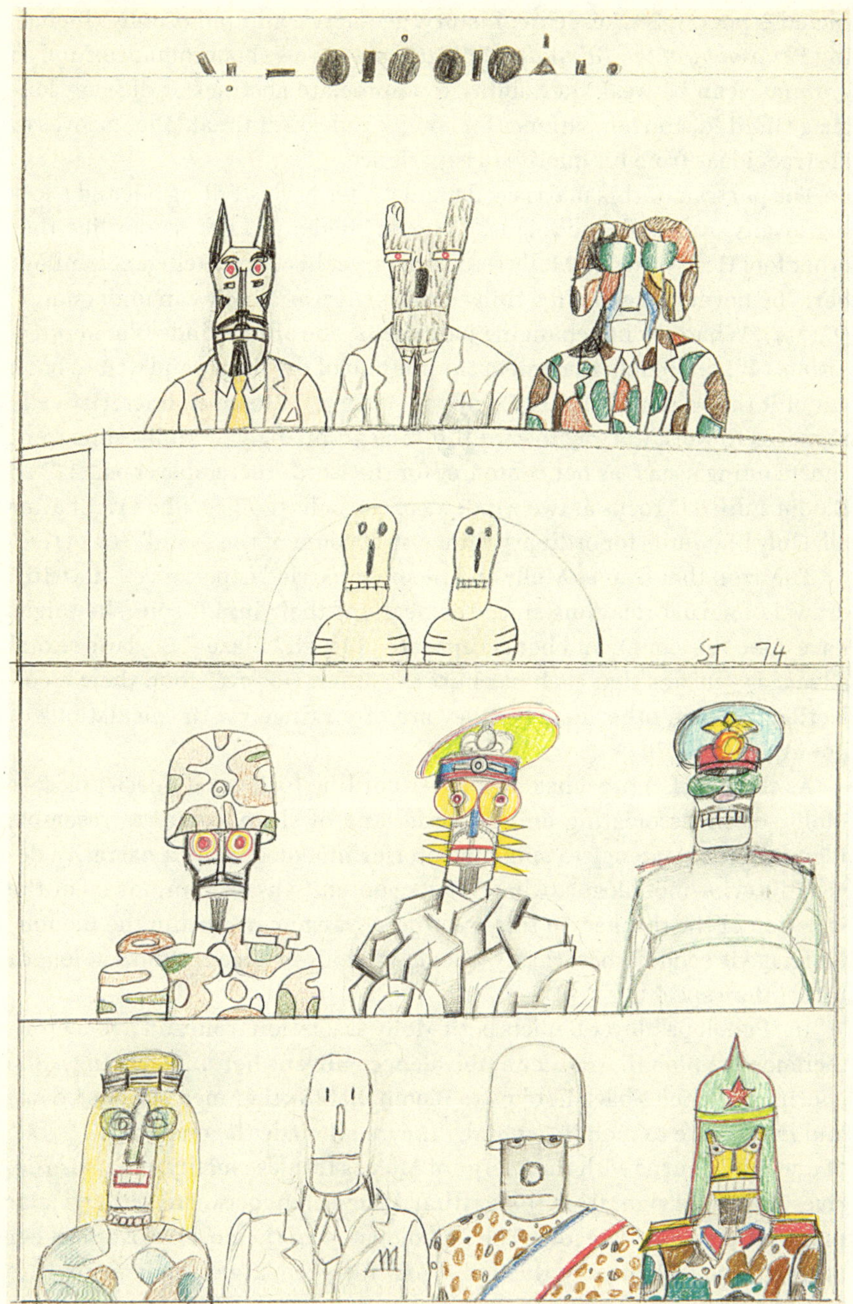

Fig. 55. Untitled, 1974. Pencil and colored pencil, with erasures, on two sheets of paper, 21⅜ × 13⅝ in. (Centre Pompidou, Paris; gift of The Saul Steinberg Foundation; photograph by Kristine Larsen)

includes poetry, Shakespeare, history, geometry, and philosophy (including *Philosophy of the Talmud*); Molly prefers novels about romance. Molly's grammar can be weak, her ability to appreciate abstract or difficult language limited, and her patience for complex ideas minimal.[8] Bloom loves to abstract ideas from his quotidian experience.

The portrait of this marriage demonstrates both a falling out and a loving loyalty. Ambivalence reigns. "[Bloom] had a few brains not like that other fool Henry Doyle," Molly remembers, yet his very intelligence annoys her: "he never can explain a thing simply the way a body can understand" (*U*, 754). Whatever her changing judgments, she always finds Bloom *interesting:* "If I only could remember the one half of the things and write a book out of it the works of Master Poldy yes" (*U*, 754). Bloom characteristically manages to work his way toward thinking admiringly of Molly's apparent shortcomings, such as her contempt for the word "metempsychosis": "Mr. Bloom smiled O rocks at two windows of the ballast office. She's right after all. Only big words for ordinary things on account of the sound" (*U*, 154).

The agon that frames Molly and Bloom's married experience—his withdrawal of sexual relations since the death of their infant son (she might have done the same), and her acceptance of Hugh "Blazes" Boylan's sexual advances—means that each has hurt the other. However fond their recollections of each other may be, they are often tinged with calculations of power.

As the novel approaches its end—according to Joyce it doesn't close—Molly, freely associating on the borderland of sleep, comes to resemble Bloom in his tendency to spin out interior monologue. As a narrative device, interior monologue, whatever its content, always reminds us of the isolation of the thinker. In this way, the estrangement within the Blooms' marriage is echoed rhetorically whenever Molly or Bloom thinks at length rather than speaking.

In "Penelope" Joyce depicts both Molly's isolation from and her deep attachment to Bloom. Another ambivalence enlivens her final musings. She continually circles back not just to Bloom, but to other men she has known and from there to men in general: "theyre all made the one way" (*U*, 751). "Penelope" churns with the energy of Molly's frank sexuality, but it also derives its playful vigor from the continual movement between her particular man and men as a category. The monologue, and the novel, close with her affirmation of Bloom, yet the final "Yes" feels too large simply to apply to just one man.

"Frailty, thy name is marriage" can be spoken by the stage character Bloom in the nighttime unconscious of "Circe" (*U*, 546). Coupledom constitutes an ongoing subject of Steinberg's drawings as well. It's an arrangement that often involves for Steinberg, as it has for Joyce, a woman and a man in simultaneous states of harmony and conflict. Viewed collectively, his images of couples amount to an extended visual essay on the relations between the sexes. Or, since he liked to think of himself as a novelist, we can read these couples as characters meriting the viewer-reader's special attention. He depicts people in groups or crowds, as members of a family, and as individuals searching for meaning, but always he returns to the twosome.

The intricacies of extended plot need not appear for us to understand that Steinberg's subject, in drawing couples, is often the issue of marital power and the unhappiness it brings. A dour (and drolly funny) pair (fig. 56), exhibited profile to profile, seems resolutely civilized and silent. A diminished version of each one lives half-tucked away in the area near the heart where feeling should be. Steinberg seems to tell a story here, but what is it? Each person may feel that only a minuscule version of him/her self can be admitted by the other, and, what's more, that such a version is trapped by the social mask of proper clothing. Then again, perhaps these are images of the possibility of communication; after all, small or not, each figure has crossed the gap of space and silence. When the power struggle between a couple is made clear, however, it's often the woman who wins (fig. 57).

Joycean nuance and ambivalence tend to accompany Steinberg's

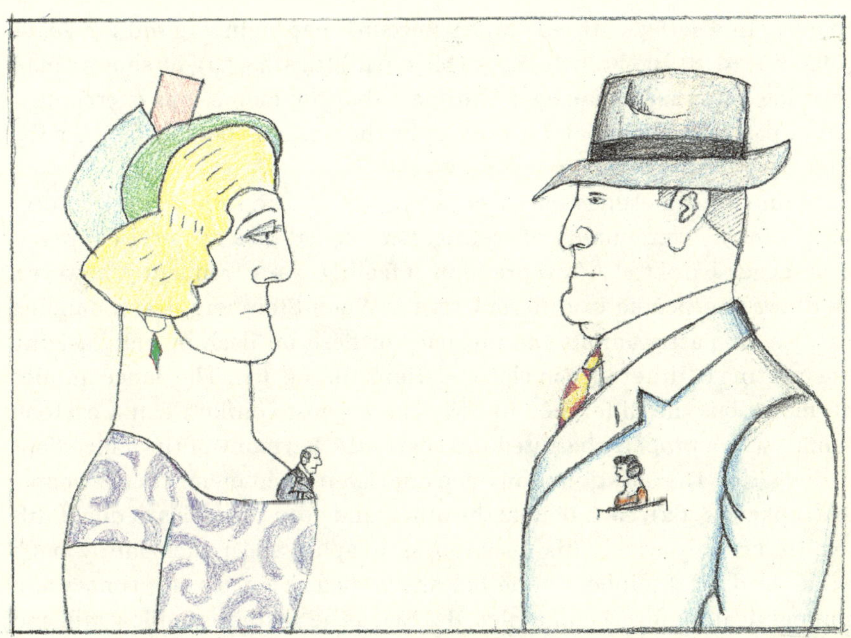

Fig. 56. Untitled, c. 1985–95. Pencil and crayon on paper, 11 × 14 in. (Beinecke Rare Book and Manuscript Library, Yale University)

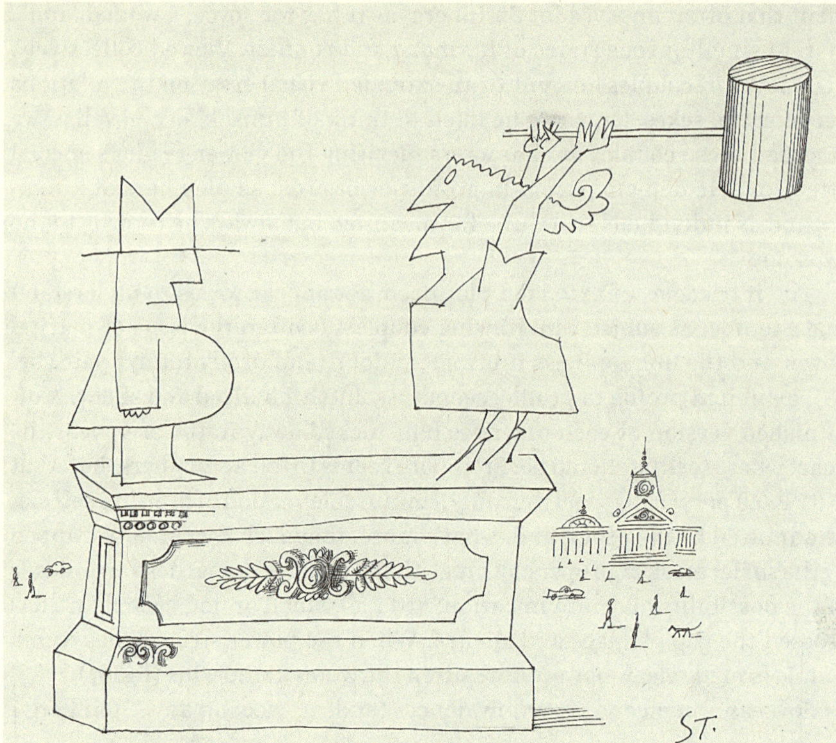

Fig. 57. Untitled, 1961. Ink on paper, 14½ × 23 in. Originally published in the *New Yorker,* October 21, 1961. (Beinecke Rare Book and Manuscript Library, Yale University)

couples. In a series entitled "Man's Burden" that Steinberg did for *Vogue* (March 1, 1948) and French *Vogue* (May 1948) (figs. 58, 59), he shows a man carrying a woman, an image of intimacy, but the man seems overcome—either partially hidden and overcome by the woman's bulk or facing away from us.

Steinberg sometimes portrays two people in the same style (fig. 60), suggesting a commonality of feeling, here belied by a geometrical precision suggestive of the very repression of feeling. More frequently, however, he draws two people in different styles. When Steinberg draws dancing couples, he partly annuls the intimacy of flesh on flesh by emphasizing the meeting of difference in close relationship (fig. 61). The dance implies harmony, but the difference in style can suggest conflict: can a cartoon woman and a properly besuited man carry the harmony of the dance floor to daily life? The question is an open one. Even when members of a couple look alike (fig. 62), each doubts the other, and even the styles of doubt differ. He actively wields his question as weapon; she nonchalantly puffs while thinking. Steinberg nonetheless sees bed as a place of intimacy and communication for a couple (figs. 63, 64), as he writes out pillow talk and

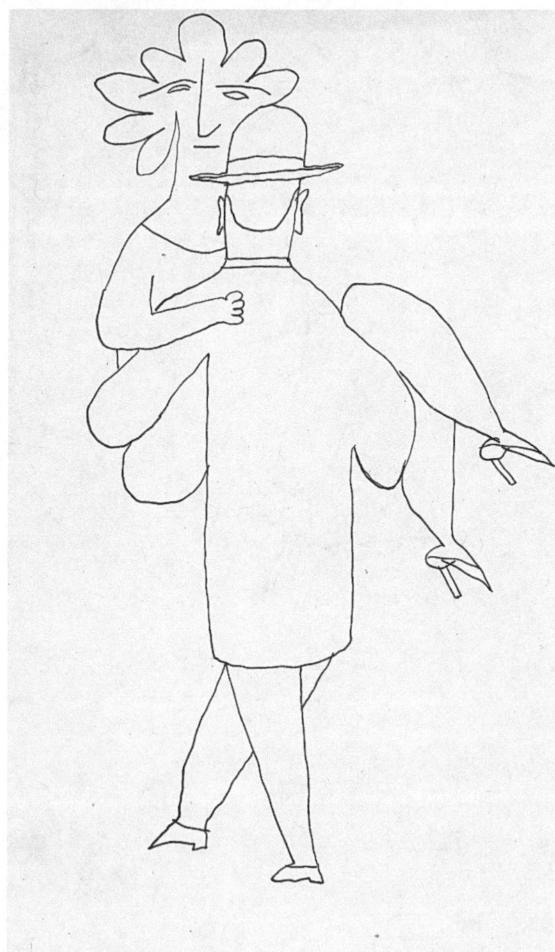

Fig. 58. Untitled, 1948. Ink on paper, 14¼ × 6¾ in. (Beinecke Rare Book and Manuscript Library, Yale University)

intermingles alphabetical beings. Drawings like these Steinberg referred to as "a parody of pornography" (*SS: I,* 152), echoing the sexually explicit thoughts of Molly's monologue. Steinberg's images of couples often pose movement against stasis: the implied lovemaking in bed, the imagined arrival of couples in postures of defiance or collaboration just before they're captured in a sketch.

Intrinsic to the quality of Bloom and Molly's relationship is Joyce's parody of popular culture. When Joyce has Bloom buy *The Sweets of Sin* for his straying wife, he epitomizes the novel's celebration of "low" culture, here pornographic. As Bloom reads, he responds: "Warmth showered gently over him, cowing his flesh. Flesh yielded amply amid rumpled clothes: whites of eyes swooning up. His nostrils arched themselves for

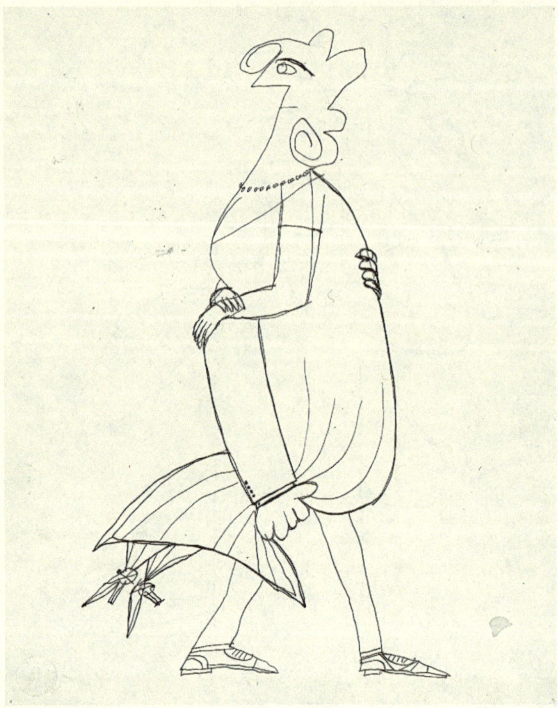

Fig. 59. Untitled, 1948. Ink on paper, 14 ¾ × 11 ½ in. (Beinecke Rare Book and Manuscript Library, Yale University)

Fig. 60. Untitled, 1957. Ink on paper, 11½ × 14½ in. Originally published in the *New Yorker,* March 30, 1957. (Beinecke Rare Book and Manuscript Library, Yale University)

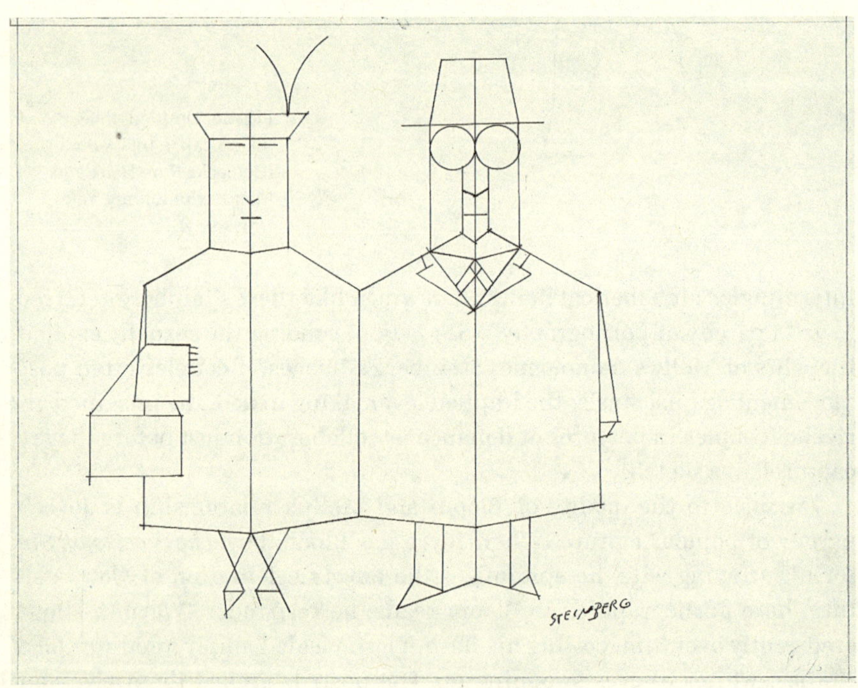

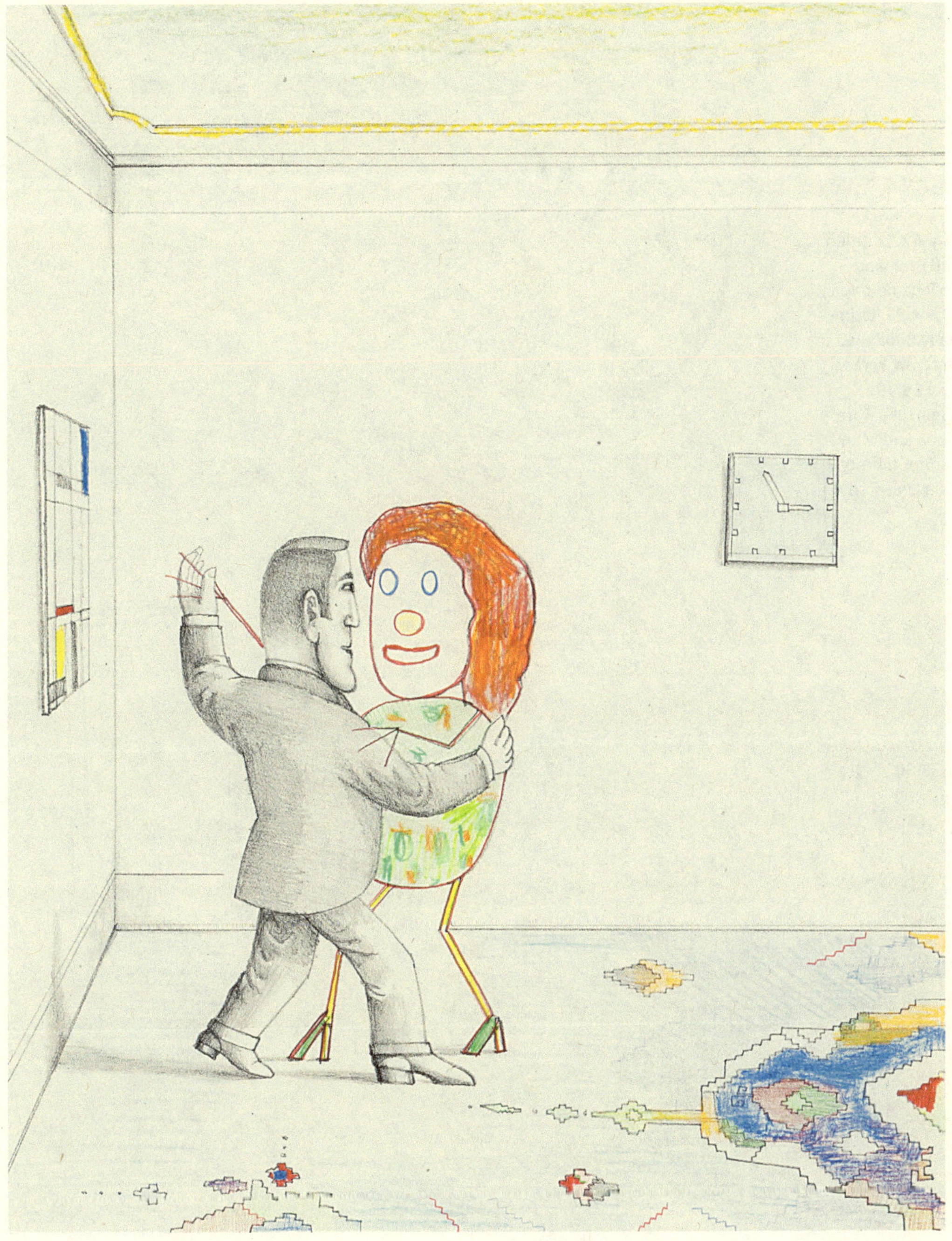

Fig. 61. *Dancing Couple (Tango),* 1965–74. Lithograph on Arches paper, with hand coloring, 30 × 22¼ in. (The Saul Steinberg Foundation, New York; photograph by Jenny Gorman)

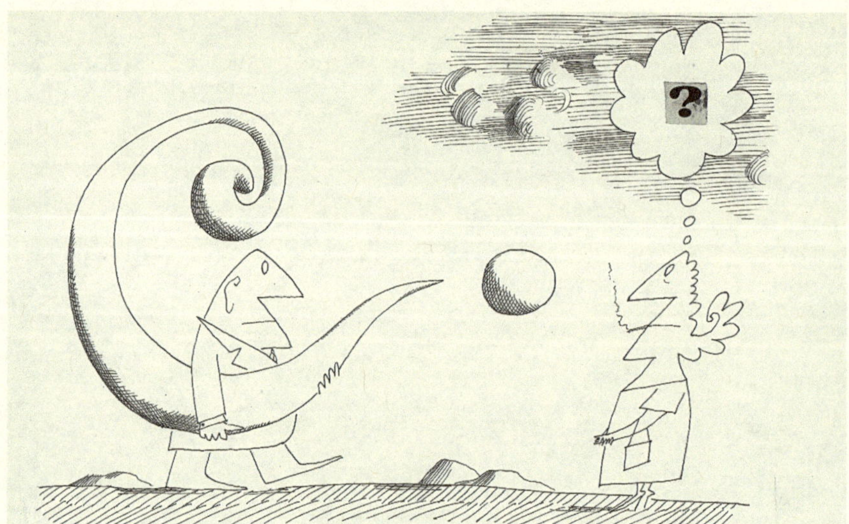

Fig. 62. Untitled, 1961. Ink and collage on paper, 14½ × 23. Originally published in the *New Yorker*, July 29, 1961. (Beinecke Rare Book and Manuscript Library, Yale University)

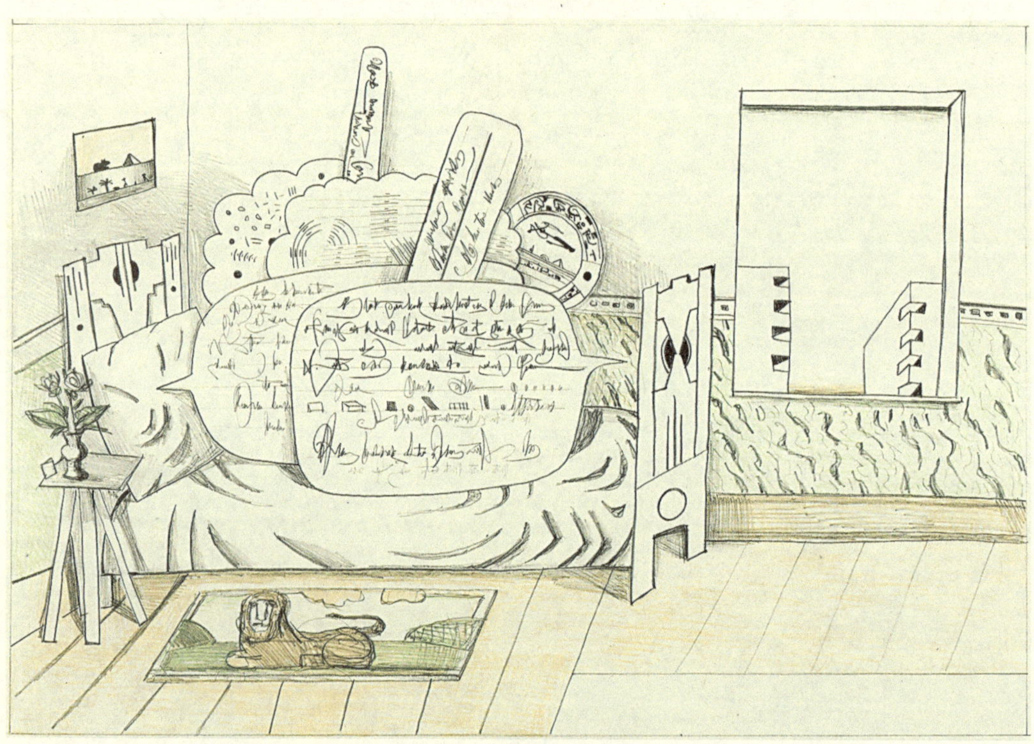

Fig. 63. *Albergo Minerva*, c. 1961. Lithograph in colors on paper, 22 × 30⅛ in. (The Saul Steinberg Foundation, New York; photograph by Jenny Gorman)

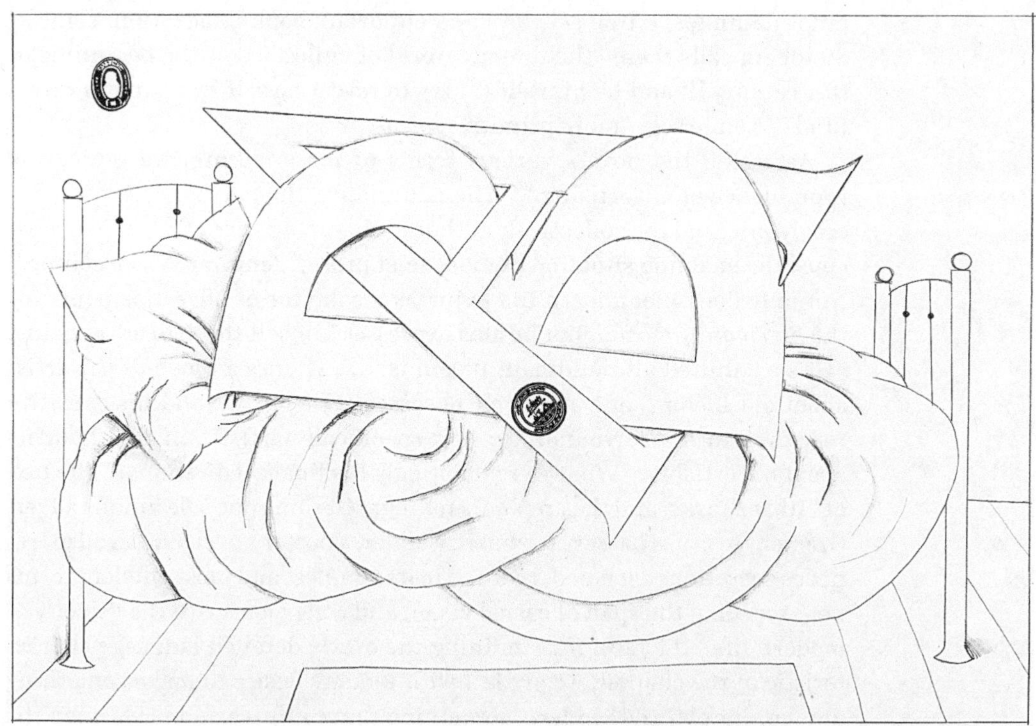

prey" (*U*, 236). "My Joyce,"[9] as Steinberg called him, wove popular culture into almost every page of *Ulysses.* Handbills, playbills, nursery rhymes, song lyrics, jingles, slogans, newspaper articles, advertisements, signs, truisms, posters, illustrated calendars, product labels, pantomime, popular scientific information, tattoos, postcards, tickets, prospectuses, magazine columns, self-help books, and more fertilize the novel. The sense of a comprehensible and commonplace world persists even through the difficult stylistic experiments that Joyce conducts. Joyce's memorialization of Dublin's popular culture equals or exceeds in importance the more arcane presence of Homer's *Odyssey.* Life on the street and in the public spaces of Dublin is—in tandem with ancient epic and a dazzling high-culture allusiveness—the basis of Joyce's modernist epic.

Fig. 64. Untitled, c. 1961. Lithograph and etching in colors with colored pencil on paper, 22 × 30⅜ in. (The Saul Steinberg Foundation, New York; photograph by Jenny Gorman)

We know that "Joyce ploughed through thrillers, patent medicine tracts, and comic books in search of their metaphorical assumptions as social images."[10] In parallel, Steinberg particularly admired the art of Richard Lindner, who "unlike most painters of our generation who derive from art reproductions, . . . derives from more primitive forms like movie posters, tailor dummies, tattoo art, toys and children's book illustration, signs."[11] Steinberg calls these "the totemic world of childhood at the beginning of this century,"[12] and he himself ("I try to reveal myself by trying to reveal Lind—") embraces "more primitive forms."

Assessing the novel's various forms of mass culture, we notice the prominence of advertising.[13] "The materiality, the pervasiveness, the hieroglyphic, and the collectively authored characteristics of advertising become the enabling situation of modernist prose," Jennifer Wicke claims.[14] Not only does Bloom earn his living as a solicitor of advertisements for the *Freeman's Journal,* but he also expresses himself through advertising. "He's a cultured allroundman, Bloom is. . . . There's a touch of the artist about old Bloom," one character observes (*U,* 235). Beyond his sensitive reactions to his surroundings, he's specifically artistic in his thoughts about advertising. "What were habitually his final meditations?" the text of "Ithaca" asks, and the answer is telling: "Of some one sole unique advertisement to cause passers to stop in wonder, a poster novelty, with all extraneous accretions excluded, reduced to its simplest and most efficient terms not exceeding the span of casual vision and congruous with the velocity of modern life" (*U,* 720). Streamlining the overly detailed language characteristic of the chapter, we are left with Bloom's desire to make something unique, simple, and modern, something that captures and plays upon the "velocity" of city life.

But, as Wicke argues, advertising is a collective enterprise, an emanation of the group. Bloom responds to signals from his culture in creating advertisements; his notions of what people will be able to absorb and appreciate strongly color his creative process. He imagines (and rejects) possible advertisements, but his imagination has itself been created by the advertising culture in which he exists. When he thinks about traveling, for example, he shows himself to be—like Nabokov and Steinberg—a reader of picture postcard captions and a supplier of cliché. Each place he might visit abroad appears with a touristic catchphrase or cliché: "The straits of Gibraltar (the unique birthplace of Marion Tweedy), the Parthenon (containing statues, nude Grecian divinities), the Wall street money market (which controlled international finance), the Plaza de Toros at La Linea, Spain (where O'Hara of the Camerons had slain the bull), Niagara land of the Eskimos (eaters of soap), the forbidden country of Thibet (from which no traveller returns)" (*U,* 727).

Joyce signals the pervasiveness of advertising by choosing a few examples and placing them repeatedly across the surface of the novel. Early in the day, Bloom reminds himself that he must take care of Alexander Keyes's advertisement; and at the newspaper office he begins to work on an advertisement for that purveyor of tea, wine, and spirits, who wants two crossed keys in a circle at the top of the ad. Design, however, isn't the chief problem. Keyes's terms for buying the ad don't pass muster with the *Freeman's* editor, so Bloom worries about the deal throughout the day. There it is, in his consciousness: at lunch, later at the pub, as his time watching Gerty McDowell draws to a close on the strand, and more than once during his cogitations in "Ithaca," where the ad is one of the causes of his "accumulated fatigue" (*U,* 728). Keyes shows up in the drama of Nighttown in "Circe," Bloom thinks about the ad again as he reads the newspaper at the cabstand, and even Molly considers it, with some irritation, during her monologue. Along the way, Bloom affirms the "modern art of advertisement": "you see, for an advertisement you must have repetition" (*U,* 323).

The novel, then, performs this repetition on behalf of Bloom, insisting that we register the importance of what seems to be just one of the many, swarming details that create the text before us. Joyce further emphasizes the Keyes advertisement by expanding the keys/Keyes pun that Bloom first points out; keyless Bloom and keyless Stephen proceed across Dublin, a watch lacks a key, a piano has keys, characters jingle keys or keep them at their backs or in their hands. If we add to such repetition the sheer number of business names that Joyce writes into his text, many of them appearing on signs, readers experience the saturation of daily life by the images of advertising.

As mentioned earlier, advertising similarly makes itself felt throughout Steinberg's works, but it's also important to realize that he was himself a creator of ads and other commercial images. He was the advertising artist that Bloom could only dream of becoming, and it's not a stretch to imagine that Steinberg enjoyed meeting Bloom the adman in the pages of *Ulysses.* Steinberg depended on the income he received from this work, and he became so popular a commercial artist that he could pick and choose which jobs to take.[15] As we've seen, Steinberg created ads for, among others, Noilly Pratt Vermouth, Emerson Electronics, Lewin-Mathes copper pipes and tubing, Nettleton Loafers, Simplicity home sewing patterns, Comptometer (adding machines), the department store Neiman-Marcus, and Lincoln automobiles. His work appeared not just in the *New Yorker,* but also in other important magazines of the day, such as *Life, Harper's, Town & Country, Mademoiselle, Vogue, Harper's, Harper's Bazaar,* and *Look.*[16]

His commercial work extended to dust jackets for books, wallpaper, fabrics, and even a television commercial for Jell-O. He worked both through advertising agencies and directly for publications; for example, *Vogue* paid him to travel to Washington, D.C., to make sketches of the scene there. Calendars and greeting cards for Hallmark were a financial mainstay for him in the 1950s and 1960s. He was commissioned to do public murals for the Bonwit Teller department store in New York, the Skyline Room in Cincinnati's Terrace Plaza Hotel, four ships of the American Export Line, and the 1958 World's Fair in Brussels (*SS: I,* 44–46, 50). Beginning in the 1960s, at the end of his first two decades in America, he stopped publishing in most magazines other than the *New Yorker,* and he did almost no more advertising art (*SS: I,* 53).

An advertisement for a D'Orsay perfume (fig. 65) provides an example of his commercial work. The image reads, "No one ever forgets Paris . . . or **Le Dandy,** the wicked, wonderful fragrance that whispers 'Someone lovely has just passed by.'" (One is reminded that Molly's perfume is specified in "Penelope.") As Joel Smith points out, "Advertising work often demanded nothing more specific than a lot of Steinbergian detail, the idea being simply to arrest the speeding eye of a reader" (*SS: I,* 44). The giant perfume bottle with its potentially crushing stopper dominates a Parisian cityscape, and this typical Steinbergian play with scale certainly catches the eye as well.

Steinberg tells Buzzi in 1947 that this commercial work is "therapeutic for me, but still more therapeutic are the money and success that come with it. So, I doubt that I'll have the strength to give up this work of mine in order to devote myself to painting" (*LAB,* December 27, 1947). Although he poses the problem as either commercial work or painting, he continues to do both, and like Joyce, he creates images of popular culture in his work. It can be difficult to tell the difference between some of his drawings and the advertisements they could so easily become (fig. 66).

Joyce portrays men as walking advertisements: "A procession of white-smocked men marched slowly towards him along the gutter, scarlet sashes across their boards. Bargains. . . . He read the scarlet letters on their five tall white hats: H. E. L. Y. S. Wisdom Helys. Y lagging behind drew a chuck of bread from under his foreboard, crammed it into his mouth and munched as he walked. . . .Three bob a day, walking along the gutters, street after street" (*U,* 154).

Steinberg, too, draws men in sandwich boards (fig. 67).[17] The message they carry is abstract, labyrinthine—the labyrinth functioning as part of Steinberg's mythology, as we'll see.

Life magazine paid for him to travel with the Milwaukee Braves in 1954 (fig. 68) (SS: *I,* 50). It was during this trip that his love of baseball originated, and he went on to create team logos. We've already noted his fascination with picture postcards that double as advertisements, for example

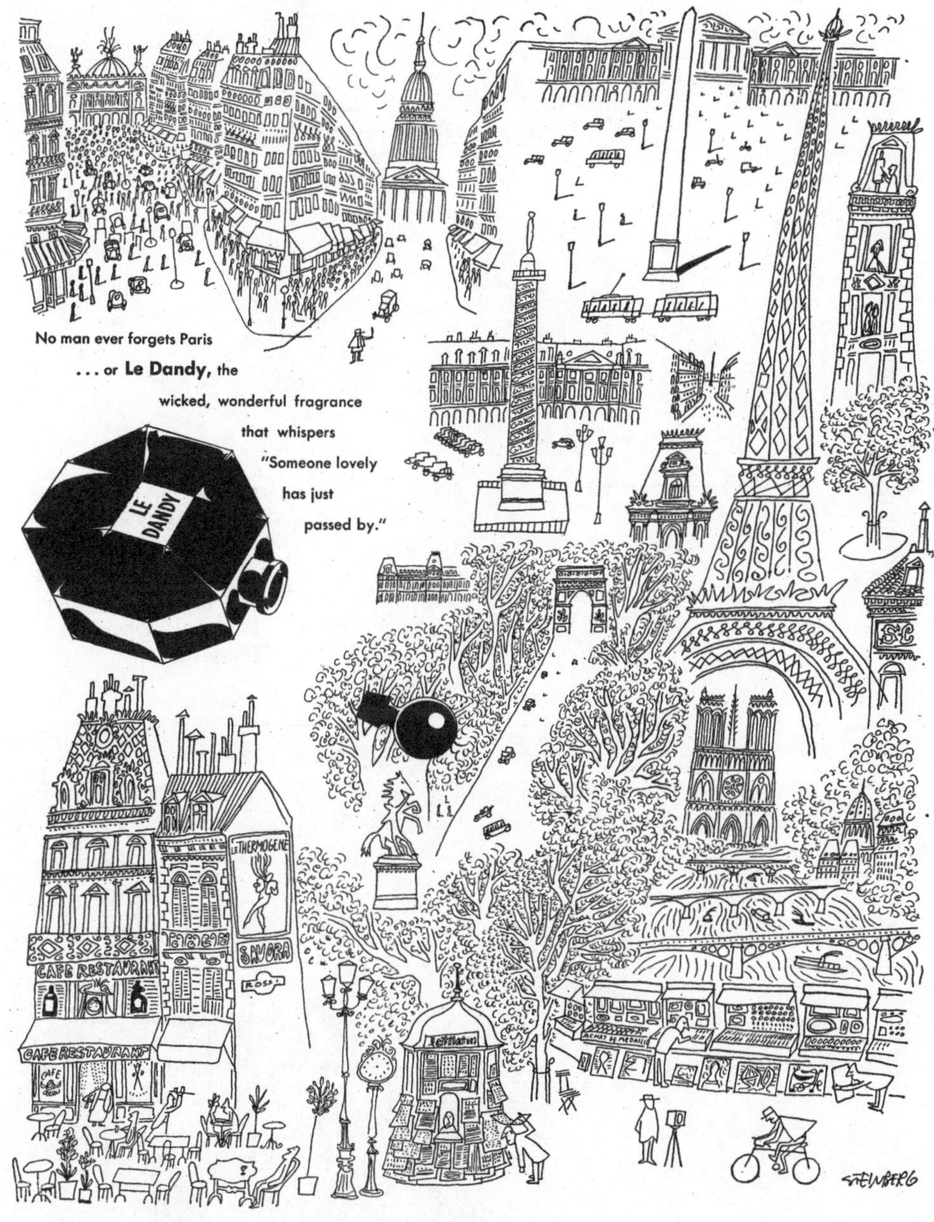

Fig. 65. Advertisement for D'Orsay perfume, as published in the *New Yorker,* May 4, 1946. (Photograph by Teresa Christiansen)

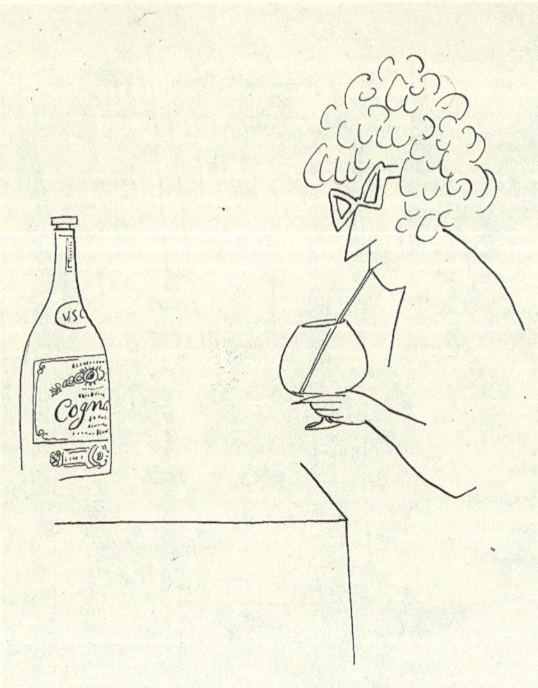

Fig. 66. Untitled, 1952. Ink on paper, 14½ × 11⅝ in. Originally published in the *New Yorker,* July 26, 1952. (Beinecke Rare Book and Manuscript Library, Yale University)

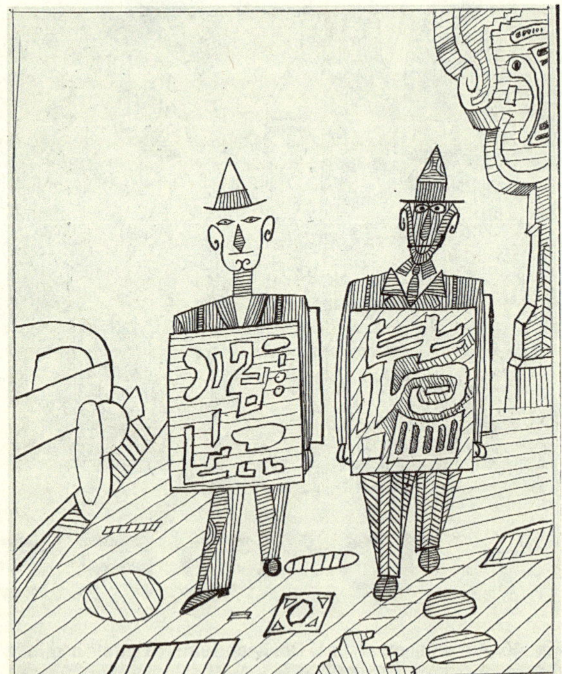

Fig. 67. Untitled, c. 1946–48. Ink on paper, 14½ × 11½ in. (Beinecke Rare Book and Manuscript Library, Yale University)

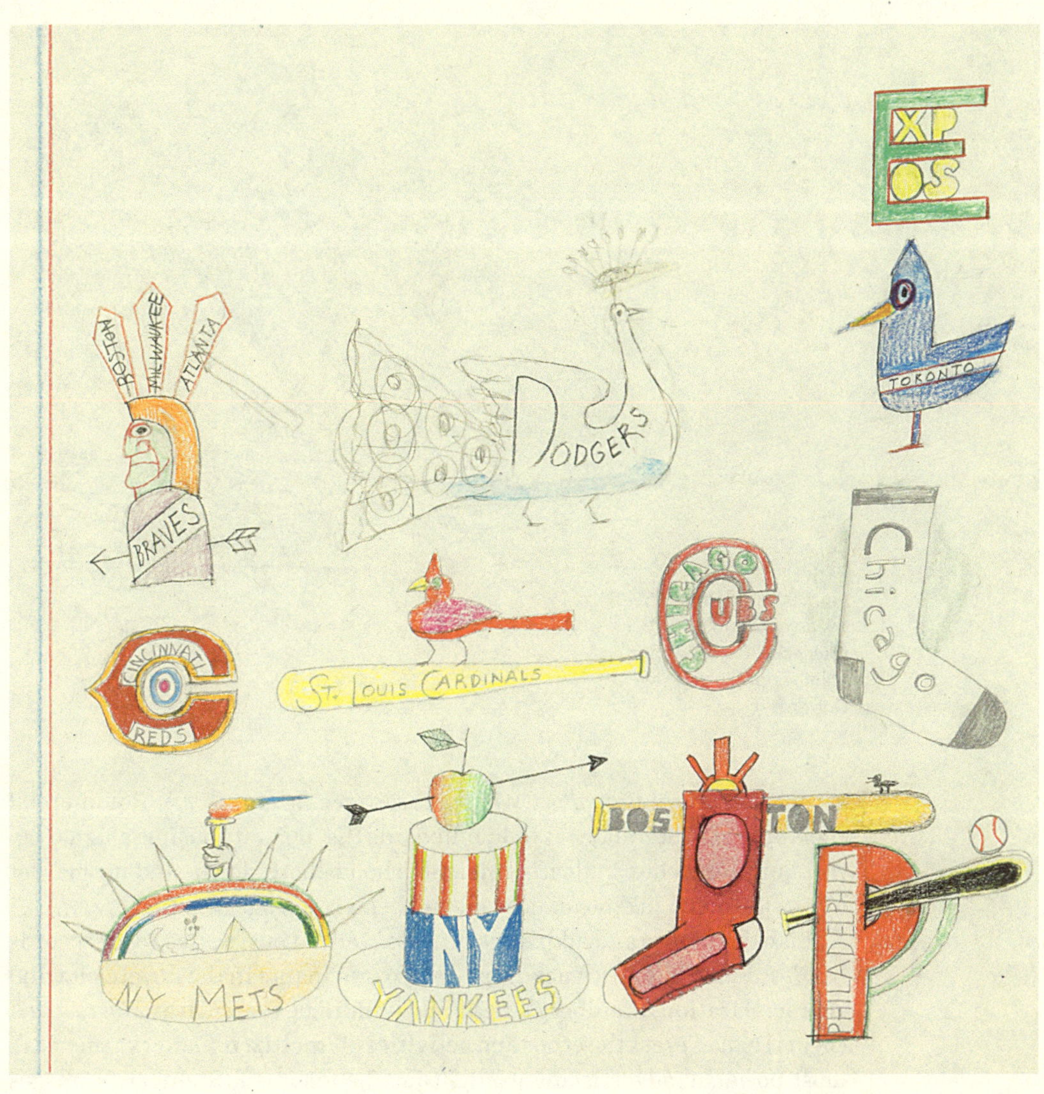

Fig. 68. Untitled, c. 1978–85. Pencil and crayon on paper, 23 × 14½ in. (The Saul Steinberg Foundation, New York; photograph by Jenny Gorman)

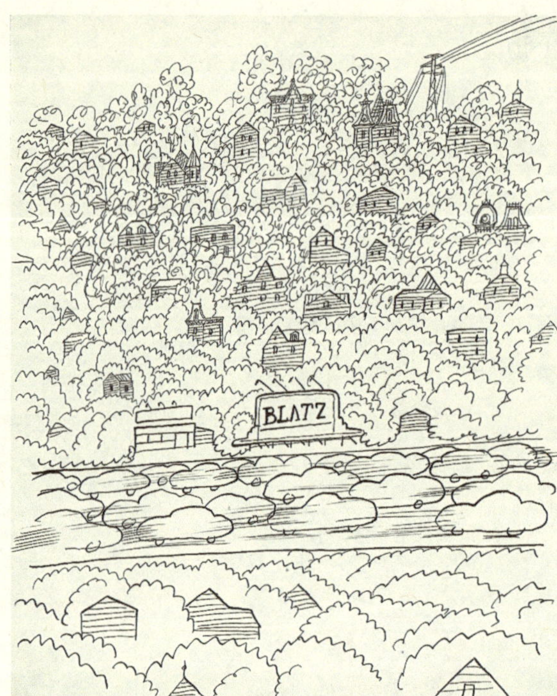

Fig. 69. Untitled, c. 1952–54. Ink on paper, 14⅝ × 11⅝ in. (Beinecke Rare Book and Manuscript Library, Yale University)

Airport Terminal Bldg. Fort Worth, Texas (see fig. 19; p. 77). Commercial signs appeal to Steinberg as well; billboards (fig. 69), city business signs (fig. 70), quick sketches indicating neighborhoods both down- and up-market (fig. 71). Diners, jukeboxes, and movie theaters engage him (figs. 72, 73).

Like the names and addresses of actual Dublin businesses Joyce records in *Ulysses,* not as static backdrop but as participants in the novel's plot and characterization, Steinberg's signs and buildings, too, such as *Marty's Deli* (fig. 74) can express the ethos and activities of its citizen-viewers. America's most powerful advertisement might just be for itself, Steinberg's images tell us, although beloved local businesses matter, too (fig. 75). And, given the "American [twentieth] Century's" embrace of change, growth, and progress, furniture brochure images and graph paper may metamorphose into whole cityscapes, as in *Furniture Street* (fig. 76).

Both Joyce and Steinberg ask serious questions. Steinberg asks about the self-creation of the artist—or any person—when he doubles his own moving hand in an incomplete image of a man who is shown drawing himself. With a simple line, Steinberg shows us a pop existential man who must draw himself into being in order to exist (fig. 77).[18] It's no accident that the PaceWildenstein Gallery entitled its 1999 show of his work *Steinberg:*

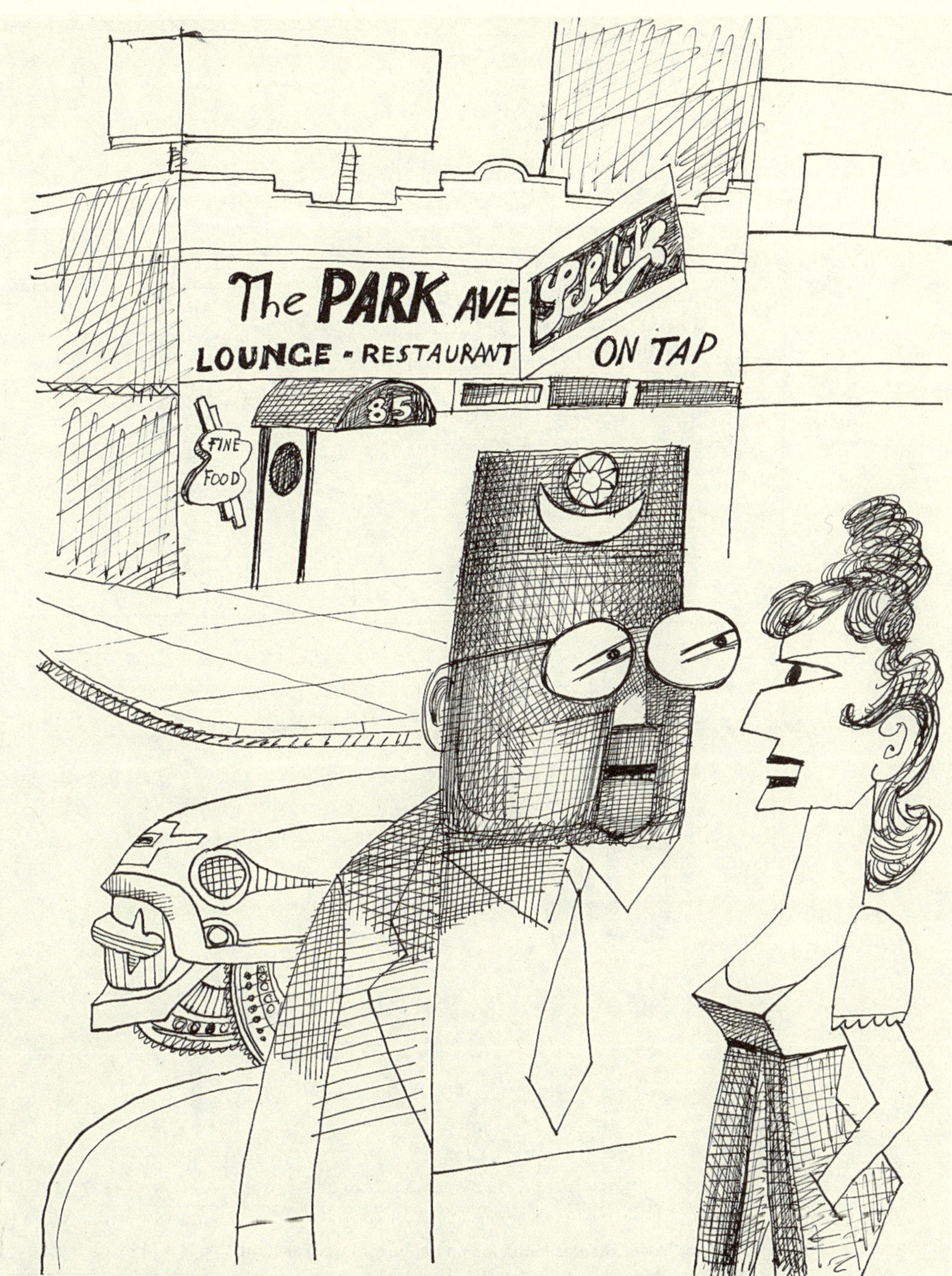

Fig. 70. Untitled, c. 1965–70. Ink on paper, torn from a sketchbook, 13⅞ × 10½ in. (The Saul Steinberg Foundation, New York; photograph by Jenny Gorman)

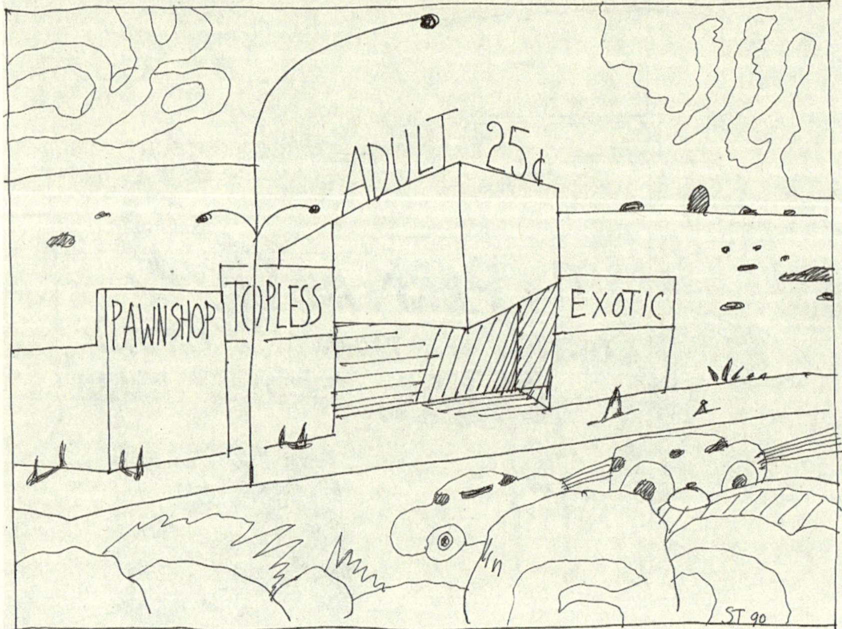

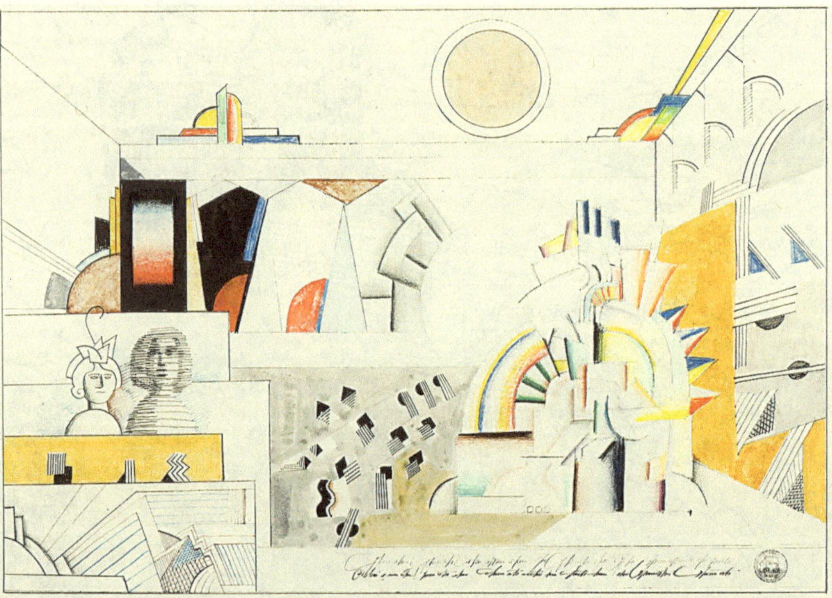

Fig. 71. *Adult Movie Theater,* 1990. Ink on paper, torn from sketchbook, 11 × 14 in. (Beinecke Rare Book and Manuscript Library, Yale University)

Fig. 72. *Juke Box,* 1968. Lithograph in color with watercolor, ink, and crayon on paper, 22¾ × 28⅜ in. (The Saul Steinberg Foundation, New York; photograph by Jenny Gorman)

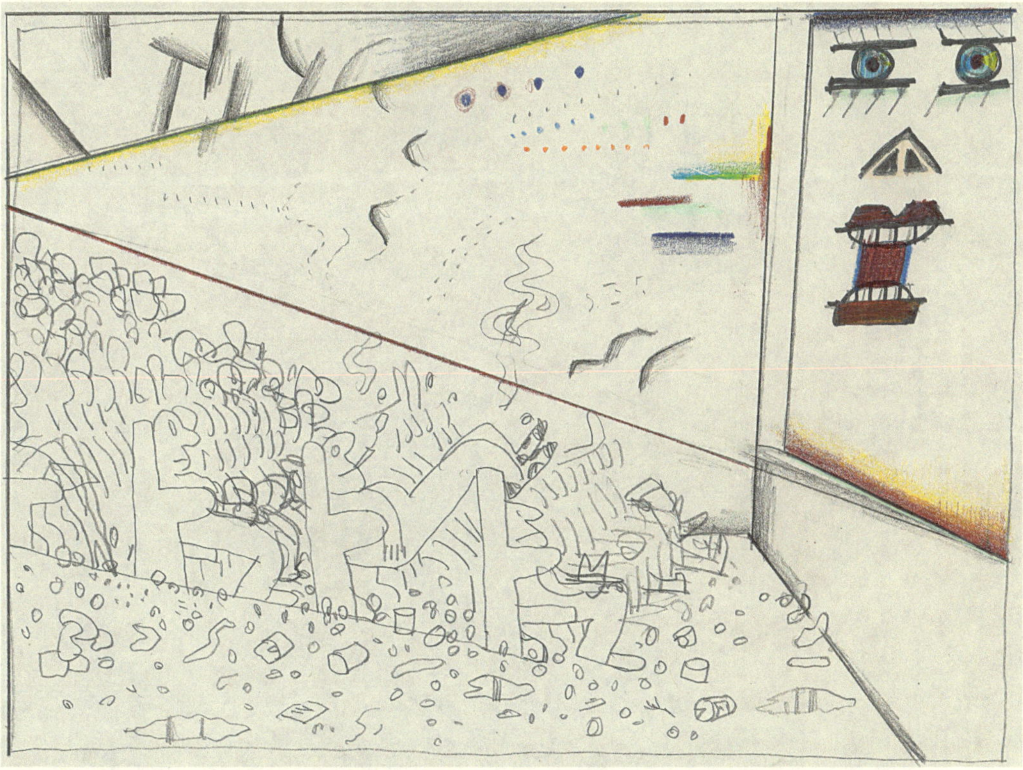

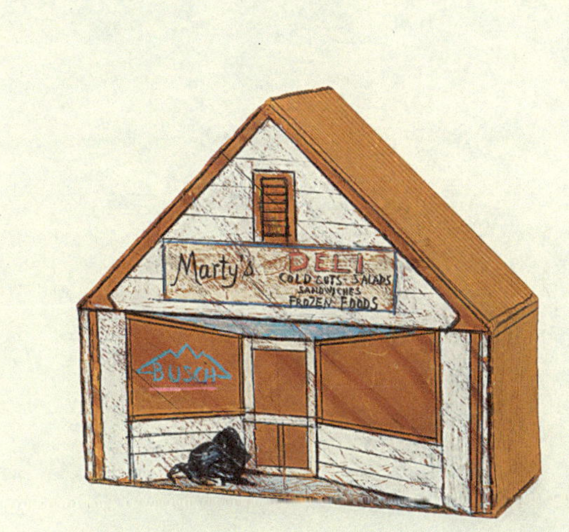

Fig. 73. Untitled, c. 1982. Pencil, colored pencil, and felt marker on paper, 11 × 14 in. (Beinecke Rare Book and Manuscript Library, Yale University)

Fig. 74. *Marty's Deli,* c. 1982–84. Crayon, pastel, felt marker, and pencil on wood, 7⅛ × 7¾ × 3½ in. (The Saul Steinberg Foundation, New York; photograph by Jenny Gorman)

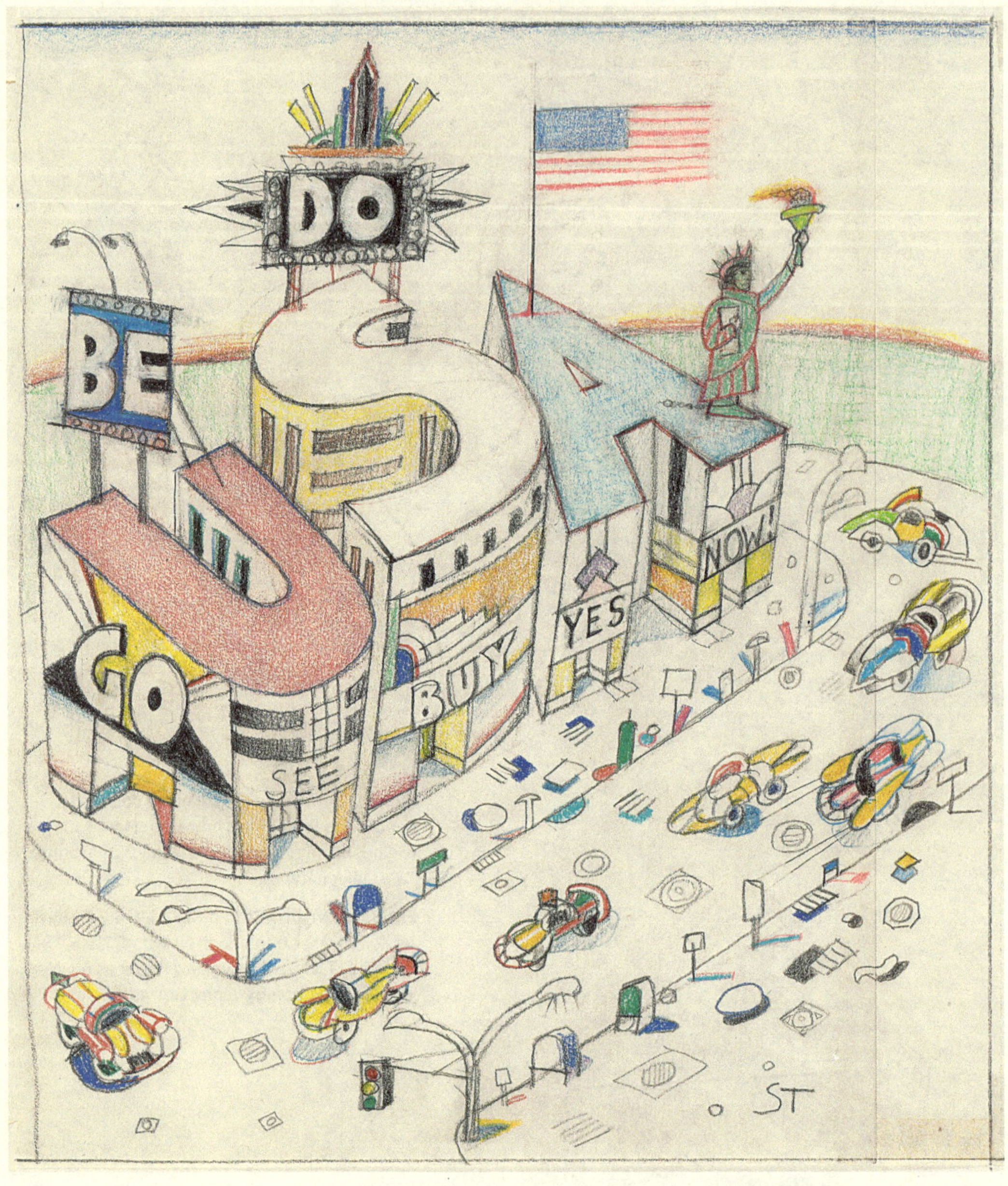

Fig. 75. Untitled, 1993–94. Pencil and crayon on paper, 14 × 12⅛ in. Cover drawing for the *New Yorker*, April 25, 1994. (Beinecke Rare Book and Manuscript Library, Yale University)

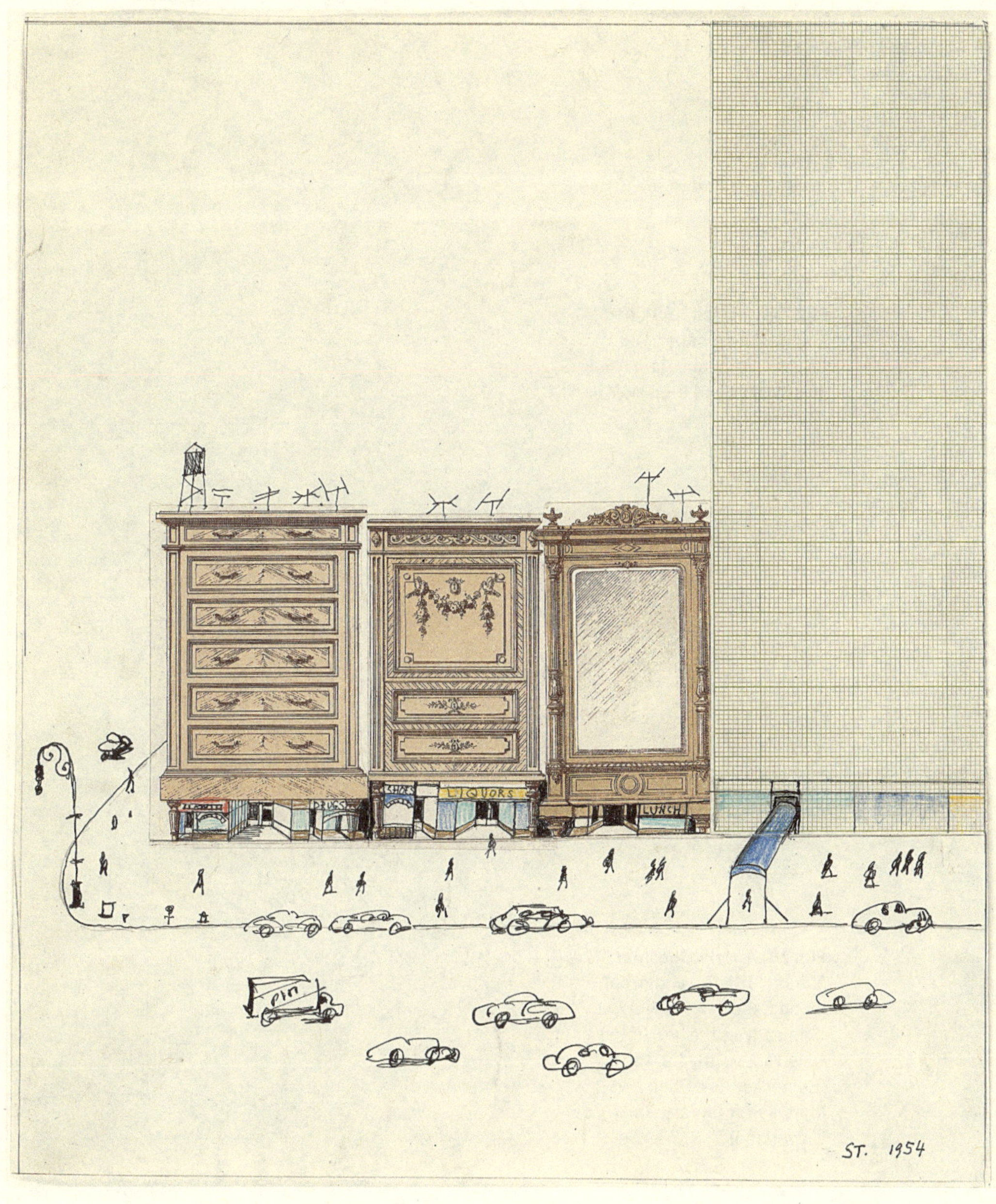

Fig. 76. *Furniture Street,* 1954. Ink, colored pencil, and collage on paper, 13½ × 11 in. (Beinecke Rare Book and Manuscript Library, Yale University

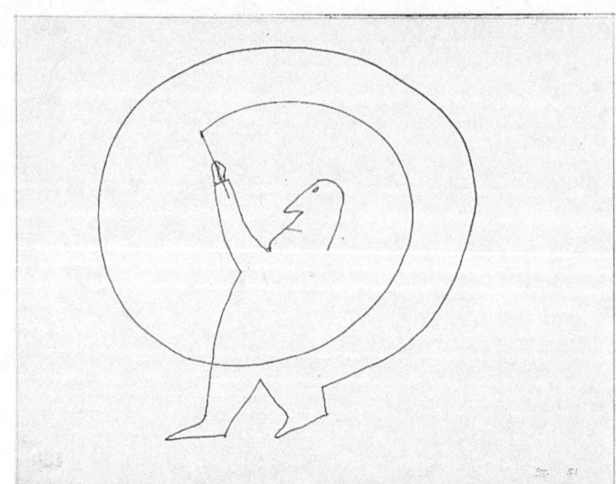

Fig. 77. Untitled, 1951. Ink and pencil on paper, 11½ × 14½ in. (Beinecke Rare Book and Manuscript Library, Yale University)

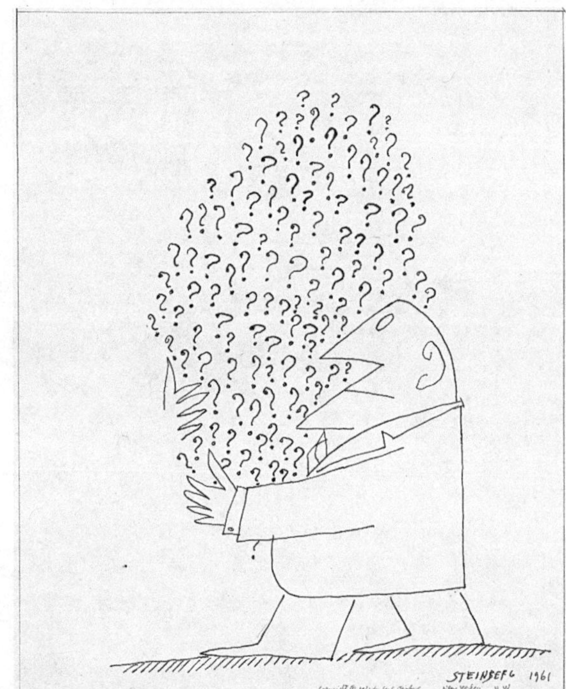

Fig. 78..*Armful Question Marks,* 1961. Ink and graphite on paper, 14½ × 11½ in. Originally published in the *New Yorker,* July 29, 1961. (Beinecke Rare Book and Manuscript Library, Yale University))

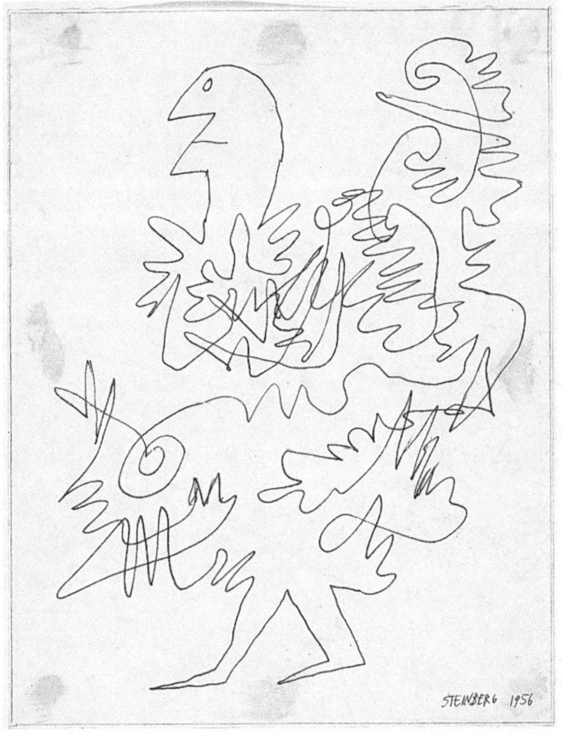

Fig. 79. Untitled, 1956. Pen and ink on paper, 12 × 9 in. (Beinecke Rare Book and Manuscript Library, Yale University)

Drawing into Being. This man without qualities figures forth, beyond self-creation, the ongoing difficulties of existence, so that Steinberg depicts him in *Armful Question Marks* as holding in his arms a swarm of questions (fig. 78) or dissolving into a large, complicated squiggle where his torso should be, as if he might keep on walking and thinking while in his heart he knows that he has lost track of who he is (fig. 79).

Here we arrive at one of the mysteries of Joyce's *Ulysses,* the question of just how he succeeds in creating Bloom as both everyman and as a special case—as an ordinary guy, yet one whose imagination, conscience, and sensibility set him apart from the crowd of minor characters who throng the streets and buildings of Dublin. We see him from many perspectives, afloat on his stream of consciousness as he creates his inner world out of the smallest experiences of a given day. We step back to judge him, and even identify with him. We don't get a detailed physical portrait of him until "Ithaca"; his appearance seems a kind of line drawing across which inner and outer must pass. He's precisely local in his travels but wide-ranging in his musings.

Steinberg liked to draw *his* everyman as a figure of coordinates (fig. 80).

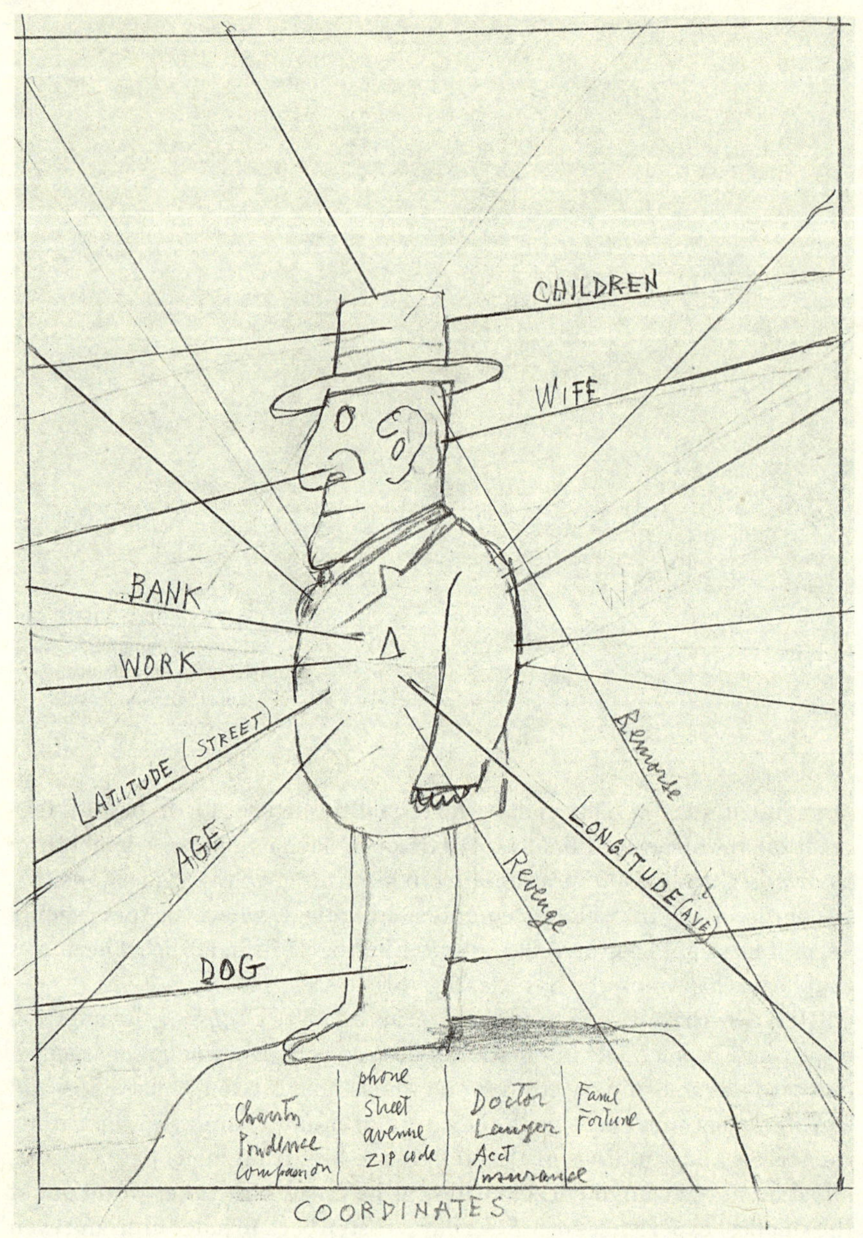

Fig. 80. Untitled, c. 1975–90. Pencil on paper, torn from sketchbook, 12 × 9 in. (Beinecke Rare Book and Manuscript Library, Yale University)

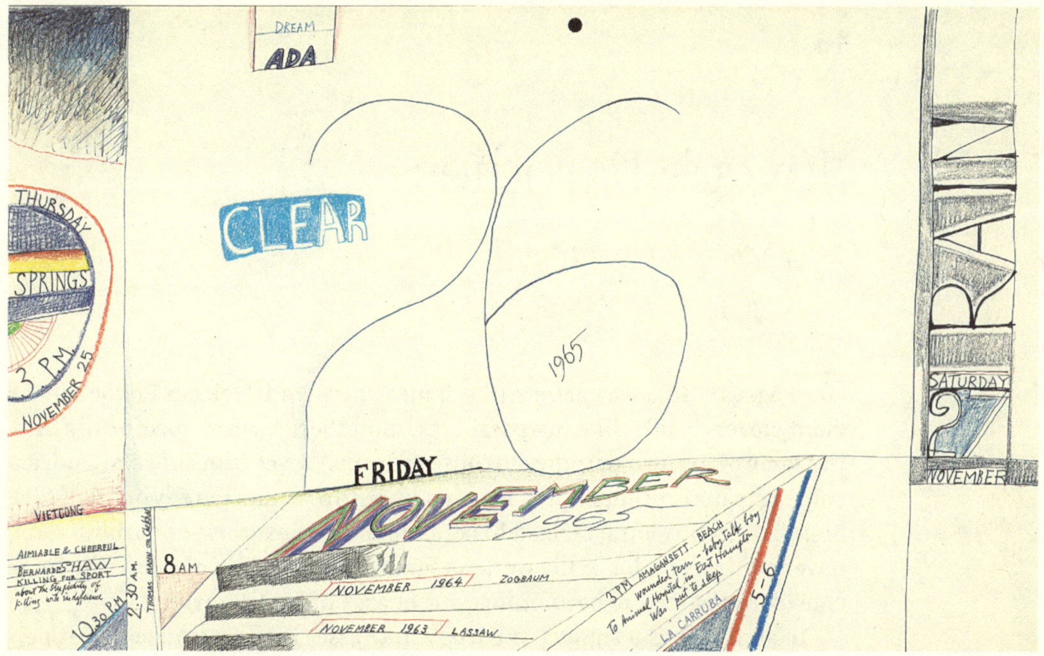

Seen from the outside, he's a buttoned-up creature of mapped generalities: "children, wife, bank, work, age, dog, revenge, remorse, latitude, longitude." He stands on the rock of generality as well: "doctor, lawyer, acct—home, street, avenue, zip code—prudence, compassion—fame, future." Yet we know that each of these categories must have a particular quality or a certain answer, so that Steinberg's coordinates remind us of the inner life of this generic man. All those coordinates converge on a perfect handkerchief triangle where his heart would be. His dual lives, inner and outer, track the continually shifting field of Bloom's characterization. Finally, like Joyce, Steinberg drew images of a single day, suggesting that one day is both every day and, paradoxically, unique to itself. Such a day for Steinberg is, among others, Friday, November 26, 1965 (fig. 81).

Fig. 81. *November 26, 1965,* 1965. Ink, colored pencil, and crayon on paper, 14½ × 23 in. (Museum Ludwig, Cologne; gift of The Saul Steinberg Foundation; photograph by Teresa Christiansen)

Beyond these shared techniques and images, the most salient aspects of Joyce's and Steinberg's mutually reverberating aesthetic worlds are those of parody, mythology, and assemblage. Turning in the following chapter to the first of these three, parody, we can begin by remembering here that Steinberg included forgery in the same family as parody (see fig. 7; p. 24), while in *Finnegans Wake* Joyce refers to *Ulysses* as an "epical forged cheque" drawn at the public's expense.[19]

16

Joyce's Parodies

"Any Repetition Is Parody"

Once again: "In a way artists like James Joyce and Jackson Pollock make giant clever frauds, like my passports," Steinberg writes, specifically linking some of his own parodies to those of Joyce.[1] Joyce himself once said, according to his brother Stanislaus, that literature "was a parody of life."[2] Like Steinberg, who characterized his creations as an exercise of parody—"You have to think of a lot of my work as some sort of parody of talent"[3]—Joyce considered parody to be an informing energy of his literary art.

To approach the subject of parody in *Ulysses* is to recognize that it pervades the work in senses both broad and narrow, just as Steinberg conceives of parody both in expansive terms ("Any repetition is parody")[4] and as particular practices, such as his rubber stamps of American icons, his faux documents, and his visual and verbal chronicling of the American landscape of motels, postcards, billboards, highways, and civic buildings. Joyce could conceive of his art as Defoe-like in its realistic details and parodic in its very mythic scaffolding. He resonates with Steinberg, who writes that "the artist, who is Robinson Crusoe . . . must invent his stories, his pleasures; he succeeded in reconstructing a parody of civilization, from scratch."[5]

Here we can only set out some aspects of the parodic richness of *Ulysses* and surmise that Steinberg reread the novel at least in part because he saw there a fellow parodist at work. We must keep in mind two notions as we construe Joyce's parodic practices: first, the wide, modernist practice of parody as repetition-with-a-difference (or reiteration) rather than as merely a ridiculing imitation of a source text; and second, Steinberg's notions of parody as related to his central fascination with "realit[ies] of the first, second, and third degrees" as he would have found them in *Ulysses.*[6] When Steinberg tells us that "drawing derives from drawing. My line wants to remind constantly that it is made of ink,"[7] he announces that he has moved beyond mere (secondary) mimeticism or parody of a "primary" reality to arrive at a third degree of "reality": his creative appropriation of works of his own or others.

Joyce takes care to represent actual people and places of Dublin within his novel—reality of the second degree, in Steinberg's terms. But he also writes a parodic, Steinbergian "third degree" of reality that, chain-like, leads to fourth and even fifth degrees of reality—the field of repetition with a difference that constitutes *Ulysses*'s pervasive parody. Through the schema he gave to Carlo Linati and Stuart Gilbert, Joyce encouraged readers to understand the entire novel as a parodic reiteration of the *Odyssey,* itself a reiteration of earlier, oral mythological stories. Hugh Kenner reveals another link in the chain: "Joyce's Dublin was in fact an eighteenth-century parody" in that his Dubliners may be said to speak the dead language of Swift and Burke as they mark and mourn "a civilization that had been smashed." Furthermore, "The music-halls parodied heroic dramas; Joyce parodied the music halls. Journalism parodied heroic elegance: Joyce parodied journalism."[8] Even the "heroic" must be understood as a reiteration of the virtues evident on actual battlefields or described in bardic poetry, so the unavailable "original" means that *Ulysses* can seem suspended in air rather than built upon solidities.

The text as a whole both embraces and (mockingly) parodies the rational grid of space and time that, however tinkered with, largely underwrites the nineteenth-century realist novel. While the novel's people, places, and events are anchored in the Dublin of June 16, 1904, its swelling of detail means that the coordinates of space and time often feel occluded, interrupted as they are by forays into the past and future, such as the medievalesque imagery of "Cyclops" or the "schemes of wider scope" for the future of "Ithaca" (*U,* 718). Space includes brief imagined forays into "elsewhere": Berlin and Jaffa ("Calypso"); Stratford, London, South Africa ("Scylla and Charybdis"); Gibraltar ("Penelope"); or even the cosmos ("Ithaca"). "Elsewhere" also includes purely textual instances of space-time, for example: the Rome or Troy of classical literature, the ancient Ireland of the parodied epic *Cuchulain of Muirthemne,*[9] the Elsinore of *Hamlet,* or the eighteenth-century Seville of *Don Giovanni* (with Bloom playing the parts of both Don Giovanni and the Commendatore).[10]

Ulysses offers several types of parody, beginning with instances of traditional, mocking parody—for example, Buck Mulligan's intoning of the mass in the opening of the novel. Such parody accounts for much of the comedy of the novel. "Telemachus" may not at first appear parodic apart from Mulligan's mockery, but everyone is acting in it, from Mulligan himself, who is parodic of the irreverent, biting, jesting stage Irishman, to Haines, who is the stock Englishman in Irish drama, to Stephen, a parodically decadent poet, and to the narration itself which is a version of "Edwardian novelese."[11] "Aeolus" parodies the examples given in handbooks of rhetoric, the bombastic verbal posing of many Dubliners, and newspaper headlines and picture captions. Joyce stocks "Eumaeus" with the trite and the clichéd, the things that "everyone knows" and repeats. "Wandering Rocks" mocks the notion that prose can capture what's going on across a city during a limited period of time, while also parodying, with its confounding interpolations, the very notion of a controlling grid of space and time. "Ithaca" mocks the catechism, the notion of rote learning from books, and even the idea that prose can fully capture the meaning of any topic it presents. "Nausicaa" parodies the prose of nineteenth-century sentimental women's fiction and ladies' magazines, what Joyce describes as "written in a namby-pamby jammy marmalady drawersy (alto la!) style with effects of incense, Mariolatry, masturbation, stewed cockles, Painter's palette, chitchat, circumlocutions, etc. etc.)[12] Indeed, every episode of *Ulysses* contains mocking parody.

But in addition to traditional mocking parody, *Ulysses* contains reiteration of texts written by others, not to mock them but to watch them grow in meaning, as in "Oxen of the Sun," an episode which we'll look at in more detail below. Such reiteration includes the creation of intertextual moments, such as when Joyce has Stephen meditate, without an explanatory gloss, on Benedetto Croce's *Estetica* (*U,* 505) or when the name of an author or the title of a work appears and quickly disappears.[13] Don Gifford and Robert J. Seidman's *Ulysses Annotated* contains references to a stunning multitude of such moments in the text.[14] Intertextuality is a principal form that parody takes in *Ulysses.*

Such intertextual parody can also expand to one of the novel's narrative techniques, the stream of consciousness, which Joyce famously borrowed from Edouard Dujardin's *Les lauriers sont coupés.* Inscribing the French *Ulysses* as a gift for Dujardin, Joyce calls himself "*Le larron* [thief] *impenitent,*"[15] just as Steinberg would later include the potentially criminal act of "counterfeit[ing]" within his family of terms associated with parody (see fig. 7; p. 24).

Finally, readers in search of reiterative parody will discern intratextuality, the repetition-with-a-difference of phrases, images, ideas, styles, memories, and events from within *Ulysses* itself. The novel's thick texture of internal allusion, of linked, repeated images, gives its parody a reflexive element; that is, it parodies not only external sources—a city, an epic—but also itself and Joyce's earlier works, as, for example, Gerty MacDowell in "Nausicaa" parodies the bird-girl in *A Portrait of the Artist as a Young Man.*

Joyce plants words and phrases early in the text that, when they reappear later, deepen and complicate their meaning. For example, the phrase "retrospective arrangement" originally appears in a conversation in "Hades" in which Martin Cunningham and Mr. Power mock Tom Kernan, a fellow Dubliner who pompously uses and reuses the phrase (*U,* 90). But when the phrase next appears, in "Wandering Rocks" (*U,* 241), we are privy to Tom Kernan's interior monologue, and he's musing about the actual General Slocum maritime disaster in New York as well as the published reminiscences of Sir Jonah Barrington, an Irish judge and historian, who discussed the Rebellion of 1798: "When you look back on it all now in a kind of retrospective arrangement," he thinks (*U,* 241). Here Kernan is depicted as a narcissist, consonant with the men's earlier mocking of him, but he's also thinking about some specific events in the history of Irish rebellions as he walks near historic sites of the struggle for independence. He's not merely a self-involved, pompous man; he also reads and thinks about history. The writing of history is always, of course, a "retrospective arrangement." However, here we learn—"Course they were on the wrong side"—that Kernan is actually opposed to Irish independence (*U,* 241). In "Hades," his fellow Dubliners criticize him for his bombast, but they do so, we learn much later, in "Wandering Rocks," in part because of his political views. Hugh Kenner writes of Joyce's "aesthetic of delay," in which he plants one word or phrase early on, then repeats it from another perspective later in the novel, so that we are constantly adjusting our understanding of passages through this parallax view.[16]

Not only does the phrase "retrospective arrangement" appear five times in the course of the novel, each time in a different context with different meanings, but it also reflexively refers to Joyce's editorial acts of returning to earlier episodes in order to enlarge them with details linking them to later episodes, his meta-"retrospective arrangement." Michael Groden, a pioneer of "genetic studies" of *Ulysses* who has studied manuscript drafts of the novel, has shown that in later drafts Joyce "added details with Homeric parallels" at the same time as he "added details of Bloom's life and thoughts, and names of Dublin residents, shops, and streets." Some of these added Homeric parallels he subtracted from the final draft. Additionally, as Joyce worked on the tenth through eighteenth episodes of the novel, he began by elaborating the technique of interior monologue and then largely replaced that method with parodic styles. As he wrote the second half of the novel, he continued to revise the earlier episodes, inserting repetitions to link the far-flung episodes of his work.[17]

Laying bare these traditionally mocking, intertextual, and intratextual parodic devices in *Ulysses* gives us the resources to think anew about types of parody in Steinberg's works, for example: his mocking of official documents; his careful drawings (as we have seen) of Rimbaud's diaries or of buildings in American cities; as well as his imitations of Braque, Matisse, Mondrian, and other modernist artists. We notice Steinberg's brief "intertextual" imitations as part of complex images, of, for example, the arts of China and Japan, or the interiors of bourgeois apartments and houses, or landscape topoi. And his intratextual reflexivity cannot fail to strike us as he visits and revisits images such as his "everyman" figure, maps, postcards, figures of American mythology, museumgoers, married couples, doodles, passages of faux calligraphy, geometric shapes, letters of the alphabet, rubber-stamped "inspectors"—and the list goes on.

It is worth pausing here to look more closely at two of Joyce's chapters. Because the book is so thoroughly parodic, a representative sample must suffice. I will concentrate on "Oxen of the Sun" and "Cyclops," the former because it is the most lavishly intertextual episode of *Ulysses,* and the latter because it parodies a variety of texts for comic effect and also spreads itself before us in a verbal Cubism that resonates with Steinberg's parodic visual Cubism.

"Oxen of the Sun" is one of the episodes that, along with "Cyclops" and "Eumaeus," Karen Lawrence has mentioned as suggesting "that language is an immense repository to be raided and cited."[18] And raid it does: "Oxen" parodies numerous English literary styles. In a letter to Frank Budgen, Joyce lists the writers he's imitating, beginning with anonymous Anglo-Saxon verse, continuing with the works of famous authors across the centuries, and ending with anonymous gouts of contemporary slang. Joyce subtly informs these parodies with aspects of earlier episodes of the novel itself, as well as with Homeric parallels, the stages of human embryonic development, and "faunal evolution."[19]

At the same time, "Oxen" mocks its own chronological plans, as Joyce seeds it here and there with details that are, upon close inspection, anachronistic.[20] Many of the entries are mocking parodies, such as the passage of Addisonian prose, sardonic in its very bawdiness, in which Joyce tries on Addison's moralizing elegance in order to chronicle the plans of *"Mr. Malachi Mulligan, Fertiliser and Incubator"* to impregnate "females":[21]

> He had resolved to purchase in fee simple for ever [*sic*] the freehold of Lambay island from its holder, lord Talbot de Malahide, a Tory gentleman of not much in favour with our ascendancy party. He proposed to set up there a national fertilising farm to be named *Omphalos* with an obelisk hewn and erected after the fashion of Egypt and to offer his dutiful yeoman services for the fecundation of any female of what grade of life soever who should there direct to him with the desire of fulfilling the functions of her natural. Money was no object, he said, nor would he take a penny for his pains. (*U,* 402)

"Fee simple for ever" parodies legal language ("fee simple absolute"). According to Gifford and Seidman, Joyce refers here to an actual person, "Richard Wogan Talbot, lord Talbot de Malahide, a retired army man and a landowner whose resistance to land reform was mild but firm."[22] He bought the island in 1814. Twelve miles east-northeast of Dublin, Lambay Island was known as a bird sanctuary—although it is here imagined by Mulligan as a sanctuary for "desiring females," or (in slang) "birds." Given that the scene of "Oxen" is the Lying in Hospital, with the laboring Mina Purefoy in the background, we can read this as a satiric portrait of a character who thinks he's being witty, but whom we see instead as crude ("an erected obelisk") and puerile. A "national fertilising farm" raises the topic of eugenics, still hotly debated in the years immediately leading up to the composition of *Ulysses.*[23] The farm's name, Omphalos, or "navel," links it to embryonic development and parturition, but it also immediately recalls the omphalos of the novel's first episode, "Telemachus," where Stephen shouts from outside a window, "To ourselves . . . new paganism . . . omphalos" (*U,* 7; ellipses in original). Here Joyce adds references to Sinn Fein, "We ourselves," and to "new paganism," the decadent sloganeering of the aestheticism of the '90s, a movement that flirted with the blurring of binary genders. Omphalos takes us to the navel of the earth (the oracle at Delphi, a "female"); and in the *Odyssey,* one of Homer's epithets for Ogygia, Calypso's island where Odysseus is stalled at the beginning of the epic, is the navel of the sea. Taken together, all of these references mean that the Addisonian style is only one aspect of the historical, political, anthropological, and aesthetic fecundity of Joyce's parody.[24]

Moreover, as scholarship has widely shown, the chapter doesn't merely mock. Its characters often quote themselves, as when, for example, Stephen "alludes to the Edenville and Tophet [hell] of his reverie on the beach."[25] Its reiterative parody likely takes some of its stylistic examples directly from authors' works, but it certainly makes use of compendia of quotations (another degree of "reality") such as George Saintsbury's *A History of English Prose Rhythm,*[26] William Peacock's *English Prose: Mandeville to Ruskin,* and W. B. Hodgson's *Errors in the Use of English.*[27] Parody of parodies appear too, as when Joyce, writing "We two, she said, will seek the kips where shady Mary is," imitates Rossetti's "Blessed Damozel," itself already a reiterative parody of Christian iconography. "Kips" (i.e., digs) and "shady Mary" insert mocking humor into the reiteration, for a parodic triple-score.

All told, "Oxen" links its patterns with patterns of the novel as a whole. For example, the very idea of a procession of styles links it to the viceregal procession in "Wandering Rocks." Its dwelling in literature echoes Stephen's propensities in *Portrait* and throughout *Ulysses.* "Oxen" resembles

"Sirens," in which Joyce experiments with the close reading of traditional literary language in order to wrest it into something strange and new. Stephen mocks Theosophical language in "Scylla and Charybdis" and "Cyclops" as surely as "Oxen" mocks Addisonian language. And so on—links to every other episode of the novel can reasonably be worked out. We can take "Oxen," too, as an epitome of the whole novel. By its cavalcade of styles, "Oxen" presents a compact reiteration of the novel as a whole, which exhibits from episode to episode its own varying discourses.

"Cyclops" also displays Joyce's playful intertextual parody. The episode takes place at five o'clock at Barney Kiernan's pub and is narrated by an unidentified "I," who, along with a character called "the citizen" (a parody of Michael Cusack, Irish nationalist and founder of the Gaelic Athletic Association), dominates a loosely developing, gossipy set of discussions circling around Irish history, politics, and local events and characters. Various Dubliners come and go. Thirty-three parodic interpolations or interruptions, "spoken" by no one (or, in parody of the *Odyssey,* by "No Man") but by the "consciousness of the text" itself, embellish this chapter of conversation.[28] Gifford and Seidman have identified the types of texts to which they refer: many of them parody (already parodic) nineteenth-century translations and versions of ancient Irish poetry and myth. Others parody newspaper articles, including reviews, sports events, and accounts of public ceremonies; Greek, Hebrew, Hindu, and Christian texts; Theosophical lore; séance talk; medical argot, a story by Washington Irving; a public meeting of a temperance league; nineteenth-century genteel fiction; a children's primer; a legislative session; a trial record; and, of course, the "Cyclops" episode in the *Odyssey.*[29]

Budgen reports that Joyce asked him, "Does this episode ["Cyclops"] strike you as being futuristic?" and that he replied, "Rather cubist than futurist."[30] Joyce refers to Futurism, a movement in the arts founded by Filippo Tommaso Marinetti in 1909 Milan which repudiated the old or traditional and advocated instead an emphasis on industrialism, up-to-the-minute technology, speed, and violence. Budgen was right to say that *Ulysses* wasn't Futurist. Far from celebrating cars, airplanes, and other machines as Futurists did, "Cyclops," for example, concerns itself with foot traffic, horse racing, palfreys, and a horse-drawn jaunting car, and it closes with a parody of Elijah's chariot-borne ascent into heaven. Exploring Budgen's notion of Joyce's Cubism will reveal the inner workings of parody in "Cyclops." One is reminded of Steinberg's parody of Cubism in *Washington, D.C. 1967* (fig. 9; p. 34).

Was Joyce aware of Cubism? Jo-Anna Isaak has approached this question by pointing out that Joyce, according to Ellmann and Stanislaus Joyce, attended art exhibitions throughout his adult life, even as his eyesight weakened.[31] Isaak argues that Joyce likely attended an exhibition of Cubist works by Harry Phelan Gibb in Dublin during the summer of 1912, and even if he didn't, he would have heard of it from his friend Oliver St. John Gogarty, the original of Buck Mulligan in *Ulysses* and Gibb's patron in Dublin. But the strongest evidence for Joyce's knowledge of Cubism lies in the serial publication of *A Portrait of the Artist as a Young Man* in the *Egoist.* In the issues where his own work appeared, Joyce would have seen "book reviews of Albert Gleizes's and Jean Metzinger's *Du Cubisme* and A. J. Eddy's *Cubists and Post-Impressionism* as well as articles entitled 'The Battle of the Cubes' and 'The Cubist Room' in which John Cournos and Wyndham Lewis, respectively, discussed current Futurist and Cubist shows."[32] It's important to realize that just as Joyce adopted the technique of interior monologue from Dujardin, he adopted—and adapted in verbal form—the techniques of Cubism within "Cyclops."

He did so, for example, by deliberately confusing the distinction between the narrated scene at the pub and the interspersed passages of parody seemingly "spoken" by the text itself, thereby creating two (and more) ambiguously related planes. The first-person narration has usually been seen as primary, the "parodic" sections as secondary. To take these parodies as merely interruptions, interpolations, or embellishments is to miss important parodic energies within the episode as a whole.[33] In fact, Joyce first wrote some of the parodies and only later the first-person narration.[34]

If we're judging by number of words, then the narrative action set at Barney Kiernan's around five in the afternoon *is* primary—there's just more of it. For all the narrator's often vicious opinions of his fellow Dubliners, for all the anti-Semitic talk that intermittently poisons the episode, this mode of first-person narration is itself comfortable to read. We're back in a prose that summons to mind nineteenth-century realist fiction: we know where we are, and we meet the people who arrive, talk, drink, listen, and eventually leave the scene.

But if we reflect on the possibility that the meaning of "Cyclops" is just as dependent on the parodic sections (which have their own set of actions) as it is on the first-person narrated action, then we're looking at two principal planes of meaning. When we read one of the so-called interpolated sections, we shift to a second, equally principal plane, and it seems Cubist in nature. Negotiating the rapid shifts between these planes creates a counterpart of the experience of viewing a Cubist canvas. Beginning in 1910, Picasso and Braque created works that turned away from an illusionistic portrayal of reality, instead proposing that "the work of art was itself a reality that represented the very process by which nature is transformed into art."[35] The "reader" of a Cubist painting must pay attention to—even summon—the various geometric forms and lines so that they almost cohere into the whole object or set of objects on view. Those objects have been painted without a sharp distinction between mass and void.

Similarly, the openly parodic interpolations diverge from a realist or mimetic view of action in the world of Dublin, on June 16, 1904. They turn the reader's attention to the components of style that each one flourishes: the specific kinds of discourse which announce themselves first as verbal rather than as windows through which we may illusionistically view important things, people, or actions. These styles invite the reader to complete them by recognizing the sources that the parodic process depends on. And what we might think of as the "mass" of these words, the subject matter which they offer as well as the distinctive styles in which they half capture that matter, itself opens out, like so many Cubist geometric shapes and multiplying planes, to the voids that surround them: the missing legends, legal documents, poems, newspapers, holy texts, handbooks or history books, séance chants, social meetings, tourist brochures, etc., from which they are supposedly lifted.

Thinking of the *relations* between these two primary planes of discourse—narration and parodic interludes—involves us in examining the very process by which they appear to have been written. Here the model of primary action with secondary parodies inserted into it breaks down even further. In fact, "Cyclops" as a whole is a field of metamorphosing elements, because these principal planes themselves fluctuate, intersecting with one another by sharing qualities that come into focus—and fall out of it—as we read.

At first, one shared quality seems to be that of inactivity. There's a static quality to the episode in both its first-person narration and its parodic interludes. The actions of the I-narrated sections—which together mark out a major plane of the episode—consist of talking and drinking, with a few movements in and around the pub to stroke the dog Garryowen or to visit the jakes. Not much happens. We can consider the episode as showing the liveliness of conversation among Dubliners, the pleasure they take in arguing, agreeing, remembering, insulting, aggrandizing—doing things with words. Yet as a chapter of talk, the narrative lacks even the movement of walking or riding through the city; what it does convey is the entrapment of Odysseus within the cave of Polyphemus. Only at the episode's close does an action larger than drinking and conversing occur.

Yet this plane breaks down and multiplies in Cubist fashion because, within the gossipy talking itself, people "do" other things. They wander the streets of Dublin, shop for food, bet on horses, attend meetings, serve as soldiers, rebel against the British, marry well or not so well, and die. Look at the narration once, and Barney Kiernan's is a curiously static little world—a series of talk balloons linked to a few, small, and (excepting Bloom) drink-addled men. Look at it again, and—just as a background portion of a Cubist painting will suddenly appear to exist in the foreground, or a transparent shape will suddenly appear opaque—it becomes a theater of actions both historic and contemporary.

The plane of the thirty-three interpolated parodies, too, oscillates in Cubist fashion between near stasis and action. Lists often appear there, and these stop the actions reported in the section. Lists matter both rhetorically and visually, as blocks of prose on the page. For example, in the fourth parodic section, we read the description of a hero, "The figure seated on a large boulder at the foot of a round tower was that of a broadshouldered deepchested stronglimbed frankeyed redhaired freely freckled shaggy bearded widemouthed largenosed longheaded deepvoiced barekneed brawnyhanded hairylegged ruddyfaced sinewyarmed hero" (*U,* 296). The very lack of hyphens in compound words causes us to look *at* the words as well as through them. As Steinberg says he draws drawing, Joyce here appears to write writing.

Following this adjectival list, a list of body parts (nostrils, eyes, mouth, heart) appears; this is followed by a list of the hero's items of clothing. One such item, "a row of seastones which dangled" gives rise to a list of "Irish heroes and heroines of antiquity." But this list breaks open—like a Cubist geometric shape that dissolves into smaller shapes—into figures who are decidedly not Irish, such as Goliath and Dante Alighieri. The list eventually becomes quite random, even chaotic. This interpolated section, one large, static list, breaks down into sublists but then reconstitutes itself into the whole "figure seated on a large boulder." What's more, lists like these from one section of parody link to lists from another, resonating across the pages of the episode much as a geometric shape repeated in a Cubist painting causes the eye to make connections across the canvas.

Additionally, the planes of pub narration and of interpolated parodies intersect in intriguing ways. As this parodic list of the seated figure's qualities ends, a brief narrative passage appears: "A couched spear of acuminated granite rested by him [the hero] while at his feet reposed a savage animal of the canine tribe . . . [emitting] hoarse growls and spasmodic movements which his master repressed from time to time by tranquillising blows of a mighty cudgel rudely fashioned out of paleolithic stone" (*U,* 297). This sentence appears in the fourth interpolated section, but it refers equally to the citizen and his cur, Garryowen, "actual" inhabitants of the pub. The enclosed lists-within-lists, the plane of parody, here open up verbally to the plane of the narrative set at Barney Kiernan's. Providing a transition between the principal planes of the episode, it belongs equally to both. Joyce repeats this type of segue across the episode.

The Cubist dissolution of forms and intersecting of planes becomes even more active when we realize that parody is actually not limited to what we have been calling the parodic or interpolated plane. Actual conversations in the pub contain parodic energies as well. The narrator has intervened in Bob Doran's florid grieving with his nasty, belittling talk, "The tear is bloody near your eye. Talking through his bloody hat. Fitter for him [Doran] to go home to the little sleep-walking bitch he married, Mooney, the bumbailiff's daughter" (*U,* 303). These conversational shards of inflation—"The noblest, the truest, says he"—and deflation within the narrated conversation are parodic of each other, the "low" depending on the "high" and vice-versa. The reader is left to tease out these mobile relations, to distinguish between a sense of "real life" depth or three-dimensionality (men talking in a pub) as well as the two-dimensionality of the purely textual nature of the parodic insertions. In the end, however, we understand that all meaning dwells between the two-dimensional surface of the page and our own imaginations.

To anatomize the breakdown and overlap of the principal planes of the episode is to experience a radical ambiguity about what counts as "real life" or "straight-up" conversation, what Steinberg might call reality of the second degree, and what counts as invasion of that imitated (third-degree) world by the parodied texts of heroism. In the former, the reader is invited to look through the words toward an imitated version of reality. In the latter, readers look *at* the words, emphasizing the autonomous existence of the text as a thing in the world. "Mockery" is one of the terms that Steinberg groups with parody and plagiarism (see fig. 7; p. 24), and here Joyce has created a scintillating veil of mockery that destabilizes the binaries of conversation and parody, or mimetic event and textually autonomous event. As Robert Rosenblum writes, "In place of earlier perspective systems that determined the precise location of discrete objects in illusory depth, Cubism offered an unstable structure of dismembered planes in indeterminate spatial positions."[36] In the space of "Cyclops," such movement rules, and Joyce leaves it to readers to construct such solidities or stabilities as they would find compelling.

It's worth standing back to think about what the parodies of *Ulysses,* taken together, imply, and how they lead us to make similar inferences from Steinberg's oeuvre. The very act of borrowing or repeating in a new context becomes a central part of the meaning of *Ulysses:* any notion of organic unity or comprehensive meaning must dissolve in the face of the sheer wealth of styles and orders of referentiality. Parody unseats certainty: the novel, through its very artificiality, reflexivity, and contingency, tells us something about the world we inhabit, the rhetorics we might encounter, and above all the enjoyment of purely circulating that stands in for the Truth we yearn for. Writing that continuously comments on writing and on what a novel might be surely struck Steinberg with fellow feeling as he made drawings that continuously comment on drawing.

As techniques themselves increasingly become subject matter in *Ulysses,*[37] like so many "characters" we come to know, so Steinberg's changing styles and media are what we remember when we come away from his work: his journalistic drawing portfolio of Russia or of theaters of World War II published in the *New Yorker;* the witty lines of his advertisements; his cityscapes that offer, like "Wandering Rocks," a dual perspective—on high and at street level; his eerie painted landscapes; the rubber-stamped figures of inspectors or American presidents, the paper bag masks, the elegant etchings. Like our reading of literary parody, which depends on sophisticated acts of decoding, Steinberg's images often present meanings that we must tease out. For every drawing that implies a "punch line," there are many drawings that hint at meanings we can only move toward, rather than arrive at, as if difficulty provides, as it does in *Ulysses,* an ongoing acknowledgment of mystery rather than mastery.

17

Steinberg's and Joyce's Mythologies

"I Enter a Labyrinth"

James Joyce and Saul Steinberg collected, parodied, and created myths. Their mocking or simply repetitive parodies of established myths metamorphose, through the power of their patterned art, into their own modernist mythologies.[1] We may follow Denis Donoghue in regarding myth as a "story told for the benefit of the community to which it is addressed: it tells the members of that community how to live, what to do, which forces they should dread." Myths have everything to do with reception: that is, they are stories *taken as* "explanatory, edifying, or admonitory," and they embody "a comprehensive ambition, to clarify human life as such." A myth speaks of "the forms of life that persist in a community through diverse conditions,"[2] and it "makes possible any number of ideas but does not commit itself to any single idea."[3] Tracing a few of these ideas will be the work of this chapter.

But how, in the first place, might we relate Steinberg's drawn and painted mythic figures to Joyce's famous "mythic method"? Certainly, one way would be to discuss specific myths that fascinated both men, such as the (Ovidian) labyrinth, and this I will do. But a slight detour through the thought of Giambattista Vico will reveal that a concern with myth and its relation to history informs both their parodic mythologizing and their mythopoesis, the creation of myth.

In 1926 Joyce remarked that Vico's theories "forced themselves on me through circumstances of my own life."[4] Although references to Vico appear more obviously in *Finnegans Wake* than in *Ulysses,* Joyce's musings reveal a Viconian strain in his thinking all along. *Ulysses,* he writes in 1920, "is an epic of two races (Israelite-Irish) and at the same time the cycle of the human body as well as a little story of a day (life). The character of Ulysses always fascinated me—even when a boy. . . . [*Ulysses*] is also a sort of encyclopaedia. My intention is to transpose the myth *sub specie temporis nostri* [from the perspective of our time]."[5] The novel as epic actually involves, according to this letter, three bodies of mythology: the Greek, the Hebrew, and the pagan Irish. Myth, however, he will transpose to the "perspective of our time," that is, to historical reference.

Vico, in both his *Autobiography* and *New Science,* argues that the antiquarian history of his day, wedded as it was to mere factuality, needs to be amended by taking into account the "new science" of mythology.[6] The historian's task, according to Vico, is "to save the logos of ancient myth and make it significant for the modern mind."[7] Myth becomes historical evidence of how civil society has been made across time, and historians need to "be attentive and responsive to the living presence of those mythical modifications of earliest antiquity which still persist in our modern mind."[8] Thus is born Vico's "New Critical Art," a method for understanding the present by exploring the ancient past, while recognizing that "fables were true and trustworthy histories of the customs of the most ancient peoples."[9] Vico entwines legend and history.

In the schoolroom scene in "Nestor," Joyce implicitly criticizes history as the memorization and recitation of dry facts, and Stephen's pupils share his frustration: "Tell us a story, sir. Oh, do sir, a ghoststory" (*U,* 25). That Joyce intends in *Ulysses* to tell "a little story," to provide "a sort of encyclopaedia," *and* to write a mythological epic ("Israelite-Irish") for his day, indicates that he, too, infuses history with mythic story. As does Steinberg: "I've finished the book . . . I've called it the Labyrinth since it contains a great variety of Minotaurs, Heroes, Ariadnes, thread, etc. A bit confused and prolix but not bad, you'll see" (*LAB,* November 21, 1960). *The Labyrinth* "save[s] the logos of ancient myth and make[s] it significant for the modern mind" by showing us the transpositions of those myths into meditations on such twentieth-century topics as celebrity, contemporary Russia, baseball, warfare, politics, and existential doubt. Both Steinberg and Joyce, then, explore mythology as a means to interweave the ancient—and even the ageless—with the contemporary.

First, Joyce. From the very beginning of his drawn-out process of composition, he linked each episode of *Ulysses* to a parallel incident in the *Odyssey.* The seventeenth episode of *Ulysses,* "Ithaca, " for example, combines incidents and images from those chapters of the *Odyssey* having to do with the "Nostos," or return home of Odysseus.[10] For each of Joyce's episodes, Don Gifford and Robert J. Seidman summarize the specifics of the *Odyssey* that appear. As previously noted, Joyce, late in the editing of *Ulysses,* added many detailed correspondences to the *Odyssey.*[11] What he didn't supply was information about how to read the many Homeric parallels within the novel's text. Perhaps they are "parallels that never meet" that "convert a realistic novel into a mock-epic"; or perhaps we can read those parallels as ennobling Dublin's people and events, so that the "mock" aspect nearly melts away.[12] Or, as Vico recommends, we can read details from epics as intersecting with the present day of the novel.

The novel hardly limits itself to manipulating Greek antiquity in relation to the Dublinesque contemporary. Instead, *Ulysses* refers to other stories of mythic heroes both risen and fallen. Bloom/Odysseus—the avenging hero—metamorphoses into such figures as Moses; Parnell; Irish rebels like Lord Edward Fitzgerald, Wolfe Tone, and Kevin Egan/Joseph Casey; and Edmond Dantès, the Count of Monte Cristo. Stephen's mother takes on the sacredness of the Virgin Mary, "Guardian of the Faith"; and Molly Bloom, through her sins of the flesh, calls to mind Mary Magdalene.[13]

Beyond the *Odyssey,* the novel echoes the Bible, Celtic mythology, Dante's *Divine Comedy,* John Milton's *Paradise Lost,* William Shakespeare's and William Blake's works, Ovid's *Metamorphoses,* Platonic myth—all for their projections of virtue, the vividness of their narrative, and the archetypal power of their characters.[14] We know that Joyce admired Victor Bérard's *Les Phéniciens et l'Odyssée,* a work which argued that the *Odyssey* is a "Greek poem with a Semitic intelligence behind it," "filled with Phoenician sea-dogs," and that "Phoenician accounts of island and coastal voyages (*periploi*) filter through the Homeric rhapsodist's ear to the tip of his Greek tongue."[15] In other words, Homer's poem is itself a palimpsest of Eastern and Greek mythology, and Joyce adopted this point of view in writing *Ulysses.*[16] Even though some critics have questioned this thesis, the novel nonetheless contains potent echoes from the East, not only of Hebrew myths including those of the Kabbalah but also of Egyptian mythology and the Bhagavad Gītā.[17] This very multiplicity of parallels and allusions provides an implied way out of the orthodoxies of "objective" history, dogmatic religion, and schools of ethical thought, a shared goal for Stephen and Bloom. *Ulysses,* then, is a novel of fluctuating mythic alternatives. Moreover, with the advantage of hindsight, we can see that Joyce creates as well as alludes to myth. Leopold Bloom, for example, has become a mythic figure in his own right, an everyday hero for the modern and contemporary eras. Molly Bloom, too, has become mythic as she has taken on for many—even some who haven't read *Ulysses*—the lineaments of female heroism or the mystery of the life force.

A strong reading of *Ulysses* requires the Viconian flexibility to move frequently between pairs that are not mutually exclusive: myth and fact, ideal and real. Stephen the aesthete might be expected to sympathize with the poet George William Russell's (A.E.'s) Theosophical or Symbolist view, expressed in "Scylla and Charybdis," that "art has to reveal to us ideas, formless spiritual essences. . . . The deepest poetry of Shelley, the words of Hamlet bring our mind into contact with the eternal wisdom, Plato's world of ideas" (*U*,185). Indeed, when John Eglinton mocks Russell, Stephen "super-politely" answers: "the schoolmen were schoolboys first, Aristotle was once Plato's schoolboy" (*U*, 185).[18]

Aristotle's realism is not to be wholly separated from Plato's idealism. From early on, Stephen acknowledges an earthiness of purpose, invoking the German mystic Jakob Boehme's belief that the modality of visual experience "stands (as signatures to be read) in necessary opposition to the true substances, spiritual identities."[19] Since Boehme, however, maintained "that everything exists and is intelligible only through its opposite," Stephen's viewing of the "rusty boot" on the strand (*U*, 37) also implies a different truth, the ephemerality and superiority of spiritual substance.[20] As the conversation in the National Library progresses, however, Stephen feels less sympathy for mystical lore, reminding himself to "[h]old to the now, the here, through which all future plunges to the past" (*U*, 186). The here and now in its physical manifestations and eternal wisdom; the empiricism of Aristotle and the idealism of Plato: Stephen holds these concurrently in mind, and so must readers of Joyce's novel.

Like Joyce's oeuvre, Steinberg's body of work presents multiple mythologies, and it does so in both obvious and subtle ways. Steinberg's four most prominent mythic presences are those of the Labyrinth, American Icons, the Crocodile, and the Nose. The first two are clearly mythical in nature—Steinberg refers repeatedly to the Ovidian labyrinth as does Joyce, and like Joyce's Celtic mythology, Steinberg's mythical emblems of the American founding and efflorescence gather across his work. The latter two—nose and crocodile—embody "a comprehensive ambition, to clarify human life as such," mythic figures that Steinberg develops on his own.[21] Taken together, these four myths enable Steinberg to blur the distinction between contemporary history and timeless legend, between free aesthetic creation for its own sake and politically engaged art.

In a 1964 appointment book, Steinberg writes, "The unimportance of everything I understand & the greatness of something incomprehensible but all important."[22] It would be an error to overemphasize this casually scribbled note to himself, but it would be equally erroneous to ignore its resonance with his work. What's mythic about it in general (we'll get to the specifics soon) is the sense that, taken together, his many images imply questions that can be answered best (and perhaps only) by myth. Steinberg asks how and with what success the artist fashions worlds, a twentieth-century version of a creation myth. The nature of Being is another of his implied explorations, pervasive in that many of his drawings reverberate in a foundationless situation and present a studied tentativeness and a mysteriousness that the reader-viewer must embrace on the way to interpretation. What stories and arrangements enable us to live together? What are the sources and outcomes of power in the world? These questions, too, elicit from Steinberg groups of images that collectively take on the power of modernist myth.

Joyce and Steinberg, as we've seen, shared an interest in the myth of the labyrinth (neither one makes a distinction between labyrinth and maze). Although Joyce signals his interest by naming one of his two principal characters in *Ulysses* Stephen Dedalus, the Daedalian floats free of Stephen as we come to recognize Bloom the father-figure as Daedalus, and Stephen the son as Icarus. For all his flights of mind, Bloom returns always to the practical, earthy preoccupations of daily life in Dublin, while Stephen, who begins his research in the physical world on the strand, ultimately prefers, Icarus-like, to fly higher, exploring the heady realms of aesthetics and metaphysics.

Joyce moves beyond characterization, however, to atomize and disperse the myth of the labyrinth across the novel. A labyrinth is a puzzle, difficult of solution, and it is only with the aid of nearly a century of commentary that readers can find their way through the novel's difficulties of style, including its rich texture of allusion and its textual wanderings and layerings that can stop the reading process in its tracks like so many labyrinthine dead ends. Joyce self-consciously wrought *Ulysses* as a labyrinth with internal repetitions and connections as a guiding thread. Again: between 1914 when he began the novel, and 1922 when he finally let go of it for full publication, he inserted multiple images so that early chapters anticipated later ones, later chapters echoed the earlier. The way through the labyrinth thus constructed requires multiple rereadings. And as readers trace paths through this patterning, the intricate text itself and the complicated city it brings to life merge, giving rise to a city of words.

The labyrinth is everywhere present in *Ulysses* but nowhere more explicit than in episode 10, "Wandering Rocks." In the schema he sent to his friend Stuart Gilbert, Joyce listed the "Technic" of the episode as "Labyrinth." Appearing at the halfway mark of the novel, it offers a *mise en abyme* of the whole. Joyce spoke of the episode as "a moving labyrinth between two banks"[23] of the Liffey: the Asian bank and the Church represented by Father Conmee (who makes his way from the presbytery in north-central Dublin to Artane, a northeastern suburb), and the European bank and the British government represented by the viceregal cavalcade (that moves from Phoenix Park to the Mirus Charity Bazaar in the southeastern outskirts of the city). Joyce's friend Frank Budgen reports that, while working on the chapter, Joyce bought a game called "Labyrinth" which he played with his daughter, Lucia, cataloguing as he went the "six main errors of judgment into which one might fall in choosing a right, left or centre way out of the maze."[24]

The primary mythic text from which the "Wandering Rocks" chapter issues is that of *Argonautica,* by Apollonius of Rhodes. It's the only chapter that isn't based on the *Odyssey,* although a brief version of Jason's successful trip also appears there, in book 12. Jason and the Argonauts conquer the Symplegades or Clashing Rocks, thought to be fatal to all ships trying to pass through, with the help of Athena, who "with her left hand [held] the stubborn rock apart, while with her right she thrust them through upon their course."[25] Joyce thus combines Ovid's labyrinth with Apollonius's near-fatal clashing rocks.

Ulysses's "Wandering Rocks," composed of nineteen tableaux, presents certain difficulties that function as temporary "dead ends" requiring of the reader rethinking (or "rerouting") through the labyrinth.[26] Perspective oscillates between a bird's-eye view and face-to-face encounters of Dubliners at specific points in the city, and the reader has to toggle between them. Joyce wrote the chapter with a map of Dublin in front of him on which he traced with red ink the routes of the Earl of Dudley and Father Conmee.[27] Yet at the same time, this chapter offers close-up views of people and places. Joyce presents both "the lived experience of the street and the abstract space of the map."[28]

The maplike quality of the chapter has a mechanical feel, as if the narration aspires to capture all that's going on in the city at three o'clock in the afternoon. Yet its close-ups can abruptly confront us with the pathos of life in just a few lines. For example, Stephen's sisters rely on charity for the food they eat:

> —Crickey, is there nothing for us to eat?
> Katey, lifting the kettlelid in a pad of her stained skirt, asked:
> —And what's in this?
> A heavy fume gushed in answer.
> —Peasoup, Maggy said.
> —Where did you get it? Katey asked.
> —Sister Mary Patrick, Maggy said. (*U,* 226)

The expression of such poverty reminds us that, in the Linati scheme, Joyce notes the "Meaning" of the chapter as "The Hostile Milieu."

But the labyrinthine "Wandering Rocks" is also hostile simply by virtue of its plethora of detail—specific streets, buildings, squares, statues, tram stops, views of the river—that can overwhelm the reader, especially one who is not a native of Dublin. Scholarly annotations register the accuracy of many business names, such as Rabaiotti's ice-cream car or "Mangans, late Fehrenbach's."[29] As those names pile up, however, unease grows. We want somehow to master all these proper nouns, to know, categorize, and decide on the significance of each. We also have to account for the characters who linger in or near the chapter's detailed sitings: we want to link their passage and the substance of their conversations to those places, but our desire is exceeded by their sheer number. In addition, we meet not only people who are present but also people only spoken of, including Dubliners as well as historical figures dating from ancient times to the present.

Hostile, too, are the chapter's thirty-one interpolations or intrusions. Within most of the sections we orient ourselves, only to come across a brief passage here and there that does not seem to belong in the episode we are reading. Some of these thirty-one intrusions look forward or backward to a different section of the chapter; they seem to be lifted from one and placed in another. The reading experience of each intrusion jolts us out of one context and into another; backward-looking intrusions set us to reexploring places we've been; forward-looking intrusions simply stymie us until we come to the section where they "belong." For example, in the first section, we follow the Reverend John Conmee, SJ, as he crosses the city, stopping to chat with people he meets, reading his breviary, stepping onto and off of a tram, making his way toward Artane. Suddenly, we read, "Mr. Denis J. Maginni, professor of dancing, etc., in silk hat, slate frockcoat with silk facings, white kerchief tie, tight lavender trousers, canary gloves and pointed patent boots, walking with grave deportment most respectfully took the curbstone as he passed lady Maxwell at the corner of Dignam's court" (*U,* 220). Father Conmee is half a mile from Dignam's court; Maginni is not one of the people whom he comes across in his journey. The reader may at first attempt to synthesize this passage with what has come before—both Conmee and Maginni, for example, walk with grave deportment, and both wear the costume of their profession. But beyond that, there is nothing internal to section 1 to explain why we are suddenly seeing Maginni. We have to wait, perhaps, until section 10, when we see him again: "On O'Connell bridge many persons observed the grave deportment and gay apparel of Mr Denis J. Maginni, professor of dancing &c" (*U,* 235). Even then the confusion isn't resolved, because this is once again an intrusion into the scene in which Bloom stands in a bookshop choosing a book for Molly. Maginni is twice a shard whose edges we cannot soften by fitting him into the contexts in which he appears.

Some intrusions are explained in later sections of "Wandering Rocks" (e.g., an intrusion on p. 229 is explained on p. 232). Or the process can work in reverse: a later intrusion refers to an earlier section of the episode (e.g., *U,* 231, 224, respectively). The "hostility" consists of not initially knowing the meaning of an intrusion, and discovering its meaning only through painstaking progress forward or backward in the text. What's more, threading through the labyrinth, the reader can make sense of some intrusions only by referring, not to their repetition within "Wandering Rocks," but to passages from earlier or later episodes in the novel, or even from *A Portrait of the Artist as a Young Man* and *Dubliners.* "Father Conmee walked through Clongowes field" (*U,* 226) appears in section 4, which takes place in the kitchen at the Dedalus home. But Conmee doesn't walk through Clongowes field during his journey across Dublin; rather he does so in *Portrait.* A few intrusions themselves form a leitmotif: a crumpled throwaway saying that "Elijah is coming" is seen three times as it proceeds down the Liffey. We know what it is because Bloom has earlier in the novel picked up just such a handbill.

Hostile, too—and therefore like wrong turnings in a labyrinth—are confusing references to people. For example, the viceroy of Ireland appears as "the lord lieutenant," while elsewhere in the chapter he is mentioned as "general governor of Ireland" and as "the lord mayor " (*U,* 249, 248, 254–55).[30] Bloom appears in the chapter as the surname of a dentist.

People, places, events, and things in "Wandering Rocks" often echo those of other episodes, so that the seemingly enclosed labyrinth extends outward to link to the labyrinth of the novel as a whole. For example, Father Conmee "passed Grogan's the tobacconist against which newsboards leaned and told of a dreadful catastrophe in New York. In America those things were continually happening. Unfortunate people to die like that, unprepared" (*U,* 221). We have heard of this catastrophe earlier, in "Lestrygonians": "All those women and children excursion beanfeast burned and drowned in New York. Holocaust" (*U,* 182). In both cases, Joyce refers to an actual article in the *Freeman's Journal,* June 16, 1904, which reported on the disaster of the burning of the steamer *General Slocum,* on the East River, in which five hundred people, many of them children, perished.[31]

When we look at the images of the labyrinth or maze in Steinberg's works, it's important to understand that he makes use of it for his own purposes rather than merely imitating Joyce's creation. Yet similarities do exist. Just as we can read *Ulysses* as a labyrinth in which repeating images create a thread through complexities, so we can take Steinberg's oeuvre as a modernist epic, reading his many images in relation to one another, finding our way. Like Joyce, who deliberately repeats images across his novel, Steinberg does the same, providing us with guides through the labyrinth of his thousands of images. Images of the labyrinth itself appear across Steinberg's many works, so that the individual labyrinths he draws are *mise en abymes* of the labyrinthine nature of his body of work.

We know that the labyrinth held important meaning for Steinberg, because, as noted above, he entitled one of his books *The Labyrinth,* telling Aldo Buzzi that, like Joyce, he has the classical myth of the labyrinth always in mind. But in a Viconian manner, his classical labyrinths slowly develop contemporary meanings of their own. The first image after the endpapers of the volume is a simple labyrinth; other pages show the labyrinth as part of a complex image including, for example, the interior of a room and a small landscape (7). Speech balloons take on the shape of labyrinths (8, 10, 12); conversations among people fill the air with competing labyrinths (22); the ribcage of a skeleton (37), the curly hair of a dog (59), even an entire figure of a woman and the rocking chair on which she sits lead our eyes into the labyrinthine (100). Balancing the labyrinth with which the volume opens, the closing pages contain a flurry of labyrinths, each one leading from "A" to "B." We read it as a labyrinth of labyrinths (250–51).

Steinberg's labyrinths suggest multiple meanings—like many myths, we can't pin them down to a single interpretation. He thought of his own creative process as the willingness to set out to goals unknown: "I enter a labyrinth.—I seek it, I start by seeking it, but the idea is not to enter a safe labyrinth, but entering something where you're really going to get lost. The trouble is not artificial. I start by looking for trouble and by finding it. The situation that becomes difficult and can't be solved.[32] Steinberg creates his own hostile, "labyrinthine" situations for making art. Always contemptuous of "make work," Steinberg sat down at his drawing table and tried each day to enter into a state of anxious but productive exploration.

As Joyce writes Dublin into being, so Steinberg draws his (adopted) city, New York. Joyce in "Wandering Rocks" creates perspectives that oscillate between bird's-eye and street-level views; Steinberg does the same (fig. 82). Drawing Bauhaus-style buildings, he seems simultaneously to be drawing labyrinths (fig. 83).

When Steinberg draws people as self-contained labyrinths (fig. 84), he's meditating on the internal complexity of others, the difficulty of knowing them. Even though some of these creatures hold conversations, spouting shapes in air that imitate their internal configurations, the drawing conveys the feeling of "the lonely crowd," a topos of mid-twentieth-century American self-understanding after the sociological study of that name by David Riesman, Nathan Glazer, and Reuel Denney. An emblem of existential questioning might be the generic man who is seated, holding a giant question mark in his right hand, his heavy head resting on his left.[33]

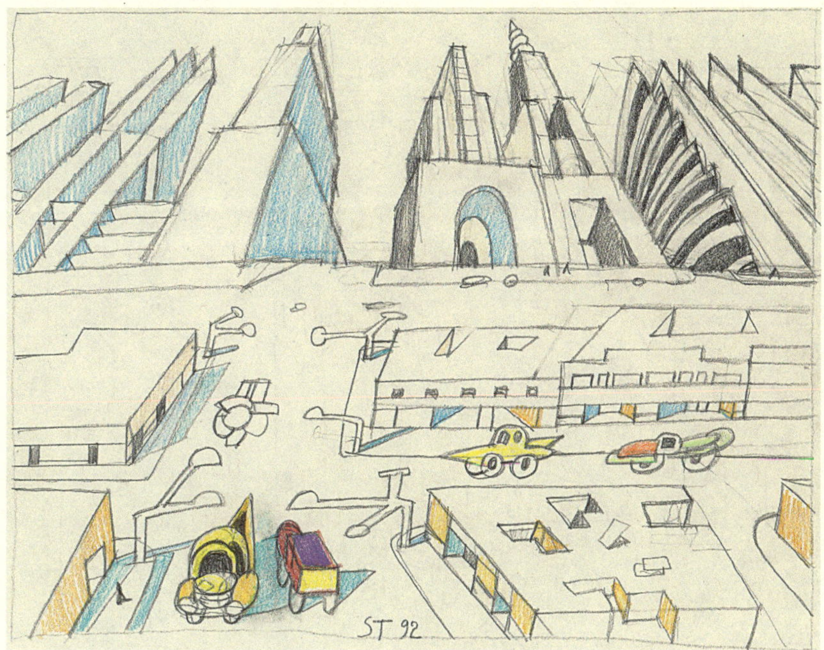

Fig. 82. *City Scene,* 1992. Crayon, black pencil, and pencil on paper, torn from sketchbook, 11 × 14 in. (Beinecke Rare Book and Manuscript Library, Yale University; photograph by Ellen Page Wilson, courtesy Pace Gallery)

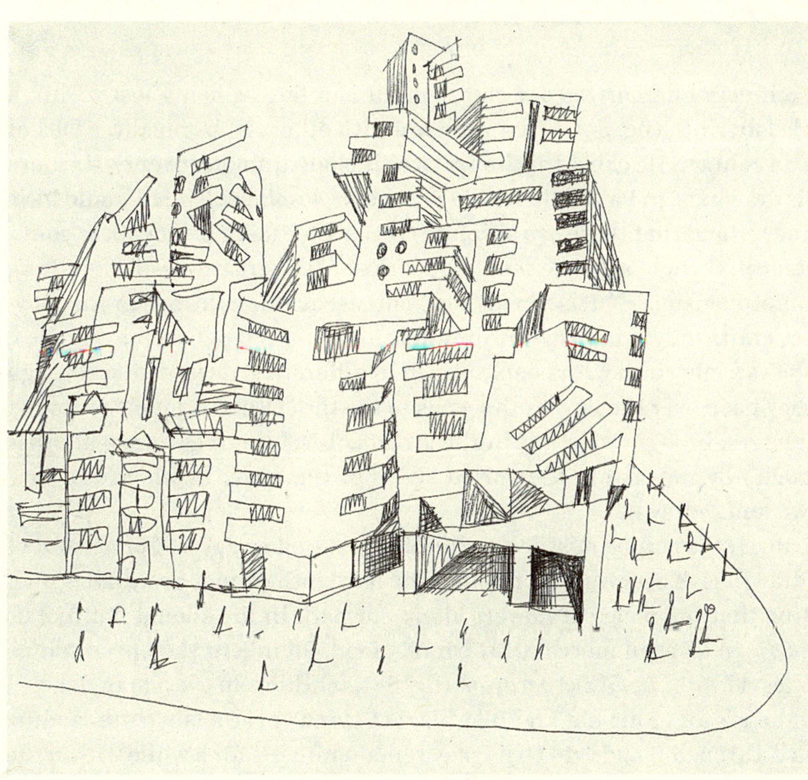

Fig. 83. Untitled, c. 1975–85. Ink on paper, 11½ × 14½ in. (Beinecke Rare Book and Manuscript Library, Yale University)

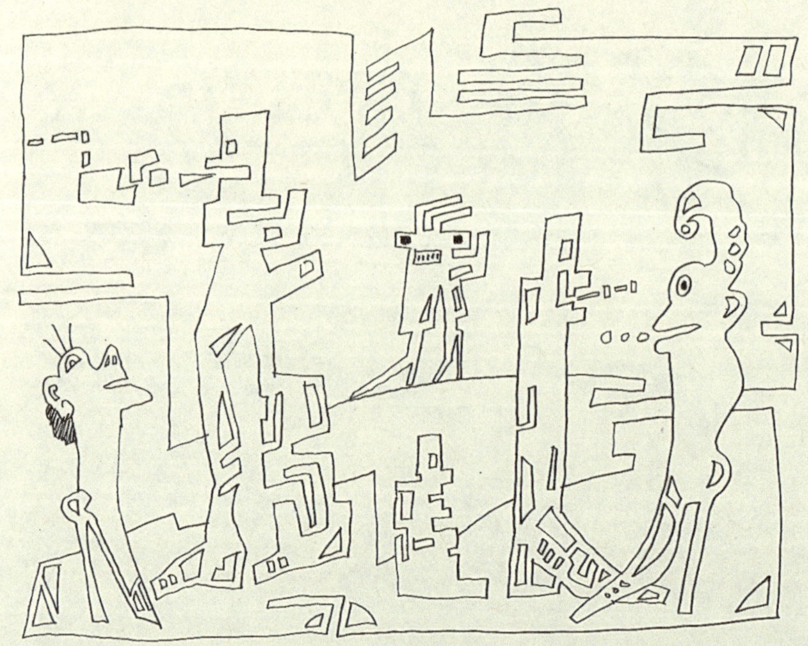

Fig. 84. Untitled, 1980s. Felt marker on paper, 18 × 24 in. (The Saul Steinberg Foundation, New York; photograph by Jenny Gorman)

Steinberg emphasizes our common human fate as being lost within a single labyrinth (fig. 85). What we share with others is, ironically, a lack of human contact. He chose this image to be included, among twenty-six more of his drawings, in Paul Tillich's *My Search for Absolutes.* Tillich would have us understand that there *are* absolute truths; Steinberg is much less confident, even though, as we've seen, he speaks of "the greatness of something incomprehensible."[34] His cloudy sky, curvaceous in contrast to his labyrinth, emits only a few rays of illumination. In a related sketch (fig. 86), he shows a labyrinth with people drawn in different styles walking through it; they peep over the labyrinth's walls to see the "Others," much as Joyce's characters, brought together in the streets of Dublin, regard one another through—by means of—the varied styles of the novel in which they are drawn and redrawn.

Labyrinths can be hostile for Steinberg as well as Joyce. For several of his drawings of everyman, a fall into the labyrinth cannot be avoided, suggesting that the pleasant flowers along our path in life should not fool us (fig. 87). In an even more darkly comic mood, Steinberg sketches what he entitles *A Life of Loud Desperation* (fig. 88), in which an everyman, labeled A at the crown of his hat and B at his feet stands near a labyrinth leading from A through B and C to D: he may remain himself for a while within the

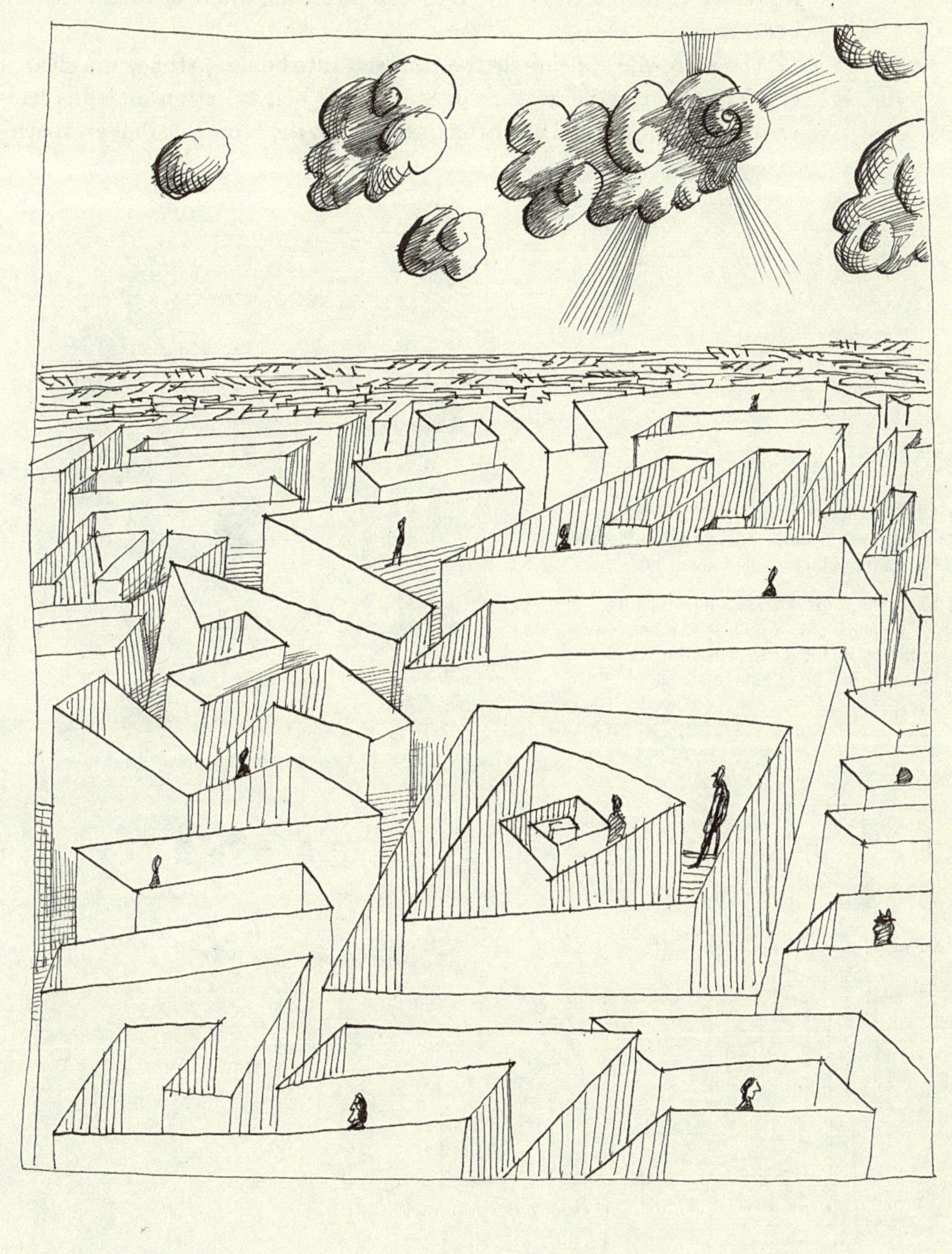

Fig. 85. Untitled, c. 1965–67. Ink on paper, 19½ × 12¾ in. (Beinecke Rare Book and Manuscript Library, Yale University)

maze, but as he reaches C and D there's no telling where or what he'll have become.

The man who appears to draw himself into being, perhaps the clearest emblem of the artist at work in Steinberg's oeuvre, often finds his hand creating a complicated maze that issues from the same line that creates his

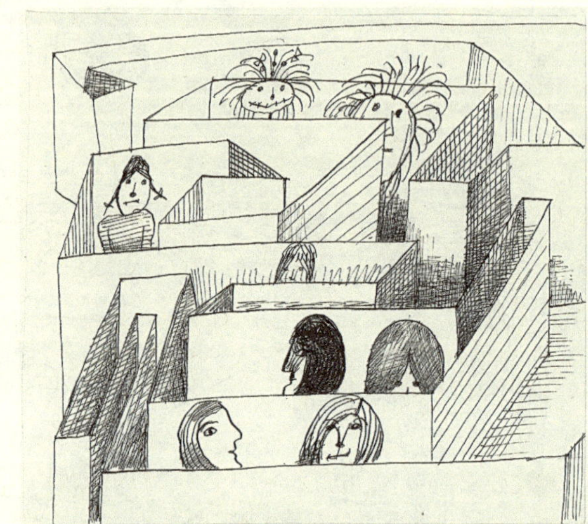

Fig. 86. Sketchbook page, c. 1965–67. Ink on paper, 11⅛ × 13⅞ overall. (Beinecke Rare Book and Manuscript Library, Yale University)

Fig. 87. *To the Labyrinth,* 1963. Ink on paper, 14½ × 23⅛ in. Originally published in the *New Yorker,* March 16, 1963. (Beinecke Rare Book and Manuscript Library, Yale University)

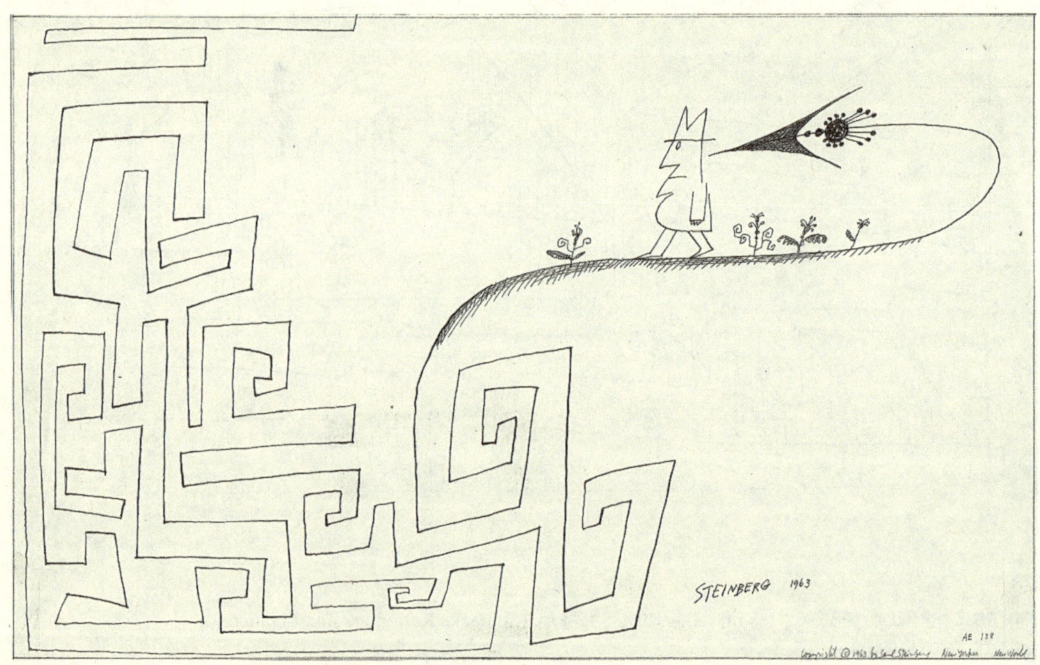

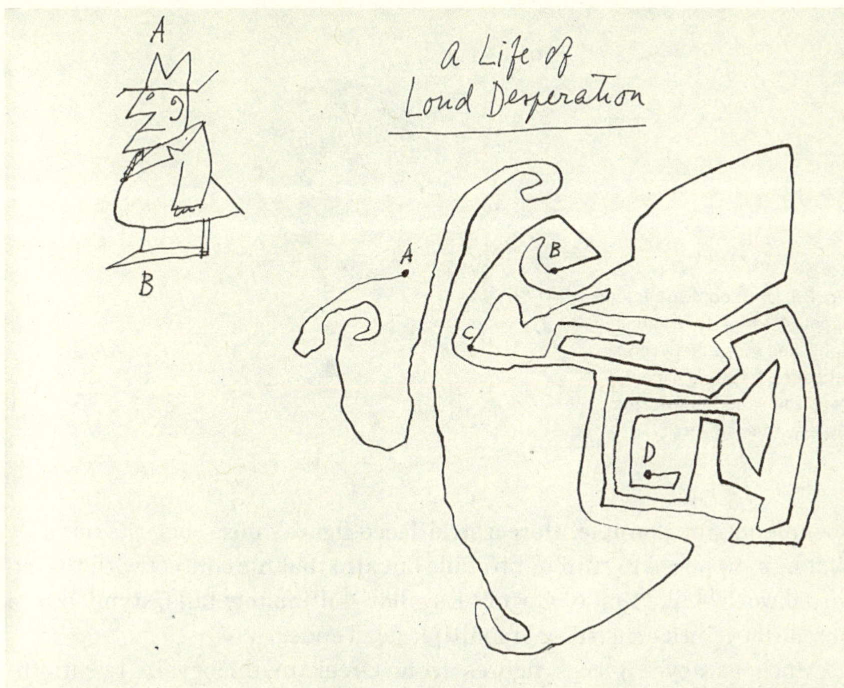

Fig. 88. *A Life of Loud Desperation,* c. 1959. Ink on paper, sketchbook page, 9⅝ × 12¼ in. (Beinecke Rare Book and Manuscript Library, Yale University)

simply drawn body, as if his anxiously held belief that each of us constitutes a simple human identity must be challenged. In drawing labyrinths as part of, or extensions of, the human body, Steinberg seems to take particular pleasure in depicting heads with protruding labyrinths (fig. 89). In this image of the brain as labyrinth, Steinberg pays homage to Van Gogh, who, he said, "was trying to paint with his baroque, comma-like, S-shaped spiral brushstrokes . . . a vision of the convolutions of the brain. Because of his madness, he thought continually of what was happening in his brain, in the labyrinths of his brain, and this obsession led him to represent the world as a gigantic, a cosmic brain: for him, nature was a brain in color."[35]

Therefore, when Steinberg draws, for example, a woman with a labyrinth for a head,[36] he refers to the brain and even to consciousness itself. When he draws a nose that becomes a labyrinth, *Nose #5* (see fig. 13; p. 48), he's not just meditating on the nose, but also showing the relation of the nose to human interiority. With his labyrinthine noses, heads, and bodies Steinberg explores the relation between human innerness and the outside world. A Russian tram conductor wears on his sleeve "*Remont,*" a Russianized French word meaning repair or restructuring. Officialdom often evokes Steinberg's contempt—note his many illegible parodies of official

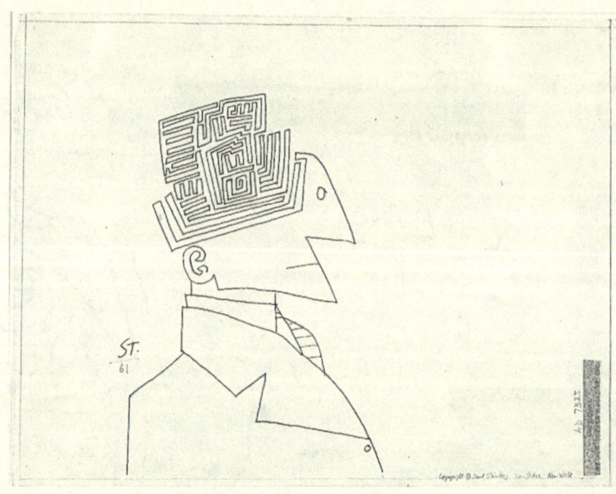

Fig. 89. Untitled, 1961. Ink on paper, 11½ × 14⅝. Originally published in the *New Yorker,* January 28, 1961. (Beinecke Rare Book and Manuscript Library, Yale University)

documents, for example. Here a straitlaced figure's nose suggests not only that he's supposed to sniff out trouble but also that his contact with the external world—like that of Gogol's Kovaliov—ultimately fails, stymied by a hostile labyrinth consisting of multiple dead ends.

Much as Joyce places figures from Greek mythology in twentieth-century Dublin, Steinberg gives his figures of ancient myth a contemporary context. In addition to labyrinths, we meet, for example, a female sphinx—complete with feathered hat, eyeglasses, the body of a domesticated cat, and the tail of a lion—presiding disapprovingly over a rural American horizon (fig. 90).

Steinberg repeatedly explores as well the contemporary mythology of his chosen country. As Joyce draws Dublin into being, so Steinberg draws the contemporary United States: "When I came here I saw the American landscape that I realized was untouched. I had a great appetite to paint it, to draw it. And I did. I drew these things that hadn't been drawn before. American women, small towns, motels and diners, and so on, but I drew them with the same carefulness that a more noble artist uses for a nude or for a still life or for an apple. It's not that I look at them as clichés. I looked at them as something that had never been seen before."[37] At the same time, and sometimes even in the same drawing, Steinberg appropriates familiar American icons or symbols ranging from the Founding Fathers to Mickey Mouse and Santa Claus.[38] He calls this "Americanerie" and mentions his plans to depict "Indians, pyramids, columns, symbols, rainbows, Niagara Falls, Statue of Liberty, sphinxes, all this stuff that's part of the American mythology."[39]

He especially enjoys bringing the varied figures of American mythol-

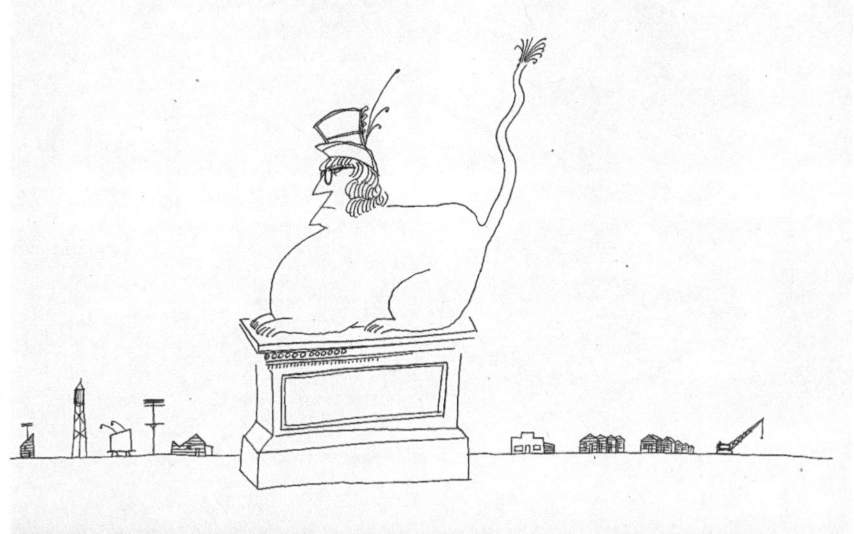

Fig. 90. Untitled, c. 1953. Ink on paper, 14½ × 23 in. (Cincinnati Museum of Art; gift of The Saul Steinberg Foundation)

ogy into complex images that generate an air of mystery as the viewer attempts to discern the statements Steinberg might be making. *The American Corrida* (fig. 91) appears to be political commentary. Here, Uncle Sam shamelessly baits with an American flag the "bull" or Native American in feathered regalia. In the front row, Abraham Lincoln, the American Eagle, Lady Liberty holding a Grim Reaper's scythe, a cowboy in a ten-gallon hat, and Santa Claus provide an audience. Interpreting the whole as political satire makes sense, in part because Steinberg stated that "I'm not art for art's sake," but rather "I'm art with a purpose and the purpose is political."[40] His mythological figures, like Joyce's, find traction in the contemporary, as twentieth-century social commentary. *American Corrida* thus implies a meaning along these lines: just as the European settling of the American wilderness involved the slaughter of indigenous peoples, so Americans today commit violent acts at home and on the world stage.

Such a reading can even become part of biographical surmise. Once we know that Steinberg viewed his life in Romania as benighted ("I had no rights. . . . My childhood, my adolescence in Romania were a little like being a black in the state of Mississippi"), it's no surprise that his images tell of American abuses of power (*RS,* 3). For this skeptical immigrant, patriotism and bravery can be mere showy falsity—a Barnum & Bailey circus or a Walt Disney production with Mickey Mouse right there on the job, Uncle Sam's backup.

To stop at this interpretation, however, would be premature. While

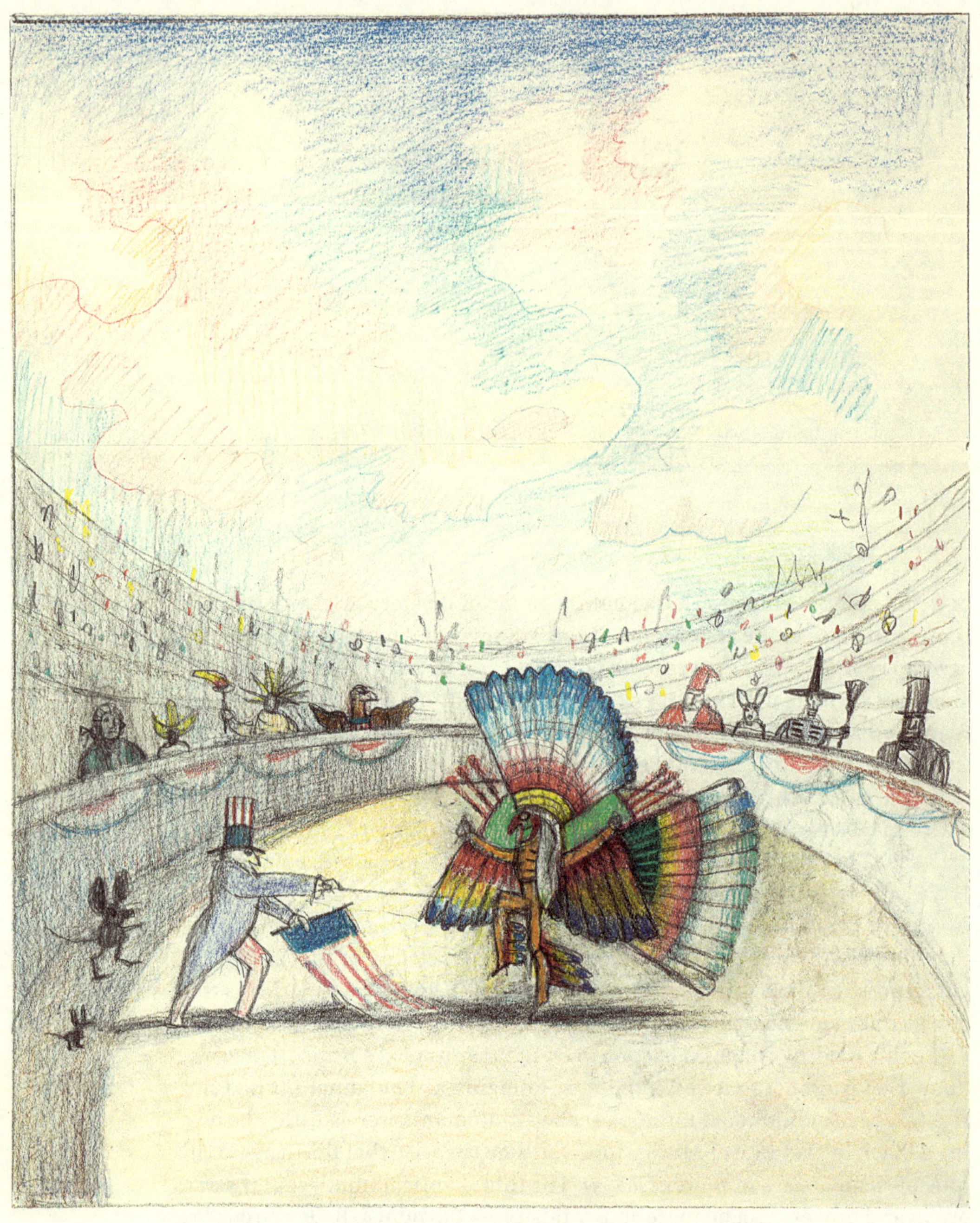

Fig. 91. *The American Corrida,* c. 1981–91. Colored pencil, crayon, and pencil on paper, 21 × 16⅞ in. (The Saul Steinberg Foundation, New York; photograph by Teresa Christiansen)

Steinberg tells some interviewers that his art is political, he tells others that social commentary is only part of his artistic practice. He uses the example of Joyce to make his point:

> But to go back to this about, on one side a certain concern with the drawing itself, on the other the social aspect of things. That's where my nature as a writer comes in. . . . Where literature comes in is if you think of another sort of influence that could be stronger—Joyce, for instance, who has these two parts. The social comment is the camouflage for his words, for his game of words, for the construction of phrases and so on. And the dialogue sometimes is, you could say, abstract, although it pretends to be social comment—abstract in the sense that it's a poetic, verbal thing, and has to do, or has not to do with people. Anyway it's a mixture. One goes from one thing to another. The same thing goes with Gogol.[41]

Here Steinberg sidesteps the phrase *l'art pour l'art* and uses instead the notions of game and abstraction. Like Joyce's art, Steinberg's is, he tells us, made of social commentary *and* what he goes on to call "the pleasures of improvisation," distinguishing those pleasures from the "labor of the journalist."[42]

Steinberg's incorporation of mythic American characters involves not only social message but also aesthetic playfulness valued for its own sake. The *American Corrida* proffers not only a look at a terrible chapter in American history but also a certain candy-colored zaniness. Perhaps Uncle Sam's spear is collapsible, perhaps at the end of this Wild West show, the rabbit will shake hands with the witch, the Native American will wander back into the movie from which he came, Abraham Lincoln will stroll back onto the penny, and everyone will take pleasure in the sheer brightness of spectacle.

Steinberg re-creates American mythology in a variety of moods. Uncle Sam and Lady Liberty, for example, may be just another couple in Steinberg's ongoing cataloguing of couples (fig. 92). But when he creates his many complex images in which multiple American symbols appear, Steinberg can catapult the mythology of the American nation into a realm of complexity that denies interpretive closure.

The lithograph *Sam's Art* is one such experiment (fig. 93). Uncle Sam/Abraham Lincoln sits with his palette at an easel. Before him towers the unfinished pyramid and eye of the Great Seal of the United States, with the word "one" suggesting the dollar bill on which it appears. *Annuit Cœptis* translates as "Providence favors [our] undertakings."[43] Behind him stands a cannon with its ammunition neatly stacked nearby and the American Eagle perched on its chase. Specifically American construction and destruction flank the artist. So far, so good—what providence doesn't take

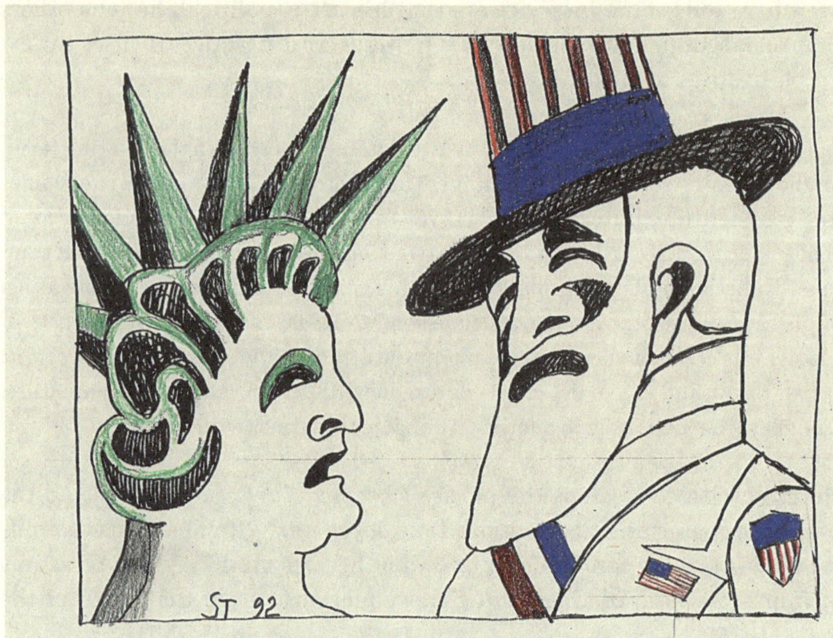

Fig. 92. Untitled, 1992. Colored pencil or crayon over photocopy, 11 × 14 in. (Beinecke Rare Book and Manuscript Library, Yale University)

care of, round shot will. Steinberg approves of the pyramid in general: "The pyramid: It is very satisfying to look at. Nothing is more right, more stable, and more representative of man's presence than a pyramid."[44]

What Uncle Sam paints, however, can't be contained by the canvas, instead erupting upward into the air, high above the eagle itself, in a series of abstract shapes culminating in clouds. The American scene's doctrinaire symbols give way to the free play of the imagination. When Steinberg's characteristic faux handwriting appears above and below the whole, its very illegibility stymies the promise of extractable meaning, of authoritative commentary or labeling. Uncle Sam, the eagle, the cannon, the pyramid, and the eye above it provide only the beginnings of meaning. They exist within a document that finally floats as free of representation and didacticism as the abstract painting within it. What begins as a nationalist mythology of strength and virtue serves as a jumping-off point for another, related story, that of cloud making, of aesthetic endeavors—Steinberg's and our own.

Steinberg doesn't rely solely on the received mythology of labyrinths and American icons. He also creates myths of his own, such as that of the crocodile. He even explicates this myth at length:

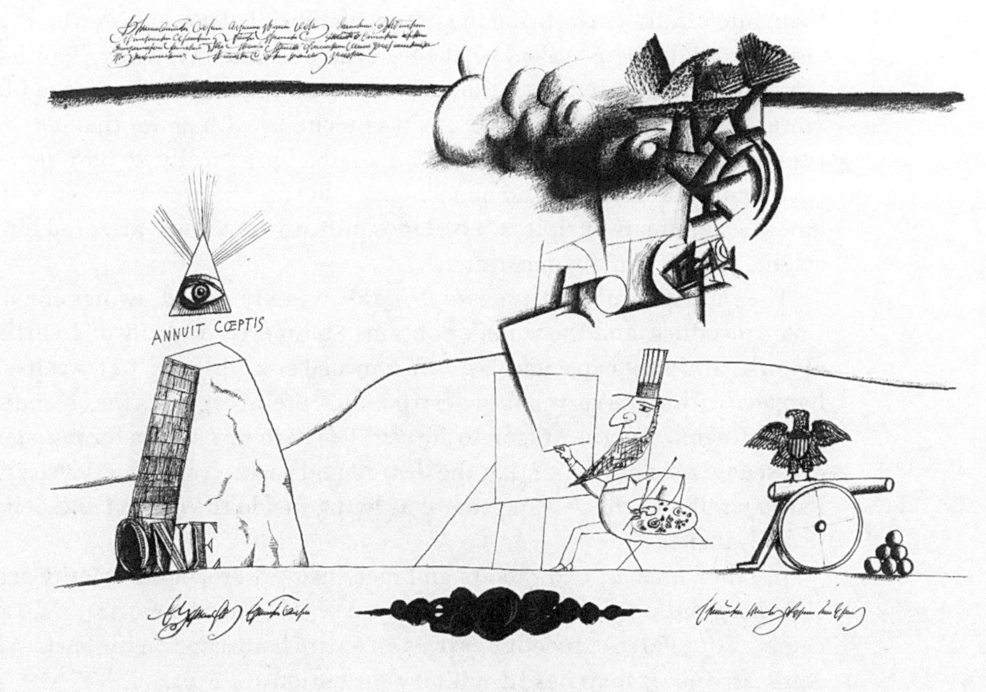

Fig. 93. *Sam's Art,* 1966. Lithograph on paper, 22 × 30 in. (The Saul Steinberg Foundation, New York)

But you know what a crocodile looks like. I know, and I don't know. The main thing to find out is what sort of technique the crocodile employs to show itself, and I found out that while, let's say, the lion is a baroque animal and some others—the hog, the fox—are maybe Gothic, the crocodile is Aztec. An extinct art. It has the rigidity of extinction, and it fits the discipline of the crocodile. I watched how they camouflaged themselves with their feet—they appear as if they are made out of mud. They want to appear like landscape, and they succeed. . . . The sides of the crocodile are disguised as—well, as crossword puzzles. The scales are made in a variety of dark green and light gray and sepia and so on, and they alternate and made some sort of a vertical and horizontal system of words. Which works all right, for a magic animal to have riddles and puzzles on the sides . . . I can relate it vaguely to the Chinese and the labyrinthine qualities of that art. The reason I hate the monster is that he is obviously part of the primitive system of nature where certain privileges were given unevenly to different species. All the armored animals are helpless and timid—the turtle, the armadillo and so on. In other words, armor is for defense, not attack. But this son-of-a-bitch is vicious, has terrific teeth, is a great swimmer and, on top of it, he's armored. So he got everything.[45]

Magic, verbal, labyrinthine, vicious: crocodiles, when Steinberg inserts them into his drawings, bring the notion of unbridled power over whatever else surrounds them. Asked what they symbolize, he responds, "Political power in general, administration in every form. . . . Just like the crocodile, power has too many advantages. . . . It's inevitable with power that it's corrupt and wicked. It's very rare, it's impossible, practically, to have power with equity and modesty and nonchalance. So I use the croc as power, and I have the hero man—helpless, a real mosquito on horseback, armored himself but just for fun, for decoration."[46]

The endpapers of *Drawing into Being* show Steinberg's drawings of multiple crocodiles, and the volume contains Steinberg's drawing of an artist at work within the capacious jaws of a crowned crocodile (fig. 94). Art itself happens within the very jaws of destruction.[47] Steinberg links the crocodile to the dragon, and the dragon to Joyce: "The hero was always for me a guy dressed up on a horse fighting the dragon and so on. Now, I see Joyce and I see myself and the Jew in general as living inside the dragon and being literally inside."[48]

In other images, two rabbits embrace inside a crocodile's toothy grin (*The Labyrinth,* 73), and two men duel there (YCAL inv. no. 5381, *NY,* December 10, 1960). A crocodile carries an entire landscape on his back (*NY,* April 21, 1962); marches in military formation (SSF 01204, *NY,* May 3,

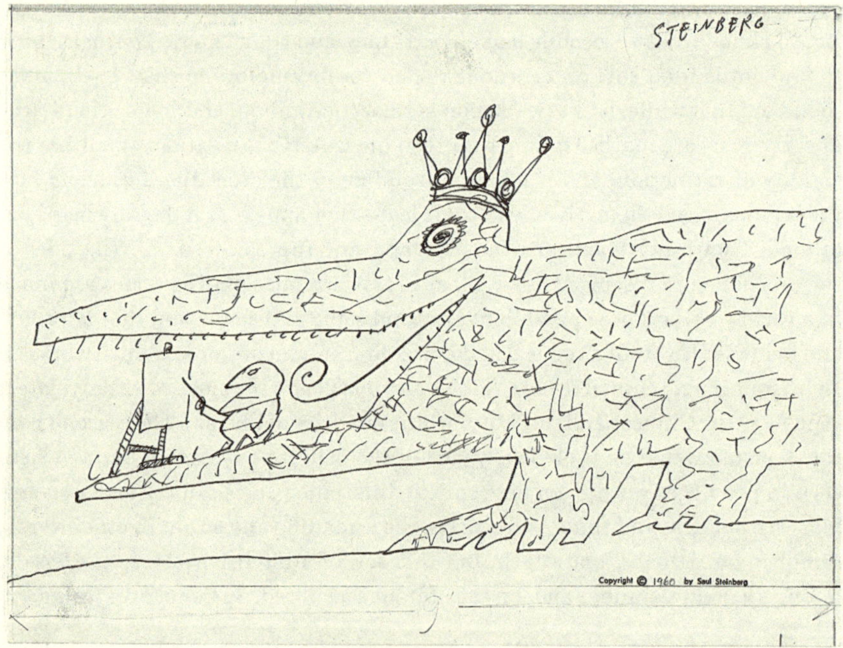

Fig. 94. Untitled, 1960. Ink and pencil on paper, 8½ × 11 in. (Beinecke Rare Book and Manuscript Library, Yale University)

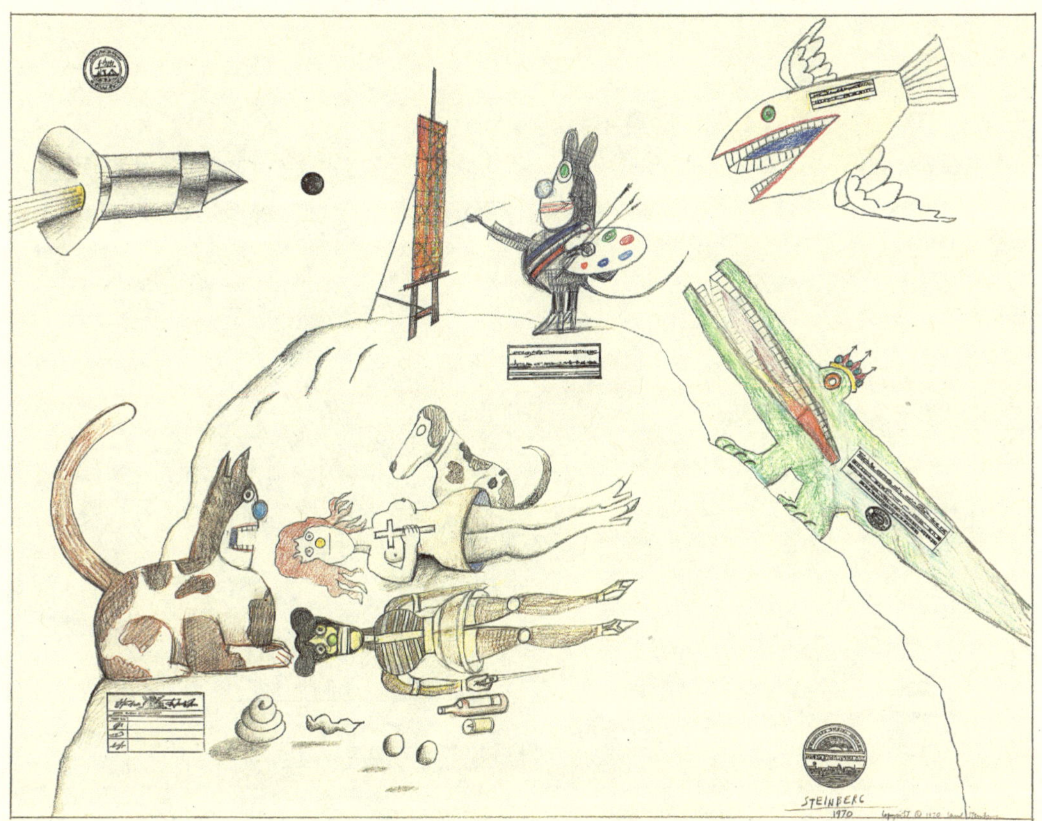

1969); approaches a poodle, peacock, and rabbit (*The Inspector,* 90); and lurks on city corners (SSF 01195; YCAL inv. no. 3467). One even drives an automobile (YCAL inv. no. 1556). When, in *Artist,* Mickey Mouse paints on an easel perched atop a hill (fig. 95), it's the crocodile climbing on human legs, and not the shark or missile, that comes closest. Other victims lie nearby in this dangerous world.

Fig. 95. *Artist,* 1970. Pencil, crayon, colored pencil, ink, and rubber stamp on paper, 22½ × 28½ in. (National Gallery of Art, Washington DC; gift of The Saul Steinberg Foundation; photograph by Teresa Christiansen)

Steinberg, like Joyce, delights in combining myths, so that we see, in *Niagara Crocodile* (fig. 96), the symbolic unfinished pyramid and eye of the Great Seal anchored among the rocks of an Art Deco Niagara Falls, along with rubber-stamped people who are dwarfed by nature and doubly threatened by an upstate crocodile in waiting. The four "seals" that Steinberg rubber-stamps and draws on this sheet, along with the illegible writing, here refer to the power of "administration" with its official documentation that Steinberg abhors—and relates to the crocodile.

While the crocodile is for Steinberg a mythic figure and a vicious "son-of-a bitch," the nose is often a mythic figure of redemptive memory,

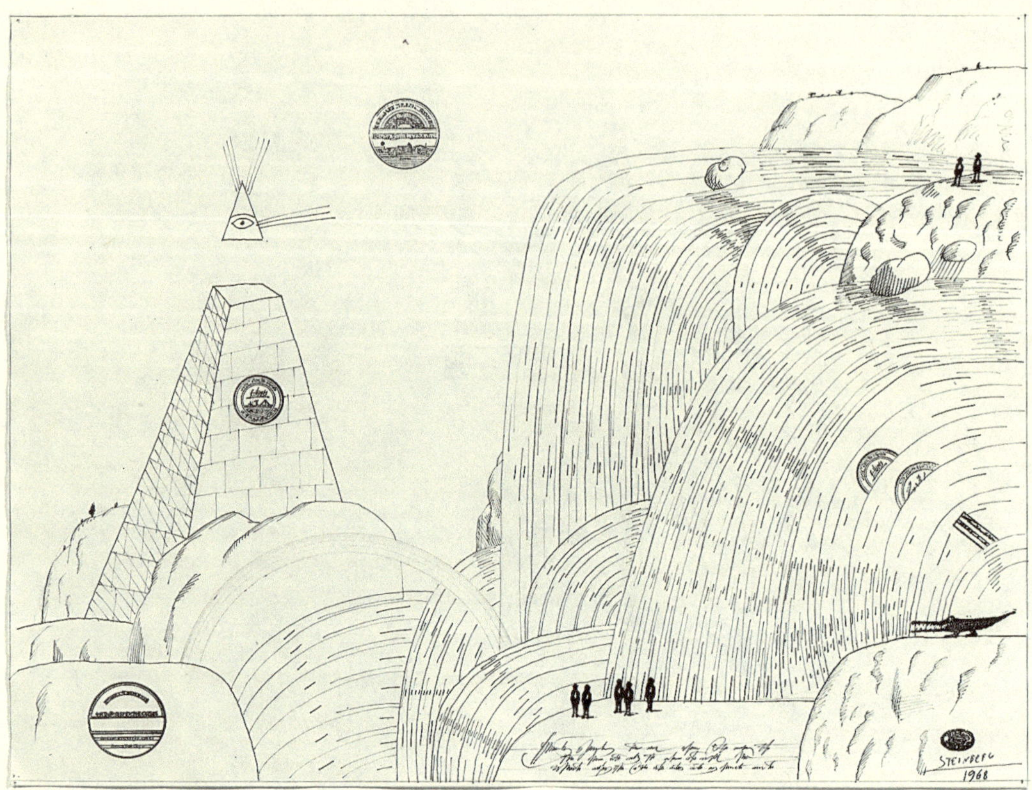

Fig. 96. *Niagara Crocodile,* 1968. Ink, pencil, and rubber stamps on paper, 19½ × 25½ (The Saul Steinberg Foundation, New York; photograph by Jenny Gorman)

a part of the "body's intelligence" that signals, wherever it appears, the literary origin of his art: "Anything that implies some sort of intelligence, of whatever kind, belongs at least partly to the realm of literature. The body's intelligence is the metaphysics of the nose."[49] It's like a second brain, concerned with matters higher, questions deeper, than the merely physical. Sometimes he speaks of his own nose as "having a brain" that can remember smells that his fleshly nose does not: "certain smells that I haven't smelled since I was a child come back to me—not to my nose, like an actual smell, but to the nose's brain" (*RS,* 4–5). Simply put, a nose sticks out, but for Steinberg it also always retains its placement as part of the skull, its seamless attachment to the place where labyrinthine brains reside.

The nose acts as a character in many of his drawings, and as such, all of his noses grow not just from faces but also from Steinberg's reading of Gogol's tale "The Nose" and Nabokov's study *Nikolai Gogol.* He's well aware of the mythical underpinnings of the noseless face: "Anyway, the symbol of something that is missing . . . it's a very old symbol . . . of sacrifice."[50] Like

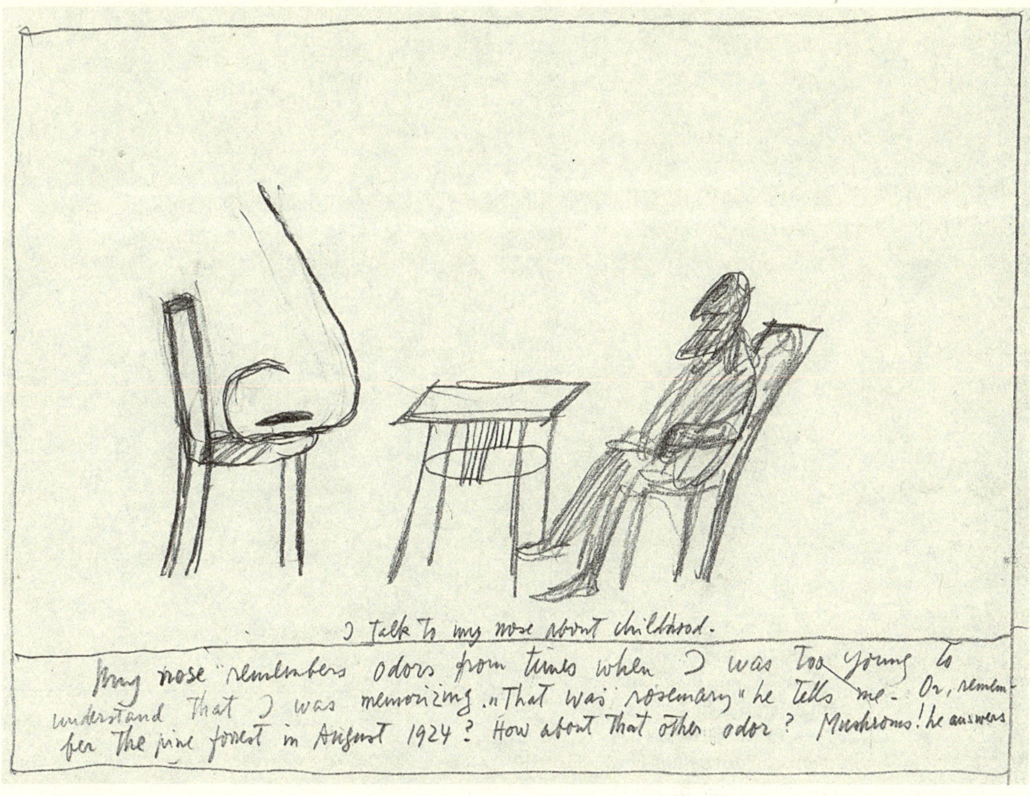

Fig. 97. *Ex-voto: I talk to my nose about childhood,* c. 1983–95. Pencil on paper, torn from sketchbook, 10¾ × 14 in. (Beinecke Rare Book and Manuscript Library, Yale University)

Gogol's detached nose, Steinberg's can converse, and it helps him remember his childhood. In *I talk to my nose about childhood* (fig. 97), one of his "ex-votos," Steinberg writes: "My nose remembers odors from times when I was too young to understand that I was memorizing. 'That was rosemary,' he tells me—Or, remember the pine forest in August 1924? How about that other odor? Mushrooms! He answers."

Gogolian noses can go astray, and the noses of some types of people, especially uniformed men, are, as we've seen (see fig. 13; p. 48), labyrinths closed off from the outer world. Some hold their noses at a distance from their faces (fig. 98). They might be versions of Gogol's Collegiate Assessor Kovaliov—men who, having lost their noses through no (or is it every?) fault of their own, now worry about how to reattach them. Then again, they might be military men who have neatly detached their own noses, leaving a void where the intelligence of the nose should be. In this formal portrait, complete with label, those geometrical shapes on the table suggest both sophisticated abstract thought and a child's blocks, as easily manipulated

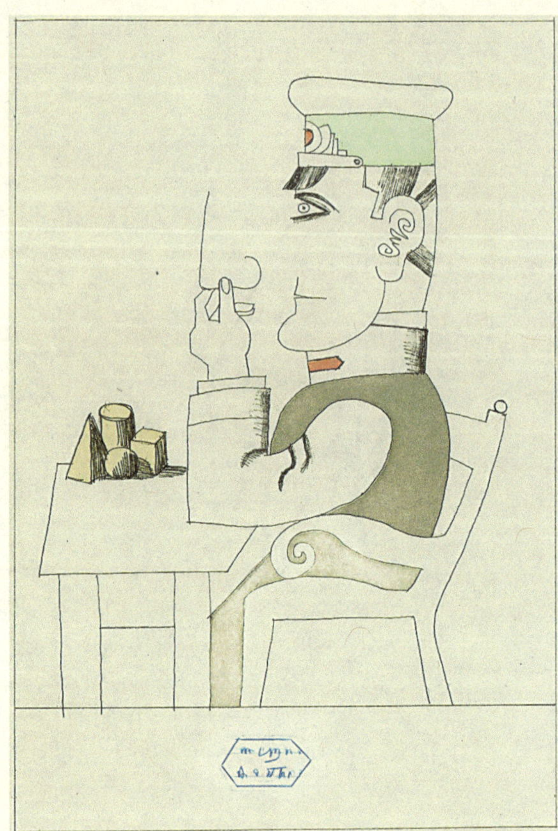

Fig. 98. Untitled (*Gogol*), c. 1984. Etching in colors, with colored pencil on paper, 23⅜ × 19⅞ in. (The Saul Steinberg Foundation, New York; photograph by Jenny Gorman)

as any Steinbergian nose militant. Even more curiously, Steinberg likes to draw faces in profile in which the nose, eye, and forehead point inward, while the mouth and chin point out (fig. 99). An unsuccesful reattachment process? A narcissistic public servant? Steinberg won't say.

In Steinberg's mythology of noses we find *Russian Noses* (SSF 05195), a dog with a thought balloon issuing from its moist little nose (*NY,* December 26, 1983), a man whose nose contains a miniature version of himself (SSF 07052), a military man whose nose dissolves into a free-form line that loops in thin air (SSF 04436), even another of his couples—this one a nose and its glasses (*NY,* July 28, 1980). He enjoyed drawing big noses early in his career,[51] and told Adam Gopnik that Harold Ross objected, saying that "Americans don't have such big noses—he was afraid—there was some trace of anti-Semitism in Ross."[52]

For Steinberg, "people are profiles," and the nose seems for him the star of the drama of personality. But the nose's story is versatile. It's a vi-

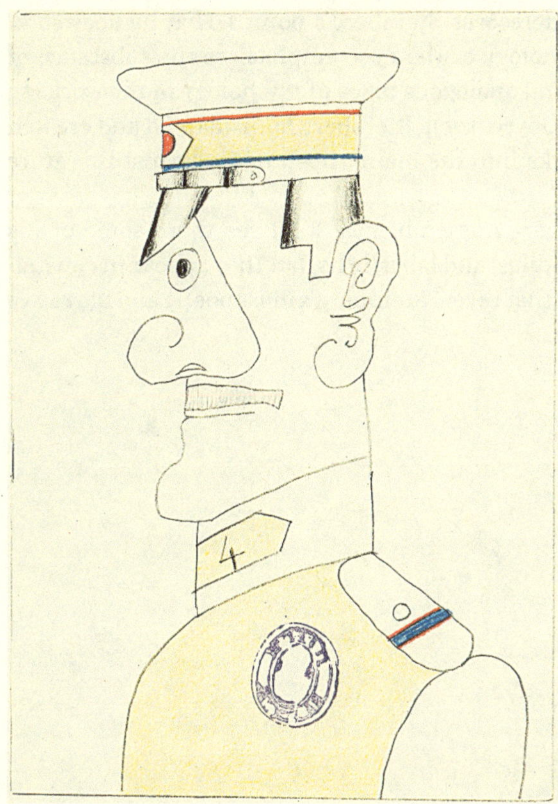

Fig. 99. Untitled, 1983. Lithograph in colors on wove paper, 11¼ × 7⅞ in. (The Saul Steinberg Foundation, New York; photograph by Jenny Gorman)

sual myth that has multiple, brief episodes, allowing its owner to reexperience the past, display the Gogolian absurdity of experience, and explore his or her own interiority. In the epic of Steinberg's oeuvre, the nose's silly authority challenges the crocodile, its universality naturalizes every immigrant, and its intelligence links it to the literariness that Steinberg so valued in art.

On what basis may we compare verbal and visual mythology? Steinberg helps us understand how he does so, when he discusses Gogol's "The Nose": "In painting or sculpture, you can't take off a nose, that would be immediately macabre. Whereas with a drawing, it's possible, it's only a line that disappears or inspires the fantasy of becoming a labyrinth, of refusing to conform to the rest of the face. Gogol reasoned like a draftsman with a line; for him, to take off a nose, it was like taking off the word nose, or even the *n* of nose, and liberating it."[53] When Steinberg likens Gogol to a draftsman who works with the lines forming letters and words, he indicates a flexible analogizing of word and image. (That Gogol was actually an amateur draftsman and painter only underscores Steinberg's point.) That he does so in reference to his own mythology of the nose emphasizes the substance of this chapter: the central and analogous place of mythology in the works of Steinberg and Joyce. Like Joyce, then, Steinberg both adapted and created myths that thrust his works into the mainstream of modernist literature and art.

Turning now to Steinberg's assemblages, we'll see there some of his mythic noses, icons, crocodiles, and labyrinths, but they appear in constellations of multiple images that reveal Steinberg's most poetic and narrative modes.

18

Steinberg's Art of Assemblage

The Drawing Table

Central to Steinberg's notion of himself as a writer was his drawing table. He explains to Grace Glueck, "A long time ago Leonardo said, '[La] pittur[a] è cosa mentale'—painting is a thing of the intellect. Certainly, so is poetry and literature and music . . . And when I make a drawing I'm just like a writer. I have a desk—a bigger desk, of course; I need more space. But I sit down and look at this piece of paper and think, what am I going to do?"[1] One answer was to replicate the very desk at which he sat. Steinberg began to create tabletop assemblages during the 1970s: "By 1971, Steinberg had begun replicating the common objects in his studio at 1:1 scale in three dimensions—casual trompe-l'oeil sculptures created by (his word) 'whittling,' assembling and painting simulacra of the objects all around him. . . . [T]he point of this strange mimetic game went beyond visual resemblance to invoke some more primal form of imitative magic. . . . [Some] he incorporated into 'drawing table' assemblages . . . which recreate the ordinariness and the mystery of the miniature stage upon which the world of his art daily came to life before him" (*SS: I,* 196).

Some of his assemblages are composed of carved items mounted on flat pieces of wood. Known as Drawing Table reliefs, also called Table Series (see, e.g., fig. 115; p. 254), they are typically encased in Plexiglas covers and meant to be hung vertically. Others are assemblages of carved or otherwise constructed elements set on tables or stands.[2] These freestanding assemblages are not, however, a wholly new experiment. Looking across his earlier works, we see a variety of two- and three-dimensional tabletops on paper, wood, and canvas that seem to lead toward the later assemblages, among them drawings and prints, oil paintings and collages, and etchings on metal plates. From beginning to end, tables appear in Steinberg's oeuvre, in all the media and genres he explores.

William Seitz, curator of the important show *The Art of Assemblage* (1961) at the Museum of Modern Art, pointed out that "figuratively, the practice of assemblage raises materials from the level of formal relations to that of 'associational poetry.'"[3] He sees assemblages as often metaphorical, in that they visually join or associate two (and more) things that are different. We might think of Steinberg's table assemblages as the lengthy fictions of his literary world, since they contain all of the "shorter forms" of his oeuvre: drawings, paintings, prints, collages, and small-scale sculptures.

Steinberg's tables are depictions of places as large as the world and as local as his own studio. They present memories, states of being, scenes of potential, and fields of patterns that point to, but never achieve, full harmony. On them, familiar domestic items retain their comforting associations while also paradoxically estranging themselves from us. Things quiver.

Food items, artists' and writers' tools, flowers in vases, toys, miniature furniture and buildings, lidded boxes, abstract shapes, talk balloons from comic books, documents, drawings, books—and much more—together form a constellation of near meaning, an arrangement in space of things that represent ordinary objects but that also tell a tale or tales that seem only just to elude us. We orient ourselves, navigate around the table, and journey through a three-dimensional still life that takes on, with our exigencies of vision, the energy of complex narrative, the associations of poetic imagery. Things juxtaposed or constellated on the tables give rise to narrative meaning as we look at them.

They are part of Steinberg's fiction writing and mythopoesis: "The objects in wood—books, pencils—are erotic characters, that is, subjects that I really love, that are for me equivalent to the gods of the house, the lares and penates."[4] To claim that these tables can be "taken" as narrative in quality is to embrace the notion that narrative is, quite simply, "the representation of an event or series of events."[5] Events here include those implied by the things on the table (e.g., a box is to be opened, a talk balloon is to be read, a brush is to be wielded) as well as our own imaginative fashioning of these already-made things into "what happens" atop the table. Even—perhaps especially—the empty spaces matter. Gaps themselves link these tables to narrative, for "it is only through inevitable omissions that a story gains its dynamism"[6] as readers supply connections.

In exploring the complexity of narrative, however, we need to recognize that narrative discourse, unlike a story, need not follow time's arrow forward; it can change (and change again) temporal direction on the impulse of its creator. Experiencing Steinberg's assembled tables, our eyes are free to dart and linger along multiple vectors. Time is, of course, inseparable from the unfolding of events in narrative, and as this chapter proceeds, it will be looking at several orders of time implied by the tables: the time it took to craft each thing on the table as well as the table itself; the specific period when each thing was crafted; remembered time as it dwells within the table's things; the time each viewer of the table takes in reading its contents; and specific references to time, such as a crafted wooden box with a specific year incised in its lid in Arabic numerals, or a faux book "published" in a certain year. Events, as we'll see, hover somewhere between the making and placing of things by Steinberg's hand and the viewer's imaginative actions as he completes what Steinberg has begun.

By now it is abundantly clear that the house of visual art forms that Saul built is self-repeating and self-enfolding. The narrative of gradually increasing dimensionality, from two to three dimensions, and on to the dimension of time, supports a traditional way of thinking about drawing: that it exists as preparation for supposedly bigger and better things, such as painting and sculpture.[7] Here on the tables, however, drawing is not the preparatory stage. Rather, Steinberg uses tabletop assemblages and wholly constructed tables—bearing as they most often do documents, pieces of "paper," wooden and painted pens, pencils, brushes, knives, or faux books—as the occasion to remind us of the acts of drawing/writing, painting, and sculpting themselves. While writing itself appears on some of his objects, the *act of assembling* his various objects is also for him a form of writing. His every table is, first and last, literally and metaphorically, a flat surface upon which he writes his associational literary-visual works.

In his three-dimensional assemblages Steinberg repeats and expands upon the previous content as well as the previous media of his life's work. Few of the things on his tables are original to them, because, like the tabletops themselves, he has done many of them before in his drawings, paintings, and prints. While we recognize in these tables images of the places, people, things, fantasies, and ideas of Steinberg's experience, they are striking in their inclusion of his own actual works of art or versions of works he had made earlier, such as a landscape oil painting on paper. Self-parody or self-appropriation characterizes his assemblages, but these prior works of art by Steinberg are within themselves derivative and parodic. His landscapes are, as we've seen, derivative of postcard scenes and also derivative of painting itself, i.e., he paints painting. Thus he places on his tables parodies—repetitions with a twist of difference—of earlier works, themselves "originally" parodic. A carved wooden pen, for example, parodies both the two-dimensional pens we see in his drawings and actual pens with metal nibs that he owned. A sense of enjoyable falsity hovers about, say, a nearly flat, roughly carved and painted wooden paintbrush, suggesting that the pleasures of replication matter as much as the things repeated, and that the material of the thing matters as much as its referentiality. He speaks of the whole as a "caricature" of a museum "but at the same time I'm plenty serious about the fact that it's a Steinberg Museum."[8]

While artists have always made use of their earlier works to inspire, even partially constitute, their later works, for Steinberg the act of self-parody constitutes a process of fictional self-creation. He confides that his tables "are also, it must be said, a representation of an autobiography."[9] Note the distinction: a representation of, not autobiography itself. Indeed, Steinberg's self-parody or modernist appropriation of his own work ("I is an Other") is also a tool of memory. Itself an aesthetic parodist, memory brings back one's earlier experience in newly enlivened but derivative forms. As we've seen earlier, Steinberg tells his friend Aldo Buzzi, "Nothing that has been deposited in the memory is lost. . . . We ought to be able to use this huge accumulation of data continually, keep it functioning, combine and multiply its elements and reintroduce them into the circuit of our thoughts" (*RS,* 5–6). He thinks of his tables as autobiographical: "In these 'Tables' I am disguised as a painter, a draftsman, a designer, in objects on my table, the pencil, that's me."[10]

Central to his memory is the table and, reflexively, the table is for him an icon of memory itself. We come to know this just by observing the frequency with which he produces tables—the very site of his imaginative, memorializing labor—across media. He has left behind an important clue, however, in one of his sketchbooks, an untitled sketch of a chair, a whatnot cabinet, and a table which he has written about on the sheet itself (fig. 100).[11] The memory he writes as follows:

> Age 6. On visit to a fancy apt. People of a higher class than my parents. I was given a red candy rabbit. I figured that if I lick it lightly it may last the rest of my life. Something happened. I was seated near a whatnot with 3 levels for bibelots arranged over embroidered doilies. I may have placed the rabbit for a moment on a doily and to my terror it may have remained glued to it. Nothing was clear to me at that age. Only fragments are remembered.* Soon after I was out in the street holding mother's hand when I realized the rabbit was gone, glued forever to the doily. No amount of luxury will ever cancel the loss of that rabbit.

He glosses his memory of the occasion: "*and things happened in fragments probably. The idea of a logical sequence came later, influenced by litterature [*sic*]." A whatnot as he draws it is a series of three tabletops; upon its middle shelf sits a red rabbit. As a writer, he has formed his own fragmentary memory into a narrative of a literary sort, and has provided us with important, but not definitive, meanings for the rabbits that appear throughout his work. They are visual reminders of the tastes, textures,

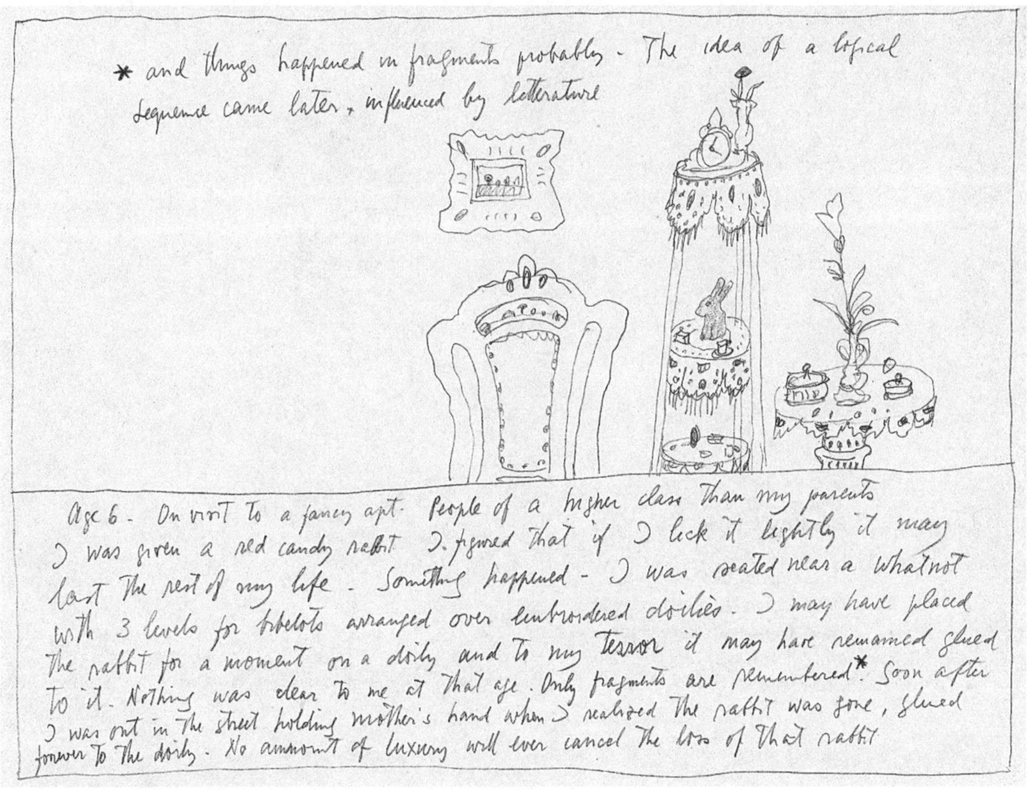

Fig. 100. *Ex-voto,* c. 1983–95. Pencil and colored pencil on paper, torn from sketchbook, 10 7/8 × 14 in. (Beinecke Rare Book and Manuscript Library, Yale University)

mysteries, and deep disappointments of childhood, and he associates them with furniture, especially tables. They are emblems of the constructive act of memory itself. As we view the rabbits that inhabit the heads of some of his characters (fig. 101), we see that, in addition to being the soft, vulnerable creatures that we all are inside, they also embody our minds in the act of remembering. Significantly, though, his rabbits often appear on tables. The toy rabbits of the *New Yorker* cover of April 20, 1981 (fig. 102) ("I grew up without toys"), cycle across the table as they do across the theater of his memory, joined there by other toys (*RS,* 6).

In 1981, too, *Rodozachari Table* (fig. 103) appears. While it doesn't present us with rabbits, it does repeat the Rodozachari flower planter appearing on the *New Yorker* cover. Rodozachari is a spoon sweet or jam-like confection, usually made by home cooks or by monks.[12] Seven years earlier, Steinberg painted *Rodozachari Watercolor* (fig. 104), where the same can appears at the top left, as a receptacle for paintbrushes. Instead of skating rabbits, we see another bibelot, this time a child's toy car. Just as images

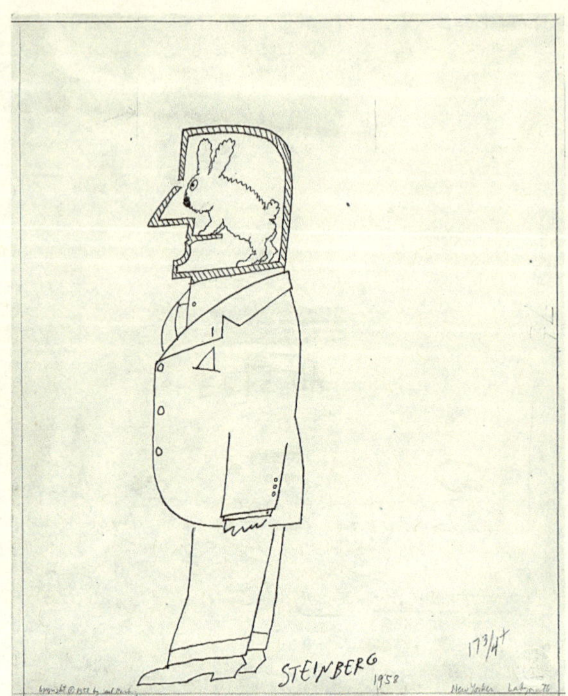

Fig. 101. Untitled, 1958. Ink on paper, 14¾ × 11½ in. Originally published in the *New Yorker,* November 1, 1958. (Beinecke Rare Book and Manuscript Library, Yale University)

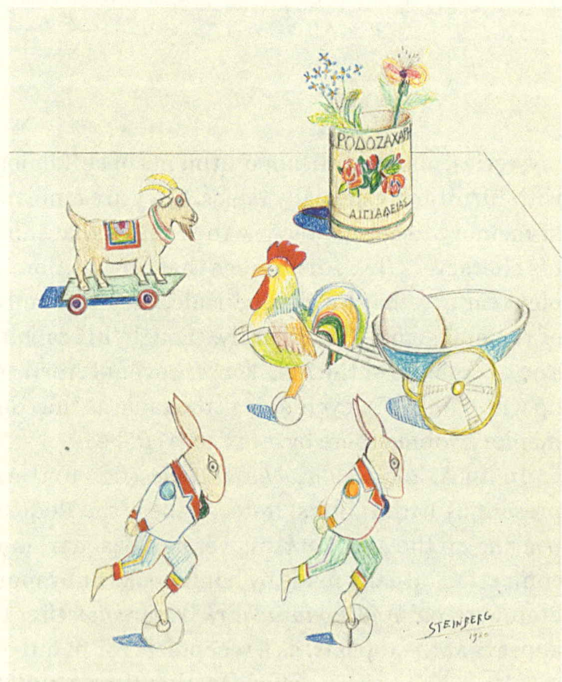

Fig. 102. Untitled, 1980. Pencil, colored pencil, and crayon on paper, 23 × 16½ in. Cover drawing for the *New Yorker,* April 20, 1981. (The Saul Steinberg Foundation, New York; photograph by Jenny Gorman)

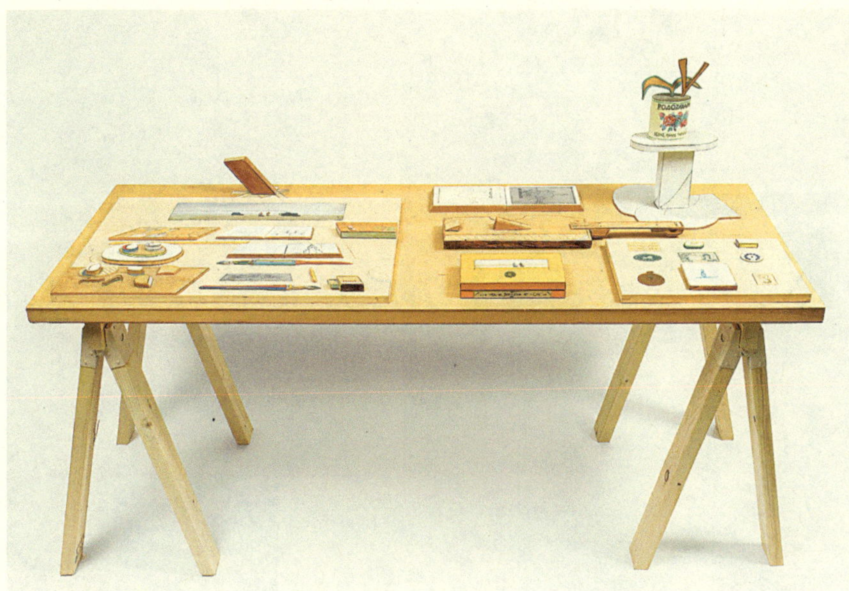

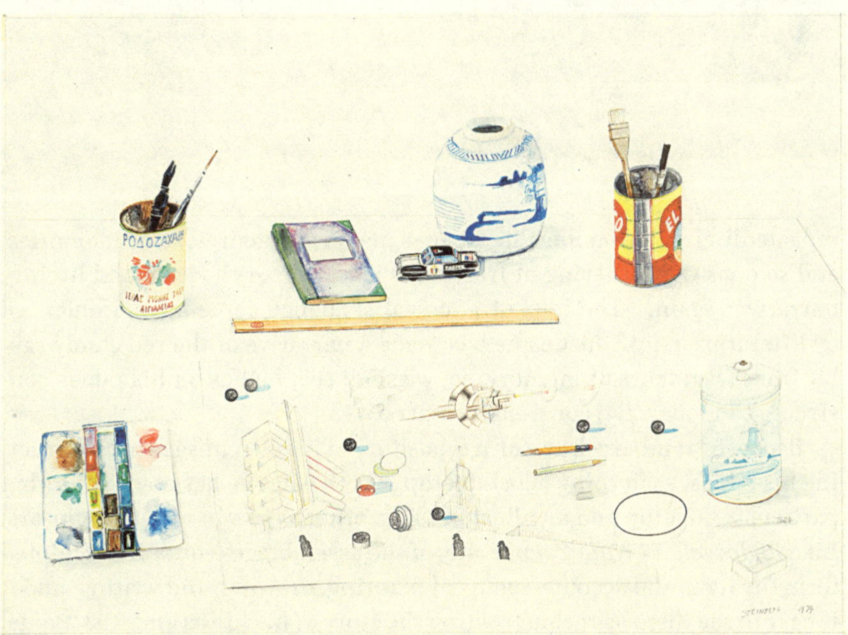

Fig. 103. *Rodozachari Table,* 1981. Mixed media on wood, 30 × 72 × 30 in. (Adam Baumgold Gallery, New York)

Fig. 104. *Rodozachari Watercolor,* 1974. Watercolor, pencil, crayon, and rubber stamp on paper, 30 × 40 in. (Whitney Museum of American Art, New York; bequest of Saul Steinberg)

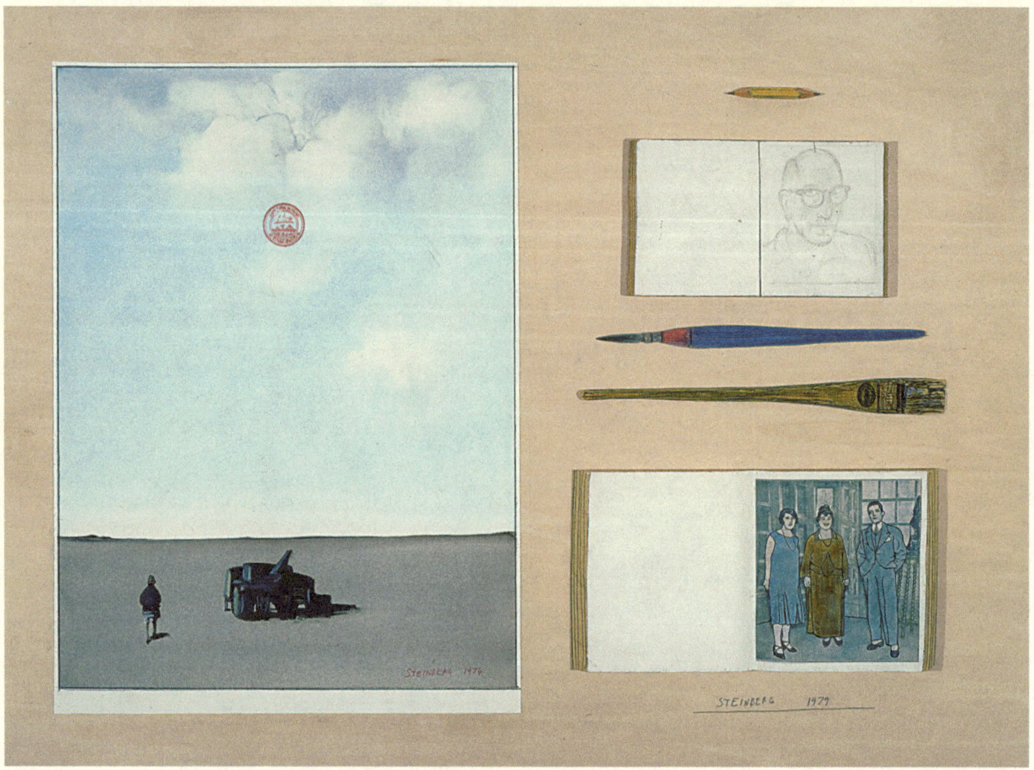

Fig. 105. *Silverpoint Self Portrait Table,* 1979. Mixed media on wood, 23 18 × 31 18 in. (Private collection)

repeatedly circulate among Steinberg's media and genres, so do memories, and so does the gathering of fragments into memory's visual and literary narrative: again, "The idea of a logical sequence came later, influenced by litterature [*sic*]." Just as he has made a narrative of the red candy rabbit from fragments of memory, so, we shall see, he has on his tables constructed a modernist, constellated narrative.

Because Steinberg draws on a repository of his own images in constructing his tables, each thing on a tabletop is both what he has made it for that particular tabletop and an allusion to his other works in which it appears. Like *Rodozachari Watercolor,* many of the assemblages contain in sculpted form the tools and accoutrements of painting, drawing, and writing, and it is easy to see them as reconstructing the story of his life as an artist. Some, such as *Silverpoint Self Portrait Table* (fig. 105) openly "state" in visual terms their autobiographical aspect.[13] It displays a carved wooden notebook that lies open to a Steinberg self-portrait. But we need not depend on the presence of a self-portrait here to establish the (often parodic) autobiographical quality of the table. A painted landscape that he made earlier, in 1974, with a soldier figure and a vehicle, overarched by a painterly sky stamped in red, forms another autobiographical passage in the assemblage—a fragment from his artistic past. Pen, pencil stub, and brush: all of them chronicle his daily life at the drawing table. The book at the bottom, open to a collaged commercial print or photograph that he has colored, extends this imaging of his life to include the arts of collage and parody, which he explored across the decades. Such items are, however, no more deeply "about" art than are his sculpted vases of flowers or carved wooden talk balloons covered with illegible writing, because these things, too, and many others, he has, in another time and on another surface, drawn, painted, or written.

Tables are the blank pages whereon he actually and figuratively practices his verbal and visual art. Maps and labyrinths; postcards, landscapes, and cityscapes; still lifes, portraits, and documents: Steinberg's favored genres, executed across multiple media, all take their places on his tables, themselves drawn, painted, or constructed of wood. Indeed, as genetic criticism has played so important a role in Joyce studies, as scholars study the many drafts of his novels to discover how they gradually came into being, so a genetic criticism establishing the history of the objects appearing on Steinberg's tables, beyond the scope of this study, remains to be written. So much happens at them: artists draw things, including their own bodies (see fig. 9; p. 34); people sit alone or in pairs locked into a relationship (fig. 106); their surfaces metamorphose into maps and mazes (fig. 107). Tables provide domestic spaces, too: pets sit below them (fig. 108), while upon them household items, knickknacks, snacks, and the tools of the artist lie. In Steinbergia, a table can open up into pure abstraction (fig. 109) or even function as a bathtub (fig. 110). A cartoonish sketch (fig. 111) makes explicit what other tables only imply: the style of the man is the style of the table.

Some of them, such as *Gulliver Table* (fig. 112), repeat the arrangements of *Library,* presenting in this case books about travel: one of Swift's satires and a second volume, *Le Dragoman,* published by "Elias Press Cairo." A dragoman is a consummately verbal person—a guide, interpreter, and translator who has to have knowledge of several languages. This is a mock version of an actual book by Rushdi Elias, published in 1965 and containing handy words and phrases for the traveler in French, English, German, and Arabic. The two books' proximity to various artist's tools may suggest that we take those books, too, as tools—as books were for Steinberg, aiding him in making his art.

Other table-like constructions only allude to literary works, such as *Gogol* (fig. 113), in which the portrait of a uniformed conductor whose nose seems reversed from the rest of his profile stands on the base of an easel, an

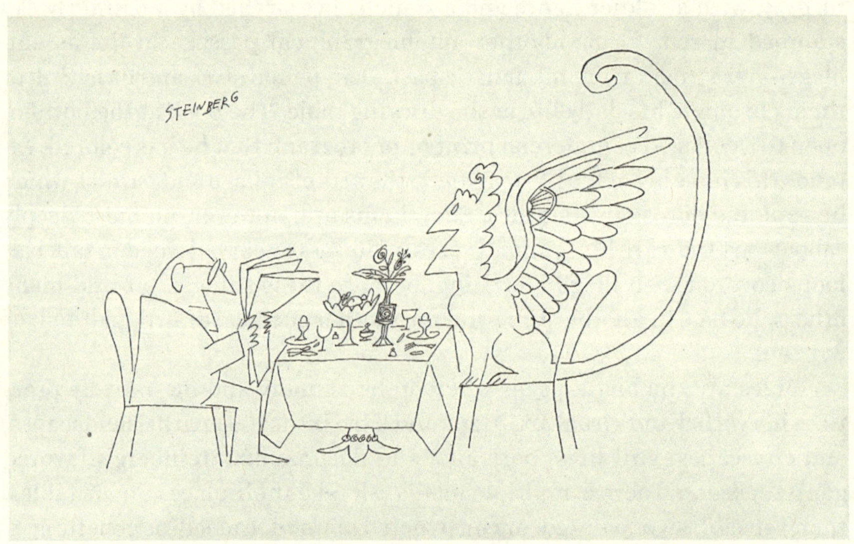

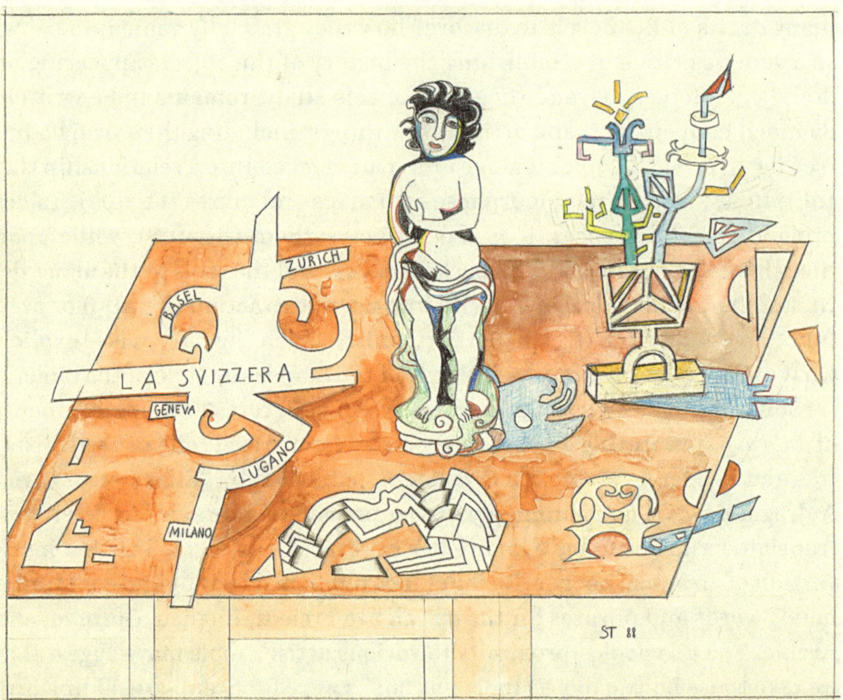

Fig. 106. Untitled, 1962. Ink on paper, 14½ × 23⅛ in. Originally published in *The New Yorker,* October 20, 1962. (Beinecke Rare Book and Manuscript Library, Yale University)

Fig. 107. *Swiss Still Life,* 1988. Watercolor, felt marker, ink, colored pencil, and collage on paper, 17⅞ × 23⅞ in. (The Saul Steinberg Foundation, New York)

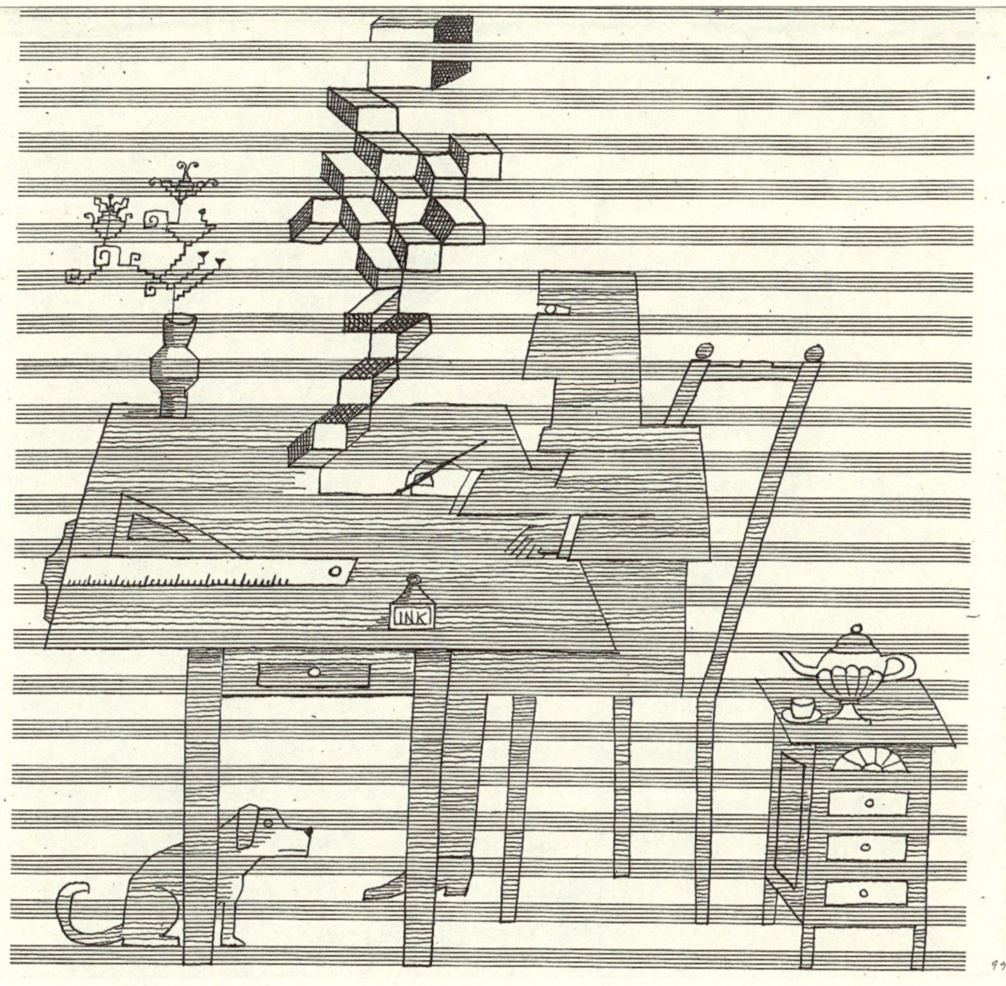

Fig. 108. Untitled, 1967. Ink on sheet music paper. Originally published in the *New Yorker,* May 6, 1967. (Kunsthalle Tübingen)

upright version of an artist's table. Sometimes a nose may join objects on a low-relief table (fig. 114). Gogol's Ivan Yakovlevich discovers in his breakfast roll a nose mysteriously detached from its owner. All the characters engage in "smelling out" the faults of others, but the nose signifies most poignantly Ivan's self-loathing and sense of guilt. Yet the familiar mythology of noses in Steinberg's work, already discussed, might here have less to do with sussing out failure and more to do with the closing line of the story: "After this . . . but here again the whole adventure is lost in fog, and what happened afterward is absolutely unknown."[14]

Steinberg's images of noses sometimes slip from their appointed stations and even detach completely, mysteriously ending up on tables in the

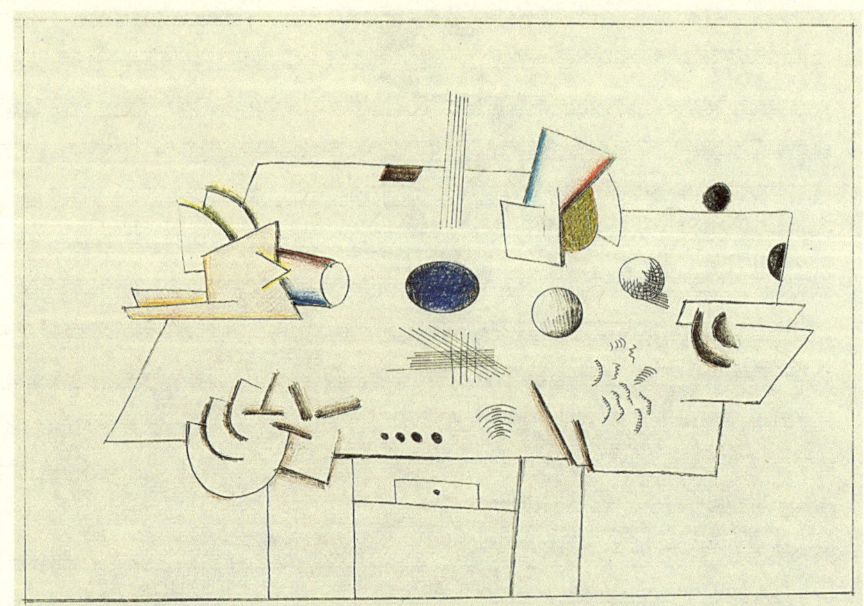

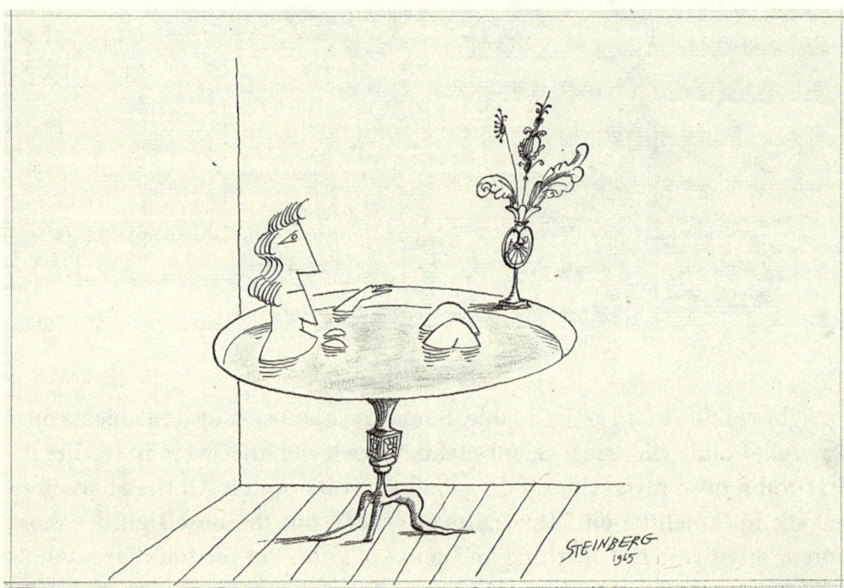

Fig. 109. Untitled, 1982–90. Etching, aquatint, and drypoint with colored pencil and crayon on paper, 18⅝ × 22 in. (The Saul Steinberg Foundation, New York; photograph by Jenny Gorman)

Fig. 110. Untitled, 1965. Ink and colored pencil on paper, 12⅝ × 19 in. Originally published in the *New Yorker,* October 9, 1965. (Beinecke Rare Book and Manuscript Library, Yale University)

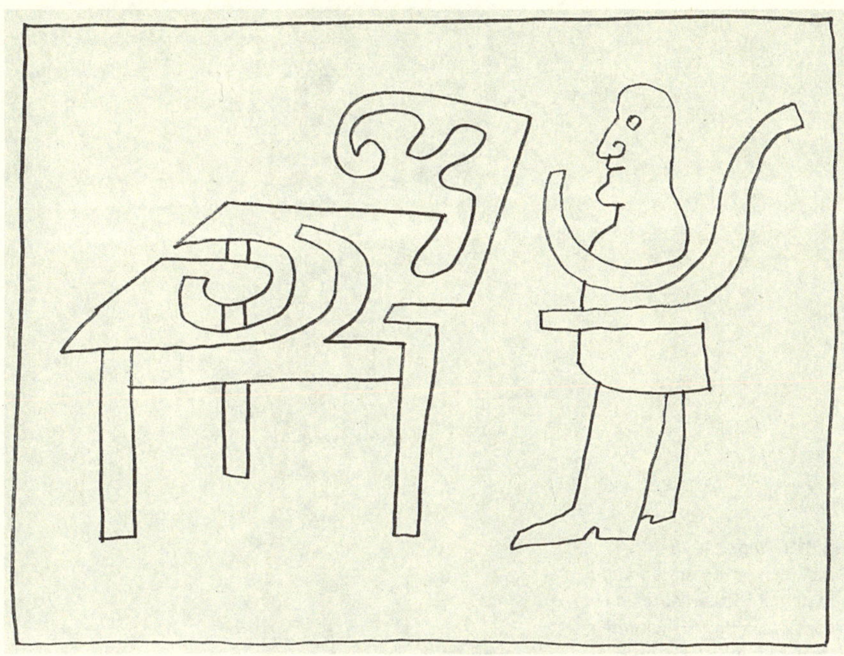

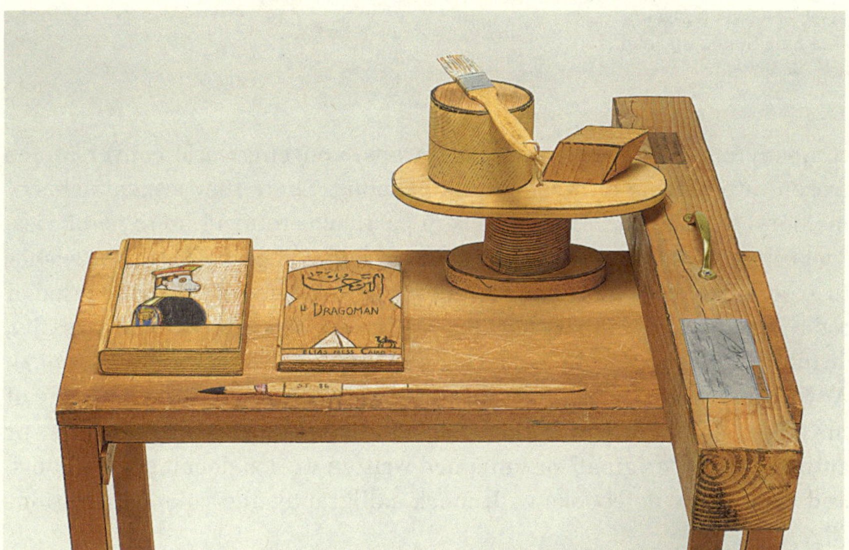

Fig. 111. Untitled, 1980s. Felt marker on paper, 11 × 14 in. (Beinecke Rare Book and Manuscript Library, Yale University)

Fig. 112. *Gulliver Table,* 1986. Carved wood with oil, colored pencil, crayon, incised and inked copper and tin sheets, metal handle and string, 36½ × 27¾ × 26 in. (The Saul Steinberg Foundation, New York)

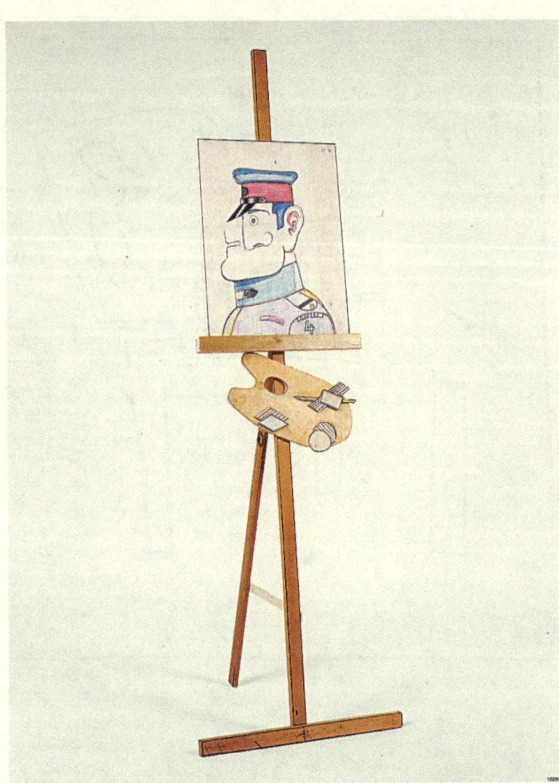

Fig. 113. *Gogol*, 1973–80. Panel: crayon, colored pencil, and pencil with erasures on wood; easel: pencil, colored pencil, rubber stamp, crayon, and carved wood on wood easel, 71 × 22⅛ × 21¼ in. (The Saul Steinberg Foundation, New York)

company of artist's tools, official stamps, and enigmatic conversations frozen into writing on wooden talk balloons. There they are emblems of memory: he tells Buzzi that smells in particular return him to memories, "deposited many years ago in the memory and now revived," and he wishes to experience these forgotten sensations within himself "with the mind of today" (*RS*, 5–6). Steinberg tells Buzzi of an unpleasant trip to Kansas City, "which I smell physically (like Gogol's Nose)" (*LAB*, November 3, 1957). At the same time, a Gogolian absurdity hovers, mist-like, about many of his tables. Some of them, rather than alluding to specific literary works or authors, carry "original" or unnamed written works: documents, albums, and even mock notebooks with mock calligraphy and color illustrations (fig. 115).

In addition to the significance of memory and autobiography to Steinberg's tables, their formal qualities and their literary qualities matter—that is, beyond alluding to books and authors, they invite us to receive them as verbal/visual fiction. In *The Art of Assemblage* Seitz identifies two simple,

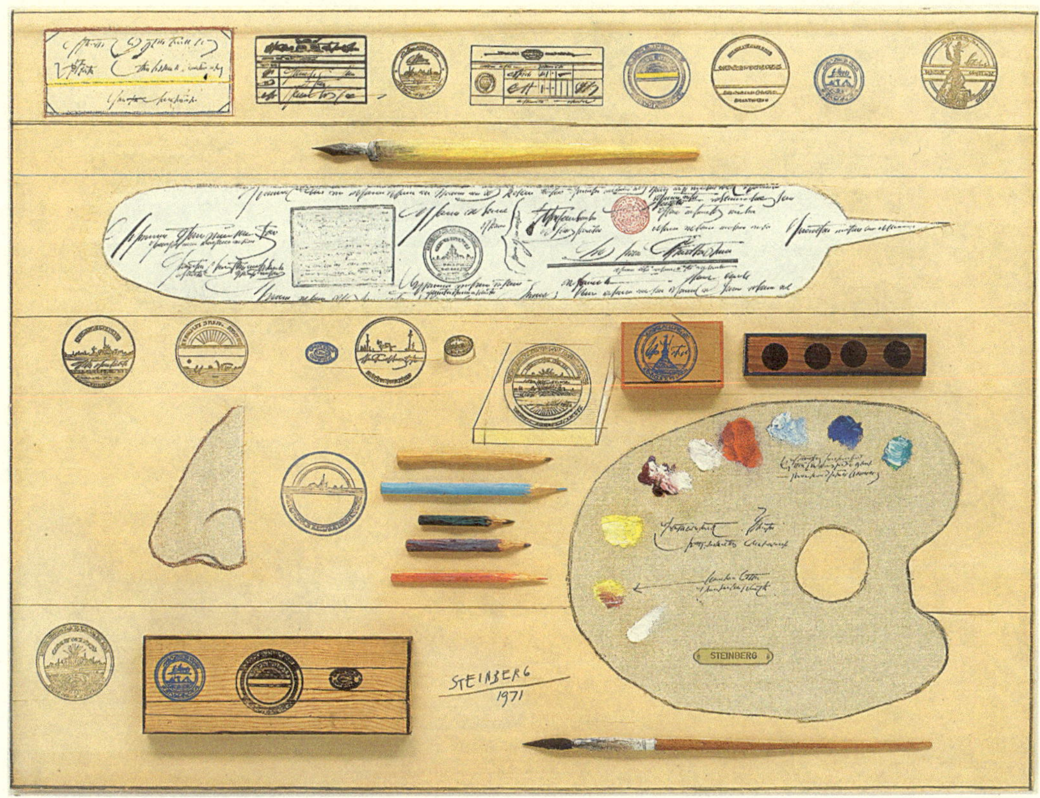

physical characteristics common to the varied works in the exhibition at the Museum of Modern Art: (1) "They are predominantly assembled rather than painted, drawn, modeled, or carved"; and (2) "Entirely or in part, their constituent elements are preformed natural or manufactured materials, objects or fragments not intended as art materials."[15] Found materials in Seitz's view are works already in progress—prepared for the artist by the outside world, previously formed, textured, colored, and even sometimes entirely prefabricated into bits of reality taken up by the collagist or assembler, thereby spanning the gap between art and reality.

Fig. 114. *Inventory,* 1971. Mixed media on wood, 20 × 26 in. (Private collection)

Steinberg, moving the art of assemblage beyond Seitz's description, crafts his own "outside" world objects, makes his own "found" items. Following Seitz's definition, we might even have to understand Steinberg's tables as parodies of assemblages, since he himself creates the works he appropriates. While Seitz's discussion of assemblage raises issues that have not been resolved, one of his conclusions remains useful for anyone looking

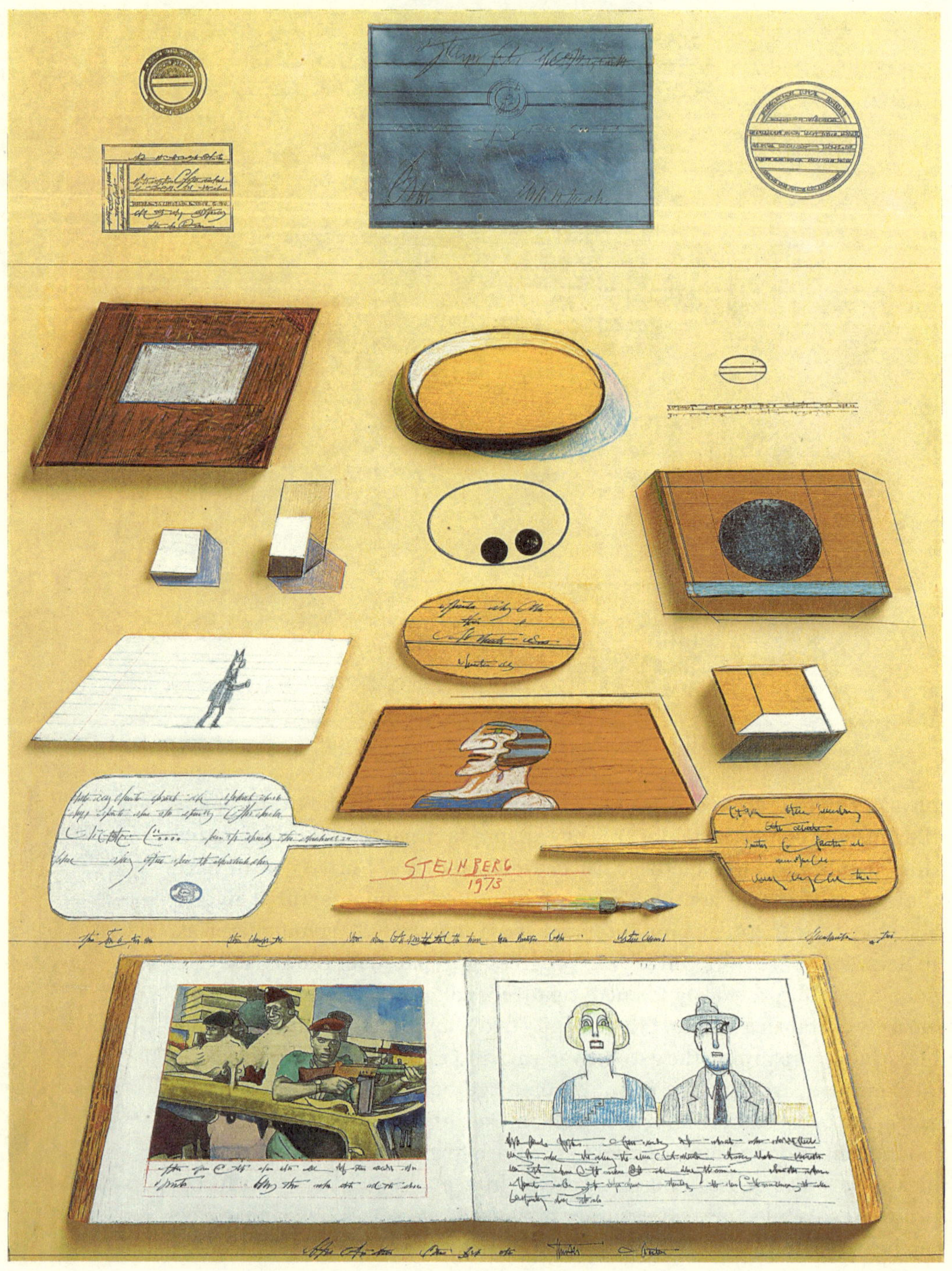

Fig. 115. *Table Series: Union Square,* 1973. Mixed media on wood, 30 11/16 × 22 13/16 in. (Institut de Dessin, Fondation Adami, Vaduz)

at Steinberg's tables—his insight that the assembler can be simultaneously a visual artist, a metaphysician, and a creator of "literary meanings." He speaks of the auras of physical materials that, in many assemblages, are "transmuted into a new amalgam that both transcends and includes its parts," leading to "significant expression." They are meant to call up viewers' intuitions and aid them in finding connections among things. Seitz understands an assemblage to be a constellation of meanings that develop through "overtones and associations" in excess of, "almost independently" of, its "colors, textures and forms."[16]

From the perspective of more than half a century later, and with Steinberg's assemblages before us, Seitz's carefully argued claims for the metaphysical and poetic nature of this kind of visual art seem truer than ever. Steinberg's assembled tables, like his drawings and paintings, invite us to read them as literary creations, many of them seemingly autobiographical.

The writing of one's own life is, of course, never just an objective telling of already existing facts. Good autobiography proceeds gingerly, sometimes hand in hand with fiction, and we do the tables a disservice when we merely comb through them for autobiographical allusions. We can read them as fictions that echo the twentieth-century experiments of Nabokov, Joyce, and other modernist writers of juxtaposition such as Ezra Pound, T. S. Eliot, Marianne Moore, Stéphane Mallarmé, and Guillaume Apollinaire. Nor need we read his tables as autobiographical at all. For viewers lacking knowledge of Steinberg's life, his tables will be assemblages of shapes, textures, and colors, or of icons of our shared human experience of books read, foods eaten, rooms arranged, landscapes inhabited, tools collected and used, money spent or saved, people known, and more.

As collaborative, strong viewers, we do best to enter the force fields of a table much as we enter a fictional modernist text that presents us with both legibility and illegibility. We look for patterns akin to those that Nabokov and Joyce, creators of novel-puzzles and labyrinths, liked to play with. Full solution is unattainable, because mystery is a goal, not a problem to be worked through and eliminated. The tables themselves begin to teach us how to look at them and read through them. When we approach them with an understanding of Steinberg's verbal imagination, these tables tell us even more. Literature, then, is not just an autobiographical key to the tables. The literary is also a valence present everywhere, a felt significance to be explored. But how do we recognize it?

First, the tables "read" like two-dimensional pages. Although they are three-dimensional, they don't demand that we view them from all sides. Rather, everything on them is arranged to be read from a fixed vantage point, like that of a reader staring at a printed page, even though the eye must take in sharp inflections of heights and textures along with two-dimensional forms. The flat base of the table itself reminds us of the page; everything placed there is as if "written" upon it. At the same time, the gaps between objects, the empty spaces, enable the "reader's" eye to move in multiple directions, not just left to right, top to bottom. Steinberg presents objects as, at the same time, texts to be read and as visual and tactile experiences. The strange interactions of his objects suggest that we "take" them as poems, stories, riddles, or dreams, not just solid things that have their being in the physical world. They resemble rebuses without solutions, the plane of the table itself providing a space in which the viewer may move about, connecting, disconnecting, and above all imagining.

Second, his tables have literary roots in the notion of "constellation." Mallarmé comes to mind, with the modernist typographical experiments of *UN COUP DE DÉS JAMAIS N'ABOLIRA LE HASARD* (1897) (A throw of the dice will never abolish chance), in which he arranges words and phrases in strangely fragmentary visual patterns across twenty pages, like so many dark objects of varying sizes that wander freely across a white surface. As he writes in that work: "NOTHING /. . . . / WILL HAVE TAKEN PLACE / . . . . / BUT THE PLACE /. . . . EXCEPT / . . . / PERHAPS /. . . . / A CONSTELLATION."[17] These important lines, scattered across two pages of poetry, arranged freely, ignoring conventions of uniform font size, capitalization, and word and line spacing, suggest the rich development of a parallel notion of constellation in modern visual art. As we shall see, *Ulysses* presents a constellation of material language. In *Calligrammes* (Steinberg owned a copy), Guillaume Apollinaire uses the letters of words to "spell out" visual forms related to their lexical meanings (e.g., a poem about rain is arranged in slanting lines down, not across, the page).[18] "Calligramme" is a neologism combining the words ideogram (a picture or symbol, not a word, used in a system of writing to represent a thing or an idea) and calligraphy (elegant or beautiful handwriting of letters and words). Mallarmé and Apollinaire lead us to take the verbal as visual, and vice versa, to see written words as both signs pointing to something else and as shapes and textures, patterns of white spaces and dark marks, in their own right.

Steinberg's assemblages demonstrate that the visual may be taken verbally, that we may "read" shapes and textures as if they were fragments of poetry or prose. Linguistic syntax floats free of its bonds to become visual, compositional syntax. Forms on a table may be read. Apollinaire's poem "Zone" suggests yet another way of thinking about Steinberg's tables. As the poem's speaker (addressing a "you" that is himself as Other) crosses gap after gap to move through such multiple and discontinuous zones as time, technology, geography, religion, and psychology, the associations he makes among them mean that finally they inhabit one zone: that of the physical presence of the poem on the page as it expands centrifugally through the reader's mind and emotions.

The notion of zones can help us appreciate Steinberg's *Rodozachari Table* (see fig. 103; p. 245), a constellation or juxtaposition of physical elements that together spell out a fiction of precise details gathered within an aura of suggestion.[19] A close reading of the table would be extraordinarily long; I offer instead only a few observations as we return to this assemblage. *Rodozachari Table* presents us with a table of zones: several major areas are delineated there, and it is the viewer's urge to move across the gaps among those groupings that sends her eyes along what is both grid and free-form fantasy. Now we're in the zone of the comfortable studio of an artist, or of a foreign and desolate landscape, or of the tabletop itself. Then again, we're occupying aesthetic zones: of music, of visual art hanging on a gallery wall, of the Pop Art–like canned goods label (Steinberg named Andy Warhol as an important influence), of the artisanal whittling of wooden objects. Perhaps, though, we're in zones of representation and Steinberg's "degrees of reality": originals and appropriations, parodies, abstractions, mass productions. All of them arise from the zone of the assemblage itself as defined by the table on which things rest.

The rhythm of looking can become that of reverie, in which associations arise as they will, sometimes leading the viewer beyond the bounds of the table. In this frame of mind, the following of the very grain of the lumber that Steinberg used to fashion the table and its contents may do the hushing crucial to reverie—or call to mind Surrealist frottage. Through our associations with the colors, forms, and textures that we see, we experience "indefinable yet precise emotions,"[20] and we may enter a world of fantasy. Yeats imagined his writing table as a potential stage for the movements of the spirit world, speaking of "all the wizard things that go / About my table to and fro."[21]

While Steinberg was never a thoroughgoing mystic in the early Yeatsian mode, his tables invite us to see a gesturing beyond their merely material presence to an ill-defined beyond. Like Apollinaire's intermittent tuning into and away from mystical channels in "Zone," however, Steinberg's drawing table planes juxtapose zones and ways of making meaning. We can take the assemblage as Symbolist-spiritualist, but also as materialist: epitomized by that label on the Rodozachari can of rose petal preserves which announces its own commodity status as a sweet made and sold at the "Ieras Mones Taxiarches" or the "Holy Monastery of the Taxiarches [Archangels]," for its members a locus of the spiritual. Rodozachari uses the ancient Greek word for rose with the modern Greek word for sugar, the brand name thus combining distant eras.[22]

Once again, why literary? We may consider this table specifically as a visual-verbal fiction—as literary in quality—if we keep in mind Steinberg's by now familiar statement: "My idea of the artist, poet, painter, composer, etc., is the novelist."[23] We pause to reflect on how an assemblage is like a novel. Paul Hunter has shown us that novels, since their eighteenth-century beginnings, have often included an element of surprise, engagement with "the unusual, the uncertain, and the unexplainable" at the same time as they value "the every-day, ordinary, and often practical."[24] The novel form shows a "tendency both to probe and promote loneliness and solitariness, and contains 'stories within stories.'" Novels originally gathered paraliterary forms: journalism, wonder books and Providence books (seventeenth-century books meant to show a divinely controlled world), sermons, and "guides, treatises, practical instruction."[25] In much the same way, we can "read" Steinberg's assemblages as modernist *Wunderkammern* and also as guides to everyday living. A life worth living, he suggests, is a life of making art, eating well, remembering carefully, watching closely, collecting, and telling to yourself the importance of what you see.

Perhaps most importantly for this study of Steinberg's assemblages, novels have always given themselves permission to digress, to include miniessays, stories within stories, or other intrusions on the plot, and thus they have roamed freely from a simple, forward narrative thrust. We can read a given table as a series of enchanting digressions, and as juxtapositions of multiple orders of things: e.g., noses, advertisements, cartoon-like speech balloons, pens and brushes, morsels of food, and pages from family photo albums.

In Steinberg's tables, we discover smaller written texts (individual objects as "chapters," as it were) within the larger text of everything on the surface of the table taken together. Meaning tends to grow exponentially there. Every object or fragment brings with it a history, its meanings outside or prior to the space in which it (now) appears, its connotations as various as readers' imaginations. To these we must add the new meanings arising from the interactions among individual objects on the table, and as we continue to dwell on these connections, we find relations among relations.

Rodozachari Table may be taken as a map, a labyrinth, a spiral reaching upward from many things to the mystery of Beauty, a document of a life lived in crossing border after border. Like *Ulysses* or *Ada,* the Table invites us to take it both spatially and (depending on the many paths our eyes may take) progressively in time. Novel and table both require rereading: a single swipe of the eye never feels sufficient. Reading from left to right, top to bottom, we see an abstract sculpture, an open book, a pedestal with a plant growing in a "tin" can, a wooden base holding multiple objects, including a painted landscape at the top, a whittled and assembled musical instrument, a hinged box, and a second flat piece of wood with some mock money in bill form at its center. This is not necessarily the order in which we first see these objects, but it is one of the several paths which the grid-like arrangement of objects and the frontality of the table inspire. Our eyes also flit randomly from thing to thing, but in doing so they also discover how to discern categories: for example, images of the human figure as they appear here and there, or of abstract shapes such as circles, or contrasting sizes of objects, or specific media, such as drawings or sculptures.

Speaking of the reflexive nature of the tables, Steinberg tells us: "I do more carpentry than sculpture. I don't use art materials. I use stuff from the lumber yard. I make pencils and rulers from lattice. My purpose in making 3-dimensional objects is to mimic my own condition. I sit in a chair and I make a chair. *It is my own civilization,* if you will. Some sort of homage to the instruments of my work. I have come to love the pens and pencils that I use" (emphasis added).[26] These tables portray "Steinberg" as the creator, like Robinson Crusoe, of his own civilization, as the maker of art about art, and as the autobiographer who writes in sculpture. He places on *Rodozachari Table* a wooden box of incised labels that seem to lie, jewel-like, on velvet (fig. 116). Here high art (sculpture) meets craft: "I worked in wood this summer," he writes. "Made sample cases and boxes for necessaries, compasses, jewelry etc. It appears that I'm trying to take up my father's trade [decorative box producer]" (*LAB,* September 29, 1981). The very making of the objects he places on these tables is, once again, a form of remembering his childhood.

His "own civilization" also includes works he has made earlier, such as that painted landscape and the mock book, and it even contains repetitions of itself—two small tabletops of flat wood bearing items that are themselves "items" placed on the larger tabletop. These mise en abymes, like a story within a novel's story, point to the degrees of reality that fascinated Steinberg from the beginning to the end of his life as a maker. If we place at the center of our attention the crudely constructed violin (he played the violin as a child and tried again to master it as an adult) (*LAB,* December 9, 1979), we can read the entire table as an act of nostalgia (fig. 116). What saves it from nostalgia's cloying pleasure is the strangeness of the juxtapositions. And that viewer at the top, drawn in the style of the art work that she observes, is familiar. She reminds us—understanding assemblage as a form of novelistic wisdom literature—that art makes us as much as we make art.

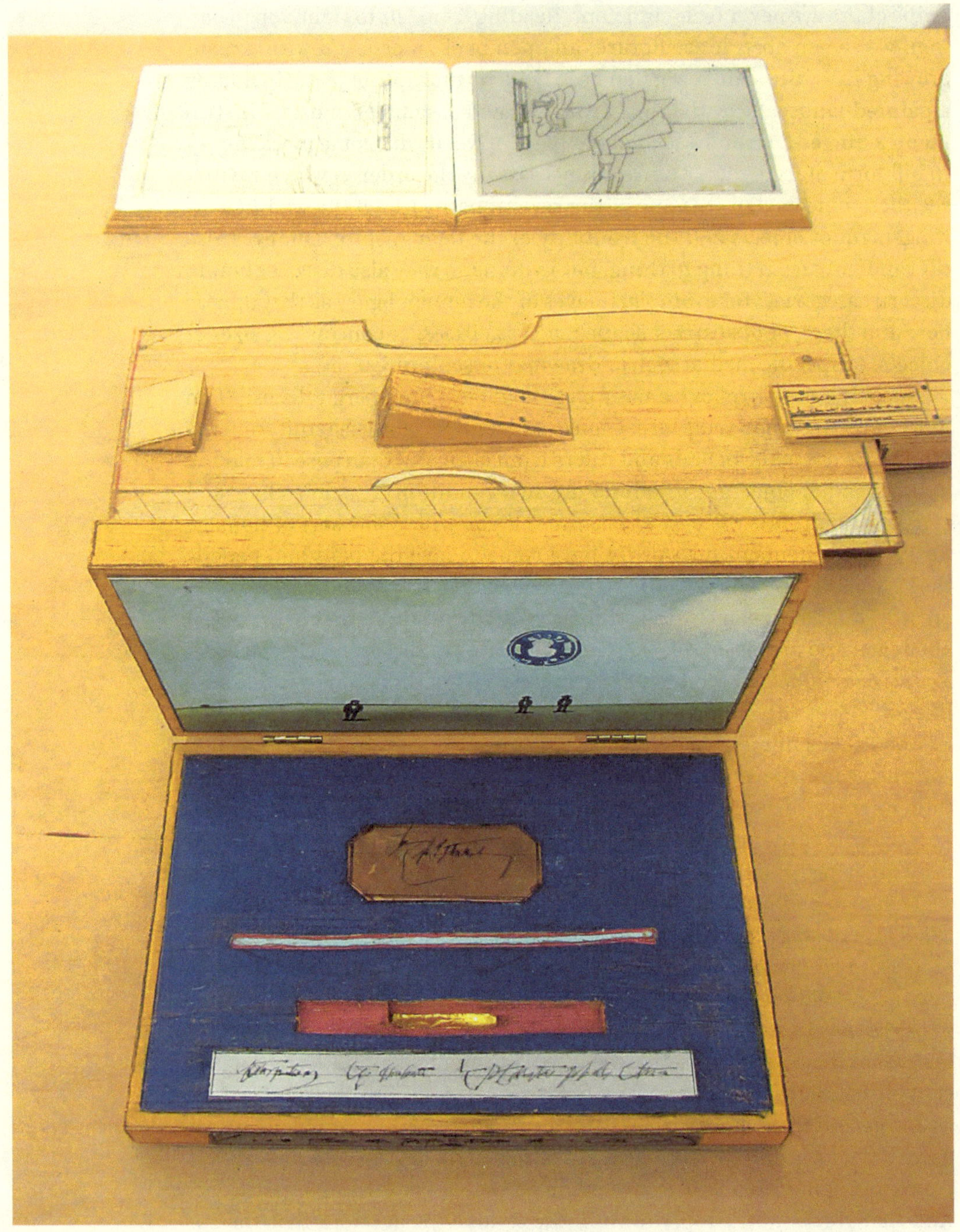

Fig. 116. *Rodozachari Table,* detail of fig. 103, with box opened.

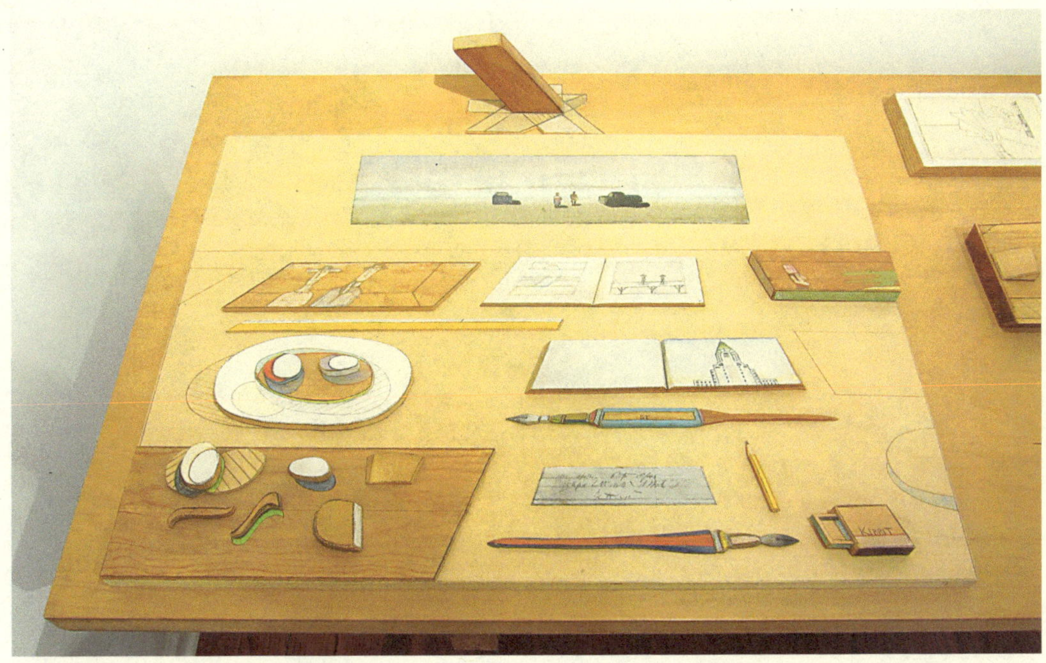

Fig. 117. *Rodozachari Table,* detail of fig. 103.

At the same time, Steinberg weakens the distinction between representational and presentational art. That matchbox (Kibrit) (fig.117) is representational; it refers to the actual matchboxes we know. It is so, however, only to a degree, because it openly deviates from what a matchbox looks like. It thus also announces itself as an object with its own being, a small piece of crafted wood. Illusion or autonomy? Representation or presentation? Memorialization or fantasy?[27] The energy emanating from these tables comes in part from such undecidability.

Those people drawn and colored on wood—we've seen them before, protagonists of Steinberg's visual tales of marital or sexual pairings. Steinberg's civilization must contain books, and there they are (fig. 117). A faux album contains an image of an Art Deco skyscraper. Steinberg's Joycean protagonist-artist—"the artist, like the God of the creation, remains within or behind or beyond or above his handiwork, invisible"—can be known through his sojourn in New York City, his architectural degree, and his love of drawing (*P*, 233).

Steinberg's mythologies in addition to the nose reappear on his tables. Here in *Rodozachari Table* is Mickey Mouse/Abraham Lincoln again, a visitor from Steinberg's American mythology, but this time appearing on a mock Dutch blue-and-white tile (fig. 118, bottom center).

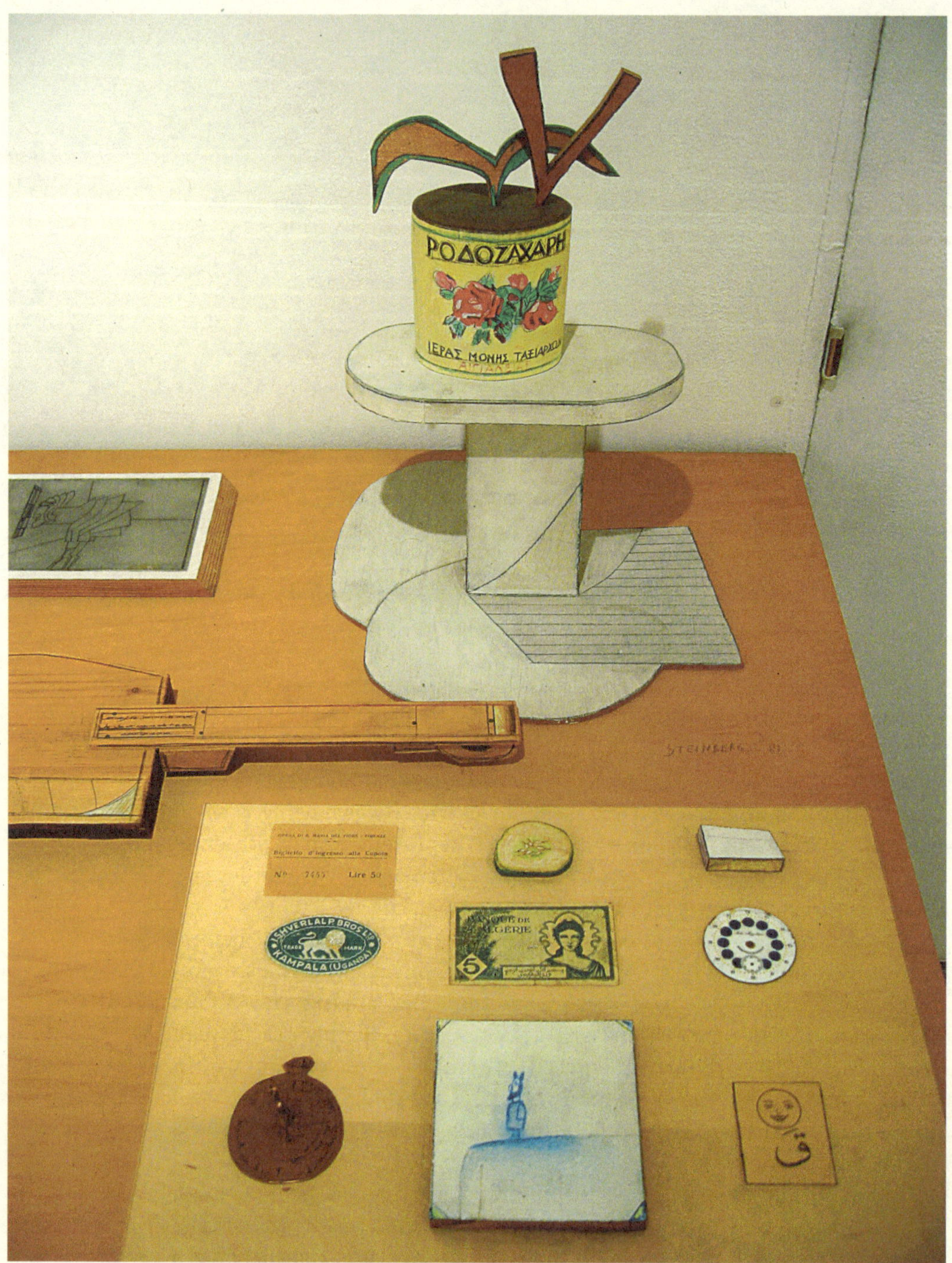

Fig. 118. *Rodozachari Table,* detail of fig. 103.

What does seem clear, after one dwells on a Steinberg table assemblage for a while, is that the *objects* on the table have become *things,* to make use of a distinction developed by Bill Brown. That is, a mere object becomes a thing when it "names a subject-object relation." Because objects on Steinberg's tables are so obviously made by his hand, each one of them contains some of his human energy, and each one seems significant, vital. Some of them even seem to oscillate between animate and inanimate, giving a sense of "the uncanniness of the ordinary."[28] The "animation and agency of the artefactual" makes itself felt.[29] The very fact that things on the table seem naively handcrafted, what Steinberg calls carpentry rather than sculpture, attests to the protagonist-artist's presence, the manifestation of his hand, which differs from Steinberg's "own" hand.

The table's vitality issues, too, from its representations of the tools of the writer's and artist's work (fig. 117). We imagine them moving in Steinberg's hand, or resting after having just now drawn on or painted the objects on the table, including themselves. Just as he registered the pleasure he felt in painting, Steinberg took pleasure in making playful table assemblages. As he tells Buzzi,

> The show,[30] yes, it went well and I made the usual trillion. . . . But what's essential is that the new things—the tables—were well displayed and I'm still pleased with them. These are new things for me and bring me closer to the rather animal world of painters. In working on them there's only pleasure, the mind is at rest, it's the happiness of a horse. . . . This new passion for wood—what fragrance!—it makes me work and even dream that I'm working. Who would have said old Saul would be revived and obsessed by work. In fact, I'm preparing a show for Maeght in October all tables. (*LAB,* March 10, 1973)

Such pleasurable energy brings us full circle to the energies of travel and exile that inform all that Steinberg made. Although *Rodozachari Table* resembles a three-dimensional still life, it also suggests world travel, beginning, as the title and the brightest colors on the table indicate, with that can of Greek sweets, now filled by the artist with imagined dirt. Our viewing pleasure includes recognition of an Algerian five-franc bill, a card or mock page from an Arabic alphabet book (the Arabic letter Q, perhaps the first letter of qibla, "direction" or "facing," appears under the little face) (fig. 118). A label from a Ugandan company shows a lion; and a Florentine ticket offers us entry to the "*Cupola.*" Steinberg's eclectic collection suggests a traveler who wanders from country to country, a tourist with careful, if eccentric, taste in mementos. That slide from a mid-century Viewmaster just might offer touristic sights (fig. 118). Just as his tables show collections of

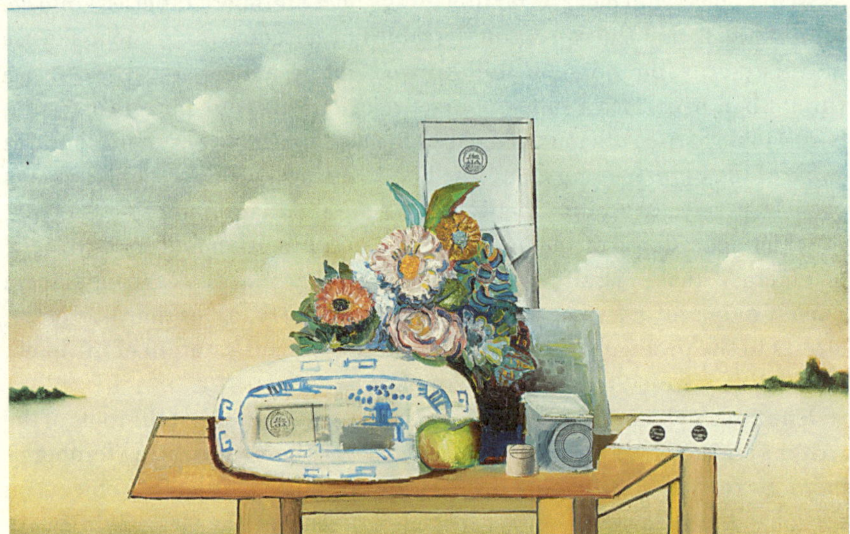

Fig. 119. Untitled, c. 1975–85. Oil and rubber stamp on unstretched canvas, 23⅞ × 38⅛. (The Saul Steinberg Foundation, New York; photograph by Jenny Gorman)

things that have come from here and there, they analogize the coming and goings of the cosmopolitan's wanderings.

This assemblage is more than a collection of things; it's also generically akin to a landscape, so that we're looking at a place as well as a still life. Cézanne painted still lifes in which molded and flowing cloths suggest hills and mountains, and Steinberg, too, meditates on the relation of landscape to tablescape or still life in a variety of ways. In his work, a painted still life may provide the foreground for a landscape, with pastel landscape painting propped up amid the flowers, fruit, and china on the table (fig. 119), a parallel to the two landscape paintings with figures that Steinberg places on *Rodozachari Table.* Steinberg even draws a perfectly hybrid still life/landscape—a stillscape (fig. 120).

In addition, the curiously static nature of his painted landscapes, such as the one we see in *Silverpoint Self Portrait Table* (see fig. 105; p. 246), suggests that we're looking at motionless figures placed on flat, deserted ground as if on a flat table. We begin to understand that on the drawing tables Steinberg's favorite genres appear and interact: the landscape, to be sure, but also the document, the labyrinth (where do we enter the table and where do we exit?), the postcard (not just sketches resembling postcards with reproductions of famous works of art, but also the dividing lines drawn directly upon the wood in a version of conventional postcard segmentation), and the portrait.

As we progress to explore Joyce's *Ulysses* as an assemblage, it's appropri-

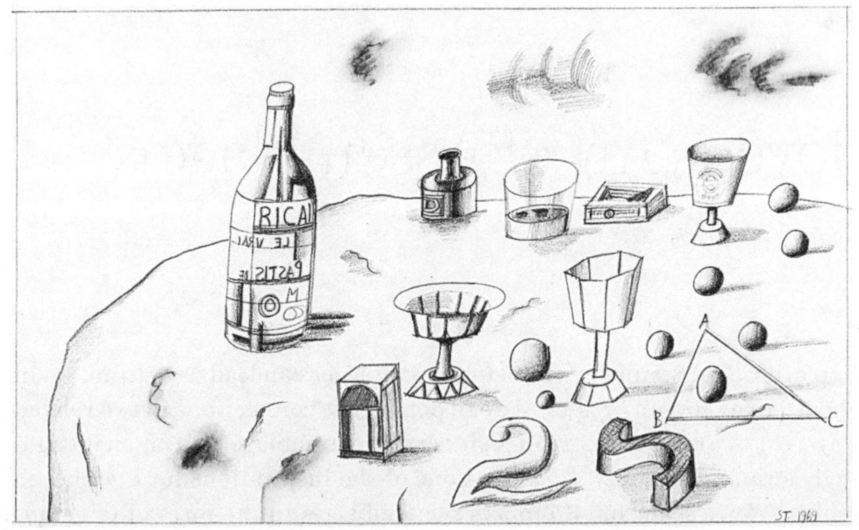

Fig. 120. Untitled, 1969. Pencil, charcoal, crayon, and colored pencil on paper, 14½ × 23 in. (The Saul Steinberg Foundation, New York; photograph by Jenny Gorman)

ate, then, to keep in mind Steinberg's literary drawing table assemblages as they memorialize and half hide his life; vibrate between representation or illusionism and autonomy; pulse across juxtapositions and gaps; present things rather than mere objects; and experiment with different styles. His assemblages flaunt their parody and self-appropriation; embody a cat-and-mouse game of the author's presence and invisibility; and mix styles and media. Above all, they summon us to the "crucible," as Delacroix called it, of an artist's studio.[31] There, Steinberg makes, collects, and arranges things, setting them in motion to become narrative events that happen in tandem with our very acts of vision.

19

Joyce's Art of Assemblage

"The Paper Studio"

Exploring Saul Steinberg's tabletop assemblages can lead us to think again about James Joyce's *Ulysses.* We can ponder the connections in two related ways: *Ulysses* itself as akin to a Steinbergian assemblage, and, as an intriguingly strong possibility, *Ulysses* as one of the inspirations for Steinberg's tables.[1] We've seen that Steinberg's assemblages in the form of tabletops or entire tables can be understood as narrative in nature, in part because things are arrayed there as if on a page we read, in part because their very juxtaposition and fragmentary nature invite us to transform them into multiple and open-ended narratives, much like the stylistically diverse episodes that together constitute the open-ended *Ulysses.* As Paul Saint-Amour has written of an assemblage made by Marcel Duchamp, *Boîte-en-Valise,* it is not a book but "an embodied regret at not being a book—a yearning for both the codex form and the condition of writing."[2] Steinberg's tables are such embodied regrets. But perhaps *Ulysses* is, in mirror image, a book that is an embodied regret at not being a visual assemblage. It's time to explore *Ulysses* itself as a would-be assemblage, a fiction whose very styles and narrative structures presage what Steinberg would come to create in his assembled tables roughly half a century later.

We can begin with a simple set of observations. As discussed earlier, many of Steinberg's tables contain handcrafted facsimiles of the tools used in drawing, painting, sculpting and writing: pens, knives, brushes, rulers, pencils, French curves. They also present, in the same bounded space, things supposedly made by such tools: documents, drawings, paintings, engravings, books, miniatures of furniture and vehicles, domestic items such as vases, boxes and tiles, and much more. His assemblages tell the story of their own making while calling attention to the artificiality of the items arrayed there.

In parallel, *Ulysses* is about both reading and writing—the crafting of its own verbal field. It's a novel *in* words that is also *about* words, about where, why, and how they are written and read. In short, like Steinberg's tables, it's self-reflexive. In it we find titles and passages from books of many genres; newspapers, songs, letters, postcards and liturgies; advertisements and shop signs with verbal as well as visual elements; things that need to be read in order to be used, such as racing forms, coins, tickets, calendars, and maps; characters who make their living by typing in offices, keeping accounts, or purveying printed matter; the writing surfaces of paper, envelopes, copybooks, and even Bloom's cuff; the reading habits of characters. Taking into account, too, the abundance and variety of allusions to other verbal works from the fields of science, literature, philosophy, theology, and history, we understand that *Ulysses* opens out upon many verbally constructed worlds.

Noticing self-reflexive textuality only begins to illuminate the possibilities of meaning that reflecting on *Ulysses* as an assemblage offers. Textuality is never the whole story for Joyce, as it never is for Steinberg. Joyce reliably opens his works to instances of nonverbal, acute, sensory experience. The novel's opening scene presents a bit of Latin text, a translation of a line from Psalm 43, but it also includes "a long low whistle of call" (*U,* 3). Rusty boots may be figures of philosophical interest for Stephen, but his own boots sensuously "crush, crack, crick, crick" along the strand (*U,* 37). We can "take" a table by Steinberg as an embodiment of self-reflexivity, or—surveying it repeatedly—as a call to the senses of taste, smell, texture, sound; as autobiographical meditations; as an array of formal elements; mythological musings; historical evidence; a domestic snapshot of "a day in the life"; and meta-artistic explorations. So, too, has *Ulysses* has proved fertile ground for critics and scholars of many persuasions: formalist, autobiographical, psychological, naturalistic, genetic, symbolic, historical, materialist, cultural, and then some.[3]

What's more, *Ulysses* invites, even demands, multiple readings, once the reader begins to notice its many subtle repetitions and patterns, just as groupings and patterns begin to reveal themselves as we meditate on a Steinberg table. Examining Joyce's Dublin bears a family resemblance to construing, for example, the things of *Rodozachari Table* (see fig. 103; p. 245), as *Ulysses* elicits multiple associations which themselves cross-associate in complex ways, slowly building to webs of meaning. Steinberg's tables can even include something like "characters," that is, portraits in various media. Imaginatively allowing these images of people to interact with other items on the table yields copious narrative. Something happens. When we do let Steinberg's people interact, the parodic *style* in which they are presented (Art Deco, clichéd family snapshot, Cubist, and so on) becomes the central element of their characterization, much as Stephen's and Bloom's qualities of being change along with the various styles and rhetorics of the book's chapters.

The reading of Steinberg's tables also involves us in an experience of bifocality: we enter into the details of each small object *and* we look at the table as a whole. As critics have surveyed *Ulysses,* their impulse has often been—in the face of its staggering multiplicity of things, characters, allusions, places—to find groups within its eighteen parts by surveying the novel as a whole from above, as it were. The specific groupings of the eighteen episodes argued for by critics—into threes, sixes, even nines—matter less than the fact of their variety. *Ulysses* seems to elicit organizing energies from its dedicated readers. And just as a combination of things on one of Steinberg's tables can function as a mise en abyme of the whole, so a single episode of *Ulysses* can represent the whole of which it is a part. "Circe," for example, seems to gather images and ideas from much of the rest of the novel, and like the rest of the novel (only more so), it deals in memories, riddles, and mysteries. The clichés of "Eumaeus" hyperbolize the all-too-common knowledge of loquacious Dubliners throughout Ulysses. "Oxen of the Sun" epitomizes the novel's exploration of multiple styles. Such an argument could be made for any single episode.

Like Steinberg, Joyce trades in differing order and modes of time. Looking at a Steinberg table, we at first acknowledge a comfortable presence of space and time: multiple objects are spread across the limited space of the table, often in a grid-like pattern, and our eyes move across that grid to the rhythm of an implied clock, item by item, tick by tock. But we've seen that the table's order tends to dissolve before our creative eyes. As strong readers we can move in many directions about a Steinberg table, skip over or linger in particular objects, circle or triangulate, emphasize or ignore.

Similarly, *Ulysses* is composed of "compartments, containers, zones, chapters, neighborhoods" across which characters move from hour to hour during the course of a single day and across which we as readers move from start to finish.[4] Time on a line is there, stretching from the death of Moses to the death of Parnell and a bit beyond, and along that line the reader can gradually organize the ever-proliferating, often confounding, details of the novel. Stephen thinks seriously about the inexorability of time's infinite passage, independent of himself; but he also thinks about shaped time and apocalypse when he "hear[s] the ruin of all space, shattered glass and toppling masonry, and time one livid final flame" (*U,* 24). As Ellmann establishes, these "premonitions begin to be realized. Time and space, once so firm and masterful, begin to crumble, and both continuity and contiguity are repudiated. The bonds that keep things and events next to or before and after each other are loosened."[5] Even before the second half of the novel, readers register that *Ulysses* is, like Odysseus the man in Homer's *Odyssey,* "polytropos," a "book of many turns" in which different modes of time matter.[6] Clock time, for example, gives way to embodied "times" felt on the pulses—good, harsh, dangerous, lost, funny. Against the backdrop of a single day, felt time can contract to a point, slow down to the idle pub talk of an afternoon, or run amuck in Nighttown. And, with Vico in mind, Joyce always threads the time of history with the time of myth.

The time of reading the novel matters, too. Spread across its pages are both abrupt changes in style *and* repetitions of significant words and phrases, an assemblage of disconnection and reconnection, tracking and backtracking, through which any phrase can serve as a vector to a related phrase elsewhere in the novel. After an initial, perhaps "straight-through" reading, the process of rereading *Ulysses* depends on multidirectional reorientations within the text and even across and out of it to include information from the by-now encyclopedic annotations to what Joyce thought of as an already encyclopedic novel.

A dialectical reading and viewing process emerges for both a Steinberg table and *Ulysses.* Each invites both the spatial view from on high and the close-up examination;[7] organized grid and multivectoral commotion; the establishment of time and space, and their dissolution. To these contrasting positions we may add others, beginning with personal and impersonal narrative. Steinberg plays a cat and mouse game on his tables, placing in proximity items that arise from his private, daily life, but these items appear equally to have sailed in from a second-degree "Steinberg's" life—not genuinely private but posed as if so. The "real" Steinberg, whoever he might be, lurks tantalizingly close, but his tables are oddly impersonal for all their autobiographical information. Does the artist include a landscape painting because he has been there, painting before it, or has it been fabricated by a someone who merely knows the rhetoric of landscape painting? Do we see a self-portrait there on a table, or a picture of a self-portrait, a work of Steinberg's "third degree" of reality? Does the table surface stand in for the "self," gathering the things placed there into a concatenated unity, or is it just a piece of wood? To all such questions, the answer must be "both." When Steinberg changed the title of his first book from *Confessions* to *The New World,* he signaled his desire to shield personal information.

In *Ulysses* as in Steinberg's assemblages, then, the personal or autobiographical exists in dialectical tension with impersonality. We know that Stephen, in "Scylla and Charybdis," argues for the autobiographical sources of great writing. *Ulysses* is more than passingly autobiographical, especially when we view Stephen Dedalus there as an appropriation of Joyce's autobiographical character in *A Portrait of the Artist as a Young Man.* Yet an early and major breakthrough in understanding *Ulysses* has revealed that much of it has been constructed and arranged in ways that can't be attributed to a traditional narrator or speaking voice, much less a lyrically composing, self-memorializing self. We discover instead that "the consciousness of the text," not a supposed person, seems to be at work.[8] Crucially for our understanding of Joyce's modernist creation, the more radically experimental second half of the novel causes us to question narrative authority throughout, much as we understand that piecing together the articles on Steinberg's tables teaches us the contingency of narrative. Playfulness outmaneuvers authoritativeness.

Keeping in mind a Steinberg table as a constellation, we find, in parallel, *Ulysses*'s simple narrative thrust interrupted by gaps and always open to reconfiguration. What happens to characters largely metamorphoses to what happens to and in language through the exploration of multiple styles or rhetorics, each one of which has a visible (in addition to legible) style as groupings of words and sentences on the page. Lost in the pleasures of lengthy catalogues or fascinated by the knee-deep clichés of "Eumaeus," the lurid drama of "Circe," or the extended catechismal session of explanation and inventory in "Ithaca," we periodically lose sight of cohesive characters and events—those standbys of narrative form. Understanding heterogeneity to be a central quality of the novel from its inception, we find nothing lacking in the narrative of *Ulysses.* Rather, its aspects of tale, myth, epic, satire, drama, encyclopedia, history, and rhetorical anthology lead each reader to assemble an understanding of what "the novel" now might be. Juxtaposition will always be its mode. Because each reader "arranges" *Ulysses* in a different way (and reassembles it anew upon subsequent readings), and because the text is so overwhelmingly rich in detail, the novel's meanings are as various and changeable as its techniques.

But what, we might ask, has happened to the retelling of the *Odyssey*? Doesn't it, according to Joyce himself, provide a fixed scheme for *Ulysses*'s turning worlds within worlds? Genetic criticism—the reading of drafts or worksheets of the novel for evidence of how Joyce conceived of it over time—has shown that he edited out some Homeric references by the stage of his final drafts of episodes. Yet the *Odyssey* gave him comfort as he wrote, supplying him with what he called fixed "ports of call." That he needed such ports and offered them as well to his early readers indicates their importance without demanding that everything in the novel be read in their light.[9]

Genetic criticism gives us other important evidence that thinking of *Ulysses* as akin to Steinberg's tables makes sense: items in both can come and go before they reach final form. Once Joyce had the "table" or *Odyssean* parallel in place, he was free to add items to it—or subtract them. Like any work of juxtaposition, an assembled work "grows by testing, rejection, and acceptance. The artist must cede a measure of his control, and hence of his ego, to the materials and what transpires between them, placing himself partially in the role of discoverer or spectator as well as that of originator."[10] Michael Groden has shown us that the published text of *Ulysses* "can't show the full range of possibilities that were in play at particular times in its past, or the ways in which Joyce responded to what was already written by retaining many of his words in an act of repetition but also by dropping, altering, and adding words in acts of invention. The published text comes to look like the last in a series of possible texts, even if a privileged one, 'a necessary possibility.'"[11]

What genetic critics call the *avant texte* does show us these acts of centripetal and centrifugal change in *Ulysses.* Each time that Joyce read a set of proofs, he was stimulated to revise to the extent that "many sections required five or six sets of proofs; some needed eight or nine."[12] Joyce worked across the total *avant texte* by "complex and nuanced incremental phases," rather than working in one way for earlier sections of the novel and another way for middle or later sections, as Groden originally thought. That is, whatever the final style or rhetoric of his various chapters, he revised in a similar, painstaking, word-by-word or sentence-by-sentence manner, as if they were so many rearrangeable things.

We know, too, that Joyce composed his material *"in blocks, with only arbitrary attempts at transition or connection"* (emphasis added).[13] Only later did he smooth transitions between blocks, doing some of the work for readers that viewers of Steinberg's tables carry out on their own. Paragraphs, especially, were things to be juxtaposed. Genetic criticism has shown us that as much as Joyce added and subtracted words, he rarely broke the integrity of an already existing paragraph. Paragraphs were discrete objects, not items that merged with or disappeared into other paragraphs.[14] They were "regulating units that could be used as frames and were made of writing itself, pure and simple. It is paragraphs, then, that allow the text to acquire in a progressive way the sense of language's independence, before or beyond characterization, mythic parallels, or the urge to universalize."[15] Joyce's paragraphs are visual "things" on the surface of his pages, often separated by a feeling of gap. Some of the herky-jerky quality of *Ulysses,* our experience of missing smooth connection, results from its mode of composition. Along with transitions between paragraphs, transitions between chapters can also seem to be lacking—only gradually can we reorient ourselves in the time and space of a new episode. Declan Kiberd has described *Ulysses* as "a collection of stories bolted with some strain together, rather than a smoothly linear narrative."[16] These gaps between paragraphs and episodes make the novel spatially similar to an assemblage with its gaps between objects and between interior groupings of objects. We might even see the novel as an assemblage of eighteen subassemblages.

Gaps emphasize, too, the materiality of language in *Ulysses,* the way in which Joyce's language not only refers to or imitates reality but also autonomously creates a reality of its own. Like Steinberg's tables, Joyce's novel both represents and presents. The space of representation and presentation matters here; genetic critics have explained that Joyce worked on *Ulysses* in space as well as time. Here, I refer not just to the "Trieste-Zürich-Paris" postscript, but also to the fact that Joyce explored the space of a sheet of white paper as he wrote. Dirk Van Hulle refers to Joyce's "paper studio": "In most—but by no means all—cases, he wrote on the right-hand pages (rectos), leaving the margins at the left and the left-hand pages (versos) for revisions and additions. The left-hand margin widened as he moved down the page. Some margins and versos are blank, but Joyce filled many others with additions, which he usually connected to the main body of the text by a line or a superscript letter."[17]

During the writing of *Ulysses,* Joyce's page, then, is akin to Steinberg's drawing table, the place where imagination issues in art objects. He puts things on pages. The giant U of *Ulysses,* S of "Stately," M of "Mr" and P of "Preparatory," as well as the large black dot with which "Ithaca" ends signal Joyce's insistence that we look at his black shapes on white, arranged on pages. Blocks of words in catalogues, short passages of centered rather than left- and right-justified prose, italic typeface, wholly capitalized characters' names and headlines, liberal leading (white space) between blocks of prose in some episodes, asterisks, even passages of square musical notation (neume): these and other typographical elements of the novel signal us to look at, not just through, the printed page.

In addition to resembling Steinberg's tables in their self-reflexive, dialectical, material, temporal, and spatial qualities, *Ulysses* is, as already discussed, a book infused with parody, a quality that returns us to the materiality of the verbal text, an invitation to understand it as a collection of things. Steinberg discusses the parodic quality of his tables, perhaps for him their most important aspect: "[On] 'The Table' . . . I did not only the drawing of a drawing, but I proposed there and in fact I executed the substance or parody of friends, of objects. I did an album which is false, in wood. I painted the pages white to represent paper. On this I drew, I made a drawing, let's say. Sometimes I made a pen out of wood, a pen case and pen, and I drew of course with real ink, although I could have made it out of something else."[18]

Ulysses overflows with a whole family of relations both internal and external: allusions, repetitions, correlations, resemblances, parallels. In this way it necessarily repeats itself in a parodic manner, if, as this study has argued all along, parody be taken in its Nabokovian and Steinbergian sense as repetition with a difference. Joyce, like Steinberg, makes use of parodic self-appropriation, the repetition with a difference of items from his earlier work.

Just as Steinberg has placed works of art made earlier in his career (or repetitions of them) on his tables, so Joyce also recycles—parodies—his own work.[19] Joyce describes *Ulysses,* early in the writing process, as "a continuation of *A Portrait of the Artist* and also of *Dubliners.*"[20] Although we read "Nausicaa's" Gerty MacDowell as a mocking parody of the bird-girl on the strand in Joyce's *Portrait,* she appears as well to have a forerunner in Polly Mooney of *Dubliners.* In fact, some thirty characters from *Dubliners* and nine from *Portrait* find their way into *Ulysses,* either making "actual" appearances or being thought of or mentioned by other characters.[21] Joyce creates parody by the liberal appropriation of his own earlier works, much as Steinberg has done in his drawing table assemblages. For example, Joyce in *Ulysses* explores again a set of concerns—desire, the visual forms that fantasy may take, sexual betrayal, mutability—that he first set out in *Giacomo Joyce,* a brief series of sketches that he never tried to publish.[22] Frightful metamorphoses, like those of "Circe," also appear in *Giacomo Joyce.*

Like Steinberg's assemblages of drawing tools, *Ulysses* refers to methods of composition. Stephen, for example, rues the fact that he neglected to pick up some library slips that could serve as free writing paper (*U,* 48). But he thinks, too, of his earlier writings ("Remember your epiphanies on green oval leaves, deeply deep, copies to be sent if you died to all the great libraries of the world, including Alexandria?" [*U,* 40]).[23]

Steinberg is careful to say that he "makes a parody of methods"[24] too—and he might well have noticed that Joyce does likewise in the parody of styles and rhetorics in the eighteen episodes of his novel. In fact, parody in *Ulysses* actually *leads* to novelistic assemblage, a recycling not just of rhetorics or discourses across the surface of *Ulysses,* but also of repeated words, phrases, things, characterizations, settings, actions rendered through these techniques. Given "Circe's" tendency to "place all figures, all analogies, all ruminations, on the plane of the visible and audible," it is perhaps easiest to grasp this section as a would-be visual assemblage.[25]

It's important to understand, though, that all of Joyce's parodic measures point to the materiality of language, our tendency to begin to see words not just as pointing devices, but also as things in themselves. Parody announces itself as artificial, and artifice claims its own contingent, rearrangeable order that moves beyond mimetic intentions. Critics have long recognized that for Joyce language is itself a collection of things to be reckoned with in their own right. Hugh Kenner states an extreme version:

> On nothing is *Ulysses* more insistent than on the fact that there is no Bloom there, no Stephen there, no Molly there, no Dublin there, simply language. To say this is by no means to surrender to the artificer's whimsical virtuosity. We and he are co-creators; characters and city have their existence in our minds . . . this is not to say, with Barthes in *S/Z,* that our reading of any book is essentially our doing. Words are prior to us, communal, entangled in human experience, registered in other books and in dictionaries. In most books [words] are brushed on to the pages, a thin wash. But *Ulysses* is the first book to be a kind of hologram of language, creating a three-dimensional illusion out of the controlled interference between our experience of language and its arrangements of language.[26]

The novel never lets us forget that "It's words, words, words we're coping with."[27] This means that "things are not [only] talked about, they [also] happen in the prose."[28] And it's not just when the writing becomes especially difficult to understand, as in, for example, the overture of "Sirens," or when cigarette smoke speaks in "Circe" (*U,* 452), that readers become conscious of the matter of language, of words on the page.

But what does it mean in reading practice to say that language functions as matter, as well as a pointing device, in *Ulysses?* Bloom's thoughts as he pages through a book provide an example of such materiality: "Mr Bloom turned over idly pages of *The Awful Disclosures of Maria Monk,* then of Aristotle's *Masterpiece.* Crooked botched print. Plates: infants cuddled in a ball in bloodred wombs like livers of slaughtered cows. Lots of them like that at this moment all over the world. All butting with their skulls to get out of it. Child born every minute somewhere. Mrs. Purefoy" (*U,* 235). We at first recognize Bloom in the act of looking at books about sex and thinking about embryonic development and childbirth. But Joyce gives us as well an arrangement of words on a page, through and about which meanings multiply and circulate as we closely examine those words.

The onomatopoeia of the passage asks us to focus on words as collections of sounds: e.g., "butting with their skulls to get out of it." The passage takes on a thickness—weight gained—as we explore its centrifugal allusions. Words become things from which we launch our reading selves. Words accrue more words. *Awful Disclosures of the Hotel Dieu Nunnery of Montreal* by Maria Monk tells of supposed priest-nun sexual depravity and infanticide. This book upon publication in 1836 caused a groundswell of Protestant, anti-Catholic response, matched by Catholic attacks on the book itself. The "crooked botched print" of the Aristotle *Masterpiece* then suggests a possible Catholic attack on Monk's book and the "crooked botched nature" of infanticide itself. The two books are closely connected in Bloom's mind: the simile "like livers of slaughtered cows" (referring either to embryos or wombs or both, it's not clear) is disgusting, just as Maria Monk portrays the "disgusting" sexual acts of monks or priests with nuns (doubled in the two parts of her name). And speaking of disclosures, the plate in *Masterpiece* shows what is usually hidden from view—the embryo *in utero.* Aristotle didn't write a book entitled *Masterpiece,* but he did discuss human reproduction in *De generatione animalium,* perhaps excerpted in the volume that Bloom the shopper examines. One "awful disclosure" of the novel has already happened offstage—Bloom's learning of the time of Boylan's visit to Molly. Another awful disclosure—that one of the "infants cuddled" has been Rudy, somehow "botched" because so quickly lost to Bloom forever—takes ghostly form within the words of this passage. Bloom has fused with the things he handles—words in a book.

More generally, we as readers fuse our understanding with the generative words on the page, moving swiftly from Dublin to Montreal to Greece; from 1904 to 1836 to ancient times; from "Wandering Rocks" to "Oxen of the Sun" and beyond through the text of the novel. The "consciousness of the text" has been at work, as have we. A wonderful, not an awful, disclosure occurs: between that consciousness and our own, a characteristic *Ulyssean* "reality" of many turns has burgeoned amid the words on the page. Dwelling there, we tell ourselves stories about words and phrases born of allusion and suggestion, much as we do when we survey one of Steinberg's arrangements of things on his tables.

In addition to the materiality of words, *Ulysses* is a table of things, as Steinberg's tables are his would-be books of things (that join his actual books collecting images he selected, such as *The Inspector*). Steinberg tells Aldo Buzzi that some of the things he made for his tables were "thoughts treated as objects," thoughts that we as readers of the table attempt to discern (*LAB,* July 16, 1964). Moreover, the very idea of the table enabled Steinberg to make things that vacillated between things as such and things as symbols ("something about something else") *throughout his oeuvre:* "My paintings are not so much paintings in themselves as parts of a table, objects of a drawing table, the painter's work table. The pencils and other things I do there are to say that this is not a painting of mine but a painting by someone else, maybe a painting by 'that painter' but not by me. In that case, I'm more an orchestra conductor than a painter doing a painting. My work says something about something else; if it's a painting it says something about painting not about the fact that this is what it is" (*RS,* 71).

Ulysses, too, displays Joyce's interest in the tendency of things to be just themselves in all their familiar appeal and simultaneously to be evocative of multiple ideas, such as the passage just explored, in which Bloom pages through books by Maria Monk and Aristotle.

"It is my idea of the significance of trivial things that I want to give the two or three unfortunate wretches who may eventually read me," Joyce writes.[29] Bill Brown discusses *things* as objects that have developed through "a mutual constitution of human subject and inanimate object."[30] As *Ulysses* proceeds, many supposedly trivial "objects"—potato, postcard, printed advertisement, mackintosh, key, soap, newspaper, biscuit tin, cup, mirror—take on the status of "things, "becoming rich with significance.[31] Although Steinberg places exotic objects on his tables, he also juxtaposes with them objects from his daily life and then lets them take on relational meanings as we interact with them and they with one another. A slice of pickle gathers meaning because he eats pickles, because it has been carved by his hand, because it is juxtaposed with other things, and because it can contain Steinberg's thoughts. Yet always, like things in *Ulysses,* it can flip back into the simplicity of objecthood. The wonderful energy emanating from both Steinberg's and Joyce's art stems in part from such fluctuation between the object and the thing.

For Joyce, some things exude energy because they possess awareness, knowledge, or even a kind of consciousness. As a young man he attended meetings of the Dublin Hermetic Society, and although he never became a Theosophist, he joined modernist artists such as Cézanne—who said his painted apples were "filled with thought"—in exploring his intuitions of an interior movement in the myriad things populating a single day.[32] Joyce also lets us watch as his characters endow things with knowledge. Stephen's certainty that things carry legible meanings waxes and wanes—mostly wanes—across the novel. The very rhythm of Bloom's thought as it lingers in thing after thing seems to half discover, half endow consciousness there. "Everything speaks in its own way," Bloom muses (*U,* 21).[33]

Things also participate in characterization. The novel gives us few direct physical descriptions of people or expositions of their personalities. We learn much about them through what they say, but also through the things associated with them. The anti-Semitic and choleric citizen of "Cyclops," for example, is introduced "with his cruiskeen lawn and his load of papers, working for the cause" rather than by a description of his person or a direct statement of his abominable qualities (*U,* 295). A cruiskeen lawn is a little full jug, and the folksong by that name celebrates the love between a drinker and his drink. Michael Cusack, Joyce's model for the citizen, was the founder of the Gaelic Athletic Association and dedicated to the systematic eradication of English games from Ireland—hence his "load of papers." Jug, papers: the narrator of the episode notes that the citizen and his things are together "in his gloryhole," which is a place where odds and ends are thrown.[34] The citizen may regard himself and his cause as superior, but both the narrator and we begin with a derogatory view—and the citizen only sinks lower as the episode proceeds. He's an alcoholic tosser, an offensive male, who has himself been tossed into Barney Kiernan's pub. Not only do his things tell us so, but also his rigid hatreds have solidified him into an object-like and objectionable man.

Steinberg's fiction-tables depend on a parodically Keatsian speech of mute objects. But the ability of *things* to challenge human speech and agency constitutes a central energy of *Ulysses*. For example, things can speak out loud ("Circe"); replace speech, when Joyce places them together in lists ("Cyclops," "Ithaca"); cut off conversation altogether (the chariot of "Cyclops") (*U,* 345); soothe with their healing beauty the pain talkative Stephen feels as he has spoken out at length—the "bless'd altars" with which "Scylla and Charybdis" closes (*U,* 218). Joyce may insist across the novel on the talismanic importance of a few things such as the potato that Bloom is careful to place in his pocket in the morning, the lemon soap he buys for Molly, the "Plumtree's Potted Meat" advertisement, or the mysterious "U.p: up postcard." Yet all objects in the novel become things once characters within the novel and we as readers react to them, and any thing within the novel can be taken as a talisman, an expression of the magic inhering in trivial, everyday life. Object to thing to talisman; talisman to thing to object: here is the metamorphic energy of *Ulysses* made physical. Steinberg's tables, too, have an aura of magic about them, as if the things of his daily life present a ritualistic gathering—and then flicker back to the quotidian.

The pages of *Ulysses* and Steinberg's tables have here resonated with each other for only a short space. Both table and novel are self-referential, spatial, dialectical, heterogeneous, metamorphic, and parodic. Both are made of things: Joyce told Jacque Mercanton: "Why regret my talent? I haven't any. I write so painfully, so slowly. Chance furnishes me with what I need. I'm like a man who stumbles: my foot strikes something. I look down and there is exactly what I'm in need of."[35] Joyce speaks here in simile, but that figure of speech nonetheless touches on his felt experience of writing as an activity of picking up and placing objects so that, thing by thing, the novel—the paper studio akin to Steinberg's drawing table assemblages—develops. A cascade of similarities flows across the imaginations of Joyce and Steinberg, across the years that separate them—and them and us—and, perhaps most importantly for the purposes of this study, across the verbal and visual media that they both explored.

Afterword

"Thought through My Eyes"

In 1970 Saul Steinberg gave a mock "restaurant menu" of books to Claire Nivola, the twenty-two-year-old daughter of his friend and neighbor in Amagansett, the sculptor Costantino Nivola (fig. 121). Steinberg had known "Tino" since their days in Italy, and Claire (nicknamed Chiaretta) from her infancy. The Joycean *nostos* (homecoming) of this study, then, is a list of books, circling back to join *Library,* with which it began. The menu, like so many of Steinberg's remarks, mentions both Nabokov and Joyce. Like *Library,* the menu is familiar in its parodic mode, which only begins with its jokey similarity to a restaurant's selection of courses. After having a rubber stamp of the figures from Millet's *The Angelus* produced for him, Steinberg impressed the menu with this parodic emblem—parody on parody. His use of *The Angelus* refers, as discussed earlier, both to his childhood and to his admiration for what Isaiah Berlin (after Friedrich Schiller) called the "naïve." Steinberg describes such naïveté as innocence meshed with the love of the beautiful.[1] Other rubber-stamped images on the menu, with their illegible "writing" within circles, mock the inscrutable imprints of officialdom.

Somewhat surprising, though, is the absence of novels from the menu. Steinberg offers, instead, various forms of life-writing—biographies, memoirs, autobiographies, letters, and journals—along with some literary criticism. We might read the list as Steinberg's own life-writing, based on the selections he has made. Beginning with Victorian explorers, the menu reminds us of his own wanderings: he has, after all, declared travel to be a "fine game" through which he discovered "what sort of man I am" (*LAB,* February 19, 1964). Joyce and Nabokov once again come to mind, with their own peregrinations. Steinberg favors books by or about artists and writers, with a king and some exiled radical thinkers supplying other complex "dishes." Or, in recalling Steinberg's sense of humor, we can savor the joke embedded in presenting Norman Douglas's *Looking Back* as a dessert choice. That memoir has no plot, but presents merely a long series of brief

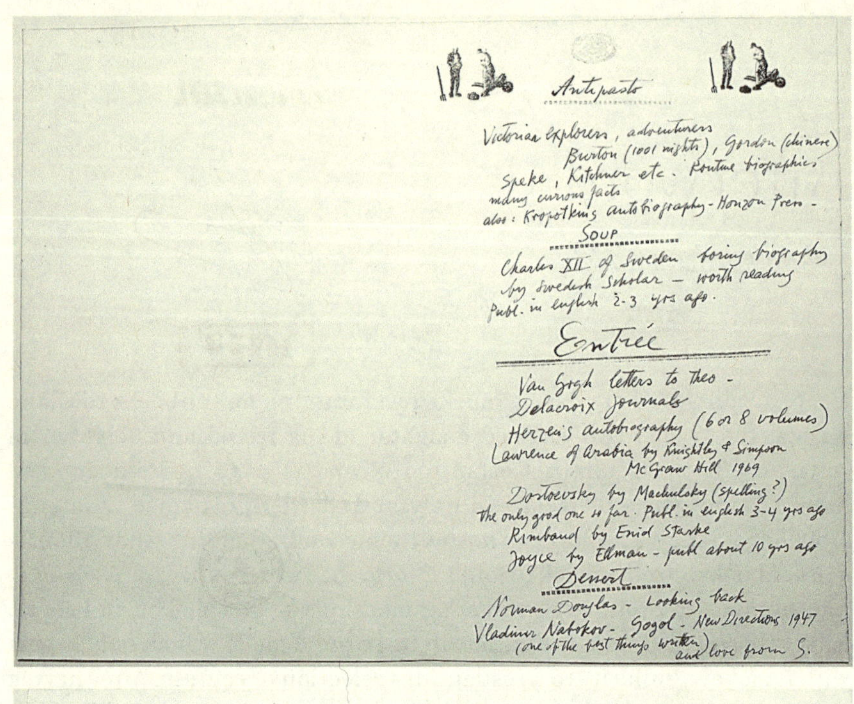
Antipasto

Victorian explorers, adventurers
Burton (1001 nights), Gordon (chinese)
Speke, Kitchner etc. Routine biographies
many curious facts
also: Kropotkin's autobiography - Horizon Press -

Soup

Charles XII of Sweden boring biography
by Swedish scholar — worth reading
Publ. in english 2-3 yrs ago.

Entrée

Van Gogh letters to Theo -
Delacroix Journals
Herzen's autobiography (6 or 8 volumes)
Lawrence of Arabia by Knightley & Simpson
McGraw Hill 1969
Dostoevsky by Machulsky (spelling?)
The only good one so far. Publ. in english 3-4 yrs ago
Rimbaud by Enid Starke
Joyce by Ellman - publ about 10 yrs ago

Dessert

Norman Douglas - Looking back
Vladimir Nabokov - Gogol - New Directions 1947
(one of the best things written)
and love from S.

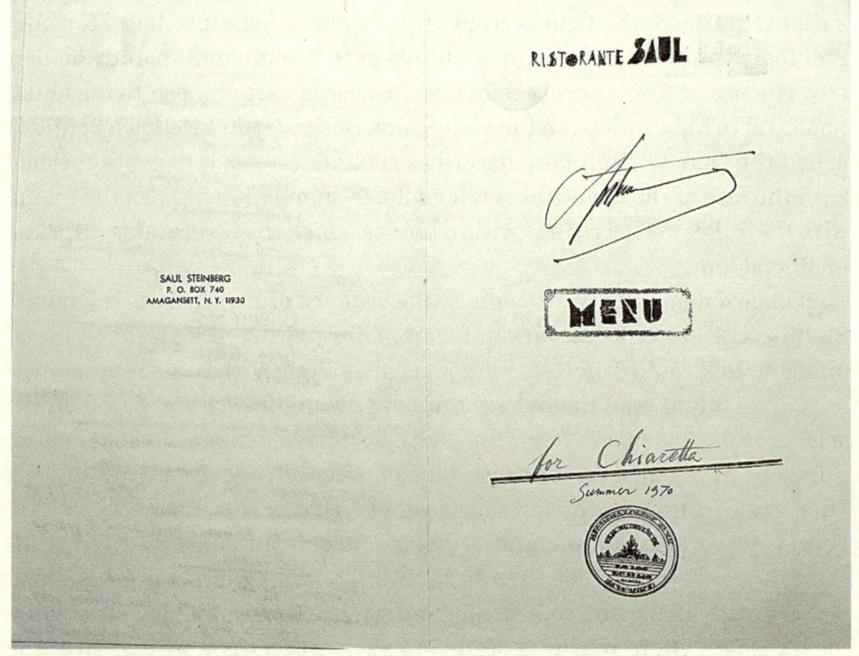
RISTORANTE SAUL

SAUL STEINBERG
P. O. BOX 740
AMAGANSETT, N. Y. 11930

MENU

for Chiaretta
Summer 1970

Fig. 121. Two-sided literary menu for Chiaretta, 1970. Ink and rubber stamp on paper, 11¼ × 14½ in. (Private collection)

character sketches and vignettes, so many bonbons. Or perhaps Claire will decide to end her meal with a taste of Gogol, via Nabokov—a serving of magical absurdity.

These instances of life-writing indicate Steinberg as the "Inspector" of others' lives while hiding his own life in plain sight across his works. "I call myself The Inspector," he writes, "and my profession is: discovery of questions, my questions being my symptoms, so to speak, as well as the symptoms of others. In other words, my answer."[2] The questions *are* the answers for Steinberg, as they must be for those of us who dwell in his thousands of images.

The questions of *Saul Steinberg's Literary Journeys* should celebrate Joyce and Nabokov, but always reach beyond them. The following questions have been addressed in the preceding chapters of this book, but only partially. There is room for more work.

What does Nabokov mean when he states, "Literature is not a pattern of ideas but a pattern of images"[3] and how does that relate to Steinberg's notion that his visual art is not just a matter of images, but also a pattern of ideas? Nabokov claims, "The story of my life resembles less a biography than a bibliography": is the same true for Steinberg?[4] And with what authors beyond those of this study did Steinberg find affinities?

More questions: what meeting of word, image, and idea does Joyce conjure with his lines, given to Stephen the inspector, "Ineluctable modality of the visible; at least that if no more, thought through my eyes. Signatures of all things I am here to read" (*U,* 37). Does the phrase "thought through my eyes" read differently with Steinberg in mind? "When one reads these strange pages of one long gone one feels that one is at one with one who once . . . ," Stephen thinks (*U,* 40), probably parodying Walter Pater.[5] To what extent is Steinberg at one with Joyce and Nabokov and the many other authors those two "great teachers" themselves parody, i.e., repeat with a difference?

Steinberg notes, in a brief scribble to himself: "The self-made man, also known as the artist—half disaster, half something never seen before" (YCAL b. 130, f. 2475). If (a big if) he is half disaster, that is nonetheless our own good fortune, but Saul Steinberg the artist, known through his works, is certainly something never seen before.

NOTES

1. Thought Images

1. For example, *SS: I,* 138, 152,168, 188, 212. See also Steinberg, *Passport* (1979), 237.
2. Glueck, "20th-Century Artists Most Admired," 78.
3. Saul Steinberg, "A Victorian Dialogue," interview by Dore Ashton.
4. Steinberg's place in art history has been addressed by Joel Smith, *SS: I;* Bair, *Saul Steinberg;* Norman, *Transatlantic Aliens;* and Melissa Renn, "The Americans Abroad: Situating Saul Steinberg's Mural for the 1958 Brussels World's Fair," in Prinzing, *Saul Steinberg: The Americans,* 15–61.
5. See, for example, Marianna Torgovnick, *The Visual Arts, Pictorialism, and the Novel: James, Lawrence, and Woolf* (Princeton: Princeton University Press, 1985); David Michael Levin, ed., *Modernity and the Hegemony of Vision* (Berkeley: University of California Press, 1992); W. J. T. Mitchell, *Picture Theory: Essays on Verbal and Visual Representation* (Chicago: University of Chicago Press, 1994); Daniel Albright, *Untwisting the Serpent: Modernism in Music, Literature, and Other Arts* (Chicago: University of Chicago Press, 2000), and *Putting Modernism Together: Literature, Music, and Painting, 1872–1927* (Baltimore: Johns Hopkins University Press, 2015); Karen Jacobs, *The Eye's Mind: Literary Modernism and Visual Culture* (Ithaca, NY: Cornell University Press, 2001). See also the journal *Word and Image* for a wealth of discussions of the relations between verbal and visual art.
6. Rosenberg, *Saul Steinberg,* 243.
7. Steiner, *The Colors of Rhetoric,* 2.
8. Schneider, *Louvre Dialogues,* 83.
9. Quoted in Ashbery, "Saul Steinberg: Callibiography," 55.
10. Ashbery, "Callibiography," 53.
11. Glueck, "20th-Century Artists Most Admired," 78.
12. Frémon, "Conversation avec Saul Steinberg," 5–18.
13. Jolanta Wawrzycka, "Translation," in McCourt, *James Joyce in Context,* 125–36.
14. Heuvel, "Straight from the Hand," 66.
15. Transcription of taped conversations between Aldo Buzzi and Saul Steinberg made c. 1974–77, preparatory to publication as *Reflections and Shadows;* translated from the Italian by Adrienne Foulke, YCAL b. 126, f. 2422; hereafter cited as Steinberg-Buzzi conversations. This passage, along with all following references to the Steinberg-Buzzi conversations, was not eventually included in *Reflections and Shadows.*
16. Shapiro, *Sublime Artist's Studio,* 26. For a discussion of his various drawing masters, see 19–26; for an account of the significance to Nabokov of *The World of Art,* an important turn-of-the-century aesthetic phenomenon in Russian culture, see 96–135.
17. Vries and Johnson, *Vladimir Nabokov and the Art of Painting,* 178–80.

18. Clarence Brown, "Krazy, Ignatz, and Vladimir: Nabokov and the Comic Strip," in Shapiro, *Nabokov at Cornell,* 251–63. See also Shapiro, "Nabokov and Comic Art: Additional Observations and Remarks."
19. Nabokov, *Bend Sinister,* xii.
20. Nabokov, *Selected Letters,* 379.
21. Boyd, *Vladimir Nabokov: American Years,* 511–12.
22. Saul Steinberg, interview by Adam Gopnik.
23. Saul Steinberg, YCAL b. 31, f. 581.
24. Steinberg-Buzzi conversations.
25. Schiff, *Vera (Mrs. Vladimir Nabokov),* 197–98.
26. Steinberg, interview by Gopnik.
27. D. Barton Johnson, *Worlds in Regression,* 13, quoting from *Drugie Berega* [Other shores] (New York: *Izdatel' Stvo Imeni Chekova,* 1954), 26–27.
28. Kramer, "Saul Steinberg: Illuminations."
29. Steinberg, spiral notebook dated April 23–July 5, 1991, YCAL b. 115, f. 2277.
30. Inventories available from *SSF.*
31. Vladimir Nabokov, "Notes to *Ada* by Vivian Darkbloom," in Rivers and Nicol, *Nabokov's Fifth Arc,* 244.
32. Steinberg, interview by Raymond Rosenthal and Moishe Ducovny, late July–August 1960, for American Jewish Committee Oral History Library. Typescript available at SSF, "Interviews," 1960.1, and at the New York Public Library (see bibliography).
33. Steinberg, interview by Rosenthal and Ducovny.
34. This excellent essay scans various positions taken by critics and theorists on the form versus context question. Its notes, while current only to 2007, provide references to important instances and analyses of the New Formalism. I have found especially useful Wolfson and Brown, *Reading for Form;* and Loesberg, *Return to Aesthetics.*

2. The "Springboard of Parody"

1. Robert P. Falk and Francis Teague, "Parody," in *The New Princeton Encyclopedia of Poetry and Poetics,* ed. Alex Preminger and T. V. F. Brogan (Princeton: Princeton University Press, 1993), 881.
2. Falk and Teague, "Parody," 882.
3. Hutcheon, *Theory of Parody,* 143.
4. Linda Hutcheon and Malcolm Woodland, "Parody," in *The Princeton Encyclopedia of Poetry and Poetics,* 4th ed., ed. Stephen Cushman (Princeton: Princeton University Press, 2012), 1002, ProQuest ebrary.
5. Hutcheon and Woodland, "Parody," 1002.
6. Lars Kleberg, "Parody and Double-Voiced Discourse," in Görenzon and Florin, *Dialogue and Technology,* 96.
7. Steinberg-Buzzi conversations.
8. John Burt Foster, "Parody, Pastiche, and Periodization," 14.
9. Steinberg, interview by John Gruen, January 19, 1978. YCAL b. 130, f. 2473.
10. Kirchner, "Parody in the Fiction of James Joyce," 26. He writes, "Parody foregrounds examples of iteration, of repetition that bring into play or emphasize in some way the trace, the difference, of the repetition rather than suppressing it, thus

avoiding the illusion of simple or pure repetition." See also Kiremidjian, *Study of Modern Parody,* 254.

11. Steinberg, "A Victorian Dialogue," interview by Ashton.

12. http://saulsteinbergfoundation.org/chronology/1941-yr/ and http://saulsteinberg foundation.org/essay/false-documents/.

13. *Oxford English Dictionary,* http://www.oed.com.proxy01.its.virginia.edu/.

14. Steinberg, interview by Eli Waldron, 1973.

15. Petherbridge, *Primacy of Drawing,* 521.

16. Steinberg, interview by Jacques Dupin.

17. Steinberg, interview by Dupin.

18. Steinberg, interview by Dupin.

19. Steinberg-Buzzi conversations.

20. Rosenberg, *Steinberg,* 256.

21. Rosenberg, *Steinberg,* 19.

22. Rosenberg, *Steinberg,* 20.

23. Steinberg, "A Victorian Dialogue," interview by Ashton.

24. Boxer, "An Assistant Tells All."

25. Rosenberg, *Saul Steinberg,* 19.

26. Hughes, "The World of Steinberg," 92.

27. Steinberg-Buzzi conversations.

28. Steinberg-Buzzi conversations.

29. Kramer, "Saul Steinberg: Illuminations," 51.

30. Petherbridge, *Primacy of Drawing,* 436n5. She goes on to say that "these words are attributed to a child in the classic text by the psychologist Marion Blackett Milner, *On Not Being Able to Paint,* London, 1950."

3. Steinberg: The Man-Pen

1. Others have commented, usually in general terms, on the literariness of Steinberg's works, often referring to Steinberg's self-characterization as a writer. See, for example, *SS: I,* 20. Also Rosenberg, *Steinberg,* 10; and Ashbery, "Callibiography," 53.

2. All definitions are from the *Oxford English Dictionary.* Steinberg's library in New York City contained three studies of graphology: R. De Salberg, *Manuel de graphologie usuelle* (Paris: Libraire Hachette, 1935); Pierre Foix, *L'influence du caractère sur l'écriture* (Paris: Albin Michel, 1954); and Oscar N. Myer, *The Language of Handwriting and How to Read It* (London: Peter Owen, 1958). Inventory, SSF.

3. Schneider, *Louvre Dialogues,* 87.

4. Rodman, "Saul Steinberg," 182.

5. Smith, *Steinberg at the New Yorker,* 30.

6. Barthes, "All Except You."

7. Schneider, *Louvre Dialogues,* 81.

8. Steinberg, interview by André Parinaud, "Steinberg: J'enseigne aux hommes à nager en les poussant dans l'eau," *Arts & Loisirs* 25 (March 1966): 51–52. *Interviews with Saul Steinberg,* typescript at SSF, 1966.1, "Comme une sténographie poétique." See also Steinberg-Buzzi conversations.

9. The colored bands of fireworks can be related to Steinberg's *New Yorker* cover of July 5, 1969.

10. Smith, *Steinberg at the New Yorker,* 172.
11. Ashbery, "Callibiography," 53.
12. Charles Baudelaire, *Painter of Modern Life,* trans. Mayne, 5–11.
13. Gustave Flaubert, *Correspondance [par] Gustave Flaubert,* v. 2 (Paris: G. Charpentier et Cie., 1889), 74, https://babel.hathitrust.org/cgi/pt?id=hvd.hwd637;view=1up;seq=82. This is a letter to Louise Colet, January 31, 1852, and the original French is "Je suis un homme-plume. Je sens par elle, à cause d'elle, par rapport à elle et beaucoup plus avec elle."
14. Steinberg-Buzzi conversations.
15. Baudelaire, *Painter of Modern Life,* 28.
16. Dore Ashton, "What I Draw Is Drawing," in *Saul Steinberg,* ed. Kosme de Barañano et al. (Valencia: Institut Valencia d'Art Modern, 2002), 153.
17. Heuvel, "Straight from the Hand," 59.

4. Steinberg: Writing Drawing

1. Shapiro, *Sublime Artist's Studio,* 219n17.
2. Calculated by Sheila Schwartz, SSF, correspondence with author, December 2018.
3. Rosenberg, *Saul Steinberg,* 10. "He is a writer of pictures . . . a draftsman of philosophical reflections."
4. Schneider, *Louvre Dialogues,* 82.
5. Gruen, *The Artist Observed,* 167.
6. Glueck, "The Artist Speaks,"115.
7. Ashbery, "Callibiography," 279.
8. Incoming Correspondence, Farrar, Straus, and Giroux, 1962–1992, YCAL b.16, f. 280.
9. Hughes, *Nothing If Not Critical,* 261; "The World of Steinberg," 95.
10. Steinberg, interview by Paul Cummings, March 27, 1973, *Archives of American Art,* transcript at SSF, 1973.1.
11. Ashbery, "Callibiography," 55.
12. Saul Steinberg, interview by John Jones, October 12, 1965, transcript at SSF, 1965.1.
13. Steinberg, interview by Jones, 8.
14. Steinberg, "A Victorian Dialogue," interview by Dore Ashton. Rosenberg, *Saul Steinberg* 10; *SS: I,* 20. Hollander, in Steinberg, *Passport,* ii, and others have commented on Steinberg's insistence that his works be read and interpreted.
15. Rosenberg, *Saul Steinberg,* 22.
16. Steinberg-Buzzi conversations.
17. For a bibliography of books by Steinberg, see Smith, *SS: I,* 268; and the Saul Steinberg Foundation, http://saulsteinbergfoundation.org.
18. Ashbery, "Callibiography," 281.
19. Wilde, *Picture of Dorian Gray,* in *Complete Works of Oscar Wilde,* 17.
20. Schneider, *Louvre Dialogues,* 81.
21. Schneider, *Louvre Dialogues,* 83.
22. Heuvel, "Straight from the Hand," 66.
23. Schneider, *Louvre Dialogues,* 81.

24. Heuvel, "Straight from the Hand," 59.

25. See Topliss, *Comic Worlds,* 181–238, for a discussion of Steinberg as a cartoonist. See *SS: I,* 36, for some useful comments on Steinberg's art in contrast to the rest of the *New Yorker* artists.

26. *Oxford English Dictionary,* s.v. "Cartoon."

27. Barthes, "All Except You," 158.

28. See Rosenblum, "Cubism as Pop Art," for a fuller discussion. For a discussion of words that function as objects in Steinberg's art, see http://saulsteinbergfoundation.org/essay/word-object-drawings/.

29. For a related discussion of the presence of letters and numbers in Nabokov's works, see D. Barton Johnson, *Worlds in Regression,* 28–46; and Shapiro, *The Sublime Artist's Studio,* 58–60.

30. Heuvel, "Straight from the Hand," 59.

5. Steinberg: Reading

1. Manea, "Made in Romania."

2. Steinberg, transcribed remarks to Rolf Karrer-Kharberg.

3. Steinberg, "Saul Steinberg: Master of Wit and Fantasy," interview by Gruen, 138.

4. Steinberg, "An Interview with Saul Steinberg," by Meg Perlman, April 15, 1975.

5. Steinberg-Buzzi conversations.

6. Glueck, "The Artist Speaks: Saul Steinberg," 115.

7. Saul Steinberg, "National Diary," January 3, 1959.

8. Fyodor Dostoevsky, *The Idiot,* trans. Eva Martin, Project Gutenberg, part 1, sec. 5, http://www.gutenberg.org/ebooks/2638?msg=welcome_stranger.

9. Saul Steinberg, *The Inspector,* n.p.

10. Glueck, "The Artist Speaks," 113.

11. Steinberg, spiral notebook dated April 23–July 5, 1991, YCAL b. 115, f. 2277.

12. Saul Steinberg, interview by Adam Gopnik.

13. Steinberg, spiral notebook.

14. YCAL, Box 32 (no f. or b. number because found only before proper cataloging by the Beinecke in 2019). The book is Roger Shattuck, *Candor and Perversion: Literature, Education, and the Arts* (New York: Norton, 1999), 60.

15. Steinberg, Sketchbook, YCAL inv. 03178.008.

16. Stendhal, *Life of Henry Brulard,* vii–xxvii.

17. Ashton, "What I Draw Is Drawing," 153 (cited chap. 3, n. 16).

18. Daniel Defoe, Charles Dickens, Samuel Butler, William Makepeace Thackery, Evelyn Waugh, W. Somerset Maugham, George Orwell, and W. H. Auden. All names taken from *LAB.*

19. Herman Melville, Stephen Crane, William Faulkner, Edmund Wilson, Saul Bellow, John Updike, Joseph Mitchell, Charles Simic, William Gaddis, Alice Munro, Ian Frazier. All names taken from LAB.

20. Leo Tolstoy, Fyodor Dostoevsky, Anton Chekhov, Ivan Turgenev, Isaak Babel, Nikolai Gogol and Vladimir Nabokov; Franz Kafka, Joseph Conrad, Eugène Ionesco, and Milan Kundera; James Joyce; Ovid, Dante, Alessandro Manzoni, Primo Levi, Italo Calvino, Giuseppi Tomasi di Lampedusa, Carlo Emilio Gadda, and Piero Chiara;

Miguel de Cervantes; Michel de Montaigne, Henri de Saint-Simon, Stendhal, Prosper Mérimée, Arthur Rimbaud, Guillaume Apollinaire, Alfred Jarry, Colette, Louis-Ferdinand Céline, Albert Camus, and Roland Barthes; Søren Kierkegaard; Thomas Mann, Arthur Koestler, and Thomas Bernhard. All names taken from *LAB.*

21. Baudelaire, *Painter of Modern Life,* 11.

22. Steinberg, spiral notebook.

23. Steinberg-Buzzi conversations.

24. Baudelaire, *Painter of Modern Life,* 9.

25. Steinberg, Appointment Book 1955, YCAL b. 107, f. 2214–15.

26. Baudelaire, *Painter of Modern Life,* 7.

27. Baudelaire, *Painter of Modern Life,* 4.

28. Steinberg, interview by Jones, 11.

29. Lallo, "Descent from Paradise."

30. Christina Ball, a translator of Steinberg's letters to Buzzi, mentions in her notes (SSF) that "Steinberg calls the book *Diari di guerra,* but most likely he's referring to Isaac Babel's *1920 Diary,* translated by H.T. Willetts and published by the Yale University Press in May 1995."

6. Steinberg: A Provisional Life

1. For a chronology of his life through 1973, see Rosenberg, *Saul Steinberg,* 234–45. See also *SS: I,* 251–67; http://saulsteinbergfoundation.org/chronology/1914-yr/; Bair, *Saul Steinberg;* and "Corrections to Deirdre Bair, *Saul Steinberg: A Biography*" at http://saulsteinbergfoundation.org/selected-bibliography.

2. For a reproduction of this map, see *SS: I,* 267.

3. Rosenberg, *Saul Steinberg,* 16.

4. Steinberg, "Saul Steinberg, Master of Wit and Fantasy," interview by Gruen, 135.

5. Gruen, *The Artist Observed,* 168–69.

6. Glueck, "The Artist Speaks," 117; see also Rosenberg, *Saul Steinberg,* 17: "By putting oneself in the uncomfortable position of the immigrant, one is again like a child."

7. Pliny the Elder, *The Elder Pliny's Chapters on the History of Art,* trans. Kiberd Jex-Blake (London: MacMillan, 1896), 175. https://books.google.com/books?id=QxsMAAAAIAAJ&printsec=frontcover&source=gbs_ViewAPI#v=onepage&q&f=false.

8. Steinberg, "Les vertiges de Steinberg," interview by Pierre Schneider.

9. Smith, *Steinberg at the New Yorker,* 19.

10. According to Boyd, *Vladimir Nabokov: The American Years,* 709n4, Nabokov wanted readers to realize that the narrator of *Pale Fire* is actually "Vseslav Botkin."

7. Steinberg and Nabokov: Wandering Men

1. Agarwal (Thompson), "Steinberg's Treatment of the Theme of the Artist."

2. Shapiro, *Sublime Artist's Studio,* 3–9, 69.

3. Gill, "Saul Steinberg's Surprise," 68.

4. Connolly, "From Biography to Autobiography and Back," para. 15.

5. Schiff, *Vera (Mrs. Vladimir Nabokov),* xi–xiv.

6. Meyer, *Nabokov and Indeterminacy,* 12, 16.

7. Barabtarlo, "Taina Naita," 60.
8. Barabtarlo, "Taina Naita," 61. For another excellent summation of the novel's complexities, see Meyer, *Nabokov and Indeterminacy,* 7–18.
9. Barabtarlo, "Taina Naita," 75.
10. Agarwal (Thompson), "Steinberg's Treatment of the Theme of the Artist."
11. Steinberg, interview by Dupin, 1978. See also "Shadows and Reflected Images" portfolio in the New Yorker, November 21, 1977, which Steinberg discusses in *RS,* 74–85.
12. Steinberg, interview by Dupin, 1978.
13. There is an entire portfolio of Steinberg's "question mark" drawings in the *New Yorker,* July 29, 1961.
14. Nabokov, *Nikolai Gogol,* 146.

8. Steinberg's Postcards

1. http://saulsteinbergfoundation.org/essay/the-postcard-as-subject/.
2. Steinberg, spiral notebook dated April 23–July 5, 1991, YCAL, b. 115, f. 2277.
3. Hedda Sterne, interview by Sheila Schwartz, October 22, 2005, transcript at SSF.
4. Manea, "Made in Romania."
5. Hélène Dufour, in *Arthur Rimbaud 1854–189: Portraits, dessins, manuscrits* (Paris: Edition de la Réunion des Musées Nationaux, 1991), 54, reproduces the Verlaine sketch of Rimbaud. Steinberg would have seen it in Starkie, *Arthur Rimbaud,* 192.
6. Bair, *Saul Steinberg,* 154, 311. See also *SS: I,* 44 and figs. 40 and 41.
7. Bair, *Saul Steinberg,* 154.
8. Notebook of advertisements, SSF.
9. Wicke, *Advertising Fictions,* 124.
10. This linen postcard was printed by the E. C. Kropp Co. and has this description on the reverse: "This building was erected by the City of Fort Worth with the aid of the W. P. A. It was designed to take care of the traffic that now exists at the Fort Worth Municipal Airport. This building is thoroughly modern being air conditioned and contains a control tower which guides traffic in and out of the airport."
11. Saul Steinberg, "My Deskmate at Matei Basarab," letter to Eugen Campus, February 12, 1988.
12. Ovid, *Poems of Exile,* 41.
13. Rosenberg, *Saul Steinberg,* 14, points out that Steinberg sometimes drew in the style of a child.
14. *San Pedro, California,* 1979, YCAL inv. no. 1610, b. 42, f. 6789, reproduced in *Repères: Cahiers d'art contemporain,* no. 30 (1986): 8; *Cheyenne, Wyo.,* c. 1979, YCAL inv. no.1709, b. 420, f. 5660; *Charlotte N.C.,* SSF 02180, 1981, which is a loose variant of the drawing used in Steinberg's "Post Office" portfolio, *NY,* March 1, 1982; *Tel Aviv,* YCAL inv. no. 1732, b. 420, f. 5681; *Bologna Via Roma,* YCAL inv. no. 3628, b. 78, f. 1570; *Paris France,* 1976, SSF 05150, reproduced in Steinberg's "Postcards" portfolio, *NY,* February 25, 1980.
15. Gruen, *The Artist Observed,* 170. Also YCAL b. 130, f. 2473.
16. Steinberg, Untitled [Ex-voto: Figures in art exhibition; Millet's *Angelus*] YCAL, SSF 03322, YCAL b. 367, f. 4907. See http://saulsteinbergfoundation.org/essay/1980s-1990s/.

17. Berlin, "The Naiveté of Verdi."
18. Steinberg, interview by Adam Gopnik.

9. Steinberg's Landscapes

1. He painted landscapes as early as the 1950s.
2. Glueck, "The Artist Speaks," 113.
3. Steinberg-Buzzi conversations.
4. Steinberg, YCAL b. 110, f. 2232.
5. Steinberg, "An Interview with Saul Steinberg," by Meg Perlman.
6. Steinberg, appointment book, 1964, YCAL b. 110, f. 2232.
7. http://saulsteinbergfoundation.org/essay/postcard-style-landscapes/.
8. Steinberg, "Take 30 in New York," interview by Adrienne Clarkson.
9. Michel, "Lorsque l'humoriste se fait peintre," *Le Monde,* June 24–30, 1970.
10. The issue of color versus line and contour has a long history, first emerging in sixteenth-century Venice—Venetian *colore* versus Florentine *disegno* (design, drawing). Associating color with the senses and line with intellect, commentators across the centuries have pointed out the contrast in terms of paired painters: Titian's color and Michelangelo's line; Rubens's sensuality of color and Poussin's clarity of contrast; Boucher's color and brushwork and David's neoclassical contours.
11. Steinberg-Buzzi conversations.
12. Steinberg, "Les vertiges de Steinberg," interview by Schneider. "Je suis amoureux des couchers de soleil, j'aime les regarder, les peindre. Les plateaux, les horizons m'enivrent. L'endroit où le ciel et la terre se touchent est la chose la plus belle, la plus mystérieuse du monde. L'essence du monde. Alors, je les peins."
13. Steinberg-Buzzi conversations.
14. Clearwater, *The Rothko Book,* 183.
15. Steinberg, "Les vertiges de Steinberg," interview by Schneider.
16. Baudelaire, *Flowers of Evil,* 29, 31.
17. "Trompe-l'oeil," Oxford Art Online, http://www.oxfordartonline.com/subscriber/article/grove/art/T039956.
18. Steinberg, interview by Dupin, 1978.
19. Baudelaire, "Crowds," in *Flowers of Evil,* 355.
20. Steinberg, interview by Waldron, July 5, 1973.

10. Nabokov's Postcards and Landscapes

1. Nabokov, *Lectures on Russian Literature,* 166.
2. See also Vries and Johnson, *Nabokov and the Art of Painting,* 16; and Delage-Toriel, "Brushing through 'Veiled Values,'" http://transatlantica.revues.org/index760.html.
3. Nabokov, *Lectures on Russian Literature,* 141.
4. I am not the first to comment on these zeros; see, for example, Zwart, "Nabokov's Primer," 219–20.
5. Wordsworth, "Lines Composed a Few Miles Above Tintern Abbey," 262.
6. James, *Varieties of Religious Experience,* 55.

7. Alexandrov, *Nabokov's Otherworld,* see index entries under "otherworld," "metaphysics," "life after death." See also Boyd, *Nabokov's Ada,* 93, 95, http://site.ebrary.com/lib/uvalib/: "It is quite possible that there are states of consciousness other than the human and that even the very pattern of the world bears witness to this, if we knew how to read the signs correctly."

11. Steinberg's Maps

1. Smith, *Steinberg at the New Yorker,* 220.
2. Steinberg, interview by Mark Rosenthal.
3. http://saulsteinbergfoundation.org/chronology/1999-yr/. *SS: I,* 267.
4. Bulson, *Novels, Maps, Modernity,* 7–8.
5. Manea, "Made in Romania," 44: "Dear Norman, Here is my magic circle: Strada Palas off Antim—Strada Justitåüiei crossing Calea Rahovei (now George Georgescu!)."
6. Wilde, "Decay of Lying," in *Complete Works,* 973.
7. Wilde, "Decay of Lying," in *Complete Works,* 982.
8. Steinberg, "Master of Wit and Fantasy," interview by Gruen, 138.
9. *OED,* s.v. "Map," n1.
10. For example, Harley, *New Nature of Maps,*150–68 ; Bulson, *Novels, Maps, Modernity,* 11.
11. Saul Steinberg, spiral notebook dated April 23–July 5, 1991, YCAL b. 115, f. 2277.
12. For Steinberg's use of furniture as maps, see http://saulsteinbergfoundation.org/essay/view-of-the-world-from-9th-avenue/.
13. Elizabeth Bishop, "The Map," in *The Complete Poems 1927–1979* (New York: Farrar Straus Giroux, 1980), 3.
14. Friedrich Schiller, *Letters on the Aesthetic Education of Man,* https://sourcebooks.fordham.edu/mod/schiller-education.asp.
15. Shapiro, *Tender Friendship and the Charm of Perfect Accord,* 229.
16. See Bulson, *Novels, Maps, Modernity,* 2, for a discussion of "oriented disorientation" in the modern novel.
17. Manea, "Made in Romania," 46.
18. Stewart, *U.S. 40,* 8.
19. Manea, "Made in Romania," 45.

12. Nabokov's Maps

1. See Feldman, *Gender on the Divide,* 220–68, for Nabokov's deep admiration for French literature.
2. Byron's and Pushkin's works also figure prominently in *Ada.*
3. Boyd, "Ada," in Alexandrov, *The Garland Companion to Vladimir Nabokov,* 4.
4. See Boyd, *Ada Online,* http://www.ada.auckland.ac.nz/, for the most thoroughgoing annotations to *Ada.*
5. Teaching Jane Austen, Nabokov would stress that "[w]ithout a visual perception of the larch labyrinth in Mansfield Park that novel loses some of its stereographic charm" (*SO,* 157). He refers here, also, to the stereographic experience of seeing right

eye and left eye images superimposed in order to give a sense of three-dimensionality, as well as the stenographic charm of visualizing, through a drawing or a diagram, the "larch labyrinth" in *Mansfield Park.*

6. Vladimir Nabokov, "Notes to *Ada* by Vivian Darkbloom," in Rivers and Nicol, *Nabokov's Fifth Arc,* 317.

7. Boyd, "Ada," 16.

8. Nabokov, *Lectures on Don Quixote,* 4–5.

9. Nabokov, *Lectures on Don Quixote,* 1.

10. Dieter E. Zimmer, *The Geography of Antiterra,* http://www.dezimmer.net/ReAda/AntiterraGeography.htm. See also Vladimir Nabokov, *Ada oder Das Verlangen—Eine Familienchronik,* 1095.

11. Boyd, *Ada Online,* annotation 18.04–07.

12. Tenderness at Esteem, Recognition, Inclination; Inattentiveness, Forgetting, Perfidy, and Pride; The Perilous Sea and the Lake of Indifference; devotion, perseverance, ardor.

13. Brinks, "Meeting over the Map."

14. Munro, *Mademoiselle de Scudéry,* 27: "[T]he group saw itself as citizens of the *pays de Tendre,* and the *Carte de Tendre* thus became a map of the group's 'homeland,' a visible sign of its sense of unity. The *pays de Tendre* had its own archives, records of major events in the country's history, which have been preserved in the *Gazette de Tendre.*"

15. Boyd, "Annotations to page 4," *Ada Online.*

16. Boyd, "Forenote, Part I, Chapter 17," *Ada Online.*

17. Zimmer, *The Geography of Antiterra,* http://www.dezimmer.net/ReAda/AntiterraGeography.htm.

18. Zimmer, *The Geography of Antiterra,* http://www.dezimmer.net/ReAda/AntiterraGeography.htm.

19. Boyd, *Ada Online,* annotation 5.06.

20. Cosgrove, *Mappings,* 11, quoting the preface to *The History of Cartography,* ed. J. B. Harley and David Woodward (Chicago: University of Chicago Press, 1987–), xv–xxi.

21. Quoted in Nina Khrushcheva, *Imagining Nabokov: Russia between Art and Politics* (New Haven: Yale University Press, 2013), 60.

22. Shapiro, *Sublime Artist's Studio,* 69–70.

23. Steinberg-Buzzi conversations.

24. Flaubert, *Madame Bovary,* 13.

25. Boyd, *Stalking Nabokov,* 361.

26. Boyd, *Ada Online,* has identified and annotated the theme of Arcady as it appears across much of the novel.

27. McCarthy, "Nabokov's 'Ada' and Sidney's 'Arcadia.'"

28. James, *Varieties of Religious Experience,* 55.

29. See D. Barton Johnson, "The Labyrinth of Incest in Nabokov's 'Ada,'" 224, for a discussion of some possible sources for Van and Ada's incest in works by Byron, Pushkin, and Tolstoy.

30. See Cancogni, ""My Sister, do You Still Recall?," 140, for a thoroughgoing discussion of the presence of Chateaubriand's works in *Ada,* as well as the widely intertextual nature of the novel.

31. Boyd, part 1, chap. 15, "Forenote," *Ada Online,* http://www.ada.auckland.ac.nz/index.htm.

32. Chateaubriand, *Mémoires de Outre-Tombe.*
33. *"Ma sœur, te souvient-il encore"* [My sister, do you still remember]: "first line of the third sextet of Chateaubriand's *Romance à Hélène* (*'Combien j'ai douce souvenance'*) composed to an Auvergne tune that he heard during a trip to Mont Dore in 1805 and later inserted in his novella *Le Dernier Abencerage.* The final (fifth) sestet begins with *'Oh! qui me rendra mon Hélène, Et ma montagne et le grand chêne'*—one of the leitmotivs of the present novel." Rivers and Nicol, *Nabokov's Fifth Arc,* 248. See Boyd, *Ada Online,* annotations to 138.05–06 and to 138.01–139.04, for further information and a slight correction to "Darkbloom's" note.
34. Boyd, *Ada Online,* annotations to 138.05–06.
35. Boyd, *Ada Online* annotations to 138.11–14.
36. Boyd, *Ada Online* annotations to 109.11–13.
37. Porter, *Chateaubriand,* 5, shows that excerpts from the works of Mademoiselle de Montpensier, Pierre Le Nain, John Milton, and François Leguat appear in a single paragraph of Chateaubriand's *Vie de Rancé.*

13. Steinberg and Nabokov: Rimbaud's Memories

1. Starkie, *Arthur Rimbaud,* 352.
2. Hélène Dufour, *Arthur Rimbaud 1854–1891:* Portraits, dessins, manuscrits (Paris: Édition de la Réunion des Musées Nationaux, 1991), 54, reproduces the Verlaine sketch of Rimbaud. Steinberg would have seen it in Starkie, Arthur Rimbaud, 192.
3. Norman, *Transatlantic Aliens,* 106a, 162.
4. For a discussion of Rimbaud's "Diary" as *illisble* (Roland Barthes's term), see Garrett Stewart, *The Look of Reading,* 67–69.
5. Steinberg-Buzzi conversations.
6. Rimbaud, "Letter to Paul Demeny," in *Complete Works, Selected Letters,* trans. Fowlie, 307.
7. Saul Steinberg, "Les vertiges de Steinberg," interview by Schneider. "L'art, pour moi, est masque. . . . Je suis dans la tradition de l'artiste: pour être soi-même, il faut être d'abord un autre."
8. Starkie, *Arthur Rimbaud,* 232–33.
9. Starkie, *Arthur Rimbaud,* 214.
10. Boyd, *Ada Online,* in annotation to 64.15, quotes the poem in French and the Fowlie English translation.
11. Rimbaud, "Letter to Paul Demeny," 307.
12. Rimbaud, "Letter to Paul Demeny," 307.
13. For a useful summary of Nabokov's views on translation, see Elizabeth Klosty Beaujour, "Translation and Self-Translation," in Alexandrov, *Garland Companion to Vladimir Nabokov,* 714–24.
14. Boyd, *Nabokov's Ada,* 22: "Nabokov's sentences often provide the illusion of continuous motion in a single direction where there have really been radical breaks, sudden shifts, silent transformations."
15. Alexandrov, *Nabokov's Otherworld,* 270.
16. Starkie, *Arthur Rimbaud,* 132–34.
17. Rimbaud, *Complete Works, Selected Letters,* 125.
18. Brian Boyd, "Ada," in Alexandrov, *Garland Companion to Vladimir Nabokov,* 16.

14. Steinberg and Joyce: Impermanent Sojourners

1. Saul Steinberg, interview by Eli Waldron.
2. Steinberg, interview by Dupin, 1978, "Interviews with Saul Steinberg" typescript SSF, 1978.
3. Ellmann, *James Joyce,* 201.
4. Bulson, *Novels, Maps, Modernity,* 81.
5. Budgen, *James Joyce and the Making of Ulysses,* 69.
6. Hegglund, "'Ulysses' and the Rhetoric of Cartography."
7. L. M. Cullen, "Dublin," 175.
8. Ellmann, *James Joyce,* 189.
9. Gillespie, *James Joyce and the Exilic Imagination,* 24.
10. Manea, "Made in Romania," 44.
11. Quick, "Molly Bloom's Mother," 223.
12. J. Mitchell Morse, "Proteus," in Hart and Hayman, *James Joyce's Ulysses,* 33.
13. Kiberd, *Ulysses and Us,* 169.
14. Senn, *Joyce's Dislocutions,* xxvi–xxvii, quoting A. Walton Litz, 'The Author in Ulysses: The Zurich Chapters," in *James Joyce: A New Language—Actas/Proceedings del Simposio Internacional en el Centenario de James Joyce,* ed. Francisco Garcia Tortosa et al. (Seville: University of Seville, 1982), 114.
15. McHugh, *Annotations to Finnegans Wake,* xix.
16. Steinberg, interview by Rosenthal and Ducovny.
17. Steinberg, interview by Rosenthal and Ducovny.
18. For a more detailed list of Jewish motifs in *Ulysses,* see Nadel, *Joyce and the Jews.*
19. Steinberg, interview by Rosenthal and Ducovny.
20. Steinberg, interview by Rosenthal and Ducovny.
21. Nadel, *Joyce and the Jews,* 5.
22. Steinberg, interview by Rosenthal and Ducovny.
23. For a discussion of Bloom as the modern Jewish Everyman, see Slezkine, *The Jewish Century,* 76–84.
24. Gill, "Saul Steinberg's Surprise," 66–73.
25. Steinberg, "Victorian Dialogue," interview by Ashton.
26. Keogh, *Jews in Twentieth-Century Ireland,* 7, 56–60.
27. Lawrence, Odyssey *of Style in Ulysses,* 101–110.
28. Budgen, *James Joyce and the Making of Ulysses,* 186.
29. James Joyce, *Letters,* 1:160.
30. Lawrence, *Odyssey of Style,* 3–15.
31. Budgen, *James Joyce and the Making of Ulysses,* 37.
32. Joyce, *Letters,* 1:157.
33. Budgen, *James Joyce and the Making of Ulysses,* 189.
34. Budgen, *James Joyce and the Making of Ulysses,* 69.
35. Bulson, *Novels, Maps, Modernity,* 69.
36. Hegglund, "'Ulysses' and the Rhetoric of Cartography," 175.
37. Ellmann, *James Joyce,* 558–59.
38. Ellmann, *Ulysses on the Liffey,* 2.
39. Frank, *Widening Gyre,* 10. For a counterargument, see Lawrence, *Odyssey of Style,* 3–15.
40. Budgen, *James Joyce and the Making of Ulysses,* 68.

41. Joyce, *Critical Writings,* 221.
42. Quoted in Hecimovich, "'With Pale Blake I Write Tintingface,'" 889.
43. Kenner, *Stoic Comedians,* 47.

15. Steinberg and Joyce: Playing with Styles

1. Steinberg, interview by Dupin.
2. Joyce, *Letters,* 1:167.
3. Ellmann, *Ulysses on the Liffey,* 186–90. The 1920 scheme supplied for each chapter: Time, Color, People [from The Odyssey], Science/Art, Meaning, Technic, Organ [of the human body], Symbols. Joyce also supplied a similar table in what is known as the "Gilbert" scheme in 1921 for Stuart Gilbert. It appears in Gilbert, *James Joyce's "Ulysses."*
4. My discussion of the multiplicity of styles in *Ulysses* is indebted throughout to Lawrence, *Odyssey of Style.*
5. Lawrence, *Odyssey of Style,* 8–9.
6. Lawrence, *Odyssey of Style,* 13 and passim.
7. Heuvel, "Straight from the Hand and Mouth of Steinberg," 62.
8. As a cursory search of the *MLA Bibliography* reveals, there is an extensive critical literature concerning Molly: her body, mind, personal history, literary precursors, and more. A fuller discussion of this complex character is beyond the scope of this study.
9. Bair, *Saul Steinberg,* 352–53.
10. Kenner, *Dublin's Joyce,* 161–62.
11. YCAL Box 75 (no f. or b. number because found only before proper cataloging by the Beinecke in 2019).
12. YCAL b.130, f. 2479.
13. For a convincing argument along these lines, see Wicke, *Advertising Fictions.*
14. Wicke, *Advertising Fictions,* 121.
15. See Bair, *Saul Steinberg,* 55, 135, 149, 154, 166, 168, 207–8, 212, 276–80, 300, 311, 42, 418, for information on Steinberg's commercial work in this paragraph. For corrections to Bair's biography, see http://saulsteinbergfoundation.org/wp-content/uploads/2016/06/Saul_Steinberg_Biography_corrections.pdf. See also *SS: I,* 242.
16. See also http://saulsteinbergfoundation.org/essay/other-magazine-contributions/.
17. See also sandwich board drawings in Steinberg, *The Art of Living,* chap. 4.
18. See *SS: I,* 37, for the notion of pop existentialism.
19. Quoted by Bruce Stewart, "James Joyce," 149.

16. Joyce's Parodies

1. Steinberg, "Victorian Dialogue," interview by Ashton.
2. Quoted in Kirchner, "Parody in the Fiction of James Joyce," 40.
3. Quoted in Hughes, *Nothing If Not Critical,* 265; "World of Steinberg," 92.
4. Steinberg, interview by Waldron.
5. Hughes, *Nothing If Not Critical,"* 261; "World of Steinberg," 95.
6. Steinberg, interview by Dupin. For a wide-ranging discussion of parody as iteration in *Ulysses,* see Kirchner, "Parody in the Fiction of James Joyce."

7. Heuvel, "Straight from the Hand and Mouth of Steinberg," 59.
8. Kenner, *Dublin's Joyce,* 11, 23.
9. Kiberd, *Ulysses and Us,* 141.
10. Hall, "Joyce's Use of Da Ponte and Mozart's Don Giovanni."
11. Kirchner, "Parody in the Fiction of James Joyce," 119; and Lawrence, *Odyssey of Style,* 38–42.
12. Joyce, *Letters,* 1:135.
13. Ellmann, *James Joyce,* 351. See Kiremidjian, *A Study of Modern Parody,* for an anatomy of parody.
14. Gifford and Seidman, *Ulysses Annotated,* 645.
15. Budgen, *James Joyce and the Making of Ulysses,* 94.
16. Kenner, *Ulysses,* 72–82.
17. Groden, *Ulysses in Progress,* 36–37.
18. Lawrence, *Odyssey of Style,* 143.
19. Joyce, *Letters,* 1:139–40.
20. J. S. Atherton, "The Oxen of the Sun," in Hart and Hayman, *James Joyce's Ulysses,* 323, 325.
21. Atherton, "The Oxen of the Sun," 326, 313–15. See also Joyce, *Letters,* 1:138–39.
22. Gifford and Seidman, *Ulysses Annotated,* 426.
23. Gifford and Seidman, *Ulysses Annotated,* 426.
24. Gifford and Seidman, *Ulysses Annotated,* 426, 17.
25. Lawrence, *Odyssey of Style,* 141.
26. Ellmann, *James Joyce,* 489.
27. Ellmann, *James Joyce,* 794.
28. Lawrence, *Odyssey of Style,* 8–9.
29. I am indebted throughout my discussion of "Cyclops" to Gifford and Seidman, *Ulysses Annotated,* for their identifications of Joyce's allusions, parodies, and historical and topographical references. The interpretation of these items is my own. See also Sean Latham, "Interruption: 'Cyclops' and 'Nausicaa,'" in Latham, *The Cambridge Companion to Ulysses.*
30. Budgen, *James Joyce and the Making of Ulysses,* 156–57.
31. Jo-Anna Isaak, "James Joyce and the Cubist Esthetic," 61.
32. Isaak, "James Joyce and the Cubist Esthetic," 26.
33. I write in order to challenge statements such as that of David Hayman, who argues that each aside, intrusion, or interpolation has "its own particular mode of mockery; . . . each is a closed structure; each is a completed action, a statement, or simply a self-contained rhetorical unit." See "Cyclops" in Hart and Hayman, *James Joyce's Ulysses,* 267. For exceptions to this tendency to read the interpolations as discrete entities within the flow of the chapter, see Nunes, "Beyond the 'Holy See'"; and Lawrence, *Odyssey of Style,* 114.
34. Lawrence, *Odyssey of Style,* 101 "According to Michael Groden, the germ of the chapter was the series of parodies rather than the first person narration." See Groden, Ulysses *in Progress,* 118.
35. Rosenblum, *Cubism and Twentieth-Century Art,* 13.
36. Rosenblum, *Cubism and Twentieth-Century Art*, 13.
37. This is by now a critical commonplace; A. Walton Litz, "Ithaca," in Hart and Hayman, *James Joyce's Ulysses,* 386, provides a good example.

17. Steinberg's and Joyce's Mythologies

1. Johnson, "Parody and Myth," 149.
2. Donoghue, "Yeats, Eliot, and the Mythical Method."
3. Patton and Wendy Doniger, *Myth and Method,* 119.
4. Joyce, *Letters,* 1:241.
5. Joyce, *Letters,* 1:146–47 ("from the perspective of our time").
6. Joseph Mali, "Mythology and Counter-History." I owe the arguments of this paragraph to Mali.
7. Mali, "Mythology and Counter-History," 35.
8. Mali, "Mythology and Counter-History," 36.
9. Mali, "Mythology and Counter-History," 36.
10. Gifford and Seidman, *Ulysses Annotated,* 566.
11. Groden, *Ulysses in Progress,* 14.
12. Harry Levin advises the former approach; Richard Ellmann the latter. For this discussion, see Groden, *Ulysses in Progress,* 201.
13. See Lowe-Evans, "Joyce and the Myth of the Mediatrix," 101, for a discussion of Mariological myth in Joyce's oeuvre.
14. Kiberd, *Ulysses and Us,* 12.
15. Seidel, *Epic Geography,* 3–4.
16. Gilbert, *James Joyce's "Ulysses,"* 86, originally made this argument.
17. Henke, "James Joyce East and Middle East," 307.
18. According to Gifford and Seidman, *Ulysses Annotated,* 194, Eglinton is a pseudonym of William Kirkpatrick Magee, man of letters and assistant librarian of the National Library in 1904.
19. Gifford and Seidman, *Ulysses Annotated,* 44.
20. Gifford and Seidman, *Ulysses Annotated,* 44.
21. Donoghue, "Yeats, Eliot, and the Mythical Method," 208.
22. Steinberg, appointment book, 1964, YCAL b. 110, f. 2232.
23. Quoted in Ellmann, *Ulysses on the Liffey,* 91.
24. Budgen, *James Joyce and the Making of Ulysses,* 125.
25. Rhodius Apollonius, *Argonautica,* trans. Edward P. Coleridge (London: George Bell and Sons, 1889), 72. https://archive.org/stream/theargonauticaof00apoli-ala#page/72/mode/2up/search/Symplegades.
26. Clive Hart, "Wandering Rocks," in Hart and Hayman *James Joyce's Ulysses,* 189.
27. Budgen, *James Joyce and the Making of Ulysses,* 124–25.
28. Hegglund, "'Ulysses' and the Rhetoric of Cartography," 178.
29. Gifford and Seidman, *Ulysses Annotated,* 265, 270.
30. Clive Hart, "Wandering Rocks," in Hart and Hayman, *James Joyce's Ulysses,* 95.
31. Gifford and Seidman, *Ulysses Annotated,* 186.
32. Steinberg, "Transcribed Remarks to Rolf Karrer-Kharberg."
33. Steinberg, *Labyrinth,* 215.
34. Steinberg, appointment book, 1964, YCAL b. 110, f. 2232.
35. Steinberg-Buzzi conversations.
36. SSF 02961, related to *New Yorker,* May 5, 1962, portfolio.
37. Glueck, "The Artist Speaks," 117.
38. See Topliss, "Saul Steinberg: The Lifeline from A to B," for a discussion of Steinberg's interest in American mythology that focuses on his social criticism.

39. Glueck, "The Artist Speaks," 111.
40. Glueck, "The Artist Speaks," 117.
41. Steinberg, "Transcript of Recorded Interview by John Jones."
42. Steinberg, "Transcript of Interview by Jones."
43. http://greatseal.com. The motto *Annuit Coeptis* was suggested by Charles Thomson in June 1782. He adapted it from Virgil's *Georgics* (book 1, line 40), written in the first century B.C.
44. Steinberg-Buzzi conversations.
45. Glueck, "The Artist Speaks," 116.
46. Glueck, "The Artist Speaks," 116–17.
47. For a discussion of Steinberg's complicity with American institutions, see Norman, *Transatlantic Aliens,* 157–96.
48. Steinberg, interview by Rosenthal and Ducovny.
49. Schneider, *Louvre Dialogues,* 83.
50. Steinberg, interview by Rosenthal and Ducovny.
51. Steinberg, *Art of Living,* chap. 5.
52. Steinberg, interview by Adam Gopnik.
53. "En peinture ou en sculpture, on ne peut pas enlever un nez, ce serait tout de suite macabre. Tandis qu'en dessin, c'est possible, ce n'est qu'une ligne qui disparaît ou à laquelle il prend la fantaisie de devenir un labyrinthe, de refuser de se conformer au reste du visage. Gogol a raisonné comme le dessinateur avec une ligne; pour lui, enlever le nez, c'était comme enlever le mot nez, ou même le *n* du nez, et lui rendre la liberté." Frémon, "Conversation avec Saul Steinberg," 5–18.

18. Steinberg's Art of Assemblage

1. Glueck, "The Artist Speaks," 113. Steinberg slightly errs here: Leonardo's maxim is "La pittura è cosa mentale."
2. http://saulsteinbergfoundation.org/essay/drawing-table-reliefs/. See also *SS: I,* 197–97, 216–17.
3. Seitz, *Art of Assemblage,* 84.
4. Saul Steinberg and Valerio Adami, *Du côté de chez les Maeght,* October 7, 1973; a film produced by Éliane Victor and directed by Jean Pierre Marchand, for Galerie Maeght, Paris. A transcript is available at SSF. "Les objets en bois—les livres, les crayons—sont des personnages érotiques, voilà, des sujets que j'aime beaucoup, qui sont les équivalents pour moi des dieux de la maison, de lares et pénates."
5. Abbott, *Cambridge Introduction to Narrative,* 13.
6. Wolfgang Iser, *The Implied Reader: Patterns of Communication in Prose Fiction from Bunyan to Beckett* (Baltimore: Johns Hopkins University Press, 1974), 280; quoted in Abbott, *Cambridge Introduction to Narrative,* 92.
7. Petherbridge, *Primacy of Drawing* 16–17: "Drawing is an independent practice, but is also identified with painting, print-making, sculpture, architecture and design, and a whole host of other traditional and contemporary media. Although always named, and maintaining its own identity, it is tied into reciprocity with these other media, although not necessarily regarded as being of equal status. This reciprocity usually invokes drawing as the free, fragmented, spontaneous and private other to the synthesized, public and finished work of painting, sculpture, or print-making,

which can also be ingested into the body of the object or performance as the spark and impulse of its origination. The incompleteness of a drawing has its own vibrating life, but also invites its completion in other media. On the other hand, a drawing can be so finished in itself that it subsumes the need for further stages of transformation."

8. Steinberg and Adami, *Du côté de chez les Maeght,* "Mais dans le même temps je suis assez sérieux sur la fait que c'est une Musée Steinberg."

9. Steinberg and Adami, *Du côté de chez les Maeght.* "Ils sont aussi, il faut dire, une représentation d'une autobiographie."

10. Steinberg, "Les Vertiges de Steinberg," interview by Schneider: "Dans ces «Tables», je suis déguisé en peintre, en dessinateur, en objets sur ma table, le crayon, c'est moi."

11. This is one of his ex-votos, which he began producing c. 1983; see http://saul steinbergfoundation.org/essay/1980s-1990s/.

12. Lucy Stylianopoulos, Fine Arts Librarian, University of Virginia, e-mail to author.

13. Rosenberg, *Saul Steinberg,* 30–32, describes a Steinberg table as "a fabrication that stands for him but also hides him. The Tables continue his autobiography in personal terms that betray no secrets."

14. Gogol, *Complete Tales of Nikolai Gogol,* 237.

15. Seitz, *Art of Assemblage,* 6.

16. Seitz, *Art of Assemblage,* 83. Seitz specifies that assemblages are "poetic" "because [their] units are loosely related rather than expository" (83). His use of the word "poetic" throughout is ambiguous: does it include fiction as well as poetry? I believe that the answer is yes, since when he speaks of the "aesthetic of juxtaposition" that is central to the art of assemblage, he mentions several writers, most of whom are poets—but he does include James Joyce. My analysis of specific assemblages by Steinberg will further show why assemblages can be taken as narrative in quality.

17. Stéphane Mallarmé, *Collected Poems,* 121–45.

18. For a richer discussion of the concept of the *calligramme,* see Leo Shtutin, *Spatiality and Subjecthood in Mallarmé, Apollinaire, Maeterlinck, and Jarry,* Oxford Scholarship Online, DOI: 10.1093/oso/9780198821854.001.0001.

19. Seitz, *Art of Assemblage,* 85–86: "The fabric of meaning woven by materials can cover the distant in time and space. . . . As element is set beside element, the many qualities and auras of isolated fragments are compounded, fused or contradicted so that—by their own confronted volitions as it were—physical matter becomes poetry. Directed, intentionally or unconsciously, by an artist's intellectual position, emotional predisposition, or any other conditioning attitude or coloration, a vast repertoire of expression—exultant, bitter, ironic, erotic, or lyrical—can be achieved by means different in kind from that of painting and sculpture, but akin to those of literature."

20. Yeats, "The Symbolism of Poetry," in *Yeats's Poetry, Drama, and Prose,* 272.

21. Yeats, "To Ireland in the Coming Times," in *Yeats's Poetry, Drama, and Prose,* 21–22.

22. Stylianopoulos, e-mail.

23. Steinberg, "Victorian Dialogue," interview by Ashton.

24. Hunter, *Before Novels,* 32, 421.

25. Hunter, *Before Novels,* 135, 39, 217, 12.

26. Steinberg, interview by Jean Robertson.

27. Rosenberg, *Saul Steinberg,* 30–33.

28. Brown, *Other Things,* 5.

29. Brown, *Other Things,* 6.
30. Steinberg exhibition at the Betty Parsons and Sidney Janis Galleries, New York, "New Work by Saul Steinberg," February 7 to March 31, 1973.
31. Petherbridge, *Primacy of Drawing,* 156.

19. Joyce's Art of Assemblage

1. Critics have long discussed the discontinuities of *Ulysses* and its spatial quality; for a summary, see Lawrence, *Odyssey of Style,* 2–3, including footnotes.
2. Saint-Amour, "Over Assemblage."
3. Fritz Senn, "Nausicaa," in Hart and Hayman, *James Joyce's Ulysses,* 310.
4. Saint-Amour, "Over Assemblage," 21, speaking not of Joyce but of Duchamp.
5. Ellmann, *The Consciousness of Joyce,* 65–66.
6. Senn, *Joyce's Dislocutions,* 128.
7. "Without altitude there can be no reading." Saint-Amour, "Over-Assemblage," 21.
8. Lawrence, *Odyssey of Style,* passim. See also Hayman, *Ulysses,* 84: "I use the term 'arranger' to designate a figure who can be identified neither with the author nor with his narrators, but who exercises an increasing degree of overt control over his increasingly challenging materials." For a refutation of the notion of an "arranger," see Benstock and Benstock, "The Benstock Principle."
9. Litz, *Art of James Joyce,* 38.
10. Seitz, *Art of Assemblage,* 38.
11. Michael Groden, "Writing *Ulysses,*" in Latham, *Cambridge Companion to Ulysses,* 8.
12. Groden, "Writing *Ulysses,*" 8.
13. Groden, *Ulysses in Progress,* 113.
14. Groden, "Writing *Ulysses,*" 9.
15. Ferrer and Rabaté, "Paragraphs in Expansion: James Joyce," 141.
16. Declan Kiberd, *Irish Classics* (London: Granta Books 2001), 467; quoted in Groden, "Writing *Ulysses,*" 10.
17. Dirk Van Hulle, "Genetic Joyce Criticism," in McCourt, *James Joyce in Context,* 117.
18. Steinberg, interview by Dupin.
19. For Joyce's recycling of unused materials from his earlier works, see Owen, "James Joyce and the Beginnings of Ulysses."
20. Joyce, *Letters,* 1:83; quoted in Groden, "A Textual and Publishing History," in Bowen and Carens, *Companion to Joyce Studies,* 92.
21. Barb Nelson, "People in the Novel," The Joyce Project, http://www.joyceproject.com/index.php?page=p,eople#.W04jW34naCQ.
22. Vicki Mahaffey, "Giacomo Joyce," in Bowen and Carens, *Companion to Joyce Studies,* 387–420.
23. Groden, "A Textual and Publishing History," 71–72.
24. Steinberg, interview by Jacques Michel, March 22, 1979, *Le Monde,* 17.
25. Hugh Kenner, "Circe," in Hart and Hayman, *James Joyce's "Ulysses,"* 364.
26. Kenner, *Ulysses,* 156–57.
27. Kenner "Modernism and What Happened to It," 105.
28. Kenner, *Dublin's Joyce,* 153.

29. Ellmann, *James Joyce,* 169.
30. Brown, *Sense of Things,* 5.
31. For a fuller discussion of things in *Ulysses,* see Paul K. Saint-Amour, "Symbols and Things," in Latham, *Cambridge Companion to Ulysses,* 200–215.
32. Kiberd, *Ulysses and Us,* 114.
33. Kiberd, *Ulysses and Us,* 114.
34. Gifford and Seidman, *Ulysses Annotated,* 316, 319.
35. Quoted in Ellmann, *James Joyce,* 661.

Afterword

1. Steinberg, interview by Adam Gopnik.
2. Steinberg, comments in "Statements and Documents," 124.
3. Nabokov, *Lectures on Russian Literature,* 166
4. Nabokov, *Think, Write, Speak,* 462.
5. Gifford and Seidman, *Ulysses Annotated,* 51.

BIBLIOGRAPHY

Abbott, H. Porter. *The Cambridge Introduction to Narrative.* Cambridge Introductions to Literature. Cambridge: Cambridge University Press, 2008.

Agarwal (Thompson), Meera E. "Steinberg's Treatment of the Theme of the Artist: A Collage of Conversations." Vassar College, December 8, 1972. YCAL b. 126, f. 2426.

Albright, Daniel. *Representation and the Imagination: Beckett, Kafka, Nabokov, and Schoenberg.* Chicago: University of Chicago Press, 1981.

Alexandrov, Vladimir E., ed. *The Garland Companion to Vladimir Nabokov.* New York: Garland, 1995.

———. *Nabokov's Otherworld.* Princeton: Princeton University Press, 1991.

Ashbery, John. "Saul Steinberg: Callibiography." *Arts News Annual* 36 (1970): 53–59.

Ashton, Dore. *American Art since 1945.* New York: Oxford University Press, 1982.

Ashton, Dore, and Art Spiegelman. "The Debate over Popular and Museum Culture: Dore Ashton and Art Spiegelman Visit High and Low at the MoMA." *Art International* 14 (1991): 60–64.

Bair, Deirdre. *Saul Steinberg: A Biography.* New York: Nan A. Talese/Doubleday, 2012.

Barabtarlo, Gennady. "Nabokov's Trinity (On the Movement of Nabokov's Themes)." In *Nabokov and His Fiction: New Perspectives,* edited by Julian W. Connolly, 109–38. Cambridge: Cambridge University Press, 1999.

———. "Taina Naita: Narrative Stance in Nabokov's The Real Life of Sebastian Knight." *Partial Answers: Journal of Literature and the History of Ideas* 6 (2008): 57–80.

Barañano, Kosme de, et al., eds. *Saul Steinberg.* Valencia: Institut Valencia d'Art Modern, 2002.

Barthes, Roland. "All Except You." In *Saul Steinberg,* ed. Kosme de Barañano et al. Valencia: Institut Valencia d'Art Modern, 2002. Originally published 1983, Paris: Galerie Maeght/Repères, éditions d'art.

Baudelaire, Charles. *The Flowers of Evil and Paris Spleen.* Translated by William H. Crosby. Brockport, NY: BOA Editions, 1991.

———. *The Painter of Modern Life and Other Essays.* Translated by Jonathan Mayne. London: Phaidon Press, 2001.

Bauerle, Ruth. "A Sober Drunken Speech: Stephen's Parodies in 'The Oxen of the Sun.'" *James Joyce Quarterly* 5 (1967): 40–46.

Benjamin, Walter. "The Collector." In *The Arcades Project,* edited by Rolf Tiedemann, 203–11. Cambridge, MA: Belknap Press, 1999.

———. "Unpacking My Library." In *Illuminations,* 59–67. New York: Schocken Books, 1969.

Benstock, Bernard. "Joyce's Ulysses." *English Literature in Transition, 1880–1920* 30, no. 2 (1987): 242–44.

Benstock, Bernard, and Shari Benstock. "The Benstock Principle." In *The Seventh of Joyce,* 10–21. Bloomington: Indiana University Press, 1982.

Berlin, Isaiah. "The Naiveté of Verdi." *Hudson Review* 21, no. 1 (1969): 138–47.

Bowen, Zack, and James F. Carens, eds. *A Companion to Joyce Studies.* Westport, CT: Greenwood Press, 1984.

Boxer, Sarah. "An Assistant Tells All, Finally and Gracefully." *New York Times,* February 22, 2004.

———. "Drawn from Life: On Saul Steinberg." *Artforum* 45, no. 6 (2007): 135–36.

———. "Saul Steinberg, Epic Doodler, Dies at 84." *New York Times,* May 13, 1999, A1.

Boyd, Brian. *Ada Online.* http://www.ada.auckland.ac.nz/.

———. "Ada, the Bog and the Garden: Or, Straw, Fluff, and Peat: Sources and Places in Ada." *Nabokov Studies* 8 (2004): 107–33.

———. *Nabokov's Ada: The Place of Consciousness.* 2nd ed. Christchurch, New Zealand: Cybereditions Corp., 2001. ebrary.com.

———. *Nabokov's Pale Fire: The Magic of Artistic Discovery.* Princeton: Princeton University Press, 1999.

———. *Stalking Nabokov: Selected Essays.* New York: Columbia University Press, 2011.

———. *Vladimir Nabokov: The American Years.* Princeton: Princeton University Press, 1991.

———. *Vladimir Nabokov: The Russian Years.* Princeton: Princeton University Press, 1990.

———. "Words, Works and Worlds in Joyce and Nabokov or Intertextuality, Intratextuality, Supratextuality, Infratextuality, Extratextuality and Autotextuality in Modernist and Prepostmodernist Narrative Discourse." *Cycnos* 12, no. 2 (2010): 3–12.

Braddock, Jeremy. *Collecting as Modernist Practice.* Baltimore: Johns Hopkins University Press, 2012.

Brinks, Ellen. "Meeting over the Map: Madeleine de Scudéry's 'Carte Du Pays de Tendre' and Aphra Behn's 'Voyage to the Isle of Love.'" *Restoration: Studies in English Literary Culture, 1660–1700* 17, no. 1 (1993): 39–52.

Brown, Bill. *Other Things.* Chicago: University of Chicago Press, 2015.

———. *A Sense of Things: The Object Matter of American Literature.* Chicago: University of Chicago Press, 2003.

Bruffee, K. A. "Form and Meaning in Nabokov's *Real Life of Sebastian Knight:* An Example of Elegiac Romance." *Modern Language Quarterly* 34 (June 1973): 180–90.

Budgen, Frank. *James Joyce and the Making of Ulysses, and Other Writings.* London: Oxford University Press, 1972.

Bulson, Eric. *Novels, Maps, Modernity: The Spatial Imagination, 1850–2000.* New York: Routledge, 2007.

Burns, Christy L. *Gestural Politics: Stereotype and Parody in Joyce.* Albany: State University of New York Press, 2000.

Caesar, Terry P. "Joycing Parody." *James Joyce Quarterly* 26, no. 2 (1989): 227–37.

Campus, Iosef Eugen. "Nature and Art (Conversations with Saul Steinberg)." In *Opening New Horizons: Critical Notes, Israel, 1960–2001,* translated by Emil Niculescu for the SSF, 1:54–56. Bucharest: Libra, 2002.

Cancogni, Annapaola. *The Mirage in the Mirror: Nabokov's Ada and Its French Pre-Texts.* New York: Garland Pub, 1985.

———. "'My Sister, Do You Still Recall?': Chateaubriand/Nabokov." *Comparative Literature* 35, no. 2 (1983): 140.

"Carte de tendre." Persuasive Cartography: The P. J. Mode Collection, 2015. Ithaca, NY: Cornell University Library, Division of Rare & Manuscript Collections. http://persuasivemaps.library.cornell.edu.

Chateaubriand, François-René de. *Les aventures du dernier Abencérage.* Translated as *The Last of the Abencerrajes,* by A. S. Kline. 2011. http://www.poetryintranslation.com/PITBR/Chateaubriand/ChateaubriandRene.htm.

———. *Mémoires d'Outre-Tombe.* Translated as *Memoirs from Beyond the Grave,* by A. S. Kline. Last modified 2015. http://www.poetryintranslation.com/PITBR/Chateaubriand/ChateaubriandMemoirs.

Clearwater, Bonnie. *The Rothko Book.* London, New York: Tate; distributed in the United States by Harry N. Abrams, 2006.

Clifford, James. *The Predicament of Culture: Twentieth-Century Ethnography, Literature, and Art.* Cambridge, MA: Harvard University Press, 1988.

Connolly, Julian W. "The Challenge of Interpreting and Decoding Nabokov: Strategies and Suggestions." *Cycnos* 24, no. 1 (2007): 155–70.

———. "From Biography to Autobiography and Back: The Fictionalization of the Narrated Self in The Real Life of Sebastian Knight." *Cycnos* 10, no. 1 (1993). http://revel.unice.fr/cycnos/index.html?id=1286.

———. *Nabokov and His Fiction: New Perspectives.* Cambridge: Cambridge University Press, 1999.

Cosgrove, Denis E. *Mappings.* London: Reaktion Books, 1999.

Cullen, L. M. "Dublin." In *James Joyce in Context,* edited by John McCourt, 173–83. Cambridge: Cambridge University Press, 2008.

Damisch, Hubert. "Tables of Evidence." *Derrière le miroir,* no. 205 (1973): 1–28.

David, Michael Levin. *Modernity and the Hegemony of Vision.* Berkeley: University of California Press, 1992.

Delage-Toriel, Lara. "Brushing through 'Veiled Values and Translucent Undertones': Nabokov's Pictorial Approach to Women." *Transatlantica* 1 (2006). http://transatlantica.revues.org/index760.html.

Dentith, Simon. *Parody.* The New Critical Idiom, 211. London: Routledge, 2000. http://search.ebscohost.com/login.aspx?direct=true&db=mzh&AN=2000035111&site=ehost-live&scope=site.

Deppman, Jed, Daniel Ferrer, and Michael Groden, eds. *Genetic Criticism: Texts and Avant-Textes.* Philadelphia: University of Pennsylvania Press, 2004.

Dick, Susan. "Tom Kernan and the Retrospective Arrangement." *James Joyce Quarterly* 18, no. 2 (1981): 147–59.

Donoghue, Denis. "Yeats, Eliot, and the Mythical Method." *Sewanee Review* 105, no. 2 (1997): 206.

Doob, Penelope Reed. *The Idea of the Labyrinth from Classical Antiquity through the Middle Ages.* Ithaca: Cornell University Press, 1990.

Elderfield, John, ed. *Essays on Assemblage.* Vol. 2. New York: Museum of Modern Art; distributed by Harry N. Abrams, 1992.

Eliot, T. S. *Selected Prose of T. S. Eliot.* New York: Harcourt Brace Jovanovich, 1975.

Ellmann, Richard. *The Consciousness of Joyce.* London: Faber, 1977.

———. *James Joyce.* New York: Oxford University Press, 1959.

———. *Ulysses on the Liffey.* New York: Oxford University Press, 1986. https://search.lib.virginia.edu/catalog/u5688109. Ebook Central, Academic Complete ed. New York: Oxford University Press, 1986.

Feldman, Jessica R. *Gender on the Divide: The Dandy in Modernist Literature.* Ithaca: Cornell University Press, 1993.

Ferrer, Daniel, and Jean-Michel Rabaté. "Paragraphs in Expansion: James Joyce." In *Genetic Criticism: Texts and Avant-Textes,* edited by Jed Deppman, Daniel Ferrer, and Michael Groden, 132–51. Philadelphia: University of Pennsylvania Press, 2004.

Flaubert, Gustave. *Correspondance.* Edited by Jean Bruneau. Vol. 244. Bibliothèque de La Pléiade. Paris: Gallimard, 1973.

Foster, John Burt. *Nabokov's Art of Memory and European Modernism.* Princeton: Princeton University Press, 1993.

———. "Parody, Pastiche, and Periodization: Nabokov/Jameson." *Cycnos* 12, no. 2 (2008). http://revel.unice.fr/cycnos/index.html?id=1441.

Foster, John Wilson, ed. *The Cambridge Companion to the Irish Novel.* Cambridge: Cambridge University Press, 2006.

Frank, Joseph. *The Widening Gyre: Crisis and Mastery in Modern Literature.* Bloomington: Indiana University Press, 1963.

Frazier, Ian, and Saul Steinberg. *Canal Street.* American Journals Series. New York: Library Fellows of the Whitney Museum of American Art, 1990.

Frémon, Jean. "Conversation avec Saul Steinberg." *Repères: Cahiers d'Art Contemporain* 30 (1986): 1–40.

Gasser, Manuel. "Steinberg as an Advertising Artist; with German and French Texts." *Graphis* 12 (1956): 376.

Gibson, Andrew, and Steven John Morrison. *Joyce's "Wandering Rocks."* Amsterdam; New York: Rodopi, 2002.

Gifford, Don, with Robert J. Seidman. *"Ulysses" Annotated: Notes for James Joyce's "Ulysses."* Berkeley: University of California Press, 1988.

Gilbert, Stuart. *James Joyce's "Ulysses"; a Study.* New York: Vintage Books, 1955.

Gill, Brendan. "Saul Steinberg's Surprise." *Horizon* 21, no. 4 (April 1, 1978): 66–73.

Gillespie, Michael Patrick. *James Joyce and the Exilic Imagination.* Gainesville: University Press of Florida, 2015.

Ginzburg, Carlo. *Myths, Emblems, Clues.* London: Hutchinson Radius, 1990.

Glueck, Grace. "The Artist Speaks; Saul Steinberg." *Art in America* 58 (December 1970): 110–17.

———. "The 20th-Century Artists Most Admired by Other Artists." *ARTnews* 76, no. 9 (November 1977): 78–103.

———. "The World, and the City, According to Steinberg." *New York Times,* December 1, 2006, 29.

Gogol, Nikolaĭ Vasil'evich. *The Complete Tales of Nikolai Gogol.* Edited by Leonard J. Kent. 2 vols. Chicago: University of Chicago Press, 1985.

Gombrich, E. H. "The Wit of Saul Steinberg." In *Topics of Our Time: Twentieth-Century Issues in Learning and in Art,* 188–94. Berkeley: University of California Press, 1991.

Gopnik, Adam. "What Steinberg Saw." *New Yorker,* November 13, 2000, 141–47.

Göranzon, Bo, and Magnus Florin, eds. *Dialogue and Technology: Art and Knowledge.* London; New York: Springer-Verlag, 1991.

Greene, Roland, and Stephen Cushman, eds. *The Princeton Encyclopedia of Poetry and Poetics.* 4th ed. Princeton: Princeton University Press, 2012.

Groden, Michael. "Joyce at Work on 'Cyclops': Toward a Biography of Ulysses." James Joyce Quarterly 44, no. 2 (2007): 217–45. http://muse.jhu.edu/journals/james_joyce_quarterly/v044/44.2groden.html.

———. *Ulysses in Progress.* Princeton: Princeton University Press, 1977.

Gruen, John. *The Artist Observed: 28 Interviews with Contemporary Artists.* Chicago: Chicago Review Press, 1991.

———. "Saul Steinberg, Master of Wit and Fantasy." *ARTnews* 77, no. 5 (1978): 132–38.

Gunn, Ian, and Clive Hart. *James Joyce's Dublin: A Topographical Guide to the Dublin of Ulysses: With 121 Illustrations.* New York: Thames & Hudson, 2004.

Hall, Vernon. "Joyce's Use of Da Ponte and Mozart's 'Don Giovanni.'" *PMLA* 66, no. 2 (1951): 78–84.

Halperin, John, ed. *The Theory of the Novel; New Essays.* New York: Oxford University Press, 1974.

Harley, J. B. *The New Nature of Maps: Essays in the History of Cartography.* Edited by Paul Laxton. Baltimore: Johns Hopkins University Press, 2001.

Hart, Clive, and David Hayman, eds. *James Joyce's "Ulysses": Critical Essays.* Berkeley: University of California Press, 1977.

Hayman, David. *Ulysses, the Mechanics of Meaning.* Madison: University of Wisconsin Press, 1982.

Hecimovich, Gregg A. "'With Pale Blake I Write Tintingface': The Bounding Line of James Joyce's Aesthetic." *James Joyce Quarterly* 36, no. 4 (1999): 889–904.

Hegglund, Jon. "'Ulysses' and the Rhetoric of Cartography." *Twentieth Century Literature* 49, no. 2 (Summer 2003): 164–92.

Henke, Suzette. "James Joyce East and Middle East: Literary Resonances of Judaism, Egyptology, and Indian Myth." *Journal of Modern Literature* 13, no. 2 (1986): 307–19.

Heuvel, Jean vanden. "Straight from the Hand and Mouth of Steinberg." *Life,* December 10, 1965, 59–70.

Hollander, J. "Steinberg at the Smithsonian: The Metamorphosis of an Emblem." In *Steinberg at the Smithsonian,* i–iv. Washington, DC: Smithsonian Institution Press, 1973.

Hughes, Robert. *Nothing If Not Critical: Selected Essays on Art and Artists.* London: Harvill Press, 1999.

———. "The World of Steinberg: With a Thinking Pen, He Has Transmuted Illustrations into Museum Pieces." *Time,* April 17, 1978, 92–96.

Hunter, J. Paul. *Before Novels: The Cultural Contexts of Eighteenth-Century English Fiction.* New York: Norton, 1990.

Hutcheon, Linda. "Parody without Ridicule: Observations on Modern Literary Parody." *Canadian Review of Comparative Literature/Revue Canadienne de Litterature Comparée* 5 (1978): 201–11.

———. *A Theory of Parody: The Teachings of Twentieth-Century Art Forms.* New York: Methuen, 1985.

Ionesco, Eugène. "Steinberg/Lindner." *Derrière le miroir,* no. 241 (1980): 1–32.

Isaak, Jo-Anna. "James Joyce and the Cubist Esthetic." *Mosaic* 14, no. 1 (January 1981).

Jacob, Christian. *The Sovereign Map: Theoretical Approaches in Cartography throughout History.* Edited by Edward H. Dahl. Chicago: University of Chicago Press, 2006.

James, William. *The Varieties of Religious Experience.* The Works of William James. Cambridge, MA: Harvard University Press, 1985.

Johnson, D. Barton. "The Labyrinth of Incest in Nabokov's 'Ada.'" *Comparative Literature* 38, no. 3 (1986): 224–55. https://doi.org/Proquest.com.

———. *Worlds in Regression: Some Novels of Vladimir Nabokov.* Ann Arbor, MI: Ardis, 1985.

Johnson, E. Bond. "Parody and Myth: Flaubert, Joyce, Nabokov." *Far-Western Forum: A Review of Ancient and Modern Letters* 1 (1974): 149–73.

Joyce, James. *The Critical Writings of James Joyce.* Edited by Ellsworth Mason and Richard Ellmann. Ithaca: Cornell University Press, 1989.

———. *Letters of James Joyce.* Edited by Stuart Gilbert and Richard Ellmann. 3 vols. London: Faber and Faber, 1957.

———. *Ulysses.* New York: Vintage Books, 1990.

Kenner, Hugh. *Dublin's Joyce.* London: Chatto & Windus, 1955.

———. "Modernism and What Happened to It." *Essays in Criticism: A Quarterly Journal of Literary Criticism* 37, no. 2 (April 1987): 97–109.

———. *The Stoic Comedians, Flaubert, Joyce, and Beckett.* Berkeley: University of California Press, 1974.

———. *Ulysses.* Baltimore: Johns Hopkins University Press, 1987.

Keogh, Dermot. *Jews in Twentieth-Century Ireland: Refugees, Anti-Semitism and the Holocaust.* Cork: Cork University Press, 2006.

Kershner, R. B. *Joyce and Popular Culture.* Gainesville: University Press of Florida, 1996.

Khrushcheva, Nina L. *Imagining Nabokov: Russia between Art and Politics.* New Haven: Yale University Press, 2013.

Kiberd, Declan. *Ulysses and Us: The Art of Everyday Living.* London: Faber and Faber, 2009.

Kirchner, James Patrick. "Parody in the Fiction of James Joyce." University of Illinois at Chicago, 1996. ProQuest Dissertations.

Kiremidjian, David. *A Study of Modern Parody: James Joyce's Ulysses, Thomas Mann's Doctor Faustus.* New York: Garland Publishing, 1985.

Kramer, Hilton. "Saul Steinberg: Illuminations." *New Criterion* 25, no. 6 (2007): 51.

Lallo, Mario Tedeschini. "Descent from Paradise: Saul Steinberg's Italian Years (1933–1941)." *Quest: Issues in Contemporary Jewish History* 2 (October 2011).

Latham, Sean, ed. *The Cambridge Companion to "Ulysses."* Cambridge: Cambridge University Press, 2014. https://doi.org/10.1017/CCO9781139696425.013.

———. *Joyce's Modernism.* Dublin: National Library of Ireland, 2005.

Lawrence, Karen R. "'Aeolus': Interruption and Inventory." *James Joyce Quarterly* 17 (1980): 389–405.

———. *The Odyssey of Style in Ulysses.* Princeton: Princeton University Press, 1981.

———. *Who's Afraid of James Joyce?* Gainesville: University Press of Florida, 2010. http://site.ebrary.com/lib/uvalib/docDetail.action?docID=10603014&ppg=1.

Lefrère, Jean-Jacques, Pierre Leroy, and Jean-Hugues Berrou. *Rimbaud au Harar.* Paris: Fayard, 2002.

Lehman, Robert S. "Formalism, Mere Form, and Judgment." *New Literary History: A Journal of Theory and Interpretation* 48, no. 2 (Spring 2017): 245–63.

Levinson, Marjorie. "What Is New Formalism?" *PMLA* 122, no. 2 (2007): 558–69.

Litz, A. Walton. *The Art of James Joyce: Method and Design in "Ulysses" and "Finnegans Wake."* London; New York: Oxford University Press, 1961.

———. "The Genre of Ulysses." In *James Joyce: A Collection of Critical Essays,* edited by Mary T. Reynolds, 109–17. Englewood Cliffs, NJ: Prentice-Hall, 1993.

Livorni, Ernesto. "'Ineluctable Modality of the Visible': Diaphane in the 'Proteus' Episode." *James Joyce Quarterly* 36, no. 2 (1999): 127–69.

Loesberg, Jonathan. "Cultural Studies, Victorian Studies, and Formalism." *Victorian Literature and Culture* 27 (1999): 537–44. https://doi.org/10.1017/S1060150399272191.

———. *A Return to Aesthetics: Autonomy, Indifference, and Postmodernism.* Stanford: Stanford University Press, 2005.

Loss, Archie K. *Joyce's Visible Art: The Work of Joyce and the Visual Arts, 1904–1922.* Ann Arbor: UMI Research Press, 1984.

Lowe-Evans, Mary. "Joyce and the Myth of the Mediatrix." In *Gender in Joyce,* edited by Jolanta Wawrzycka and Marlena G. Corcoran, 101–11. Gainesville: University Press of Florida, 1997.

Mali, Joseph. "Mythology and Counter-History: The New Critical Art of Vico and

Joyce." In *Vico and Joyce,* edited by Donald Phillip Verene, 32–47. Albany: State University of New York Press, 1987.

Mallarmé, Stéphane. *Collected Poems.* Translated by Henry Weinfield. Berkeley: University of California Press, 1994.

Manea, Norman. "Made in Romania." Translated from the Romanian by Patrick Camiller. *New York Review of Books,* February 10, 2000, 44–46.

Marshall, Brenda K. "Sebastian Speaks: Nabokov's Narrative Authority in 'The Real Life of Sebastian Knight.'" *Style* 23, no. 2 (1989): 213–24.

McCarthy, Penny. "Nabokov's 'Ada' and Sidney's 'Arcadia': The Regeneration of a Phoenix." *Modern Language Review* 99, no. 1 (2004): 17–31.

McCormick, Kathleen. "'Just a Flash Like That': The Pleasure of 'Cruising' the Interpolations in 'Wandering Rocks.'" *James Joyce Quarterly* 24, no. 3 (1987): 275–90.

McCourt, John, ed. *James Joyce in Context.* Cambridge: Cambridge University Press, 2008.

McCullough, David W. *The Unending Mystery: A Journey through Labyrinths and Mazes.* New York: Pantheon Books, 2004.

McHugh, Roland. *Annotations to Finnegans Wake.* Baltimore: Johns Hopkins University Press, 2006.

McShine, Kynaston, ed. *Joseph Cornell.* New York: Museum of Modern Art, 1980.

Melchionne, Kevin. "Collecting as an Art." *Philosophy and Literature* 23, no. 1 (1999): 148–56. https://doi.org/10.1353/phl.1999.0021.

Meyer, Priscilla. "Black and Violet Words: 'Despair' and 'The Real Life of Sebastian Knight' as Doubles." *Nabokov Studies* 4 (1997): 37–60.

———. *Nabokov and Indeterminacy: The Case of "The Real Life of Sebastian Knight."* Evanston: Northwestern University Press, 2018.

Michel, Jacques. "Lorsque l'humoriste se fait peintre—Les parodies de Steinberg." *Le Monde,* June 24, 1970.

———. "Retrospective Steinberg à Saint-Paul-de-Vence: Je fais un métier d'equilibriste." *Le Monde,* March 22, 1979.

Munro, James S. *Mademoiselle de Scudéry and the Carte de Tendre.* Durham: University of Durham, 1986.

Nabokov, Vladimir. *Ada oder Das Verlangen—Eine Familienchronik.* Translated by Uwe Friesel. Reinbek: Rowohlt Verlag, 2010.

———. *Ada, or Ardor: A Family Chronicle.* New York: Vintage International, 1990.

———. *The Annotated Lolita.* Edited by Alfred Appel Jr. New York: Vintage, 1991.

———. *Bend Sinister.* New York: McGraw-Hill, 1974.

———. *Lectures on Don Quixote.* Edited by Fredson Bowers. San Diego: Harcourt Brace Jovanovich/Bruccoli Clark, 1983.

———. *Lectures on Literature.* Edited by Fredson Bowers. New York: Harcourt Brace Jovanovich/Bruccoli Clark, 1980.

———. *Lectures on Russian Literature.* New York: Harcourt Brace Jovanovich/Bruccoli Clark, 1981.

———. *Nikolai Gogol.* New York: New Directions, 1961.

———. *Pale Fire*. New York: Vintage International, 1989.
———. *The Real Life of Sebastian Knight*. Norfolk, CT: New Directions, 1959.
———. *Speak, Memory: An Autobiography Revisited*. New York: G. P. Putnam's Sons, 1966.
———. *The Stories of Vladimir Nabokov*. New York: Alfred A. Knopf, 1995.
———. *Strong Opinions*. New York: McGraw-Hill, 1973.
———. *Think, Write, Speak: Uncollected Essays, Reviews, Interviews, and Letters to the Editor*. Edited by Brian Boyd and Anastasia Tolstoy. New York: Alfred A. Knopf, 2019.
———. *Vladimir Nabokov: Selected Letters 1940–77*. Edited by Dmitri Nabokov and Matthew J. Bruccoli. New York: Harcourt Brace Jovanovich/Bruccoli Clark Layman, 1989.
Nadel, Ira Bruce. *Joyce and the Jews: Culture and Texts*. Basingstoke: Macmillan, 1989.
Norman, Will. *Transatlantic Aliens: Modernism, Exile, and Culture in Midcentury America*. Baltimore: Johns Hopkins University Press, 2016.
Nunes, Mark. "Beyond the 'Holy See': Parody and Narrative Assemblage in 'Cyclops.'" *Twentieth Century Literature: A Scholarly and Critical Journal* 45, no. 2 (1999): 174–85.
Ovid. *Metamorphoses*. Translated by Rolfe Humphries. Bloomington: Indiana University Press, 1955.
———. *The Poems of Exile*. Translated by Peter Green. London: Penguin Books, 1994.
Owen, Rodney Wilson. *James Joyce and the Beginnings of "Ulysses."* Ann Arbor: UMI Research Press, n.d.
Pamuk, Orhan. *The Naive and the Sentimental Novelist*. New York: Vintage, 2011.
Patton, Laurie L., and Wendy Doniger. *Myth and Method*. Charlottesville: University of Virginia Press, 1996.
Pearson, Roger. *Mallarmé and Circumstance: The Translation of Silence*. Oxford: Oxford University Press, 2004.
———. *Unfolding Mallarmé: The Development of a Poetic Art*. Oxford: Clarendon Press, Oxford University Press, 1996.
Peterson, Dale. "Knight's Move: Nabokov, Shklovsky and the Afterlife of Sirin." *Nabokov Studies* 11, no. 1 (2007): xi–xii, 25–37.
Petherbridge, Deanna. *The Primacy of Drawing: Histories and Theories of Practice*. New Haven: Yale University Press, 2010.
Porter, Charles A. *Chateaubriand: Composition, Imagination, and Poetry*. Saratoga, CA: Anma Libri, 1978.
Power, Arthur. *Conversations with James Joyce*. London: Millington, 1974.
Praz, Mario. *Mnemosyne: The Parallel between Literature and the Visual Arts*. Princeton: Princeton University Press, 1970.
Quick, Jonathan. "Molly Bloom's Mother." *ELH* 57, no. 1 (1990): 223–40.
Rimbaud, Arthur. *Complete Works, Selected Letters*. Translated by Wallace Fowlie. Chicago: University of Chicago Press, 1966.
Rimmon, Shlomith. "Problems of Voice in Vladimir Nabokov's 'The Real Life of

Sebastian Knight.'" *PTL: A Journal for Descriptive Poetics and Theory of Literature* 1 (1976): 489–512.

Rivers, J. E., and Charles Nicol, eds. *Nabokov's Fifth Arc: Nabokov and Others on His Life's Work.* Austin: University of Texas Press, 1982.

Rodman, Selden. "Saul Steinberg." In *Conversations with Artists,* 181–85. New York: Devin-Adair, 1957.

Rosenberg, Harold. *Art & Other Serious Matters.* Chicago: University of Chicago Press, 1985.

———. *Saul Steinberg.* New York: Knopf, 1978.

———. "Saul Steinberg's Art World." *Art News* 65 (1966): 51–54.

Rosenblum, Robert. *Cubism and Twentieth-Century Art.* New York: Harry N. Abrams, 2001.

———. "Cubism as Pop Art." In *Modern Art and Popular Culture: Readings in High and Low,* edited by Kirk Varnedoe and Adam Gopnik, 117–32. New York: Abrams, in association with the Museum of Modern Art, 1990.

———. "Picasso and the Typography of Cubism." In *Picasso, 1881–1973,* edited by Sir Roland Penrose and John Golding, 49–75. London: Paul Elek, 1973.

Rosenthal, Mark. *Artists at Gemini G.E.L.: Celebrating the 25th Year.* New York: Abrams; Los Angeles: Gemini G.E.L, 1993.

Ryan, Marie-Laure. "Toward a Definition of Narrative." In *The Cambridge Companion to Narrative,* edited by David Herman, 22–36. New York: Cambridge University Press, 2007.

Saint-Amour, Paul K. "Over Assemblage: *Ulysses* and the *Boîte-en-valise* from Above." *European Joyce Studies* 15 (2003): 21–58.

Schiff, Stacy. *Vera (Mrs. Vladimir Nabokov): A Biography.* New York: Random House, 1999.

Schneider, Pierre. *Louvre Dialogues.* New York: Atheneum, 1971.

Seidel, Michael. *Epic Geography: James Joyce's "Ulysses."* Princeton: Princeton University Press, 1976.

Seitz, William Chapin. *The Art of Assemblage.* New York: Museum of Modern Art, distributed by Doubleday, 1961.

Senn, Fritz, ed. "Book of Many Turns." *James Joyce Quarterly* 10 (1972): 29–46.

———. *Joyce's Dislocutions: Essays on Reading as Translation.* Edited by John Paul Riquelme. Baltimore: Johns Hopkins University Press, 1984.

Shapiro, Gavriel. *Delicate Markers: Subtexts in Vladimir Nabokov's "Invitation to a Beheading."* New York: Peter Lang, 1998.

———. "Nabokov and Comic Art." In *Nabokov at the Limits: Redrawing Critical Boundaries,* edited by Lisa Zunshine, 213–34. New York: Garland, 1999.

———. "Nabokov and Comic Art: Additional Observations and Remarks." *The Nabokovian* 59 (Fall 2007): 21–31.

———. *Nabokov at Cornell.* Ithaca: Cornell University Press, 2003.

———. *The Sublime Artist's Studio: Nabokov and Painting.* Evanston: Northwestern University Press, 2009.

———. *The Tender Friendship and the Charm of Perfect Accord: Nabokov and His Father.* Ann Arbor: University of Michigan Press, 2014.
Shattuck, Roger. *The Banquet Years; The Origins of the Avant Garde in France, 1885 to World War I: Alfred Jarry, Henri Rousseau, Erik Satie [and] Guillaume Apollinaire.* Rev. ed. New York: Vintage Books, 1968.
Slezkine, Yuri. *The Jewish Century.* Princeton: Princeton University Press, 2004.
Smith, Joel. *Saul Steinberg: Illuminations.* New Haven: Yale University Press, 2006.
———. *Steinberg at the New Yorker.* New York: Harry N. Abrams, 2005.
Starkie, Enid. *Arthur Rimbaud.* Westport, CT: Greenwood Press, 1978.
Steegmuller, Francis. *Flaubert and Madame Bovary.* New York: Farrar, Straus and Giroux, 1968.
Steinberg, Saul. *The Art of Living.* New York: Harper, 1949.
———. *Dal Vero.* New York: Library Fellows of the Whitney Museum of American Art, 1983.
———. *The Discovery of America.* New York: Knopf, 1992.
———. *Steinberg: Drawing into Being.* New York: PaceWildenstein, 1999. Exhibition catalogue.
———. *The Inspector.* New York: Viking Press, 1973.
———. Interview by Adam Gopnik, 1992. YCAL, b. 130, f. 2475.
———. Interview by John Gruen, January 19, 1978. YCAL b. 130, f. 2473.
———. Interview by Jacques Dupin. Typescript, January 11, 1978. SSF.
———. Interview by Jean Robertson. In brochure published for the exhibition "Saul Steinberg." Ohio: Columbus Museum of Art, 1986.
———. Interview by Paul Cummings. Transcript, March 27, 1973, Archives of American Art; transcription at SSF 1973.1.
———. Interview by Mark Rosenthal. Transcript, 1995. SSF.
———. Interview by Raymond Rosenthal and Moishe Ducovny. Transcript, August 1960. **P Oral History Box 74 #4. New York Public Library.
———. Interview by Eli Waldron. *Publishers Weekly.* July 5, 1973. YCAL b. 130, f. 2464.
———. "An Interview with Saul Steinberg." Interview by Meg Perlman, April 15, 1975. SSF 1975.1.
———. *The Labyrinth.* New York: Harper & Brothers, 1960. Reprinted by New York Review of Books, 2018.
———. *Lettere a Aldo Buzzi, 1945–1999.* Milano: Biblioteca Adelphi, 2002.
———. "My Deskmate at Matei Basarab." Letter to Eugen Campus, February 12, 1988. Typescript, Archive A: Selections from the Romanian Correspondence of Saul Steinberg, SSF. Translated by Emil Niculescu. Published in *Apostrof* 10, no. 12 (1999).
———. "National Diary," January 3, 1959. YCAL b. 108, f. 2220.
———. *New Work by Saul Steinberg.* New York: Sidney Janis Gallery, 1973. Exhibition catalogue.
———. *The New World.* New York: Harper & Row, 1965.

———. *The Passport.* New York: Harper, 1954.

———. *The Passport.* With an introduction by John Hollander. New York: Vintage Books, 1979.

———. *Reflections and Shadows.* With Aldo Buzzi. Translated from the Italian by John Shepley. New York: Random House, 2002.

———. *Saul Steinberg: Recent Work.* Pace Gallery, 1987. Exhibition catalogue.

———. *Saul Steinberg: Still Life and Architecture.* New York: Pace Gallery, 1982. Exhibition catalogue.

———. *Saul Steinberg: The Americans.* Edited by Andreas Prinzing. Cologne: Museum Ludwig, 2013. Exhibition catalogue.

———. "The Saul Steinberg Papers." Uncat. Mss 126. YCAL.

———. "Statements and Documents: Artists on Art and Reality, on Their Work, and on Values." In "Visual Arts Today," special issue, *Daedalus* 89, no. 1 (1960): 124–26.

———. "Steinberg: J'enseigne aux hommes à nager en les poussant dans l'eau." *Arts & Loisirs* 25 (March 1966): 51–52.

———. "Take 30 in New York." Interview by Adrienne Clarkson, Canadian Broadcasting Co., aired January 1968. Transcript. SSF.

———. "Transcribed Remarks to Rolf Karrer-Kharberg for His Film, 'Das Maskenhafte an Saul Steinberg: Bericht Aus Der Welt Eines Großen Zeichners,' Süddeutsche Rundfunk," 1967. YCAL b. 128, f. 2446.

———. "Typescript of Recorded Interview by John Jones with Saul Steinberg," October 12, 1965. SSF.

———. "Les vertiges de Steinberg." Interview by Pierre Schneider. *L'Express*, October 22–28, 1973, 54–55.

———. "A Victorian Dialogue with Saul Steinberg." Interview by Dore Ashton, undated, c. 1954. YCAL b. 130, f. 2468.

Steiner, Wendy. *The Colors of Rhetoric: Problems in the Relation between Modern Literature and Painting.* Chicago: University of Chicago Press, 1982.

———. "'There Was Meaning in His Look': The Meeting of Pictorial Models in Joyce's 'Nausicaa.'" *University of Hartford Studies in Literature* 16 (1984): 90–103.

Stendhal. *The Life of Henry Brulard.* Translated by John Sturrock. New York: Penguin Books, 1995.

Stewart, Bruce. "James Joyce." In *The Cambridge Companion to the Irish Novel,* edited by John Wilson Foster, 133–52. Cambridge: Cambridge University Press, 2006.

Stewart, Garrett. *The Look of Reading: Book, Painting, Text.* Chicago: University of Chicago Press, 2006.

Stewart, George R. *U.S. 40; Cross-Section of the United States of America.* Boston: Houghton Mifflin, 1953.

Strier, Richard. "How Formalism Became a Dirty Word, and Why We Can't Do Without It." In *Renaissance Literature and Its Formal Engagements,* edited by Mark D. Rasmussen, 1–16. New York: Palgrave, 2000.

Stuart, Dabney. "'The Real Life of Sebastian Knight': Angles of Perception." *Modern Language Quarterly* 29 (1968): 312–28.

Taylor, Brandon. *Collage: The Making of Modern Art.* London: Thames & Hudson, 2004.

Toker, Leona. "'The Dead Are Good Mixers': Nabokov's Versions of Individualism." In *Nabokov and His Fiction: New Perspectives,* edited by Julian W. Connolly, 92–108. Cambridge: Cambridge University Press, 1999.

Topliss, Iain. "Saul Steinberg: The Lifeline from A to B." In The Comic Worlds of Peter Arno, William Steig, Charles Addams, and Saul Steinberg, 181–238. Baltimore: Johns Hopkins University Press, 2005.

Turner, R. A., and G. W. Turner. "The Nature of James Joyce's Parody in 'Ithaca.'" *Modern Language Review* 64 (1969): 759–63.

Varnedoe, Kirk, and Adam Gopnik, eds. *Modern Art and Popular Culture: Readings in High and Low.* New York: Abrams, in association with the Museum of Modern Art, 1990.

Verene, Donald Phillip. *Vico and Joyce.* Albany: State University of New York Press, 1987.

Vries, Gerard de. *Silent Love: The Annotation and Interpretation of Nabokov's "The Real Life of Sebastian Knight."* Boston: Academic Studies Press, 2016.

Vries, Gerard, de, and D. Barton Johnson. *Vladimir Nabokov and the Art of Painting.* Amsterdam: Amsterdam University Press, 2006.

Waldman, Diane. *Collage, Assemblage, and the Found Object.* New York: Abrams, 1992.

Wawrzycka, Jolanta W., and Marlena G. Corcoran, eds. *Gender in Joyce.* Gainesville: University Press of Florida, [1997].

Webb, Michael. "Saul Steinberg: Walking a Fine Line." *Graphis,* no. 324 (1999): 102–7.

Wicke, Jennifer. *Advertising Fictions: Literature, Advertisement & Social Reading.* New York: Columbia University Press, 1988.

Wilde, Oscar. *Complete Works of Oscar Wilde.* Edited by Vyvyan Beresford Holland. New York: HarperPerennial, 1989.

Willer, Thérèse, and Iain Topliss. *Saul Steinberg: L'écriture visuelle.* Strasbourg: Musées de la ville de Strasbourg, 2009.

Wolfson, Susan J., and Marshall Brown, eds. *Reading for Form.* Seattle: University of Washington Press, 2006. https://search.lib.virginia.edu/catalog/u4819320.

Wood, Michael. *The Magician's Doubts: Nabokov and the Risks of Fiction.* Princeton: Princeton University Press, 1995.

Wordsworth, William. "Lines Composed a Few Miles above Tintern Abbey." In *The Poetical Works of William Wordsworth,* edited by E. de Selincourt, 2nd ed., 2:262. Oxford: Oxford University Press, 1940.

Yeats, W. B. *Yeats's Poetry, Drama, and Prose: Authoritative Texts, Criticism.* Edited by James Pethica. New York: W. W. Norton, 2000.

Zwart, Jane. "Nabokov's Primer: Letters and Numbers in 'The Real Life of Sebastian Knight.'" *Philological Quarterly* 82, no. 2 (Spring 2003): 213–34.

INDEX

Italicized page numbers refer to illustrations